Y0-BZL-394

EYE OF THE BEHOLDER

Praise for EYE OF THE BEHOLDER

Other books by Lowell Cauffiel:

Masquerade
Forever and Five Days

EYE
OF THE
BEHOLDER

LOWELL
CAUFFIEL

PINNACLE BOOKS
KENSINGTON PUBLISHING CORP.

http://www.pinnaclebooks.com

For my brother John, the closer.

AUTHOR'S NOTE

Eye of the Beholder is not a "fictionalized" version of the Diane King murder case, but is based on court and police records, more than 300 hours of interviews with key participants, eighteen months of research and other proven methods of journalistic discovery. Sections entitled "From the View of Bradford King" are King's own words, compiled from six months of taped prison interviews. They represent Mr. King's version of his case and his personal history. Several individuals in this story, in consideration of their privacy, have been assigned pseudonyms. Their names appear in italics in first reference.

ACKNOWLEDGMENTS

The book is not possible without the support and cooperation of good people. Many of their names already appear in this work. Specifically, I would also like to thank my agent Russell Galen, editor Paul Dinas, my attorney Michael Novak, Peggy Bourn and the Michigan Department of Corrections, and forensic psychologist, Dr. Michael Abramsky, who served as a consultant in the testing employed in this work.

Finally, no work is possible without support of my family and Bill's many friends.

"And I have heard she is beautiful: Is she?"
"Beauty is in the eye of the beholder."
    —from "Molly Bawn,"
    Margaret Wolfe Hungerford

INTRODUCTION

*On its best blocks, Marshall makes the Midwest seem
like the sweetest place on earth.*
— *The New York Times,* June 23, 1991

A mass media instructor explained to me once why people will keep glancing at a television that's on in the background, though they may be fully engaged elsewhere and nothing of any real interest is on the screen.

"The TV has this moving electronic beam," he said. "It scans left to right across more than five hundred lines of the picture tube, creating a complete image every twenty-fifth of a second. The conscious eye sees this as a TV picture. But the unconscious picks up that demonically fast moving beam. Since the dawn of man, movement has meant *be on alert.* So you keep checking that TV set in the local bar or storefront or your friend's living room, whether you want to watch it or not."

A twenty-eight-year-old man named Michael Perry from the Cajun country of Lake Arthur, Louisiana, wanted to watch television very much. When authorities tracked him down in a Washington, D.C., hotel, they found seven television sets, stacked one on top of another in a pyramid, like some kind of electronic altar at the foot of his bed.

A few weeks earlier, Perry had blasted his mother, father, brother, and two neighbors into oblivion with a shotgun. His rampage came after he'd returned from California where he'd unsuccessfully tried to contact singer Olivia Newton-John at her Malibu ranch. After his Lake Arthur murders, Perry drove north to the nation's capital to stalk Supreme Court Justice Sandra Day O'Connor. He'd become obsessed with both women by watching them on TV.

The killings landed Michael Perry on Louisiana Death Row. "The Eye," Perry used to call himself. He drew big single eyes on his TV screens in blood-red magic marker. He wrote slogans like "War" and "Why" in reverse, as if the images on the picture tubes were trying to write him back.

It was one of those strange coincidences that journalists get when they spend months obsessing on a subject. I was looking at police photos of Perry's TV pyramid when a free-lance reporter from Kalamazoo, Michigan, I'd met at a conference, called. It was early February 1991. The reporter had breaking news about a Battle Creek anchorwoman named Diane Newton King.

"Another victim for your book," she said. "Diane King was being stalked by an obsessed fan. She was shot to death right in front of her kids in the driveway of her home."

But Diane Newton King would not be another candidate for the book I'd been planning about the celebrity stalking in America.

In the days ahead, I waited for news of an arrest, the apprehension of some reclusive schizophrenic or possessed loner. That's the way it usually went.

No arrest came.

The Diane Newton King case lingered on as the latest in a series of highly publicized, violent cases: John Hinckley and Jodi Foster. Mark Chapman and John Lennon. Arthur Jackson and Theresa Saldana. Robert Bardo and Rebecca Schaeffer.

In the two years preceding the King murder, stalking coverage was everywhere from talk shows to *The New York Times*.

Theresa Saldana was lobbying against the prison release of her knife-wielding attacker. A twenty-eight-year-old shipping clerk sent more than five thousand threatening letters to Michael J. Fox. David Letterman dodged visitations from Margaret Ray. There were stalking stories about Johnny Carson and Janet Jackson and local deejays and TV news people and folks who hardly qualified for Andy Warhol's fifteen minutes of fame.

At times, it seemed America was paying a price for its worship of celebrity. But public figure obsession also had been one of the entertainment and TV industry's best kept secrets. Reporting the phenomena only encouraged it, the conventional wisdom went for many years.

That philosophy changed in 1989. Behind the scenes, new research for the Department of Justice was fueling the star stalker flap in the mass media. The study was conducted by Newport Beach psychiatrist Park Dietz, one of the country's leading criminal experts. (Dr. Dietz led the psychiatric team in the prosecution of John Hinckley.) The psychiatrist delineated the stalking phenomena by studying the files of Gavin de Becker, a Hollywood security expert who provided protection and threat assessments for dozens of top Hollywood stars. Both Dietz and de Becker gave interviews around the country for two years, helping lobby for new statutes. In 1990, California passed the country's first stalking law. More than forty states have followed.

Michigan did not have a stalking law when Diane Newton King was killed. And Battle Creek, the western Michigan city where she worked, was not a city known for obsessive pathology, but for the American quest for healthy breakfasts.

In 1991, metropolitan Battle Creek was Michigan's third largest city geographically, but had a population that hardly exceeded ninety thousand. Its roots remained solidly agrarian. Kellogg's, the Post Division of General Foods, and Ralston Purina were still the main employers. Ralston's grain silos as well as office buildings defined the modest downtown skyline. City limits gave way to rural countryside rather than suburban sprawl.

Celebrity sickness seemed to have hit the heartland with the

murder of the city's most popular anchorwoman. This became
only more poignant when I drove out to the nearby small town
where Diane, her two preschool children, and her husband,
Bradford J. King, lived.

The headline in the *Marshall Chronicle* read: **DIANE KING
HARASSED BY LETTERS, PHONE CALLS.** It was topped by:
"Music Boosters plan spaghetti supper, See page 2."

Marshall, Michigan, was typical of small-town America.
"The Town of Hospitality," as the town of 6,900 calls itself, was
also much more than that. The former stagecoach stop midway
between Detroit and Chicago is a Midwestern testimony to the
pursuit of excellence, when it comes to appearances at least.

Named after John Marshall, the first chief justice of the U.S.
Supreme Court, the town was so sure it would be the state's
capital in 1839, a white pillared governor's mansion was built
on the town's high ground overlooking the Kalamazoo River.
The district became known as Capitol Hill. But one vote in the
state senate put the capital in Lansing in 1847. However, Marshall prospered as a trade and farming center for the lower
region of the state.

Now, much of the town is a National Historic Landmark
District. There are forty-six historical markers, at last count.
The coming of the Michigan Central Railroad inspired the
nation's first railroad union and launched a thirty-year building
boom that ceased just in time to preserve Marshall's small-town
character. A lawyer and a minister conceived the state's public
education system under a local oak tree in Marshall. A runaway
slave named Admad Crosswhite was tracked down in Marshall
by Southern bounty hunters in 1846, but town elders refused to
turn over the fugitive.

But visitors didn't need markers to find Marshall's classic
heritage on its maple-lined streets. Historians consider the town
one of the nation's foremost representations of the best in small-
town American architecture, its designs brought west by New
Englanders who settled many of Michigan's communities.
Today, Marshall's biggest event is its annual house tour, which
draws people from around the United States to walk through
meticulously kept Victorians, Queen Annes, Gothic Revivals,

Italianates, Carpenter Gothics, Romanesques, and Tuscan and Italian Villas.

" 'I don't know you. What house do you live in?' " one newcomer reported being asked at her first local business district meeting. "People have a real pride in their homes in Marshall," she added. "You *are* somebody if you live in Marshall, Michigan."

In recent years, homeowners have celebrated the rich, extroverted palette of the nineteenth century on their homes. Variations of green and gold snap up Victorian gingerbread. Scrolled cornice and deep sashes are delineated in blue, garnet, and gray. When a visiting official from Biloxi, Mississippi, asked the head of the Marshall Historical Society for a copy of the city's color ordinance, he replied: "We don't have one. All we have is good taste and peer pressure."

The Brooks Memorial Fountain is the town's center, donated by late 1920s mayor Harold C. Brooks to honor his father. The local businessman patterned the fountain in 1930 after the Grecian Temple of Love at Versailles, sans the nude of Aphrodite in its center. A town patron for six decades, Brooks bought up historical houses and offered prizes to residents with the best garden, lawn, and home.

Mainstreet Marshall stretches east from the fountain on Michigan Avenue. The broad thoroughfare offers two hardware stores, dentist offices, a travel agency, a Rexall drug store, gift shops, an office supply, a bakery, three banks, a photo studio, a restored post office, several pubs, and three cafes named Ken's, The Dugout, and The Coffee Pot, where two people can still get lunch for under five bucks. More elaborate dining waits at Schuler's, an old family spot famous among travelers on Interstate 94. More than a dozen antique shops reside in town. In one storefront resides the American Museum of Magic, a twelve thousand volume, private collection of the instruments and memorabilia of illusion, kept by a retired newspaperman who opens the collection for private tours and world-class magicians like Copperfield and Blackstone when they play the state.

The old money came from railroads and patent medicines

and the Brooks Appliance Company, the town patron's family business which made hernia trusses and rupture supporters and sold them around the world. The old headquarters on Michigan Avenue still has a sign that reads "Personal Fittings." The company motto: "Brooks Supports the World—And Will Never Let it Down."

The last big murder in or around Marshall was nearly thirty years back. A man killed a local restaurateur's wife with a letter bomb because he refused to sell his eatery.

Through the years, Marshall has remained largely white, Protestant, and Republican. In 1991, Marshall's new money— new folks with the new trappings—was coming from transplanted urban professionals like Diane and her husband Bradford J. King. She was a newswoman, he a criminal justice instructor at Western Michigan University, forty-five minutes west. Like many other couples who hustled and spent their way through the eighties, the Kings appeared to be seeking a simpler, more rural life. They were restoring an old farmhouse south of town.

Diane Newton King was a new kind of murder victim for all of the Midwest. Electronic media appeared to have brought killer and victim together. Electronic media would cover the consequences as well. The anchorwoman was a citizen of a new kind of town that extended beyond Marshall or the "Cereal City." It was a community measured neither by location nor conventional population nor streets of smart Victorians.

Diane Newton King's killer was in that community, too.

It extended to any eye captured by that quick electronic beam.

PART ONE

Early Impressions

Early impressions are hard to eradicate from the mind. When once wool has been dyed purple, who can restore it to its previous whiteness.

—Saint Jerome

1

He stood up in an est meeting, his gesture not part of the training or any particular practice or custom. He just rose unexpectedly, and everyone listened and watched.

"I love Diane," Bradford King said. "I love Diane, and one day I'm going to marry her, too."

On July 21, 1984, it was hard to miss when he did.

The ceremony was held in the First Unitarian Church of Denver, on the corner of Fourteenth and Lafayette, where Dwight D. Eisenhower married Mamie. Diane wore a white satin skirt and silk jacket with rolled hems. She wore a white blouse, hand painted with yellow and bright red stars. Brad wore a white dinner jacket and slate slacks. His tie and cummerbund were lavender, and Diane carried lavender orchids. A pair of bagpipers in Scottish kilts flanked them at the altar, the tall pipes of the church organ serving as their brassy backdrop.

They'd written out their vows. They'd underlined certain words for emphasis.

He said, "Today and always, I chose you to be the one I stand beside in life. You are the one I will love, support, and serve as we grow and expand in our aliveness."

She said, "I pledge myself to having this marriage be magical and fun, inspiring, fulfilling so that at the end of my life I can know that because of your love and support I went far past my dreams."

When it was over, the pipers puffed up their bags and led Bradford and Diane King outside to the street, where they turned and kept right on going. They stopped traffic and people as the pipers led them to a nearby restaurant for the reception, their instruments still wailing.

Other rituals would come in time.

Marler, their first child, was born March 6, 1988, four years later, in Grand Junction, Colorado. It was well after Diane had established herself as a star TV reporter at KJTC-TV. She named the boy after her late father, Herbert George Marler. She also gave herself a new name, taking the surname of her stepfather, Royal Newton.

Diane Newton King.

It had a rhythm. It sounded contemporary. It sounded authoritative on the air.

Both Diane Newton King and Brad wrote letters to their new baby in a memory book. Diane not only dated her entry on the fifth day of the fifth month, but she noted the exact time as well: 10:47 P.M.

Dear Marler,

Giving birth to you was the hardest task I've ever known. I would never have changed the experience again. When I saw your head be born I cried because until that very moment I never really could imagine a little human being existed in my womb. The first thing you did is scream immediately. Then as quickly as you screamed, you stopped. I'm so proud of the fact that you bear my complexion. My pug nose and beautiful dark brown hair and eyes. I'm always thrilled to see you wear your daddy's ears and lips and have the same sparkle in your bright eyes. Every time I look at you I realize truly what a miracle it is to have the ability to give birth and realize how very privileged I am to have you. I know there is a god and he created you for me to give all the love I can. You see, before you were born I did not know my being had an empty space. But when you were born I realized you filled a big void and gave my life meaning I didn't know existed. Marler I will commit my life to you and always be here for you whenever you need me or we need each other. Forever your mother. I love you, Mommy.

Two and a half months later Brad made his entry. He wrote of Alissa, his daughter by his first marriage, back when he was considered command material on the police department of Pontiac, Michigan.

Dear Marler,

Seeing you born was one of the great experiences in my life. Having you as part of my life has given a new meaning to our relationship with your sister. Also this new opportunity is yours and mine to live through. Thank you for contributing to me, Alissa, and your mother. Just as I love your sister I love you also. Things I can give you are many. But the most important is to be always questioning of all that goes on in your life. If you do not question you cannot learn and grow. You have a proud heritage and I promise to learn and experience all you can. I gave you a football when you were in the hospital. You are a big boy for your age. Every dad wants a son to be successful and I'm no exception. I'll teach you about sports and business and just having fun. Everyone says you are a beautiful baby. I couldn't agree more. You look so much like your mother and me. No one can mistake you for anyone else's son. I promise to be there for you all the time. We can solve anything by just discussion. Thank you for making a difference in my new life. I love you, Dad.

The boy was baptized in a Catholic church in Colorado. Diane, herself half Mohawk, was learning about her Native American roots. Brad had studied the ways of the Lakota and other Western tribes. They decided to meld native spirituality into the Catholic ceremony. First they smudged everyone who watched with burnt offerings of the sacred medicines of cedar and sweet grass.

Then, after the baby had been christened, everyone circled them. Brad held Marler up, presenting the child to his elders. Brad then held the boy higher. He presented their son to the East and the West and the North and the South. Indians called these the sacred four directions, the center being where he stood.

* * *

They named the second child Kateri, born on November 20, 1990. She was healthy, beautiful, and blond. Diane and Brad King had moved to Michigan, settling finally in a farmhouse just outside the Marshall city limits. Brad was working as a criminal justice instructor at Western Michigan University. Diane was the morning anchor at WUHQ-Channel 41, the only TV station with news located in Battle Creek.

They planned more blending of native tradition and Catholic ritual for Kateri's christening, scheduled to be held at St. Mary Catholic Church in Marshall on Sunday, February 24, 1991, at 11 A.M.

But on Saturday, February 9, at 6:49 P.M., a call came in to the Marshall Police Department on the unrecorded line. That meant the caller had just dialed zero and an operator had patched him through.

There was crying and yelling at the same time.

"I need help!" a man's voice shouted.

Then a woman. The controlled voice of a telephone operator.

"You have them, sir."

"Please, I need help!"

Joe Delapas, the dispatcher on duty, tried to make sense out of the hysteria. The man was saying something about his wife. That she was on the ground, near her car. He found her there, coming back from a walk.

He screamed, "There's blood coming out of her mouth and she's not moving!"

Delapas got an address and dispatched a Marshall Firefighters Ambulance Unit from the fire hall just south of town.

"Unknown medical." Location, 16240 Division Drive.

The operator offered the caller's phone number. Delapas asked the caller to identify himself.

"My name is Brad King."

Delapas called the Calhoun County Sheriff's Department dispatcher on another line. Division Drive was in Fredonia Township. That was the sheriff's jurisdiction.

When he returned to the caller, the man named King was still crying, sometimes yelling, repeating the same things. His wife was in the driveway. He'd found her there, coming home from a walk. "It was very hard to understand him," he would later note in his report. "Let alone keep him calm."

The dispatcher tried to steady him by talking to him, asking him to stay on the line.

"Why did this have to happen?" he kept saying.

"Oh, I want to be with her," he said more than once.

In winter, Michigan ground could be as white and hard as cast plaster. But this week a thaw was underway. On February 9, the National Weather Service in nearby Battle Creek had logged a high of forty-three degrees at five o'clock as the sun had poked through the clearing clouds, headed for a 6:06 P.M. sunset. The farm tracts south of Marshall would need a few more days of unseasonable temperatures to make deep mud. Soy and corn stubble textured most of the fields. Snow lingered only in the shadows or where it had drifted on shorter, colder days.

Sheriff's deputy Guy Picketts had to go home for the flashlight. He'd forgotten it when he reported for the afternoon shift and another night of traffic control across the 744 square miles of territory known as Calhoun County. So, during dinner time's predictable lull, Picketts swung by his house on Mansion Street, not a half-dozen blocks east of the Brooks Memorial Fountain.

Two other sheriff's deputies were out and about that night in separate cruisers, waiting for dispatches. One car covered the eastern side of the county, the other the west, which included the Marshall fringe. The dispatches usually started after dinner. That's when the all-day drinkers got home. That's when the family fights started.

The first radio call went to the west car, eleven miles from Marshall near the county's border: "Unknown trouble. Address: 16240 Division. Subject says he was coming home from a walk and found his wife laying in the driveway."

Deputy Guy Picketts heard the call and west car response from the hand-held radio he'd taken with him into his house. The address piqued his interest as much as the call. He knew the address well.

"I'm responding," he said, grabbing his flashlight and heading out the door. "I'm here in town."

Guy Picketts sped west on Mansion Street, then south on Old 27. The county cruiser leaned through the traffic circle, its lights painting the Greek Doric shapes of the Brooks Memorial Fountain in flashing shades of red, white, and blue. Halfway around, Picketts was headed south again on Old 27. He passed a rescue unit in the first block, its nose just poking out of the Marshall Fire Station. He saw the ambulance in his mirror and surmised it was also heading for 16240 Division Drive, two and a half miles away.

The view out the cruiser's front window changed quickly. Small bungalows gave way to an old canning plant and light industrial buildings. A set of tracks. A lumberyard. A feed granary. A trio found in many rural Michigan towns. After the Kalamazoo River bridge the horizon flattened. Picketts rocketed past a golf course on the left. A Moose Lodge on the right. At Brooks Field Airport, a yellow wind sock hung limp.

Checkered asphalt and a slice of light on the horizon greeted Picketts as he turned west onto Division Drive. Only a dozen houses lined the mile of road west of Old 27. All but three homes were on the north side. The house at 16240 Division was on the south. It was the second home a half mile down the road.

Guy Picketts was marking his thirteenth year of police work. Nine years with the county. Four years with Marshall PD. He knew 16240 Division Drive better than any police officer in Calhoun County. He'd lived with his parents in the old, two-story farmhouse in the sixties. He'd spent another three years there in the seventies raising his own. Picketts knew the house. He knew the farm's red-and-white Victorian barn. He knew the 510 acres that surrounded both and the stream called Talmadge Creek that bisected the back property.

The deputy turned left into the two-hundred-foot driveway, eyeing the yard as he drove up the slight incline, past a stand of cedars and crooked oaks. The Victorian barn on his left, outbuildings and a cement silo straight ahead. A tan station wagon was parked just beyond the barn. A silver Jeep Wagoneer was parked in the branch of the driveway that jutted off toward the house. The Wagoneer's grill faced the side porch entrance; the passenger side faced the deputy.

Guy Picketts saw the body as he passed the Jeep and parked. She was two feet from the Wagoneer's left rear tire. She lay on her back, her legs folded under her at the knees. Her dark, straight hair was spread around her head on the gravel. Her arms extended over her head. Her palms faced up.

Approaching, Picketts heard something. A young boy, a preschooler. He was in the last throes of crying himself out. He was in a child seat in the backseat of the Jeep, his upper body restrained. Next to him, in a smaller car seat, was an infant. She was silent, but apparently alive, her tiny limbs assuming the still shape of her little jumpsuit.

Picketts fell to his knees next to the woman. She was in blue-and-white running shoes and baggy powder blue lounge pants and a gray "Operation Desert Shield" sweatshirt. Picketts noticed a wisp of frothy blood near her nostril. He placed his fingertips on the cardioid area of her neck. Her skin was soft and smooth and warm.

There was no pulse.

Now muffled shouting was coming from inside the house, well beyond the facade of the side porch. Picketts jumped to his feet and moved toward the noise, thirty feet away.

More yelling, still muffled. He saw movement beyond the porch door, inside the house itself, in what he knew to be the dining room. A second door on the porch, one that led to the kitchen, was open.

Then Picketts could see the figure of a man silhouetted on the porch.

"Help her," the man shouted. "Help my wife."

"They're on their way," Picketts shouted back.

Picketts strained to make some kind of identification. It was all happening very fast. The Marshall rescue unit had pulled to a stop in the driveway behind him. Picketts spun around and pointed out the body to two emergency medical technicians as they ran from the ambulance, one carrying a duffel bag of emergency equipment.

The rescue unit later logged its time of arrival at 6:54 P.M.

One EMT dropped his duffel bag as he fell to his knees at the woman's side. The other started searching for a pulse.

"Nothing."

The other EMT tried.

"I think I've got something."

Then, he thought he heard a breath. Maybe one faint, desperate breath.

One EMT sprinted to the ambulance to get an intubation kit and a defibrillator. He also sounded a general EMT alarm that the crew had a probable cardiac arrest. The other EMT cut open the woman's sweatshirt, pulled back the garment to expose her white bra and the skin of her upper chest.

Picketts was heading to the porch now as the man on the porch stepped out the door onto the sidewalk. But the EMT called out.

"My God," he said. "I think she's been shot."

Picketts turned. Headed back. He shined his flashlight on the woman's chest. There was a quarter-inch hole just to the right of her sternum, just above the bra line. A drop of blood trickled from the wound. One of the paramedics was feeding an intubation tube down her throat now.

"Try not to disturb anything," Picketts said.

The deputy turned around and approached the man again. Gotta get a handle on this, he thought. Right now.

"Your name is?"

"Brad King."

"And that's your wife?"

"Diane."

"Do you have any weapons?"

"Only a shotgun."

"Is there anybody else on the property?"

"No."

"I want you to stay right here," he said, holding out both his hands for emphasis.

The man stood motionless, his arms hanging at his sides. He stood on the sidewalk, just off the porch, some twenty-five feet from the body.

Guy Picketts would get a good look at him a little later. Brad

King was an odd-looking fellow. He was wearing Maine boots, green camouflage pants, and a loose camouflage shirt. His head was covered with a stylish wide-brimmed hat in striking red felt, something L.L. Bean called "The Crusher." The man had dressed up its crown a bit further.

A blue jay feather poked out handsomely from its band.

2

"I'm not sure what I got out here," Deputy Guy Picketts told the county dispatcher. "But I need some help *now*."

Three county cars and two Michigan State Police cruisers were speeding toward 16240 Division Drive within five minutes of the first dispatch. All carried cops who recognized the alarm in Deputy Guy Picketts's voice.

Picketts needed a lot of help. He didn't know if the shooter was still on the property. He knew little about the man near the porch. He had two EMTs who needed space, maybe protection. In seconds, a medical emergency had turned into a crime scene that needed to be secured and preserved.

Confusion introduced itself into the scene. The cardiac alarm was sounding beepers on volunteers all over Marshall. A third EMT parked his truck on the road and ran across the lawn to the house. He tried to scurry past Brad King, who was sitting on the porch steps. The EMT thought a heart attack victim was inside. King stopped the stranger in street clothes.

"Hey, you can't go in there."

"I'm here to help. Where is everybody?"

King pointed to the Wagoneer, which had blocked the EMT's view of the emergency at hand.

They were working frantically, trying to save the life of Diane Newton King. A mercury vapor lamp on a barnyard pole lit automatically with the ensuing darkness. When Guy Picketts heard an EMT say something about transporting the victim to the local hospital, the deputy ran to his squad car. He returned with his 35mm Kodak autofocus camera.

"Can I get some pictures?"

"Can you do it while we work?"

The deputy snapped six photographs. Horizontal and vertical views, taken a few steps back from the victim's feet, and points beyond. A leather key wallet lay not a foot from her legs in the gravel. Nearby there was a leather hair band. The deputy's small flash reached twenty or so feet into the scene, not deep enough to reveal Brad King standing back in the darkness.

One of the EMTs was having trouble intubating her, which meant feeding a tube down the victim's trachea for a fail-safe air passage. One EMT began CPR while somebody ran to the ambulance to get a light. Inside, the EMT asked other responding paramedics to hold off. He didn't want to "clutter the scene with extra people," he later noted. But soon, two more emergency workers would be on the scene.

The next police officer to arrive was a fifteen-year veteran named Harold Badger, a man who, with or without his sergeant stripes, could have been a stand-in for actor Aldo Ray. Badger had raced from his desk at the sheriff's headquarters just around the corner from the Brooks Memorial Fountain and drove up the driveway at 7 P.M. Two Michigan State troopers were seconds behind his rear bumper.

Picketts led Badger to the body, quickly briefing him, pointing out the bullet hole in Diane Newton King's chest. Badger pointed out something else.

"What about this?"

There was a small hole in the victim's pants. It was front and center, ten inches below her waist. One of the EMTs pulled down the waistband, revealing an apparent small-caliber bullet wound a half inch above the pubic hairline.

The two state troopers were approaching the porch now, where they found Brad King sitting on the steps. He no longer was wearing a hat. His head was smooth and shiny, the style of a balding man who'd decided it was easier to shave what hair he had left than comb it. They noted later in their official report that King's face was in his hands and that "it appeared the subject was crying."

Badger later recalled first seeing Brad King pacing, between the kitchen door on the porch and the sidewalk just below the steps. He never came farther forward than the spot where Picketts had earlier told him to stay. When Badger approached, identifying himself, he tried to make a quick assessment of the scene.

"What happened?"

King said he had been out walking earlier. When he returned he'd found his wife lying next to the car.

"Walking where?"

"Back in the fields." King motioned to the acreage south of the barn and the house.

"Have you seen anybody?"

"No," he said, shaking his head.

"Did you hear any gunshots today?" Badger asked.

"Quite a few."

Badger turned to the two state troopers, who were still standing near the porch. "Stay with him, will ya?"

At 7:04 P.M. a third county car turned into the driveway at 16240 Division, the west car that had been patrolling near the county's border. A twenty-year veteran deputy named Bill Lindsay had made the trip halfway across the thirty-mile-wide county in eleven minutes.

Badger pulled Lindsay aside, pointing to Brad King and the troopers near the porch.

"That's the husband and I want you to stick with him."

Lindsay summoned King into the porch.

"I thought it was best to get him out of there," Lindsay would later explain. "Some of the things a paramedic does can upset family."

Back at the body, one of the paramedics succeeded in the second attempt at intubation. A respirator filled Diane Newton King's lungs with cool oxygen, but she failed to breathe on her own.

One paramedic went to the ambulance to notify Oaklawn Hospital in Marshall of the victim's condition. They wanted the emergency room ready for her arrival. CPR continued. They put a headboard underneath her, then lifted her onto an emergency cot. The maneuver dislodged her breathing tube, and she had to be intubated again.

There was little blood, considering Diane Newton King was an apparent gunshot victim. The penetration was small-caliber, and there were no exit wounds. Some blood ran from the corners of her mouth now, down her cheeks, spotting the collar of her sweatshirt. It apparently was coming up her trachea, from an internal wound near her lungs.

Finally, paramedics strapped her onto a cot and carried her to the waiting ambulance. Inside, two paramedics flanked her, continuing the CPR. Someone closed the ambulance's back doors.

It was 7:08 P.M., twenty minutes from the first police dispatch, fourteen minutes since the ambulance had arrived at 16240 Division. The vehicle swayed and groaned as it made its way out the stone driveway. It turned right on Division Drive and sped away toward Marshall, its siren wailing, its light bleeding into the cold, sweeping darkness of the country night.

Her children were still in the car.

Picketts and Badger had met near the Jeep as Diane King was being moved to the ambulance. Picketts kept looking at the big red Victorian barn. The exterior was well lit, not only by the barnyard vapor lamp, but by two motion-detecting floodlights glaring from under the eaves of the house.

A high barn gable faced them. Below was the main barn door. It was wide open. There was a closed double loft door above the entrance, surrounded by three attractive double hung windows with muntins. To the right of the main entrance was another section, the barn's stable area, sheltered by another roofline stretching south.

"I used to live here," Guy Picketts said. He remembered living there and he remembered shooting varmints with his .22. He shot a lot of varmints in that barn.

Picketts was looking at the stable section of the barn now. He looked at Sergeant Badger then back in the same direction Diane Newton King appeared to have been facing when she collapsed. The white stable door on the first level was closed, but Picketts was looking higher.

"Harold," he said. "Look at that loft door."

The loft door was the sliding variety, three-by-eight-foot, trimmed in white. It was suspended over a handsome wood silhouette of a trotting horse.

The door was open slightly. Someone would later measure the space at seven inches.

"We better check the area here," Sergeant Badger then said. "And we better check that barn."

The two pulled semiautomatics from their holsters and made a quick survey of the yard around the house, then headed for the large, open barn door.

The barn wasn't lit so they had to use their flashlights. They moved forward with sneak-and-peek movements. They found a tractor and garden tools and plastic tarps. They found miscellaneous junk scattered on the plank floor. Picketts knew there was a tack room under the stairs to the loft. He shined his flashlight inside. A black mule plow harness hung on the wall. Beneath it, a young Doberman pinscher lay sleeping in some straw.

Picketts and Badger worked their way up a dozen narrow steps to the loft. They stayed low as their view opened up at the floor line. Upstairs it was wide open. The air smelled old and dusty. The floor was scattered with straw and some remnants of corn. The high ceilings and open space seemed to amplify their voices over the murmurs of more personnel arriving outside.

Picketts approached the open loft door he'd spotted earlier outside. There was a mound of straw in front. The deputy walked slowly forward, sweeping his light in front of his feet.

Something shined back. In the straw. A brief reflection.

Picketts stooped down just to the right of the opening in the loft door.

"Harold," he called, "come take a look."

It was the same color as the floor cover, various shades of

yellow. It was the same diameter as well. But unlike straw, brass threw a discernible reflection.

Badger reached into his breast pocket and pulled out a black-and-white Bic Round Stic pen. He set it down, pointing the tip at the object. They'd leave it there for the detectives. That would make it easier for them to find it.

A spent .22 caliber casing wasn't exactly easy to spot poking upwards out of the countless strands of straw.

The various versions of what Brad King did and when he did it as his wife's body was put into the ambulance and taken to the hospital would later be detailed in official police reports, statements, and court testimony. The emerging picture would be contradictory, ambiguous at best.

Right after Diane Newton King was removed from the driveway, King would later say, he approached Harold Badger on the sidewalk off the porch.

Badger later recalled asking some questions.

"Do you have any weapons on you?" Badger asked.

King responded, "I've got a shotgun. It's broken down." He gestured toward the house. "Next to the washer and dryer inside."

Badger later recalled noticing King's boots at that time. They were clean and shiny.

"That car is packed," Badger continued. "Was she getting ready to go somewhere?"

"She was coming home," King said. He added she'd been in the Detroit area, visiting family.

"Can I get my kids?" King asked.

"Go ahead," Badger said.

King walked to the car, opened the rear door. Marler had unstrapped himself from the child seat. He took the boy into the house, sat him on the couch inside, then returned for Kateri.

Sometime during this period, King asked Badger about his wife's condition.

"I don't know how she's doing," the sergeant answered.

Inside the house, King asked to make a phone call. He wanted to call someone to care for his children.

"He wanted to be with his wife in the hospital," Deputy Bill Lindsay later noted in his report. By now, the undersheriff of Calhoun County, James McDonagh was outside on the property and in command. King's request was relayed to the undersheriff, who consented.

"I hope she's all right," King told Lindsay.

He also commented to Lindsay on the law enforcement protocol. "I understand that you guys have a job to do," he said.

King phoned a couple in Battle Creek, friends of the family. They'd be there as fast as they could.

Lindsay sat on the living room couch with Brad King, eyeing the interior. The farmhouse was smartly furnished. Patterned rugs stretched across hardwood floors. The windows were done with colorful valances decorated with Southwestern patterns, colors of earth-red and deep aquamarine, distinctly Native American in design.

The deputy relied on a number of calming techniques for dealing with rural emergencies and emotion charged scenes. Lindsay had spent the first couple of minutes doing what he liked to call "getting the horsepower on somebody." He asked Brad King for his name, his address, a phone number, a date of birth.

"If a subject is forced to think of specific things of which he has ready knowledge," Lindsay later explained, "it takes his mind off of what might upset him."

"Where are you employed?" Lindsay asked.

"Western Michigan University."

"And your wife?"

His wife was the morning TV anchor at WUHQ-Channel 41, the ABC affiliate in Battle Creek.

King explained he'd spent a dozen years as a cop himself, on the Pontiac Police Department just north of Detroit. At Western Michigan University he taught criminal justice classes.

Lindsay saw a book sitting on his coffee table: *Zen and the Art of Archery*.

"You a bow hunter?" Lindsay asked.

Yes, he replied.

At 8:17 P.M. the telephone rang. King answered the phone. It was Freida Newton, the mother of Diane Newton King. She wanted to know if Diane had made it home from Detroit safe and sound.

"There's been an accident," Brad King said.

At 7:20 P.M., Barbara and Nuri Elgutaa, the couple Brad King had called earlier for help with the children, arrived at the farmhouse. Barb Elgutaa had known Diane King for eight months. Her two children had played with Marler. Later, she would recall the scene she found at 16240 Division that night:

"I walked in the house. There were two police officers in the dining room area. There was one on his way out. There was one in the kitchen with Brad, and the children were sitting on the couch. The first thing I did was look over, the first thing I saw was Marler and Kateri. I heard them crying before I even got up to the door. Marler was in shock. He was sitting on the couch, just staring.

"Brad was preparing a bottle. Kateri had been crying for a long, long time. I would guess an hour. Well, he was fixing a bottle, washing it off, picking a nipple, slowly doing, washing things off, mixing. And I just looked at him, and the first thing I thought was, are you in shock? What are you doing? The children are by themselves. There was nobody in there. My husband was in the other room with the police officer. He was somewhere in between.

"I looked at Brad, then he started to cry. And I looked at him, and I was already crying. And my first instinct was to go to those children. I wanted to get in there by those kids. And he looked at me as I came in, and that's when he started to cry. And I walked over, and I said, 'What happened?' And he just said, 'Oh Barb.'

" 'Okay,' I said. 'I'm going to get the kids. I'm going to take them back with me. . . . We'll just grab 'em the way they are. Don't worry about anything.'

"He said, 'I'll go to the car . . . Diane had some stuff packed in there.'

". . . Brad picked up Marler and walked, carried him all the way out to the car, and Marler cried, the whole time. And he put him in the car, and I settled him down, gave him gum and sat him by my kids, and he cried, and Kateri started crying, but then my husband held her, and Brad just grabbed some bottles and . . . one of the blue bags that was in the car, from the (Jeep).

"Before we left I stood outside the car and said, 'Where is she?'

"He said, 'At the hospital.'

"And I said, 'She can't be alone. I'm gonna take these kids back, get them settled, and meet you at the hospital.' "

By 7:30 P.M., parking was at a premium at 16240 Division Drive, and more arrivals were expected. The sheriff's department was trying to locate its two detectives, who were off duty for the weekend. Earlier, Sergeant Harold Badger also had requested a special unit provided by the Michigan State Police. The unit out of the Battle Creek post usually arrived in a royal blue station wagon. It had become standard procedure in recent years on major crimes, especially when there was evidence of a fleeing felon from a known location. As Brad King waited in the living room with Deputy Bill Lindsay, the gathered forces of the sheriff's department milled around outside, most of them waiting at the head of the driveway.

They were waiting for two detectives and a tracking dog.

A neighbor named Doug Nielsen had seen only one police car and one ambulance at the King residence when he and a friend came back from Marshall earlier with two large pizzas just before 7 P.M. Now Nielsen was struck by the escalation of manpower as he, his wife, and a group of friends passed the King place again. They'd left the pizza at home with a half-dozen kids, ages three to fourteen. They were heading for dinner and drinks in town.

When Nielsen approached the King driveway, he slowed. He stopped to talk to the deputy posted at the end of the driveway.

"What's going on?"

"I have to ask you to leave," the deputy said.

Nielsen did not want to leave. He was concerned as well as curious. There had been a rash of break-ins in the neighborhood in the past year. His house was on the north side of Division Drive, not a quarter mile away. He'd had electronic equipment ripped off and a .22 rifle stolen months ago. Earlier that day he'd seen a strange car parked on the road.

"I just want to ask you . . . I've got some kids—"

"I said you'll have to leave." Harsher now.

Nielsen persisted. "Hey, wait. Is it okay to leave a bunch of kids home alone next door? It looks like something really terrible has happened out here."

The deputy peered into the car for a second. "No, everything's okay now. Your kids will be fine. Now, please go ahead. We need the room."

Three hours later, when they came back from town, Nielsen saw a State Police K-9 station wagon parked on the property. He saw a figure with a flashlight hunting in the distant fields behind the King house.

My God, he thought, they're looking for somebody.

"My first reaction was they don't know nothin' about nothin'," he later recalled. "I was mad that somebody had chased me out of there when it was obvious they didn't have that situation at all in hand.

"Everything wasn't *okay*. Everything wasn't okay at all."

3

It was one of the more wacked-out things he'd seen in his twenty years as a cop. In fact, it had a Hollywood feel to it.

The original complaint had been on Detective Jack Schoder's desk for a couple of months, the note stored in the evidence room. The letter had lots of crazy shit going every which way. Different sizes and styles of type. Cut-out patterns all haphazard. The placement erratic. Scotch tape holding down the letters.

A lot of work by some very fucked-up individual, Schoder thought.

It read:

you Should Have Gone to Lunch WITH me

Now it was waiting over in the property room, the legal-sized paper that held the whole paste-up stained purple from Ninydrin, a chemical used to mark amino acids left by sweat and produce fingerprints. There was one print on the corner of the page. It was unidentified. As far as Jack Schoder was concerned, that's what was holding everything up.

The original report laid out the complaint. Al Lehmkul, one of the deputies on the road, had picked up the note after Diane Newton King called the department the night before Halloween. She said she'd found it in her mailbox, the place most local folks knew as the old Zinn farm, 16240 Division Drive.

She told Lehmkul she'd started getting calls at Channel 41 in the spring from a man in his twenties or thirties. He said his name once, but she never got it again and forgot the damn thing. He spoke slowly and deliberately. Like a mental patient on Lithium, she said. The guy wanted to know how to get into the business, about schools, training, and shit like that. She told him to check out a community college, a couple other things.

He kept calling. Sometimes three times a week. The receptionist started screening her calls, not difficult because he always asked for "Diana." Then they stopped. But then at the end of the summer, he somehow got through again. He told her he liked the way she looked. He wanted to go to lunch with her, she reported.

That's when, as far as Jack Schoder understood it, Diane Newton King politely told the guy to fuck off.

She was nine months pregnant when she got the letter. She was scared shitless, Lehmkul said. The note wasn't postmarked.

"She figured the wacko followed her home," he said.

Schoder told Lehmkul he'd give it a look, get the thing over to Battle Creek city lab for latents. Not six weeks later, Lehmkul was back at the old Zinn place. This time he talked to Diane

King's husband Brad. He'd reported an attempted B&E at the house earlier that day. Lehmkul stopped to pick up a fan letter his wife had received at the station. King wondered if it had anything to do with the complaint. Lehmkul said they sat down and talked for maybe an hour. King was home alone. They traded some stories. King said he'd put in a dozen years himself at Pontiac PD. They had taken some security precautions at work and home since the letter, he said. They had a Doberman. He seemed to know his stuff.

Jack Schoder thought he was giving the complaint the appropriate priority. Three people had handled the note: Diane, another anchor named Cindy Biggs Acosta, and Cindy's husband, Juan. She'd taken the thing over to the Acostas' house after finding it in the mailbox. Schoder made two phone calls and a trip out to the old Zinn place trying to get elimination prints from Diane Newton King.

"Diane, it's important I get your prints," he told her in December.

She started rattling off dates, a lot of them her social calendar for the month of December. "Man, it was like she was trying to impress me with all the things she had to do," he later said. Finally, Diane and Cindy Acosta showed up at the department to be printed. But as of February, he was still waiting for prints from Acosta's husband. The couple had moved to Venezuela. Maybe there was some more to do. Do some more checking on the letter the husband had come up with.

"I was working on it, but Diane didn't seem to be exceptionally concerned," Schoder later said. "I gave it the same kind of priority she did."

For the first part of Saturday evening, February 9, Jack Schoder's priority was spending an evening with his wife at the Fraternal Order of Police Valentine's party being thrown at an American Legion hall in Battle Creek.

Jack Schoder liked being a county detective. He liked the more laid-back pace. Mostly, the job was a lot of B&Es where nobody sees anything because the farmhouses are so damn far apart. They got a murder-and-a-half a year, and a genuine armed robbery now and then. But as he liked to tell the guys from Battle Creek city, he had time to work them.

"I gotta work five a week," he'd say.

On the warm days, Jack Schoder also liked to draw the ball long off the tee and come into the green high and left to right with his irons. On a good day he was shooting in the mid-seventies. Jack Schoder liked golf, and he liked people to like him. He was not very good at the hard-ass thing, so he didn't play it. He had a lot of old sixties terms still on the tip of his tongue, something probably left over from a short stretch in college and four years in undercover narcotics. He'd gotten into the business when his father gave him a job in the jail, then learned the rest riding with deputies. The old man ordered him to get rid of that goddamn Central Michigan University haircut.

"He couldn't get me to cut my hair as my father. But when I joined the department I had to cut it, man. Back then, he was the sheriff." It was a story Jack Schoder still liked to tell.

On February 9, Jack Schoder was still stirring his first whiskey and Coke at the legion hall when the beeper went off. Schoder was not pleased to hear about a shooting somewhere south of Marshall. Already, police work had pissed on his Saturday. All morning, he and volunteers sifted through pungent black mush in a burned-down, converted, one-room schoolhouse, looking for evidence in a homicide followed by an arson fire. They worked on a plastic tarp over the foundation. It had been awfully cold and smelly and wet.

Schoder left his wife at a table with friends and drove home to get his department car, a gray 1987 Grand Prix. He was looking in the rearview mirror, near the photos of his two little boys in the visor, when he saw the Michigan State Police K-9 unit come up quick, then blow by him on I-94, running code.

Jack Schoder got on the radio, talking with headquarters about calling his partner out of the same FOP party. Suddenly, he heard the voice of Jon Olson, the sheriff of Calhoun County. The sheriff sounded mighty pissed.

"Jack, it's *Diane King*."

Well, sorry, Sheriff, Schoder thought. I only knew it was a shooting. I mean, I really didn't know the chick that well.

Then it hit him.

By the time he hit the Marshall city limits, he was wondering if he had done the appropriate investigation on the file from Al Lehmkul.

Jack Schoder was hoping he had not seriously fucked up.

When detective Jim Stadfeld arrived at the same FOP party in Battle Creek minutes after his partner Jack Schoder left, someone told him at the door he'd been called to a shooting.

"Oh bullshit," Stadfeld said, laughing.

He hung up his coat and ordered a drink.

Finally, somebody convinced him it wasn't a practical joke. By 7:45 P.M., the other half of the Calhoun County Sheriff's Department Detective Bureau was out the door and on the road.

County born and bred, Jim Stadfeld, forty-six, liked living in the town of Marshall and serving where he could. The detective bureau was only part of the picture. Stadfeld did some PI work on the side and served as treasurer for Marshall Township. Unlike his partner, there had never been a cop in his family. But when he was hired by the department, he made damn sure his estranged father learned about cops real quick.

Stadfeld told the story this way: "One of the very first things I did as a policeman was book my real father in jail. I'd only met him twice, and both times were in a courtroom on child support. I turned twenty-one in March and was hired on Memorial Day in the same year. I was working in the jail. I went over to the Friend of the Court and told them my mother wasn't getting any child support, and never had."

A deputy picked the old man up. Stadfeld processed him in the lockup. "I asked him, 'Do you know who I am?' He looked at me real seriously and said, 'I don't have a clue.' So I informed him who I was. Then I booked him. And that's the last time I've seen him, in fact."

On February 9, Stadfeld stopped at his home in Marshall and changed into jeans and a sweater. He also picked up his

Cannon E-1 camera. He wanted his own for evidence work. The one the county supplied was a hopeless antique. That had become their system in their eight years together. Jack Schoder handled most of the people. Jim Stadfeld usually handled the evidence and the scene.

This was out of necessity more than anything. Jim Stadfeld had been to evidence school. He was not short on expertise, but on major felonies he sometimes found himself short on time. Crime scene documentation was its own job, something that could keep a detective from chasing other things he should. He and Schoder had complained about this, but nothing had changed in the department.

Maybe that was something Jim Stadfeld could work out when he became undersheriff. His old friend Jon Olson had promised him the job when it opened up. Earlier that year, Stadfeld had spent three months at the FBI Academy in Quantico in management school, getting ready for the job.

Jim Stadfeld *was* the detective bureau for a while before he was joined by the former sheriff's son. Some around Calhoun County said they were local law enforcement's odd couple. Schoder was gangly, animated, and emotional. The shorter Stadfeld was reserved and studious, more likely to smolder, more likely to look at the big picture, and play it safe.

Jim Stadfeld thought they complemented each other. They'd had their problems just like anybody that saw each other as much as they did. Christ, they'd worked together for nine years.

At 8:20 P.M., Stadfeld was almost on Schoder's bumper when they pulled in front of 16240 Division, parking on opposite sides of the street.

Schoder's mouth was going as they walked toward the head of the driveway. "Holy shit, Jim, this is Diane King. Jim, remember this is the lady. Jim, remember the letter. We've got this threatening letter. Oh, fuck. This is it, man."

Stadfeld didn't know about the file. He didn't know what the hell Jack Schoder was talking about.

"Jack was a basket case already," Stadfeld later said.

Waiting at the end of the drive was Undersheriff James

McDonagh, the second in command in the department, the man whose job Stadfeld was scheduled to take when he retired.

McDonagh and Guy Picketts walked them through the setup. They saw the blue wagon of Michigan State Police K-9. McDonagh said a trooper and his dog were working the property behind the barn, looking for the shooter.

"The husband is in there," McDonagh said, pointing to the house.

It was a homicide now, the undersheriff said. Diane Newton King had been declared dead on arrival, minutes after she was wheeled into the emergency room.

"Well, we better get a warrant," Stadfeld said, volunteering. They better get a warrant before they started doing any more searching on the property. He'd head back to the department and start typing the thing up.

Sergeant Harold Badger joined the gathering of sheriff's personnel in the driveway, as well as Deputy Bill Lindsay. Somebody had to tell King of his wife's death, Badger said.

"I've dealt with him before, on the letter thing," Schoder said, volunteering. "I'll go in there."

Lindsay said he'd go, too.

"I don't know, Jack," the undersheriff said. "He's a weird lookin' son of a bitch."

"Whatya mean?" Schoder said, puffing on a smoke.

"He's in full army fatigues. Jack, the sombitch just looks strange."

Deputy Bill Lindsay figured somebody developed what they called the "step method" for guys on midnights. It was the worst, delivering bad news to loved ones as they rubbed the sleep out of their eyes. In the step method you broke the news in increments: "There's been an accident. Your wife was seriously injured. They tried CPR. They took her to the hospital. They took her to the emergency room. They worked on her. They tried their best. But, I'm sorry. . . ."

In the step method, you didn't just blurt it out that somebody was dead.

"Brad, they worked on her real hard out there," Lindsay began.

"I know," Brad King said.

He was on the living room couch. Jack Schoder and Sergeant Harold Badger stood by.

"They got her to the hospital," Lindsay said. Step two. "She—"

"Yeah, Brad, she's dead," Jack Schoder interjected. "She didn't make it, man."

King buried his face in his hands, his elbows resting on his knees. He sobbed, then shuddered.

Schoder put his arm around him.

"Brad," he said. "I'm sorry for you, man."

It lasted a minute or so. When King stood up, he was out of breath.

"Brad, do you got family out here?" Schoder asked. "What can I do to help you?"

King gave Schoder a name and number: a friend in the Detroit area named Randy Wright. Schoder called the number and reached his wife. She said her husband was out, but she could probably reach him.

"Please, have him call me at the sheriff's department," Schoder said.

Schoder knew Detroit was two hours away.

"Brad, you got some church people or anybody you want me to call? A minister, maybe?"

It took a few phone calls. The pastor wasn't home, nor was his assistant. Finally, the detective was told that some people from the First Presbyterian Church in Battle Creek were on their way.

King was motionless on the couch.

"Now, Brad," Schoder said, "it's really important, 'cause you're the only person out here, you know what I mean? I gotta talk to you, man. I know it's a bad time, but I gotta talk to ya."

King nodded. "Sure. I understand."

Jack Schoder asked Sergeant Harold Badger to drive King to headquarters in Marshall. He'd catch up with him later.

It would be quiet there, and he could run some tape.

4

The air was still and cold, the kind of conditions Trooper Gary Lisle knew made a scent hug the rugged ground. Gary Lisle knew his German shepherd Travis was working. His dog's ears were straight up and he was pulling. But alone, without an escort in the darkness behind the farmhouse, Lisle preferred that whomever he was tracking was not hiding and well-armed.

The undersheriff had briefed the forty-four-year-old trooper when he arrived at 16240 Division Drive at 7:55 P.M. They had a shooting, the undersheriff said. They believed they'd found the spot up in the loft where somebody fired a round. There was a shell casing in the barn loft. The husband told them he was on the property out back. He found the body when he returned.

Lisle wanted to know exactly where police and emergency workers had walked. No one had gone farther than the cement silo fifty yards south of the barn, the undersheriff said.

"Has there been anybody up there since you found the casing?" Lisle asked, pointing to the barn. He was hoping the area hadn't been adulterated with the scent of a half-dozen cops. Not everyone knew the tracking rule: You protect the area from unnecessary contamination.

"No, no one's been up there," the undersheriff said. "I'll have Picketts go with you, and you do whatever K-9 does."

Lisle was surprised when he reached the top of the stairs to the loft. "They said no one had been up there," he would later recall. "But in the loft there was kind of a half semicircle of officers standing around."

Near the loft door, he saw the Bic pen on the straw, then the casing.

"Everybody's stayed away," somebody said.

Gary Lisle had confidence in Travis. He liked to brag about the animal to other policemen and signed his name to his official reports with a small paw print. He'd testified about Travis dozens of times in court. They had worked more than eight hundred tracks together since he picked up the shepherd from donors who'd called the state police K-9 program ten years ago. He found a note taped on the door: "Dear Trooper: The dog is out back. His name is Travis. He won't bite you. Good luck."

He was six months old, black with gold skullcap and shoulders, and chained to a tree. "There was a doghouse, and that was his whole world," Lisle said. "He craved attention."

The need for a pat on the head was used to train him to track suspects and find property. He'd hunted down bank robbers and B&E men in city neighborhoods. He'd found a wandering, disoriented mental patient. He'd saved Gary Lisle from an ambush by a couple of felons hiding in a swamp. Travis had found revolvers thrown out of cars during street crimes and dimes tossed in open fields during training demonstrations. Gary Lisle kept a log. Travis had helped make an arrest on the scene in one in ten calls.

The training literature explained scent this way: The human body has about sixty trillion cells. These cells die and are lost at a rate of fifty million cells a second. Bacteria attacks them, producing gas that rises from a person like a plume. More scent comes from human sweat, in three varieties. One kind is a temperature regulator. One kind native to the forehead, palms, and underarms. One kind triggered by fear or apprehension. These chemical compounds and other personal and environmental variables formed a scent unique to each individual.

Travis, Lisle firmly believed, had developed a special talent in his senior years. They often did not have to eliminate tracks left by police officers and bystanders. A fatal shooting four years ago confirmed it. Travis tracked a scent out of a scene contaminated with policemen and paramedics, across a field to a road where they found skid marks. After their arrest, the felons confirmed they'd fled from there in a waiting car.

"Right then I knew my dog was picking up what some people call the fear scent," Lisle later explained. "When you're scared you've done something, your heart is racing, you throw off a scent. My dog picks that up, because he's been running these people for years."

Gary Lisle was counting on that talent when he coaxed Travis over to the .22 casing in the straw. Figuring a gun ejects to the right, he pointed his hand to the left of the casing and gave the dog the command.

"Track."

The shepherd's nose went down, and his ears and tail went up. He pulled Lisle out of the loft and down the stairs. At the bottom of the stairs, the Doberman in the tack room began barking. Travis stopped, looked momentarily, then kept going, pulling out of the barn door at a forty-five-degree angle. He pulled for seven feet, then turned straight south, heading down the lane that led from the barnyard toward the cement silo.

When they headed out of the barnyard, Lisle had a police radio, a Maglite thirty-thousand-candlepower flashlight, and Guy Picketts with him as an escort. Lisle considered the cement silo the first test. If the dog tracked past the silo, he knew Travis wasn't following a police officer's scent. When the dog pulled past the structure, Lisle began thinking about the husband. He wondered if the husband had been in the barn for some reason and how far south he'd walked.

Gary Lisle wasn't able to ask Guy Picketts those questions as the dog pulled south. At the silo, somebody in the command had called the deputy back. Before he had a chance to explain that he didn't particularly like tracking down an armed killer without any backup, he'd found himself alone with the dog. The incidental light from the barnyard well behind them to the north. He had to keep his eyes on the dog, praising him when needed. He had to go with it now and count on his partner for protection.

"If he doesn't have that tension on the lead, he doesn't have a track," Lisle liked to say. "If he doesn't have that tension, he's just out sight-seeing."

Travis was still pulling, and pulling hard.

The dog stalked a variety of surfaces. The lane was mostly a mix of dormant pasture grass and hard packed dirt. In shadowed swales or open ridges vulnerable to high drifting, some snow still covered the ground. About 250 yards from the barn they came to a creek, its water the color of tannin. The stream was noisy and fast, to the point where it had carved new paths for itself around an old tile culvert that once had run under the vehicle lane. A felled utility pole and a plank now served as a makeshift bridge across the gap.

Travis pulled across the plank, Lisle sweeping his light in front of him as they did. On the utility pole where it met the south bank, Lisle saw a heel impression. Remnants of water, ice, and mud outlined a ripple pattern on the pole's creosote-soaked wood.

Over the creek, Travis pulled slightly southeast for ten yards or so, into a knoll bordered by the stream, a marsh to the east, and a line of saplings and bushes to the south. There was a small patch of snow. Lisle's light picked up two more footprints. Both appeared to be a right boot. One was facing north, the other south. The trooper noticed the deep heel impression. It left a horizontal pattern of a half-dozen, thick, serrated lines.

"I'm thinking, I only have two prints," he later said. "I figure they're the husband coming and going. But we continue anyway, until we're absolutely positive before we restart."

Lisle turned around briefly. He could still see the glow of the barnyard in the distance. He carefully stepped around the footprints. The dog pulled on.

Travis pulled due south into the stand of saplings and brush. It was a deer trail, but looked more like a tunnel through the wispy branches. There were more patches of snow and more footprints. The Maglite revealed the same heel pattern, but now they were all headed due south.

Out of the stand of small trees, the snow cleared. Travis pulled abruptly left, heading east. The dog began working the edge of a farm field, staying on its grass covered border, avoiding the plowed dirt. Lisle knew the creek was somewhere to his left. But his flashlight couldn't reach it. The damp darkness and the chill had layered the area with fog.

About one hundred and fifty yards east of the lane, Travis pulled northeast, left again, following a deer trail, into the marsh itself. It was not smooth going. There were mounds of marsh grass, between them depressions of soft mud and slush.

Just inside the bog, Lisle spotted another heel impression,

imbedded in one of the soft depressions. It looked similar to the
sole he'd seen earlier on the trail.

Twenty yards ahead the rushing creek split the marsh. Travis
pulled hard toward the stream. Lisle shortened his lead. Lisle
caught up to the shepherd just as he reached the edge. Travis
had his head down, near the water. The stream was high,
caressing the bangs of swamp grass that hung over its banks.

The dog stopped because of the natural barrier, Lisle figured.
A little praise. "Thatta boy, Travis. Track 'em out."

The dog leaped and landed in the middle of the stream,
which was about eight feet wide at that point. Lisle realized he'd
failed to give the dog enough slack.

He ran downstream several yards, looking for a narrow spot
to broad jump the water. He found Travis on the other side,
shaking himself dry.

His tail and ears were up.

"Thatta boy. Track 'em out."

The dog tracked northeast out of the marsh, then due north
across a wide open field of soybean stubble. The field was hard
packed or frozen, so solid Lisle worried about the dog's paws in
the sharp soy stubble. He could see the barn several hundred
yards away now on the left, to the west. He knew the road had
to be ahead, maybe three or four hundred yards away.

They came out of the field near a small Michigan Gas Utili-
ties pipeline station on Division Drive. Travis turned left, pulling down its berm. When they approached the driveway to
16240 Division the dog angled for the entrance. Just inside the
driveway, where the undersheriff and other police had been
standing earlier, the German shepherd's head came up.

Lisle knew his dog, and he knew he'd lost the track. They
were two hundred feet from the barn, two hundred feet from
where they began. The dog essentially had made a large circle,
a circle maybe three quarters of a mile in length.

With patrol cars in the driveway and unmarked units parked
along Division Drive, Lisle knew the dog's confusion presented
a couple of possibilities. The person they were tracking could
have jumped in a car at the foot of the driveway. Or, the area
simply had become too contaminated with other scents.

The trooper tried working Travis deeper into the driveway, but Travis remained disinterested. Lisle eyed the barnyard as Travis continued meandering. He did not see the undersheriff or any deputies. He did not see the husband he'd been told about.

Gary Lisle wanted to keep the dog working. He wanted to return to the area east of the barn and to do some more searching. He wanted to make sure the track didn't pick up again somewhere out in that field.

He'd use his radio, Gary Lisle decided. Switch it to the frequency for the Calhoun County Sheriff's Department. He had to tell somebody about those footprints, especially the one he'd found in the swamp.

"I figured they might be real important," he later said.

5

The offices of the sheriff's department sit beneath two floors of cells that constitute the Calhoun County Jail. The building is vintage 1950s, a poured concrete structure that seems to have suffered more with time and foot traffic than the district courthouse which shares the same block.

When Jack Schoder arrived, he found Brad King in the first-floor break room. He was hunched over a long lunch table, not a step or two from the department's commercial-grade Bunn coffee maker and a bulletin board tacked with everything from birthday announcements to lost and found.

"Can I get ya a coffee?" Schoder asked. "Juice?"

No, Brad King replied.

"Brad, you were a cop," he said. "You understand, man. I've got to get everything I can from you tonight."

Yes, he understood.

Schoder suggested they walk down to the squad room. There

was another table there, a smaller one. It was old, gray, and scarred from clipboards and flashlights slid across its surface, three times every day, seven days a week. There were a couple of chairs and two IBM Selectronics for typing reports. There were small lockers for weapons and varnished wooden mailboxes. The room was empty. All the deputies were either on the road or at the scene.

What Jack Schoder did not realize as they sat down was that the county dispatcher had been quite busy in another part of the building. He'd been fielding anxious phone calls from the family of Diane Newton King. Her stepfather had called repeatedly, asking what had happened, begging to know her condition.

"You'll have to wait until the detectives get in," the dispatcher had told him.

Jack Schoder sat on one side of the table, Brad King on the other. King hung his head in grief, then rubbed his bald top with his right hand. Schoder placed a Panasonic Microcassette recorder between them and turned it on.

"The following will be a conversation with Brad King, two-nine-ninety-one. It is about a quarter after nine. We're in the squad room."

Schoder paused, then continued. "I guess we just need to talk to you Brad here about anything we can that might help us shed some light on it. I guess in terms of what you heard or what you saw, or how you came upon this. I know it's going to be difficult to go through it so, so damn soon, but why don't we just start from right there, Brad?"

King cried briefly, his shoulders shaking.

"Okay," he said.

There was a long pause.

"Well . . . I went out for a walk." He stopped to sniff. "I don't know what time. Maybe six or a little after. I was home alone. My wife and kids were on their way home from Detroit."

King stopped, apparently unable to think of anything more.

"Okay," Schoder suggested, "they were in Detroit."

"Yeah. Sterling Heights."

"Okay. What were they doing?"

"Visiting Grandma."

"Her mom?"

"Yeah."

"Okay. When did they leave, Brad?"

"They left Thursday, in the morning. After I went to the university, I think. When I talked to her she said she left the house about ten-thirty."

"Okay, had she planned this visit for a while?"

"Yeah."

He'd stopped crying, answering more matter-of-factly now.

"How long had she been planning on it?"

"Maybe two weeks."

Schoder paused. He was wondering who knew Diane Newton King was gone. He continued. "Is this something she was pretty excited about? I mean, talked about at work?"

"I know her boss knew about it 'cause she didn't do the news on Friday. Someone else did it, you know. I guess her boss did it for her. I don't know. I didn't watch the news."

Schoder asked for the name of her boss. As it turned out, the detective knew the man. He went back to the subject of Diane's return.

"She's due back into work tomorrow?"

King corrected him. "No, Monday."

"I'm sorry," Schoder said. "Tomorrow's Sunday, right. Who all knew she was going?"

"Family in Detroit knew. As far as at work, I would guess probably everybody she works with knew she was gone."

Schoder nodded. "In terms of her plans on when she was arriving back home. Was that set when she left?"

King took a second to answer. "No. Well, it was set that she was coming home today."

"Today?"

"Yeah, but the time wasn't set."

"It wasn't set as far as——"

"No. In fact, I didn't know when she was coming home. She called me today. I don't know what time it was. Maybe, noon. I don't know. Somewhere in there. She called me twice. She called me this morning sometime."

Now, King began to cry.

"Yeah, we can break here, man," Schoder offered. "Anytime you want."

King pushed on. "She said she'd be leaving after talking to her cousin . . . she hadn't seen her in a while . . . who was coming over to her mother's. Then she called me later and said she was leaving later than she had planned because of her cousin. She wanted to spend more time talking to her cousin, and—"

Schoder interjected, "What's her cousin's name? Do you know which one?"

King rubbed his head. He looked lost.

"Her parents will probably know," Schoder offered before he could answer. "I can probably get that from them."

King stammered, apologizing.

"We'll get it later," Schoder reassured.

King continued. "Anyway, then she was gonna go to her sister's, 'cause her sister's kids wanted to see our kids. And then she was gonna come home. And I said, well, you know, just let me know when you're comin' home, when you leave, so I can, kinda have an idea of when you'll get here."

"Sure."

"So her mother called me, and I think that was about four-thirty. And, said Diane and the kids had just left. So . . . I . . ."

King paused then continued, "I had been takin' a nap at that time."

"What? When the mom called there?"

"Yeah. I laid back down for a little while. . . . Then I . . . decided I'd take a walk. Just kinda wake myself up. I usually take one back through the property whenever it's a nice day."

"How many acres you got back there, Brad?"

"Well, there's five hundred. It's not mine."

"You have access?"

"There's a lane back there."

"A lane?"

"Yeah, a lane that leads back to the creek. Walk through the brush, come out to another lane. . . ."

"Where'd you go on your walk?"

"Across the creek. Just straight down the lane, on the other side of the thick brush there. It's a deer trail out in back there. Follow that to get through the brush."

"Yeah. . . . Do you remember what time it was you took off on your walk?"

"Around six."

"Took off about six?"

"It was around then. I walked back a ways, and just kinda sat on one of the old bales of hay for a while."

Schoder paused. "How far are you from the house?"

King was thinking.

"Quarter mile?" Schoder offered. "Half mile?"

"At least a half mile, if not more. Closer to a mile."

"That far away, back in there?"

"I walked quite a ways. Hard to judge."

"So you went back and just kinda sat, and then you figured it's about time for them to be gettin' back home."

"Yeah, it was dusk. Just startin' to darken up. I don't know what time it was. I didn't have a watch with me or anything. By the time I got back to the house it had gotten a lot darker than when I started walkin' back."

"Yeah."

"Saw her layin' there, by the car."

King paused between the next few sentences.

"I ran over. Grabbed her. Called to her. Shook her. And she was just motionless."

Schoder was still thinking about what King might have heard. "Let me ask you, and it's an obvious question. I'm sure you would've mentioned it, but did you hear anything at all in the solitude of being out there?"

"No, I could hear the traffic from the expressway."

"That's it, huh?"

"Yeah. I . . . I don't know. I thought I heard a gunshot. But it sounded like it came from way at the other end of the property."

"That's not unusual to hear out in the country."

King agreed. "No, I didn't pay any attention to it. I mean,

I was hearin' 'em off and on all day today. People were, I don't know, rabbit huntin' or poachin' deer."

"Okay, you thought you heard one gunshot?"

"Yeah, but I didn't pay any attention to it. I'd heard gunshots all day. I have no idea what kind of gun it was. Can't tell, far away anyway."

Schoder returned to the time factor. "You come up there, then you go in the house. Okay, can you give me an estimate from the time you heard that one shot?"

He couldn't.

King seemed stumped.

"Are you a half hour away?" Schoder asked.

"Oh must've been."

King thought about it some more. "I kinda walk briskly when I go out there . . . especially comin' back, cause there's not much to see when it's gettin' dark. I guess I . . . I can't figure out how long it took." King sighed deeply.

"Okay," Schoder said.

"Fifteen minutes maybe. I don't know."

Schoder wanted to know if he'd seen or heard anything walking back to the house.

"Damn car door slam, or two doors slam?" the detective suggested.

"No."

"Tires peal out? Engines run?"

"Nope," King said, shaking his head.

"Not a goddamn thing?"

"Nothin'. Totally quiet around there. Totally *quiet*. Like it always is. My car was sittin' there. I walked up. Soon as I saw the Jeep . . ." His voiced trailed off.

"So you went up, shook her. And she was kinda motionless, huh?"

His voice was getting lower. "I cried, I knew something was wrong with her. Called to her . . . couldn't even. . . . I have the sheriff's department on speed dial."

"You have a speed dialer?"

"Yeah, I couldn't even remember the number, so I just pushed 'O' for the operator."

"Yeah."

"I told 'em I wanted, needed the police, and then . . . I don't remember much of the conversation. She gave me, I guess it was the Marshall Police Department."

"Yeah."

King was barely audible.

"Seemed like it took forever. . . ."

The detective reached for the tape recorder and turned it off. The phone was ringing in the squad room.

Jack Schoder listened to the dispatcher on the telephone.

The dispatcher was upset. "Jack, what the hell am I supposed to do? The family is on the phone and they know something bad has happened."

Shit, why hasn't this been handled by somebody else? Schoder thought. I'm not going to tell them there's a death in the goddamn family over the phone. That wasn't the way it was done. I got a shitload of things to do.

He came up with a quick compromise. "If they want to talk with Brad," he told the dispatcher, "that's fine with me."

The dispatcher put the call through. It was Royal Newton, Diane King's stepfather.

Schoder handed Brad King the phone.

"Brad, it's your in-laws."

King reached out and put the receiver to his ear. He said one sentence.

"Diane is dead."

He began crying again and handed back the phone.

"Hello," the detective said. "Hello."

There was no one on the line.

Brad King continued crying for about a minute. Jack Schoder was worried now. He wanted to keep the interview flowing, but now he thought he'd lost his subject.

"Is everything going to be okay?" he asked King, motioning toward the phone.

"Well, there's going to be some real problems there," King said, sniffling.

Schoder wasn't sure what he was talking about. He pushed the record button on the Microcassette again. He tried to think of something to bridge them back into the interview.

But it was King who brought them back on track.

"Where were we?" he asked.

Schoder offered a fragmented summary, then they were interrupted again. Someone had brought in a consent form for Brad King to sign. Schoder explained that they needed permission to search everywhere on the property. They might also have to call the landlord, Frank Zinn.

"He's just checking to make sure you have access to all the buildings," Schoder said. "And you appreciate that—having been a cop."

King said he understood. He offered directions, which buildings were locked, which weren't.

"Okay, so let's try and get back to where we were. You waited, and it seemed like a long time for help to arrive, and I guess we can note what the hell happened from there."

Schoder wanted to move into the area that had been troubling him for hours: The phone calls. The note in the mailbox. The viewer that had been bothering Diane Newton King.

"Let me ask you: Over the last few days, or few weeks, if ah, there's been any strange activity at all in the neighborhood, anybody driving by that you've noticed, or that you and Diane talked about."

"No," King said, his voice on the edge of crying.

"Has she received any of those calls?"

"No. Not since . . . the letter."

"That goes back several months."

"Yeah, he wrote the letter." And, King added, someone had called the station when she was on maternity leave in the fall, wanting to know if she'd had the baby yet.

"Called the office?" Schoder asked.

"Yeah, called the office, the main number. Yes. And the receptionist wasn't giving the information out. . . ."

That was the only call King knew of since the series of harassing calls culminated in the threatening letter on October 30.

Schoder digressed for a while. He spent a couple minutes asking about Diane's trip to the Detroit area prior to the murder. King said his wife had gone there on Thursday to hear a speaker at a Salvation Army conference. Then she'd visited her family, staying at her mother's house in Sterling Heights.

Schoder wanted to pin down if Diane King's exact time of return was known to anyone besides Brad King.

"She didn't talk to anybody other than me about it. And she just said, I'll be coming home, you know, Saturday, and we hadn't settled on a time."

King volunteered more information about her return: Diane's plans were fluid. He didn't know the exact time of her arrival back in Marshall until his mother-in-law called him "to let me know when she left."

Schoder moved back to the threats at work again. He recalled them having a brief discussion about the threatening letter.

"I guess it was actually last summer?"

King corrected him. "It was fall."

"Fall."

"Yeah, I was at the university when she called me when she found it."

"Okay."

"Maybe in October."

"And she's not brought that up or had any more problems in the last few weeks?"

"No," King said, firmly. "Would've been on the phone with you if we had."

"Yeah, I talked to her not too long ago, you know."

"We always tried to be careful," King added.

The interview continued, often rambling back and forth in subject matter, consuming nearly an hour's worth of tape. They talked about the Doberman. Schoder had seen the dog in the tack room.

"You guys, you have a pet dog?"

"More like a lover than a dog," King said. "Still a puppy. Yeah, she doesn't bark."

"She doesn't bark?"

"Only at animals. She wouldn't, if you walk up she won't bark. She'll just jump up on you like if she's loose."

"Was the dog loose?"

No, King said. He didn't take her on walks. He was worried she might try to chase down the deer on the property.

They also talked about Diane's schedule. Following her maternity leave, she'd been back in the anchor's slot at WUHQ since the first of the year. She left the house between four-thirty and five in the morning weekdays. Usually she was home by two in the afternoon.

"Who takes care of the children?" Schoder asked.

"I do. Except on Thursday. They go to day care, because I have to leave for the university."

Finally, Schoder got around to asking Brad King what he did for a living.

"Okay. What do you do, Brad?"

"I teach. I teach at Western."

"What, are you a professor?"

"I'm an instructor. I don't have my PhD yet."

Brad King chuckled momentarily, then stopped.

"How many classes do you teach over there?"

"I'm teaching one right now."

"So you only work one day a week?"

"Yeah. Last semester I had three."

"So then you're around the house all the time?"

"Yeah."

"Except Thursday. At least this semester."

"Yeah."

They talked about cars. Diane had a car. He had a car. They were visible most of the time when they were parked.

"I guess I'm trying to think if I was kind of watching the house, and picking up on a routine, you know what I'm saying?"

"Yeah, we're pretty routine to tell you the truth," King said.

Schoder explained how he and his wife parked their cars at his house.

"I don't know what I'm going to do," King said.

"Yeah, it's a real difficult situation," Schoder said. "To say the least."

King was gasping now. "God, I loved livin' out there, but I don't know. . . ."

"Be pretty tough."

"I don't wanna take the kids away from there. They love it. Well, my son loves it so much." King's voice strained, but he did not cry.

Schoder asked King about the age of his children.

Marler would be three in March, King said. Kateri was only three months.

As King calmed, they talked about extended family. He said his family was in Texas. His mother and brother lived there, though the family were Michigan born. They discussed the possibility of King's mother-in-law coming from Sterling Heights to help watch the children. King didn't like that idea.

"Yeah, she's gonna watch 'em," King said. "That's gonna be a problem. I don't want them to go with her."

It was the second time in the interview that Jack Schoder noted conflict between Brad King and his in-laws.

Schoder changed the subject back to the shooting. He was still focused on that obsessed fan. "Let me ask you Brad, can you just think of anything at all that might help us have an idea as to what the hell happened there? Any indication of any feelings that you've been getting from Diane that—"

King interrupted, seemingly dismissing the stalker. "No, in fact, last time we even discussed this problem was when she was home on maternity leave. You know, haven't heard from this guy. . . . We were watchful."

He reiterated, they had tried to be careful, just in case. They had watched for strangers in the neighborhood, people scoping out the house. There was no place near the farmhouse for someone to spy on them without being noticed. King pointed out he would have seen somebody stalking earlier in the day.

"I would have had to notice it," King added.

And as for today, King said, "I was outside almost all day."

"Were you?"

"Yeah, I was working on the porch. I was in and out of the house. In and out of the barn."

"You remember what time you laid down?"

"What time did I say my mother-in-law called to say—"

"About four-thirty."

"I probably had been down a half hour, maybe an hour. I don't know, somewhere in there."

"Okay."

"I really didn't, you know, pay attention to the clock."

"Right. You're not wearing a watch, I see."

"No, I carry a pocket watch in my jeans."

Schoder nodded at his army pants. "Not in those?"

"No, in my jeans upstairs in my room."

"Okay."

King apparently realized that Schoder was curious about his clothing. "I just, you know—"

Schoder answered for him. "You're just hanging around in your fatigues today?"

"Yeah, 'cause I was working outside."

Back to the time again. Schoder asked him to pinpoint some key times throughout the day.

King said he woke up at 8 A.M. He started working outside the house around ten o'clock. Diane called him once from Detroit before he went out.

"Oh, I did leave the house," King added.

"Did ya?"

"I went and got a McDonald's for lunch."

There was a McDonald's in Marshall, a few minutes' drive from the farmhouse. When he returned he worked outside more, let the dog run around, then took the nap.

"Tryin' to pin times down again. Four-thirty. What caused you to think it was four-thirty you got that phone call?"

"Well my mother-in-law said that Diane was on her way home. So I looked at the clock on the VCR to see what time it was, so that I would—"

Schoder finished for him. "Estimate?"

"Estimate when she was gonna get home."

"Yeah, how long does that trip take?"

"Oh, about two hours and fifteen minutes, give or take."

"That's not pushing it."

"Not pushin' it." And Diane wouldn't speed with the kids in the car, he added.

"So we've got that locked in," Schoder said. "That was at four-thirty."

"Yeah."

Schoder began answering King's questions for him. "Because of the VCR time, then you crashed out again. The phone call probably didn't wake you all the way up?"

"No."

"Okay."

"I was sleepin' pretty good. I laid back down but couldn't get back to sleep. So I just laid there. I turned the TV on. Don't remember what was on."

"Sports?"

"No, I don't like watchin' sports on TV. I don't know what it was."

There was a long pause. "I didn't even really watch it," King continued. "I just turned it on to turn it on."

"Have noise."

"Yeah."

Finally, King said he could only guess. It was probably around six o'clock when he decided to take the walk. "I did not look at the clock. I just kinda looked outside and said: Well, if I'm going to go for a walk I better do it now. It'll wake me up. By the time I get back, Diane and the kids will be coming home and we'll go get a pizza and have dinner."

King said he closed the blinds and turned on the light in the living room because he knew it would be getting dark when he got back.

Schoder wouldn't let go of the time issue. He wanted to know more.

King said, "I'm just saying it was around six based on . . . how light it was out. You know, it was starting to get a little dark, but it was still pretty light out. And I thought, well, you know a little twenty-minute walk and I'll be back in time."

"In time for Diane."

"She wouldn't have been home more than a minute, couple minutes or, you know, ten minutes or five minutes, and the truth is I figured I'd be back before she was."

"Yeah," Schoder said.

King repeated it. "I really didn't even think that she'd get home before me."

Schoder wanted to know if he locked the house.

Yes, King said he kept the house locked when he was gone.

"Are there any guns in the house?"

"A shotgun."

"That's it."

Yes, and it was disassembled, King added. He said he hunted deer and rabbit with it.

Schoder summarized the times again, making sure he'd understood correctly.

Then he turned off the tape recorder. That was it for Brad King. For now.

6

Randy Wright spent the first forty-five minutes on the car phone with his wife Cathy. Miles, memories, and shock filled the rest of the trip.

In the well-appointed silence of his Lincoln Continental, Randy Wright kept coming back to the threatening letter. Diane had mentioned it when they entertained the Kings during the holidays.

"Randy, I'd like to tell you I'm not scared," she said. "But I can't."

"Well, Diane, I'd be careful," he said. "Watch yourself."

Considering a recent rash of publicity about obsessive fans, Randy Wright figured it wasn't prudent to just blow something like Diane's letter off. Now, he wondered if he shouldn't have done more.

Randy Wright had done well for himself dispensing counsel. His home and corporate law practice were both in Birmingham, one of Detroit's most pampered suburbs. Real estate. Banking. Conflict resolution. International deals from Mexico to Russia. He did not do criminal work or divorce. He preferred working with people that were on the upside of the cycle. When it came to friends, however, loyalty was what counted. Too many people, he thought, bailed out when everything turned to crap.

Randy's wife had tracked him down at an indoor soccer game for his seven-year-old son and given him Jack Schoder's number.

"She was shot," the detective told him. "We think it's a homicide."

He sounded concerned. "Brad doesn't seem to have any family or anybody around and he's asked for you, Mr. Wright. Frankly, a person in this situation I really hesitate to just send him out on the street, you know. I don't know what to do with him. He can stay here as long as he wants, but at some point he is gonna want to leave. And I hesitate to have him be alone."

Randy never hesitated. Brad King was a friend. Not his best friend, but a *good* friend. They'd never hunted or fished together, or chummed around much. But they had wives and kids, and they'd always kept in touch.

Marshall was more than two hours by freeway from Birmingham, too long to ponder the fragments of information from the detective, not long enough to cover everything he knew about the couple he'd help match into a perfect fit.

The memories covered twenty-five years. They met at Western Michigan University, where they'd roomed together in the dorm. They pledged Tekes, or Tau Kappa Epsilon. Brad was what they used to call "a face man." Former high-school quarterback. Money, clothes, and looks. Randy became the chapter president, graduated from Western, and rose to lieutenant after he joined the Army. In Vietnam, he led a platoon through the Quasion Valley. In 1970 it was straight guerilla work. Combat.

Booby traps. Infections. And sixty-day patrols into hell. On one patrol, the combination whittled his platoon from forty men to ten.

Brad didn't go to Nam, but that never slid between them when the war was over. When Brad graduated from Western, he became a Pontiac cop. Randy Wright always figured that was some kind of war of its own. It didn't surprise him when Brad became disenchanted with police work after fourteen years.

What surprised him was when Brad announced he was leaving his first wife Gail when his daughter Alissa was still toddling around. Hoping to help them save the marriage, he introduced Brad and Gail to est.

The self-empowerment program had been chronicled by Tom Wolfe in his "Me Decade" essay and lampooned in the movie *North Dallas Forty*. Its name was a cerebral acronym for Erhard Seminars Training, named after founder Werner Erhard. Randy experienced it as a series of rigorous training sessions that considerably enhanced his self-worth and worldview. He took what he needed from the training and moved on. Others went off into the deep end with it.

Est couldn't save the first King marriage, but it helped set the stage for the second. Randy Wright first spotted Diane Marler when she was an est volunteer. Somebody coined the word vivacious for gals like her. She was an ROTC candidate at Wayne State University and seemed to have an endless supply of drive and personality. She also wasn't afraid to test people, challenge their assumptions, make them think.

Ten years ago, Randy Wright thought old friend Brad King needed a good kick in the pants, and Diane Marler might provide the perfect boot. After separating from Gail, Brad was thirty-five and dating women Randy guessed were in or hardly out of their teens. "Children," Randy used to call them. One day, Randy pulled his old friend aside.

"Brad, at least you ought to date an adult, you know," he told him. "I know this gal. She's single. She's sharp. And she's gorgeous. And, Brad, she's certainly no child."

Brad King walked right over and introduced himself when

Randy pointed her out at an est function. Not a year later they were living together in Colorado. Brad fell hopelessly in love with her on the first date, he later said. From the day he met Diane, Randy Wright had suspected Brad would.

The truth was, Randy Wright liked Diane King as a friend every bit as much as Brad. In the last, dark miles on I-94 between Jackson and Marshall, Michigan, the attorney struggled with the news that she was dead. More unbelievably, Diane was *murdered*.

As he saw the Marshall exit approaching, Randy Wright knew he was on his way to mourn as well as help.

Detective Jack Schoder met him at the entrance of the Calhoun County Sheriff's Department. In the break room, he answered some questions. The detective wanted to know how long they had been friends, how they'd met.

"You know, I knew her," Schoder said after Wright finished. "I knew Diane."

Schoder said he was working on a complaint Diane made that she was being harassed, he said. He sounded apologetic.

"Oh really," Randy Wright said. He was surprised. Diane had not mentioned that the matter had gone that far with the authorities.

Schoder was apologetic, defensive. "Man, there was no real evidence to think it was going to turn to this," he said, shaking his head.

Wright had not meant to imply any blame.

"Did they have trouble?" Schoder asked. "With their marriage?"

"We just saw them over Christmas," Randy said.

That night, they'd all sat around the Wrights' fireplace, having holiday drinks. Diane did most of the talking. Diane always did. Brad listened patiently. He always seemed content to let her talk, occasionally offering up a wisecrack, punctuating it with that Jack Nicholson grin he had. Brad had always been pretty laid-back, "Mr. Go-With-the-Flow." Diane could talk for hours about kids, TV, and career plans, about politics, peace or war. Randy and his wife used to laugh about it.

"My God, I wonder if she ever breathes," Cathy always said.

During the Christmas visit, Diane was talking about how she'd fallen in love with motherhood. "Hey, I like this mother thing," she told everybody. "I thought last year that I wanted to be on a station in Detroit or Grand Rapids. Now all I want to do is be a stay-home-mom. I wish Brad could go full-time at Western. Then we'd be all set."

But the homebound mom had ambitions, mainly, a video company she was calling Two Worlds Productions. She wanted to produce Native American education films for public schools. She had her eyes on funding from sources ranging from the Kellogg's Foundation to the National Geographic Society. At the farm, she wanted to get some livestock and board some horses, maybe put Brad to work refinishing antiques and start a cottage industry of crafts. Yet, she'd also sent out resume tapes to a TV-talent agency for a possible placement.

That was the Diane Newton King, Randy Wright knew. She always had something going. She put her choices on parade and did most of her thinking aloud.

"No, I didn't notice any marital problems," Randy told Jack Schoder. "Nothing I was aware of, at least."

The way Diane talked about her schedule and agenda, he didn't think she would have the time to work something like that in.

They made their way to the squad room. Brad was sitting at a table with some people from his Presbyterian church. It was an odd contrast, the camouflage gear and his countenance. His shoulders were stooped and collapsed inward. He looked like he'd been crying for hours.

"He looked like he was in total despair," Randy later said.

King stood and embraced him, weeping.

"Oh, Randy. Randy, she's dead. She's dead, and what am I going to do?"

Later, Jack Schoder summoned Randy Wright into the hall.

"I'm worried, Randy," Schoder said, puffing nervously on a cigarette. "I'm worried about his emotional condition."

Randy shook his head. "What can you say about something like this?"

"It's important that you take care of him," the detective told him. "I need you to watch him. I'm worried about him."

Randy Wright agreed. Schoder left to attend to some police business.

After the church people left, Randy Wright just listened. Brad rambled from subject to subject. Mainly, he was worried about the kids. Himself.

"Randy, what am I going to do?" he kept asking. "Do they know how this happened? Why did this happen?"

"I don't know, Brad. They haven't told me much at all."

As midnight neared, they began talking about leaving. They wanted to go to the funeral home in Marshall where Diane's body had been taken.

Jack Schoder discouraged them when he returned. "I doubt if anybody's up there," he said. "It's pretty late."

Randy Wright wondered about the farmhouse. Brad needed a change of clothes.

"We have to freeze the scene," Schoder said. "We have lights out there, and we're gonna have the place tied up for a couple of days."

"Well, we're not going to sit here for a couple of days," Wright said. "Brad, let's get a motel."

The detective suggested the Arborgate, a motel near the freeway on the edge of town. The detective was eyeing Brad's feet, his Maine boots with the rubber bottoms and leather uppers.

"Listen, Brad," he said, "we're going to be going back out there looking for tracks."

King interrupted him. "Here."

He pulled off the boots and handed them to the detective.

"Let me get you something," Schoder offered.

The detective returned after a trip upstairs.

Randy Wright thought what had happened to his old friend was downright pathetic. Brad King was wearing jail slippers when they left.

7

It was a madhouse, Denise decided. The whole family had come together at the old homestead, and now the little ranch house on St. Joseph Street was a madhouse.

Darlene, her eldest sister, was shouting. She never did put up with nonsense. And now she was yelling at their stepfather Royal about the nonsense with the telephone.

Royal was adamant. "Now, there's no sense calling, damn it. There's just nothing we can do right now."

Everyone wanted Royal to call the sheriff out in Marshall again. Everyone wanted to know what had happened. Why was Diane dead? How did it happen?

Who did it?

"I'll be damned if I'm just going to sit here," Darlene said. "I'm going to call them myself."

Royal stood up. "Listen, who do you think pays the phone bill around here?"

He walked to the telephone. When he sat back down, he cradled it defiantly in his lap.

Freida, their mother, sat nearby. She was rocking back and forth in silence. She, at least, had spoken to Brad earlier.

Brad. Why wasn't Brad calling now?

Because of Brad, she thought, here we are fighting Royal. Dear Jesus, what has happened to my sister?

A ringing telephone had shattered all their nights. Darlene, the oldest sister, had already been with their mother for a couple hours. She and her husband had sped over from her house seven miles away in Utica when all anyone knew was there had been "an accident."

Denise was the youngest, thirty-two now. She and her husband, Don Verrier, had just tucked their children in when Royal called.

"You've got to do something bad," Royal told Don.

Don didn't know what he was talking about. Royal sometimes didn't make any sense.

"Don, you have to tell Denise that Diane is dead."

"Dead? How?"

"We don't know. We only know that she is dead."

"Where's Brad?" Denise asked, grabbing the phone.

"He's at the police station."

"They think *he* did it?"

"What do you think?" Royal said.

Allen was a year older and out with his girlfriend Nancy. The message was waiting at her house. He was so upset he threw up in the driveway as they ran out to his car to come over.

Gordon was the oldest. Quiet, unassuming Gordy. He was eating his birthday cake for his forty-first with his sixteen-year-old daughter Kim by his first marriage, when the telephone rang.

Now they were all there with Mom and Royal. Royal was seventy, but still as wiry as the day their mother brought him home. He fought Hitler in Europe with the Canadian Second Division and was the man who married their mother and took on an instant family. But they all thought he was a cranky dictator, and the tragedy of the night hadn't changed that a bit.

"We need to keep trying," Darlene persisted.

"We are not going to bug those people anymore," Royal said. "They've got their hands full."

Royal was looking through the phone book now, deciding who he was going to call, which relatives and friends would receive the horrible news.

Denise joined the conflict. "Royal, what is wrong with you?"

She pointed at her mother. She was still rocking, catatonic with grief.

"Your wife . . . she just lost her baby. Mom just lost a child. And you want the phone. What is wrong with you?"

"Hell with it," somebody said. "Let's just go to a phone booth and call."

"Phone booth? I'm just gonna go home," Darlene threatened. "You know, Royal, I don't need your goddamn phone."

Brad, Denise thought. *Why doesn't Brad call?*

* * *

They had to rehash Diane's three-day visit. Talk about what she did, where she went, what happened, as if that might somehow make order of the chaos, as if that might somehow keep her from leaving all their lives in an instant.

On Thursday, Diane arrived with the kids to the house on St. Joseph Street. She came around noon after delivering the morning news breaks, the way she always did, when "Good Morning America" was on Channel 41 in Battle Creek. Diane had made several such weekend visits without Brad since the baby Kateri was born. Without Brad around, they talked about a lot of mother and girl stuff. And as far as they knew, Brad was content to stay behind to work at the university and tinker with his hunting and his projects, like the porch he was building out at the farm.

Diane was in exceptionally good spirits. Channel 41 gave her Friday off so she could attend a speech in Detroit by General Eva Burrows, the head of the Salvation Army who'd come from England to dedicate the new Detroit headquarters. Diane was on the Battle Creek board of directors for the church. The event wasn't far from the house on St. Joseph in Sterling Heights, a half hour north of downtown Detroit.

On Thursday, Diane told Denise she wanted to leave Marler and Kateri with their grandmother. Brad would pick them up on Sunday or maybe Monday.

"Brad and I could use the time alone," she said.

But Kateri had a cold, and Frieda reminded her she was still feeding her daughter from the breast as well as the bottle. Maybe she shouldn't leave Kateri, Freida suggested.

"But I'll be happy to keep Marler," she said.

Freida and Marler were very close.

"Well, if I'm going to take one, maybe I better take them both," Diane said.

Diane talked to Kateri as though the three-month-old infant could understand. She always was talking to her kids. "Boy, wouldn't your daddy be surprised to see you," she said.

It wasn't the only plan subject to change that weekend. On

Friday, Diane complained to her cousin Elaine Wash that the kids weren't feeling well.

"I probably shouldn't go to that speech," she said.

No, she decided when her future sister-in-law Mary Kozak, Gordon's fiancée, dropped by on her way to Oakland Mall. Instead, she should go shopping. She'd just received a $275 clothing allowance from Channel 41. Mary wanted to pick out a ring for her wedding, which was a month away. Diane, in fact, had a new engagement ring. Brad had taken her original band, had it mounted with a big one-karat diamond, and presented it to her for Christmas.

"Isn't it beautiful?" she was telling people. "I have no idea where Brad ever got the money."

"I wish Gordy and I had a chance to get up to your farm," Mary told her during the ride. "But he's always so busy. I should just come up without Gordy."

"Why don't you just come back with me, Mary?" she asked. "Go ahead, come back with me this weekend."

No, Mary admitted, she was too busy with the wedding scheduled for March 9.

The shopping trip lasted a good four hours. Diane helped Mary pick out a wedding band at Service Merchandise, then pulled Mary from store to store at the mall. They hit a sale at Winkleman's, laughing themselves silly as Diane modeled three or four dozen dresses. She found a dress in cardinal red with white lace for Gordy's wedding and an identical one in deep green for Kateri's christening. A hundred dollars, marked sixty percent off. The design seemed to call for one size up on her petite five-foot-two frame.

"Oh my God, I've got to buy this dress in a nine," she said. "Mary, don't you dare tell anybody I'm in a nine."

As they drove back, they talked about Diane singing at the wedding. She had a professional's soprano.

Then, she turned to Mary like a light had just gone on.

"You know I just thought of something, Mary. There's no way I can leave Kateri with my mother for the weekend. I'm still breast-feeding."

Friday night, Diane was supposed to stop at Denise's house

in Mt. Clemens, but ended up staying late chatting with her old high-school girlfriend, Gina Zapinski. When she returned to the Newtons, she lay on the bed with her mother for a couple hours, watching TV into the early morning. Marler curled up next to her. She rested her head on Freida's stomach. She put Kateri on her own tummy.

On Saturday, cousin Elaine came over. They saw each other maybe a half-dozen times a year. Elaine Wash was twenty years Diane's senior with three grown children of her own. Diane had promised to show her how to make baskets out of paper bags and twists. Diane had three of them in the works, one for Kateri, one for Freida, and one for her stepdaughter Alissa.

Diane talked about wanting the weekend alone with Brad. "You know, I need some quality time alone with my husband," she said.

Elaine, married more than thirty years, read between the lines. "When somebody says something like that, you know that something's up. I never worried about 'quality time' with my husband. You have kids. You're together. And that's that. It's one of those terms people use who are having trouble. It's one of those terms marriage counselors use."

The subject of the obsessed caller came up as they folded the bags into weaving strips. She talked about the letter and the scratch marks on the doorplate.

"Maybe you ought to just get a gun and load it," Elaine said. "Keep it up on the refrigerator where nobody can get it."

"I can't live life looking over my shoulder," Diane told her. "I can't live like that. I've just got to go on living like it doesn't make a difference."

Elaine told her how she'd taken karate classes years ago. They began laughing.

"Yeah, if somebody attacked me, I'd be thinking about am I pushing off the correct foot for this kick?" Elaine said. "We're just not programmed for violence when it comes. We're not programmed. They are. We just can't live like that."

There were hints of simpler days. Diane's big plans for the farm in Marshall reminded Elaine Wash of her Sundays in the fifties, when Diane's father Herbert was alive. The Marlers rented a farm on Fourteen Mile Road near Schoenherr. Family congregated on every Sunday. Leaves were changing colors or a pig was being slaughtered or there was a new pony to ride. Freida was always running to the store to get more food for unexpected guests. Even when the family moved to St. Joseph Street, there was little more around them than woods and a riding stable up the road. Over the years sprawl and subs filled in the space.

"She wanted a farm, like when she was a child," Freida said.

"She wanted to recapture those memories, those times," said Elaine.

On Saturday, as they wove baskets, Freida worked on a customer in her home beauty shop, a little cottage business she had. The customer had a baby sheep for Marler, a lamb born on her son's farm. Darlene was offering her another Doberman, plus she knew somebody looking for a home for their horse.

"Oh, my Diane would love that," Freida said.

Freida sometimes put "my" in front of her name.

"You should have seen my Diane's eyes light up when I told her," Freida later recalled. "Little Marler was just as thrilled as she was, running around talking about the sheep and the ducks he was getting."

There had been several calls to Brad over the three days. They heard her talking to him a couple times on Saturday. Nobody paid much attention to the calls. She was on the phone in the other room.

Then, in the late afternoon, Diane decided to head back to Marshall, deciding to take Marler and Kateri home. Not only was Kateri still sick, Marler was clinging to her. He didn't want to leave his mom.

Elaine Wash helped her pack up. They strapped the kids into the car seats. Diane wanted to call Brad to tell him she was leaving, but Royal was using the telephone. She asked her mother to do it. With all the stalker nonsense, she wanted Brad to know her schedule, especially when she would be getting home near dark.

Freida and Elaine and Diane all said goodbye with hugs and kisses. Freida waved as her daughter drove off. The trip was usually two hours and fifteen minutes. Home was 120 miles away.

Freida Newton lingered a bit outside. It was a balmy day for February. She picked up the playthings Marler had left in the yard. A toy tractor. Tonka trucks. When she got inside, she telephoned the farmhouse in Marshall. Brad answered the phone.

"Diane's on her way home now," she said.

"Okay."

That was it. Words had never linked them.

Freida eventually lay down on the couch to watch TV. Diane always called when she got home. She didn't and Freida dozed. She woke at 8:15 P.M., nearly two hours past the time Diane would have arrived home.

Freida thought about calling, decided against it, then changed her mind again.

Brad answered the phone.

"I'm just calling to see if Diane made it home okay."

"There's been an accident," he said.

She thought it was a car accident.

"Where are the kids? *How* are the kids?"

"The kids are fine."

"Where is Diane?"

"She's in the hospital."

Freida was angry. "Why aren't you with her?"

"They won't let me," he said.

He wouldn't talk to her. He never would talk to her.

"I'm on my way," she said, hanging up the phone.

Royal had stopped Mom. That's the way Denise understood it. He insisted on calling the hospital first. The hospital had referred him to the Calhoun County Sheriff's Department. He'd made several calls there, but couldn't get anything from the dispatcher. Finally, after 9:30 P.M., he'd reached a detective named Jack Schoder who had put Brad on the phone.

"All he said was, 'Diane is dead,' " Royal told everyone.

Royal later had gleaned a few more details from another call to the detective. She'd been shot. Brad said he'd been out walking on the property. He'd found her in the driveway.

When Brad didn't call, it was just a matter of time before the stones started flying. Everybody began questioning Brad's role. He knew Diane didn't like coming home to an empty house. Why had Brad taken a walk? Why wasn't he there to meet her? Maybe he *was* there to meet her. Maybe he'd sent the letter. Maybe he'd made the harassing calls.

"No," Denise said. "He couldn't have done it. He *couldn't* have done this or made the calls. Diane would have recognized his voice. She'd recognize her own husband's voice. Those are his kids. You can't shoot the mother of your kids."

Everyone is just thinking crazy, she thought.

Why doesn't Brad call?

He was a natural target. The family outsider. And boy, he seemed to relish the role, despite Diane's best efforts. For years, Diane had puffed about his best qualities and tried to minimize his standoffish ways. Diane, they always suspected, signed his name to cards and letters. Diane forwarded greetings from him when she visited. Diane was his best promoter, but face-to-face Brad undid her finest work.

Nobody really clicked with Bradford J. King. Maybe some of them never forgave him for the times he and Diane tried to con the entire family into taking est training years ago. Or the fact that she'd left the Army after they started dating. Or that he stood around like Yul Brynner with his arms crossed in his stylish baggy pants.

Everyone had their own reasons, Denise thought, particularly their mother. Brad was always right on Diane's tail. Tagging along. Watching Diane. Watching them.

"He's like a damn puppy dog at your heels," she said.

But when you got right down to it, Brad just wasn't a good provider. Everyone knew that's what Freida thought. He was a sponge artist who packaged himself as some kind of modern man. He let Diane carry the family load.

"Brad is just plain lazy," Freida had said more than once. "And he's a liar."

"What kind of lies?" somebody would ask.

"Don't ask me for specifics. He's just a liar. He contradicts himself. It's his logic. There's something wrong with him. He has a way of changing his logic. He thinks he's got everybody fooled, but he hasn't fooled nobody."

Everyone was still trying to make sense out of his disappearing act a couple weeks ago. Diane was supposed to meet a cameraman from Channel 41 at the grand opening of an archery shop opened by rock star Ted Nugent in Jackson on a Saturday afternoon. Brad took off to wash the car a mile up the road, but disappeared for two hours. Diane was fuming. He finally called, saying he'd soaked the engine and stalled the car.

"Why didn't you call earlier?" Freida asked. "Diane's waiting."

"I didn't have a dime."

"You just called now."

"I borrowed change from a guy at the car wash."

Then Diane went out to find him and he wasn't at the car wash. When he returned, he said he'd gone to a different one. It didn't seem to bother him a bit that he'd fouled up her assignment.

"God knows what he was up to," Freida later said.

Denise's husband Don thought Brad did his share to keep the atmosphere tense between him and the family. Brad liked to bring up subjects he knew would kindle acrimony. Controversial views of crime. Haughty social commentary.

"Brad liked to grind the axe with the family," Don said. "He had idiosyncracies, and he liked to grind them in. I could get into an argument every time if I wanted to, but I just ignored him. I have better things to do."

There were plenty of differences to exploit. They came from different worlds.

Freida grew up on Kahnawake, a Mohawk reservation south of Montreal. Her mother Cecilia was wrapped across the knuckles if she was caught speaking Mohawk in the public school. Freida never got past the seventh grade. They were a people caught between two worlds ever since salvation came canoeing westward, delivered by Jesuits out to save the savages of the New World.

Herbert Marler, Diane's natural father, was an Englishman, a Canadian iron worker. Freida met him when her brother brought him home from the high steel. The Mohawks from Kahnawake bolted structural iron for bridges from Brooklyn to Mackinac. Freida's father went into the hole with a couple hundred tons of wire and beam and thirty-five other dead Mohawks when the Quebec City Bridge collapsed in 1907. No wonder Freida had little respect for Brad's laid-back life-style. Men not only worked all day where she came from, they often died on the job.

The iron legacy made Herbert Marler's death all the more foolish when doctors ruptured his pancreas during a botched-up gall bladder operation in 1966. He'd gone into the hospital for a backache, been misdiagnosed, and given the wrong medication. He was only thirty-five. Diane was nearly ten, Denise seven. The final malpractice payout was nearly $300,000, but it took a few years. Freida met Royal, a machine repairman, while she was working as a waitress in his brother's bar.

While Freida went to beauty school and played darts with Royal down at the LaSalle Club, the Kings were hosting bridge parties or entertaining local physicians and judges. Brad's father Willis was a World War II hero and a small-town banker. Brad said he wore nothing but hand-tailored suits. Brad had his own golf pro before he was in junior high and could still score in the low eighties. Brad's mother Marge was a Michigan State University graduate, a banker's daughter from a small northern Michigan town. They met in a military hospital where she worked as a dietician and Willis was nursing his war wounds.

Diane always said they had bucks.

"I just think Brad thinks he's better than us." That's what brother Allen Marler said.

Denise Verrier simply felt she didn't know Brad King. She didn't know who he was. Brad kept most everything to himself. He didn't let anybody in. That alone could be irritating.

In a way, Denise could argue, his behavior on this horrible night was right in character. But she kept thinking, why doesn't he find a way to get to the phone? Can't he feel what we're feeling? Lord, we're *her family*. Doesn't Brad realize all this mystery would drive any family nuts?

As midnight approached, the whispering began, the plotting. With Royal commandeering the telephone, everyone began splitting off into small groups, looking for ways to outwit the man sitting at the end of the couch.

Don and Allen came up with a reasonable solution.

"We're going up there," Don said. "Allen and I are just going to drive up to Marshall to find out what's happening up there."

They left with little fanfare. Denise was glad they were going. She was glad Don was driving. Allen looked in no condition emotionally to be behind the wheel.

Their mother had left the living room. She'd gone to her bedroom to be alone. Someone should stay with her, Denise decided. She would stay with her, though she really wanted to go to Marshall. She wanted to go to the hospital and be with her sister. She wanted to hold her, tell her she loved her, tell her goodbye while her body was still warm.

Then, she wanted to find her brother-in-law and ask him what in the world was going on.

8

Trooper Gary Lisle made his way back to the boot print in the marsh and points beyond, letting Travis roam without his collar. "Free searching," trainers called it. He wanted to give the shepherd the opportunity to pick up any other fresh scents that might have been left by a recent intruder in the area.

The dog found none.

Deputy Bill Lindsay was waiting for the K-9 team at the footbridge over the gurgling culvert. They'd agreed to meet there when Lisle radioed that he'd found footprints that might interest investigators.

Lisle shined his light at the small trees and brush to the south of the stream. "There's a heel print on the log here. I've got some north. I got some going through the trees there in the snow."

The trooper pointed east in the direction of the marsh. "And I got one more way back over there on the deer trail."

Lisle suggested the sheriff's department get an evidence technician back in the area with a camera and some casting plaster.

"You know, those foot impressions may be pretty important," he added.

That would have to wait, Lindsay said. Everyone was back at the department, he said, getting a search warrant together. The evidence people hadn't arrived yet.

"Well, let me know when they do. I'm going to rework this area. I'm looking for any other tracks out here."

Lindsay nodded. "I'll pass it along."

The deputy disappeared into the darkness, heading back toward the barn and house.

Lisle and Travis free searched for two hours. They made an extensive search of the field south of the creek, then roamed west. Except for the strip of marsh that bordered the creek and cut diagonally across the land tract, it was wide open farmland, the fields marked by fence and tree lines. The vehicle lane that stretched south from the barn to the creek resumed fifty yards on the other side of the stream.

By 11 P.M., Lisle was back in the barnyard. The only police vehicles left were his station wagon and a county cruiser posted at the end of the driveway. Fog smothered the area. Pillows and travel bags were still piled in the back of the Wagoneer. The mercury vapor lamp over the Jeep was buzzing like a million flies on a carcass.

Lisle kneeled down with Travis, giving him a good head rub, giving him his just reward. He walked the dog over to his station wagon, eventually loading him in the back.

Gary Lisle was still waiting to show someone those footprints.

He looked at the county cruiser idling at the end of the driveway in the fog.

As he walked toward the road, he flirted with the idea of using his own camera. He had one in the car. No, he thought, this was a Calhoun County Sheriff's Department case in Calhoun County territory. This was the sheriff's scene.

"I'm there to assist," he later explained. "I'm not there to take over their investigation. If someone would have said take your camera and go take some pictures, fine. But I'm not just going to start doing it, especially when their crime scene people were expected. You just don't go trouncing out there and start shooting pictures, possibly destroying evidence, before they arrive."

Inside the cruiser, Deputy Bill Lindsay was sitting behind the wheel, his police radio occasionally crackling. Lisle told him about the dog's work, how the track circled back to the driveway. Still, no one had debriefed him about the work he'd been called there to do.

"Look, that footprint's back there, but I'm gonna have to leave," he told Lindsay. "My people are going to be upset if I have too much overtime when I'm not working that dog."

Lindsay nodded.

Lisle had a suggestion. He'd go home, get Travis squared away, and wait for a call from the department. He could tell the detectives about the track, brief them well in advance of his written report.

"Just have them call me at home whenever they get here. I'll come back and show them where it's at."

"Got it," Lindsay said.

At 11:47 P.M., Gary Lisle hit the road with his blue Michigan State Police K-9 wagon, Travis eventually lying down in the back, his nose nestling into his shoulder.

Unlike his dog, the trooper felt unsettled, despite the way Travis had locked onto that track from the busy barn loft. Gary Lisle didn't like the way the crime scene at 16240 Division Drive was being processed. There were just too many loose ends.

"I figured this was probably going to fall down big-time," he later told another investigator. As he drove off into the fog, for a second or two, Gary Lisle wished he weren't involved.

Back at the sheriff's department in Marshall, Detective Jim Stadfeld had faxed a search warrant for 16240 Division Drive to a local magistrate for his signature. The transmission "disappeared somewhere in fax land," and had to be resent, Stadfeld later said.

It wouldn't be the only information lost or misplaced as police worked on into the darkest hours of the night, kicking off what would become one of the most extensive homicide probes in the history of the state.

As the county detectives waited for another fax transmission, Jack Schoder took a phone call from a probation officer in Battle Creek. The woman officer told the detective she dated one of the state troopers who'd been out at the scene earlier. Brad King was bad news, she said. He'd worked as a probation officer for the district court in 1990, but was fired, she said.

"Brad did it," she said. "I just know Brad did it."

Schoder found a couple things about King a little bewildering. Something definitely appeared amiss in the way he'd handled the in-laws, cried, then effortlessly changed gears to continue the interview. He also wondered why King hadn't demanded to leave the station earlier to be with his wife's body. He'd kept the guy there until 11 P.M. before he'd even talked about the funeral home.

"So, what about this guy?" Stadfeld asked.

"You know, he's a strange one, Jim. It's like he didn't even want to see his wife."

While such impressions about King's demeanor would later be recalled by officers on the scene, the time, place, and source of the most fundamental notification in the investigation would not be noted and would be forever lost. No one would be able to say when or where Brad King was told that his wife had been felled by gunshots. An EMT had shouted that out to Picketts, but it was unclear whether King ever heard the remark. Jack Schoder and Bill Lindsay certainly had informed him she had died, but had not provided a cause. Schoder talked about gun-

shots with King in their interview, but he never informed him
on tape that Diane King was a gunshot victim.

Ten minutes after midnight, the two detectives, a crew of
deputies, and an assistant prosecutor drove back to 16240 Division Drive with the signed search warrant, even though Brad
King also had given his written permission to search the property and house. The combination gave them free reign. But
despite Jim Stadfeld's own complaints about his department's
limitations in gathering evidence, the detectives passed on one
available option. The Michigan State Police Crime Lab would
dispatch a crew to process a scene such as the King property
when called. The lab offered state-of-the-art technology. Evidence techs also freed personnel for other pursuits, such as
talking to witnesses, deputies, or dog handlers called to the
scene.

Stadfeld would later justify the decision. "There have been
times when we've called in the state crime unit. They did have
the philosophy that if you called in the middle of the night
they'd say just hold the scene till the morning. Then you're
stuck posting people at the crime scene until they decide when
they want to get there. In retrospect, it probably wouldn't have
been a bad idea. On the other hand, I look at the crime scene
itself, and it was a very clean crime scene. It wasn't like you had
three bodies in a house and blood in every room. It was a very
clean and easy crime scene to work."

At least it seemed that way at first.

When Schoder returned to the property he met up again
with Deputy Guy Picketts, who'd gone home and changed into
boots and warmer clothes. Schoder was still in the coat, tie, and
trenchcoat he'd worn to the FOP party. Schoder told Picketts
he wanted to walk back south of the barnyard where Brad King
said he'd been. He wanted to verify King's story.

Schoder pulled Brad King's boots out of the backseat of his
Grand Prix. "He was wearing these," Schoder said, showing
them to the deputy.

The two men walked south of the barn, past the silo, to the
makeshift footbridge at the gurgling culvert. Picketts found a
footprint by the stream, then crossed the plank to the south side

of the creek. He pointed his flashlight toward the small knoll slightly southeast. It was one of the first impressions Gary Lisle had found earlier.

"They look like the boots," he shouted to the detective. He shined his flashlight farther south. "There's another one over here, Jack."

Schoder stood at the north side of the stream, straining to see ahead in the darkness. He saw no reason to cross the creek. He wasn't dressed for it. Besides, those footprints were right where they should have been, according to the story Brad King had given him.

"I didn't see those footprints at that point as anything other than corroboration of what Mr. King said," he later said. "I'm really happy Guy found those, and I'm happy to look at them. But I didn't see them as significant enough to cross the creek, or I sure as shit would have on a murder case. I would have waded the creek if I thought it would have solved the case."

Jack Schoder headed back to the barnyard, Picketts following. There was plenty of other work to do. Jim Stadfeld snapped pictures of the victim's hair band and key wallet in the driveway. Schoder had deputies measure the Jeep's location, triangulating its position from various reference points. Stadfeld photographed the Jeep's exterior and interior. Diane King's blue parka was sprawled across the front passenger seat, a beverage squeeze bottle nestled in its folds. A couple of cassette tapes glimmered on the console. A large, overstuffed purse sat on the floor. An eyeglass case poked out of the top.

Schoder was still thinking about the stalker reports and the break-in reported at the house in December. Brad King had pointed out a scrape on the lock plate of the kitchen door to the deputy who took the report back in December. Stadfeld photographed the lock, then Schoder removed the mechanism and packaged it as evidence with three screwdrivers also on the porch.

The deputies searched the interior of the farmhouse. In a small attic over the kitchen they found storage boxes. In one labeled "Camping Equipment and Tools," they found a blue fishing box. Inside they found gun cleaning tools and solvent.

They also found two small boxes of ammunition, one made by Winchester, the other by Remington. They were .22 caliber.

Farther back in the attic they found a wooden gun case. In a lower compartment were two cleaning rods. Both were old and cryptic, one with the larger circumference used for a shotgun. The other was thin, the size often used for a .22.

They tagged the .22 ammo and rod.

Outside, they looked for footprints, but they were looking nowhere near the marsh. They not only didn't know about the impression well east of the footbridge—where Brad King said he had *not* walked—Jack Schoder didn't even know the path of the dog track had circled back to the farmhouse. Deputy Bill Lindsay later noted in his report that he'd informed the under-sheriff of Gary Lisle's work. But the undersheriff was gone now. Somehow the news hadn't reached the detectives at the scene.

The detectives and deputies were looking for impressions in more difficult settings. They stretched a lead chord from the house to the barn, powering up high-intensity lights and aiming them at the barn floor, hoping to pick up some kind of pattern in the dust. There was nothing worth photographing. A half-dozen cops and a dog had already trampled through the structure.

Upstairs, they looked for more footprints in the loft with similar results. Jack Schoder measured the distance of the open loft door and triangulated the position of the shell casing in the straw. Stadfeld snapped the casing's picture, then took it into evidence.

By 4 A.M., the forces of the Calhoun County Sheriff's Department huddled outside in the driveway to make an important decision. The assistant prosecutor had left more than an hour ago.

"We tried to evaluate what we'd done," Schoder later said. "We figured what more we could do."

Any investigation can be second-guessed. Any investigation has mistakes. The investigation of the murder of Diane Newton King would start with ample opportunity for both. In his taped interview with Brad King, Jack Schoder had failed to determine exactly where King had walked on his jaunt back onto the property. No pictures or casts had been made of the boot prints the department knew about, let alone the one that they did not. No one in authority had debriefed Gary Lisle. His message that he was waiting at home and available apparently had been lost in the night.

The department had also ignored what other investigators would call "a real gift." Guy Picketts used to live on the property and knew it, but the command had put him to work early on directing traffic at the foot of the driveway. And, as "simple" as the crime scene might have appeared, it was an appearance packaged in darkness. Neither Jack Schoder or Jim Stadfeld had seen the scene in the revealing light of day.

Jack Schoder's day had begun twenty hours ago in the damp, burnt basement of a schoolhouse crime scene. A cold front was moving into the area now. By 4 A.M., the temperature had dropped to the mid-twenties, clearing the fog that covered the area earlier.

"Man, it was awful cold out there," Schoder later recalled.

At 4:20 A.M. Schoder and Stadfeld made the decision to clear the scene. This meant the property would no longer be posted with a deputy. In fact, the house itself was more vulnerable. The lock was gone in the side porch door at 16240 Division Drive.

Some of them met back at the sheriff's department in Marshall, some gathering in the break room to warm up with hot coffee. That's when Jack Schoder would later recall that somebody finally told him.

"Hey, Jack," somebody said. "You know the dog track."

"Yeah."

"Did you know that dog track ended up back at the house?"

From the View of

BRADFORD KING

I dressed that way the whole weekend. My camouflage pants. Long johns. My camouflage flannel shirt. My red hat. I wore it hunting or when I was at the house, working outdoors. I wore those hunting clothes when I worked.

When I was a cop, I was always prepared for any situation, for any weather. In the trunk I always kept a pair of coveralls, and in the winter, a warm jacket, hat and gloves, and rubber boots to put over my shoes. I had an extra flashlight. I had evidence bags, pens, pencils, paper, a clipboard. Because I would forget things, or run out during a crime scene or have to crawl under a house and not want to do it in my good clothes.

That's what you did. That was part of the job. Being ready for anything.

Jack Schoder failing to cross that creek because he was in street clothes was not only a matter of not being prepared, it was just plain bad police work.

If, as a police officer I would have been called to the scene of Diane's murder, my primary focus would have been the husband. In most of the cases it *is* the husband. I'd go with those statistics at first. That would be my primary focus until something told me otherwise. And, even though if I felt it might not be the husband, I would have had to have taken the position, until the evidence told me otherwise. And then maybe I could say, okay my gut feeling isn't right.

It would be process of elimination. I wouldn't have assumed a thing. I would have locked that property up tighter than a drum until I was done with it. I wouldn't have turned that house over until I was done with it. And, if that meant I had to stay up for two days in a row, I would have. If there was a footprint I would have cast that sucker, or photographed it. I would have recorded it so that it was identifiable and could be attributed to a particular piece of footwear. I would have walked the dog up to the husband. I would have done everything I could. I wouldn't have missed a beat.

Myself, I never grew up wanting to be a cop. I never really planned it. I didn't want to go to Vietnam. You could get a deferment for being a teacher or a police officer. I didn't believe in the war. We were Preppies. I guess that's the word to use. Short hair. Nice clothes. Took a shower whether we needed to or not. But there were a lot of people who didn't agree with the war that didn't drop out of society.

When I got out of college I wanted to teach high school. I was applying to teaching jobs everywhere: Pontiac, Flint, Grand Blanc, Waterford, you name it. And there just weren't any. They were taking people with master's degrees or people who had been teaching already. But Gail, my first wife, found one. She found a teaching job right away in Pontiac at the junior high. And she liked it. She never left until she got pregnant with our daughter.

Gail's dad was a cop, a captain in the Pontiac Police Department. He said, "Well, why don't you try it. You're gonna get drafted, or join the department." So I put in the application and they accepted me. I went to recruit school and went to work.

My dad was okay with it. He was proud of it, actually, because he could tell people, "My son is a policeman." And when he'd introduce me to them, he was proud. My mother never said a word. Just said nothing. I don't think she liked it. Then, after I'd been at it a couple years, she figured I was going to stick with it, especially when the war ended and I no longer needed the protection from the draft.

Randy and I never talked about it a lot. But he said, "You did your Vietnam. You just did it differently than I did." Because I certainly took a profession that didn't leave me out of harm's way, by any stretch of the imagination. And you know, it's funny. It took Randy coming back and posing that question for me to even see that. I didn't even consider it harm's way. It never crossed my mind.

When I started I was uniformed, marked car, predominantly with partners in the worst areas of town. Pontiac was like a small Detroit. It's a bit smaller than a Detroit precinct in terms of police manpower, but as far as square miles it's about the same size as one precinct in Detroit.

The only time I thought the job was dangerous was during this time when my partner and I almost got shot. We were on the afternoon shift. We were parked off the side of the road writing some reports, catching up on our paperwork, when two kids walked up behind us. My partner was driving. We saw them in the rearview mirror.

"The son of a bitch has got a gun," my partner said.

All of a sudden this gun comes sticking through the window, a sawed-off .22. He pushed it up, and the kid never fired it. I'm already out of the door on the ground. Then the kid took off running and turned back and pointed the gun at my partner. Well my partner drilled him right there. I forgot all about the other guy. I knew he was behind me, so I hit the ground and rolled over. I saw he was running. When that gun went off he got scared. He had a gun in his hand. He was getting ready to blow me away. They were high. They were just going to go kill some cops. So I took off after that kid and said, "If you don't throw that fucking gun away I'm gonna blow your ass off, man." He took that gun and just tossed it and laid down on the ground. He didn't want to die. We got them both.

I think it was in 1973 when I applied for an assignment in plainclothes with what we called a crime patrol unit. We worked with unmarked cars, sometimes cars borrowed from used car lots so they didn't look like detective's cars. It was a street crime unit. I was on the unit for a year. We staked out areas with high street crime, or worked tips, like somebody was going to rob the corner grocery store. Well, after doing that in Pontiac, at least, we had an impact, so we outlived our usefulness. They disbanded the unit.

I had a pretty good variety of jobs in police work. They assigned me to vice squad for six months. I went back to uniform for a few months. Then they started a surveillance unit attached to the detective bureau. Whatever the detectives had that required surveillance, we worked it. We worked some extortions. We worked surveillance on an auto theft ring. We cleared out almost two hundred cases on that one.

Once I started on the surveillance unit, I began graduate school full-time. Once my mother realized I was going to stick with police work, she said if you're going to do this for a living, go to Michigan State and get your master's. Even before she mentioned that, I'd already decided I should get some education in the area. So, I started out at Wayne State University, then applied at Michigan State and was accepted. I received a master's in criminal justice. Graduated in 1977. The federal government paid for it. The Law Enforcement Assistance Administration paid the tuition.

After that, I went back to uniform, but then was assigned to the juvenile division as an investigator. They call them a counselor, or liaison, with the high schools. I was assigned to Pontiac Central. I already knew everybody up there because I was a student teacher there during college. I wanted the job when it became vacant. There was one white officer and one black officer. When the white officer left on a promotion, I got the job.

We had an office in the high school. The juvenile division of the department assigned our cases because the juveniles were usually students in our school. That's how we got our investigative case load.

Our jobs started early in the morning like the teachers. We had responsibility for providing security. As the kids were getting off buses, we were outside watching. There were some pretty tense moments. Outsiders were not allowed on school grounds. If you were not a student, you were trespassing, and the school district would prosecute. We knew who belonged and who didn't belong.

They'd had police officers in Pontiac schools since the mid-sixties. It was a community relations program as well as a crime program. We got to know the kids. They got to know us. When the kids weren't in class, we knew where they were. I don't think there was a week that didn't go by there wasn't a fight, and usually a weapon was involved. We were there to assist the teachers. We knew who the criminals in the school were because we dealt with them on a regular basis, on school grounds and off. In the summer, if Pontiac Central students were involved in a crime, my partner and I got the case. So we investigated everything from runaways to homicides. It worked well. The program is still underway.

I did that seven years, until 1980. I enjoyed those seven years—a lot. The job had some pretty good perks to it. We got our own car. We didn't have to go through the car pool. Then, they had a downsizing of the program because the school district was having money problems and they cut back to one officer. So I lost my job. I was back on the road for about six months, maybe a little longer.

Finally, I was assigned as the training director, which was the job I held until I left. I coordinated all the training schools where we sent people and kept records of who was trained at what. I developed in-service training. One was a refresher course police officers had to take every year.

I was in the process of developing a yearly in-service training for detectives when I left. I didn't even tell them that because I knew they'd get crazy if they knew I was doing it. I'd been at a seminar for police trainers and ran across a guy who had developed some unique firearms training. So I brought that concept home and was refining it for us. You could buy plastic cartridge casings, put .357 primer in them, and load harmless dental cotton as slugs for training sessions. I was going to put policemen in situations where guns were drawn on them, then train them to protect themselves in that kind of situation. The other thing I wanted to do was use this Sears building we had downtown that had been vacant a long time. A car would be given a call at the Sears building, an armed robbery, a hostage, or whatever. It would be their training call. They would go in and deal with it right off the road, just like if it were real, except it was controlled.

Sometimes I wish I'd stayed. But I'd grown up. I was just too mature for the job. The politics burned me out. I got close to the politics in that position because I reported directly to the chief's office. I got to see more of the corruption, not criminal corruption, but political corruption, corruption within the organization. The politics. I had this budget. It was my money and I could spend it. But they would take it away and use it somewhere else in the department.

Well, I think it was probably about the third or fourth time I'd been in the chief's office and bitched about this budget thing, when I finally refused to do it. I was ordered to do it, and I refused the order.

Two weeks later I gave my resignation. The total was fourteen years on the department, 1969 to 1983. To me, police work was like a game. It was outsmarting the bad guy. That's all it was: A game to outsmart the bad guy.

I did the est training when I was still in the juvenile division. One of the things the training did was make me more aware of my ability to do things, to have things the way I planned them to be. To create it *my* way. It was also when I got really in touch with the fact that I'm a great teacher. I'm a great teacher, because, well I just am. There's no *because* about it.

I really enjoyed teaching at Western Michigan. I had been away from being a criminal justice practitioner long enough to be objective about the profession, and yet be able to say things that are factual. Because of my experience, nobody could tell me I didn't know what I was talking about. There's a level of deficiency in the education of practitioners in the justice system and I think that's what creates a lot of the problems. I felt I could impact that.

I tried to strip the veneer off police work. I did it for a purpose. Students needed to know, number one, that cops aren't saints. These people are human beings that screw up. These people, in fact, screw up and as a result screw up other people's lives.

I tried to free students from their illusions. In the fall semester in 1990, I gave my Introduction to Criminology students the assignment to design the "perfect crime." I had a sociology professor do that to me once, too. I had everybody in class get in groups. They were to try to commit a crime, describe how it was committed, then see if they could get through it without being caught. They had forty-five minutes. Then we took a break, came back, and each group described their crimes to the rest of the class.

"We'll see if we agree with you," I told them.

Well, nobody could. Everybody says there's a perfect crime. But there is no perfect crime. As they would mention things, I would throw things in as well as the rest of the class.

"What about this?"

"Well, we didn't think about *that.*"

It was an exercise to show that as a group of human beings, you cannot plan that. I don't even think one human being can plan the perfect crime. There's always evidence. A perfect crime has no evidence to be gathered. I don't think anyone is capable of that.

But people live with the illusion that there is such a thing. I chose to demonstrate it, let them demonstrate it for themselves, because telling students isn't going to make it sink in.

That's how I taught. I let them teach themselves.

PART TWO

No Better Rule

Take nothing on its looks; take everything on evidence.
There's no better rule.

—Charles Dickens

1

By Sunday evening, western Michigan TV stations were carrying reports about the killing. But on Monday morning, WUHQ-Channel 41 in Battle Creek opted not to cover the shooting as a murder story. The station suspended its local news breaks between "Good Morning America" entirely. They were breaks normally anchored by Diane Newton King.

An announcement ran instead. It urged viewers with any informatin to call police, and concluded: "Diane was an important part of Channel 41 and will be greatly missed. Our deepest sympathy is expressed to her family." Soon, the station would also establish a trust fund for the children.

Diane King had been greeting morning viewers for two years, providing a three-minute news segment just before "Good Morning America" and two five-minute time slots allotted by the network at the half hour. Channel 41 didn't have noon, five, or eleven broadcasts. Other network affiliates were located in nearby Kalamazoo and Grand Rapids. All three cities formed the same western Michigan TV market ranked thirty-eighth in the nation.

Diane Newton King *was* the TV news in Battle Creek. To produce thirteen minutes for viewers, the newswoman and a small staff of a half dozen put in hours of preparation, overtime, and legwork. King not only anchored the morning news, she spent the rest of her morning and early afternoon reporting local stories in the field. King also helped work up a periodic local magazine segment called "41 News Prime Time." She had signed on at Channel 41 in early 1989 after leaving a reporter's job in Grand Junction, Colorado, to pursue a career in her native state.

Some of the half-dozen reporters that showed up in front of the station on Monday morning had worked with her on stories. They found the front doors of the station locked, its flag at half-staff, and security guards posted around the property. The station was a red brick and white sash building, classic pre-World War II military fort construction. The building once served as the headquarters of a surrounding Fort Custer, a massive troop staging facility in the second war, and the subject of one of Diane King's prime-time documentaries.

Eventually, Mark Crawford, the station's vice president, emerged to make a statement. Crawford said he was unsure when the regular newscasts would continue. "We made the decision fairly late yesterday that it was both inappropriate and impossible for us to expect any of our staff members to go on the air and deal with the story and treat it as a routine news story."

It wouldn't be, not by any stretch.

The Battle Creek *Enquirer* ran a page one headline: TV AN-CHOR SLAIN. Under it: FRIENDS REPORT HARASSMENT. A staff writer had reached Diane King's former boss in Grand Junction, KJCT-TV station manager Jan Hammer. He said he'd talked to Diane King two weeks earlier. She'd told him she was being stalked. She had received calls and the cut-out letter, he said.

"It's a little known part of our business," Hammer told the *Enquirer*. "It goes on all the time."

The subject fueled the first question to Mark Crawford outside Channel 41.

"Obviously concern for a stalker is high," someone asked. "You have guards around here."

Crawford refused to discuss security measures, the letter, or anything else about the stalker. "I wouldn't tell you if it were true or false," he said.

Confirmation or not, the story already was making national and international news wires. It was driven by more than the fact that a TV newswoman was killed. The basic components provided the kind of high contrast that feeds the instant-story business: An electronic age celebrity felled by the primitive impulses of obsession and murder, all set in a postcard-perfect town near a city represented at every breakfast table in America.

And what a crowd it drew.

WUHQ executives would deny more than 250 requests for interviews in the days ahead. Crawford and other managers asked staff not to discuss their anchor with journalists. Everyone complied, though the reporters came in waves, up to a hundred showing up at the station in the first week alone. One tabloid TV show would offer cash for comments. Another would try to sneak into the building, a photographer posing as a messenger, his camera hidden in a delivery box. For two days, a woman identifying herself as a nationally known therapist approached Mark Crawford with an offer, saying she represented "A Current Affair." She offered "free" trauma and grief counseling to the station staff in trade for interviews. Crawford stuck to the policy.

Everyone was working on variations of the same story: Diane Newton King had been stalked and murdered in front of her own children, simply for being bright and beautiful and on TV.

By midweek, news crews would stake out territory around St. Mary Catholic Church in Marshall, site of the funeral. "Inside Edition" would borrow electricity from Winston's Pub in Schuler's Restaurant. *People* magazine would dispatch stringers to pick up local color. "Hard Copy," "A Current Affair," "Unsolved Mysteries," and all three networks would want information. Interested publications would range from the *Los Angeles Times* to *Good Housekeeping* magazine to the *London Times*.

In Battle Creek, the story was no less sensational, but was handled with less attention to glamour and stereotype. Television news people find a measure of celebrity in many Midwestern cities, even in towns the size of Detroit, where anchors' personal lives and professional moves often make page-one news. But in death, the Cereal City accorded Diane Newton King a due amount of respect.

The anchor's local visibility exceeded her TV exposure. She had hosted fashion shows and visits by soap opera stars at local malls. She had served on the board of the Salvation Army and co-chaired a task force for the Food Bank of Southwestern Michigan. She had emceed ice shows and Sesame Street productions at local venues. She had taken part in the annual Battle Creek Christmas Parade, but also made herself available for much less elaborate processions in nearby small towns.

"Diane was a vibrant person," her own priest would say at her funeral Mass. "She was excited about her new baby, Kateri, her son, and her husband. She was an exciting person on television. She loved her work. She loved the service she provided through that medium. And she was excited about the traditions of her Native American background."

Fifty percent Mohawk, Diane King wanted to make an impact on Native Americans across the country. She attended large powwows in the Midwest and Colorado, celebrations that feature dancing, trading, and prayer. In Denver, she served as chapter president of the National Organization of Native American Women. In 1986, Indian Women of America had named her the country's Outstanding Young Woman.

As local newspapers put together her obituary, the list of postmortem accolades lengthened: Distinguished ROTC graduate. Former Army officer. The Native American Advisory Committee for the United Arts Counsel. The Kings belonged to two churches. Diane was a Catholic; Brad, a Presbyterian. On Sundays, they attended St. Mary in Marshall then drove fifteen miles to Battle Creek for services at First Presbyterian.

"I think the thing that struck me about Diane was that she was really sincere," the executive director of the arts counsel told a newspaper covering her death. "She really cared."

Outside the station's big, brick building, reporters speculated among themselves about Channel 41's commitment to its devoted anchor. Maybe the station had not taken the threats seriously.

"Why would people in the news business not give a single goddamn interview?" more than one groused.

Maybe Channel 41 had really screwed up.

* * *

Thirty miles west, at the campus of Western Michigan University in Kalamazoo, the first headline in the *Western Herald*, the campus newspaper, would read: **WMU PROFESSOR'S WIFE SHOT, KILLED; NO ARRESTS MADE.**

Across the mall from the campus clock tower, the news had spread through Sangren Hall by Monday's first bells. Sangren was the campus home of Western's criminal justice program, taught by a dozen full-time and three part-time faculty, one of whom was Bradford J. King. King had joined the program in the fall of 1989. King's resume impressed program administrators, not only his tenure with the Pontiac Police Department, but his background in training and rehabilitation for several Colorado health agencies.

Faculty considered King professional, competent, and helpful. He looked out for colleagues, bringing them articles and videos they could use. Colleagues knew him as exceptionally easygoing and well-liked by students. King spent considerably more hours on campus than other part-time faculty, who often had other jobs. He also had an office. He had his name on his Sangren office door.

Police at Pontiac PD confirmed faculty impressions. "When I first hired on, I worked with Brad on patrol," a sergeant would later say of King. "He was very quiet and reserved, kind of laid-back. Brad was very congenial. He had a good temperament. Not much bothered him."

King's Pontiac service record didn't approach the lofty exaltation of his father's two World War II Purple Hearts, but it did show a cop who could excel beyond the call of duty. The city counsel cited him for "meritorious service, bravery, and valor" while working an extortion case in 1973. The next year he was cited for busting two thieves working hospital and industrial parking lots, an arrest that cleared up nearly two hundred similar complaints. Another certificate came for taking down the perpetrator of thirteen thefts at Pontiac Central High School. Back on the streets in 1981, King ran down a pair of suspects on foot after a gas station heist. Grand Trunk Railroad praised him for a larceny investigation, as did Pontiac Silverdome officials for his work on a crackdown of bootleg merchandisers during the 1982 Super Bowl. One Pontiac woman wrote the police chief to cite King for apprehending a fleeing house burglar in another foot race, then taking time afterwards to find the radio the thief had tossed away into the night.

Brad King consistently scored high marks in performance evaluations in Pontiac. In 1979, after King accumulated nine years of duty, his chief William Hanger wrote in an application evaluation for a graduate study program in management:

> For the past several years Brad King has been assigned as a police school counselor. In this capacity, he not only has shown a great deal of discretion in terms of making decisions, but maintains a daily staff relationship with the school's management administration personnel. He has always demonstrated an interest in pursuing educational activity, both on and off the job. He is progressive in his thinking, and accepts management's positions with a good level of comprehension. It is my opinion that both his activities and his attitude are oriented towards a goal of someday becoming a member of the management team.

Brad King taught criminal justice for six years at Henry Ford Community College in Dearborn while he was with the Pontiac Department. He taught for one semester at Kellogg Community College in Battle Creek before joining the Western faculty.

"It was nice to have somebody teaching that class who was doing a very good job, who was doing it consistently," said Ron Kramer, a professor who would later go on to head the program. "It was nice to have someone who seemed to take the sociological approach to the subject and wasn't just telling war stories. He was very knowledgeable about his field."

Western's CJ program itself was popular. Almost two-thirds of the university's sociology students were CJ majors, pursuing careers in corrections and law enforcement administration. The program also offered a criminology doctorate, something King himself had in mind.

The news of Diane King's death also spread on Western's fraternity row. Brad King was a faculty advisor to Tau Kappa

Epsilon, the same chapter where he had served as historian twenty-five years earlier. He had a following of young Tekes who he helped with chapter business and fraternity ritual. They bought him beers at local campus bars. He sometimes dropped by the house after class to engage in philosophical musings or offer advice and counsel. When the Kings moved into the farmhouse in Marshall, several Tekes formed a cleanup party and spent a Saturday working on the farm. King brought his wife to formal fraternity functions, showing off the local TV celebrity at chapter parties.

The Kings showed up at department faculty parties as well, always well-dressed and articulate. Diane Newton King made contacts among her husband's circle. In January, she helped organize a symposium on the Gulf War, recruiting people from the university and covering it with Channel 41 cameras. She interviewed Ron Kramer. She was a former Army officer. He was an antiwar activist, but had come to admire the wife of his teaching colleague.

"I really liked Diane a lot," he would recall of her months later. "She was a delightful woman. A beautiful woman. She was very, *very* nice. Full of life. And very well-liked by people who got to know her. They seemed like a very happy couple, by all outward appearances, at least."

Two thousand miles away, on both sides of the Colorado Rockies, people learned the news in shocked agreement. The Kings had left many friends in Denver and Grand Junction.

Debbie Rich, a reporter at KJCT, recalled them as exceptional. "They were always dressed to kill. I mean, they looked *good* together. But more than that, they were seekers. They were always looking for ways to improve their relationship, understand it better, become a better couple."

Brad King was not threatened by his wife's success, she said. He relished it. "I remember a New Year's eve, when she was hosting a local show," Rich recalled. "He sat there, glued in front of the TV that night, commenting on her. 'Doesn't she look great. Look at that dress. Doesn't she just look fantastic.' "

In Colorado, they appeared the quintessential New Age couple, their lives defined by the human potential movement, driven by eighties careerism and spiritualized by the environmentally correct American Indian movement. Like many est graduates, The Training, as acolytes called it, shaped the Kings' lives long after est ceased to be contemporary. In fact, the *Philadelphia Enquirer* once suggested Werner Erhardt, the program's founder, had created Yuppies with his me-oriented teachings.

The Training was a grueling two-weekend ordeal run by charismatic trainers who confronted groups of a hundred or so trainees who paid $250 to $600 to find themselves locked in hotel ballrooms, sitting for hours on hard chairs. Trainers kept them from avoiding frequent confrontations by limiting breaks or even trips to the bathroom. The Training's goal was to provide a "breakthrough" experience, a life-changing disposal of emotional baggage and discovery of true, empowered self.

Describing the est experience often was elusive for graduates, a fact that seemed to help them as they were sent out to recruit new paying customers for the seminars. Drill sergeant methods shattered resistance at seminars. Then trainers dished up an eclectic blend of group therapy, Eastern mysticism, gestalt psychology, and sensitivity training to hearts and minds made willing. People were directed to sit across from one another, staring into each other's eyes for long periods. Trainers singled out people, breaking them down, sometimes humiliating them as they pushed deep into their psyches. The goal near the end was to "get it." To accept responsibility. To take control. To be the master of your destiny. To define your own life.

While many of the half-million people who took The Training found renewal, est was not without its critics. Some charged it preached amorality. There was no right and wrong. No social standard. Only a mystic psychopathy of sorts. Erhard was accused of profiteering and running an authoritarian cult. He repackaged a more palatable version of est as The Forum in the mid-eighties. But by early 1991, his empire was nearly crumbled, facing lawsuits and charges of tax evasion. His wife charged him with abuse. His twenty-eight-year-old daughter labeled him a "total control monster."

Brad and Diane King not only had taken The Training to its limits, they both had worked for Werner Erhard and Associates. Brad left the police department to work as a recruiter for the organization in Cincinnati and Denver. In 1983, Diane left the Army and moved to Colorado to be with her fiancé and work briefly for the organization. The couple eventually distanced themselves when some of Erhard's own Denver staff became disenchanted. But the Kings, like other est graduates, put some of The Training to work in private enterprise. Brad King led management seminars for a Colorado consulting firm. The two of them led business seminars on dual-career marriages.

In Denver, Diane decided she wanted to put her communications degree from Wayne State University to use. She started by making a cold call on a twenty-year TV veteran anchorwoman in Denver named Reneylda Muse, asking for advice on how to break into the business.

Muse tried to discourage her. Diane King was twenty-nine, too late to start. She warned her of innumerable hurdles and exceedingly slim odds. Muse told her she would have to start in the small markets, where stations counted on the allure of the public eye to draw job candidates and paid a poverty-level wage. Diane's resolve was almost delusional.

Six years after that conversation, the KCNC anchor got the news of Diane's death in a call from Brad King himself. She dug out an old letter dated May 22, 1985. It was the thank you letter Diane had sent for the leads Muse had given her. The end read: "Once again, thank you for everything. I will get this job, and I'm not stopping until I get exactly what I want."

Muse later recalled, "Out of all the people that contacted me for help over the years, I found her the most impressive, without question."

Diane began as a lowly production assistant and researcher at KRMA-TV Channel 6, a PBS affiliate in Denver. She made hardly $8,000 a year, but she had a foot in the door somewhere and time to put together an audition tape. Within six months, Diane King had pounced on the opening at KJCT-TV in Grand Junction, a market ranked 180th in the country. Station manager Jan Hammer hired her for $13,000 a year on the basis of her audition tape.

Hammer had seen his share of youngsters looking for a start, but nobody like King. "She worked long and hard to establish and build sources and she worked hard on those sources," he told the Battle Creek *Enquirer* for the murder story. "She was probably the most aggressive we've had since I've been here."

A town of only thirty thousand residents, Grand Junction had a potential TV audience triple that in the Grand Valley. Ranching, mining, and recreational interests drove the local economy along the western slope of the Rockies. Diane King covered everything from police stories to local politics to mental health. She fancied herself an investigative reporter. She demonstrated to viewers that security had lapsed at the Grand Junction airport by hiding metal in the airport waiting areas when metal detectors were turned off at night. The next morning, she retrieved them, as someone would a gun, outwitting the system. Soon, she was hosting a news talk show on weekends.

Some remembered her as possessing some of the best personality traits of a successful reporter, traits that might not serve someone so well in other jobs. She was focused under pressure. She knew how to apply compliments and charm when she needed a favor. She knew how to throw a well-orchestrated tantrum if that didn't work. The word "No" did not mean no, it just meant she had to try a different approach.

Not everyone was so enamored inside KJCT. She had a running feud with a news director named Mike Moran. Diane King told friends she wanted Moran's job. She told them he just resented her because she was a woman competitor.

Moran thought she pushed too hard inside the station. Well after her murder, Moran told the Kalamazoo *Gazette:* "I had to sit her down so many times to break up fights with employees and remind her that I'm her boss and she has to be more tactful because future bosses may not be so understanding."

Others, hearing about the murder, remembered the sensitive, searching sides of the Kings. Steve Boas, a Colorado custom furniture entrepreneur, and his wife, Donna, befriended the Kings through est in Denver in the early eighties. Donna

Boas was a seminar leader. Steve was starting his own business. Diane King was working for est. Brad was trying his hand at different jobs.

Many months after the murder, the couple would sit in their great room remembering the Kings, a vista of the Rockies jutting skyward just to the west of their Boulder home.

"Her clothes were always perfect," Donna Boas recalled. "Her house was always very tidy and very clean. She was very conscious of that. Closets, everything, was always perfect. She sought perfection. She didn't always get it. But she always tried."

"She was the powerful dynamic of that relationship," Steve Boas added. "Brad, he would sort of revel in what she was up to, be it going on staff, going off staff, or just the way she did it. When she was starting up with Channel 6 here, he'd always sit back and be excited, as though he were living his life through her as well."

"She was just fearless," Donna said. "I remember when she told me she was going to go into TV and she wanted to be an anchorwoman. I looked at her and said, 'That's nice, Diane.' I figured maybe in a couple years. Within six months she was in there doing it. I was just amazed. Whatever she wanted, she went after it and got it."

"He had a real sense of humor," Steve said. "Good-natured. Life was just rolling off his back."

"Even when he had no money, it didn't seem to bother him," Donna added.

"And, that's one of his strengths, and one of his weaknesses," Steve said. "He never really got fazed by stuff."

They both remembered Brad and Diane's affection for one another. He seemed to worship her. Diane made frequent public displays of her devotion.

Donna Boas said, "He would say something, and she'd sit right on the couch in front of everybody and point at him and say, 'Brad King, I love you.' Then she would turn to everybody, nodding, and say, 'Brad King. *That man*. I love that man right *there*.'

"It was really something to see."

2

Randy Wright called the sheriff's department before Sunday breakfast. They just wanted to pick up some clean clothes for Brad at the farmhouse. He was surprised when someone told him they already were done with the scene.

He'd never been to the farm. After he walked through the door, evidence of mother and child struck Randy Wright. He saw Marler's drawings tacked on the refrigerator with magnets. A neat stack of books and crayons. Bath toys placed around the tub.

He volunteered to unload the Jeep as Brad shuffled around the first floor. He thought his old friend shouldn't have to endure that. He put Marler's duffel bag on the dining room table, but hung up Diane's clothes in her closet. He thought it might be easier for Brad if he kept those out of sight.

All morning, Brad appeared to be in a state of shock. When he wasn't crying, he was vacant. That was the Brad Randy knew. His personality had always covered those extremes. He could be tearfully sentimental among friends, then sit deadpan for hours. The tragedy only amplified those two extremes. He found himself talking for him, keeping the conversation going with visitors who would stop by.

Randy Wright had considered the worst. He'd thought about Brad, where he said he was and what he said he was doing during the shooting. They had talked over everything a half-dozen times with each other. Allen Marler and Donald Verrier also had demanded some answers in the early morning hours at the Arborgate Motel.

"Now, you know, I did think it out," Wright later recalled. "Did this guy kill his wife? Is he off his rocker? Am I going to expose myself to danger? I mean, this stuff is going through my mind. I began looking and ruling things out, like a physician might rule out some kind of virus."

He ruled out that Brad was violent. In twenty years he'd

never seen the man lose his temper. He never saw a cruel streak
or a drinking problem, unlike a number of cops he'd known. In
fact, the opposite was true. Brad was patient and tolerant. He
was into self-awareness and sensitivity. Brad took est and psychology and human issues much further than Randy ever
wished to.

Randy also decided Brad's story made sense. Diane *was*
being stalked. A copy of the search warrant they found on the
dining room table seemed to confirm it. It detailed what police
knew for a local judge. The paperwork reported Diane's position in the driveway, the open loft door and the shell casing
discovered in the straw. Police were looking for small-caliber
weapons and ammunition. It listed the shells and cleaning rod
they found in the house. He didn't find the discovery alarming.
He knew Brad had guns and liked to hunt.

The house also swayed Randy. He'd done enough divorce
work when he was a young attorney to know what a home in
crisis looked like. "When you walked into a house and go from
room to room you can tell," he later recalled. "You can tell
when people are depressed, or when there's big trouble, or
when there's alcoholism. In this house I instantly recognized:
This is a really healthy place for these kids. She's a great mom
and she's paying a lot of attention to what she's doing. There's
nothing wrong here, I said to myself."

The same could be said for Brad, Randy decided. His old
friend gave him a little house tour. There were professional
family portraits everywhere. Brad talked about the future, as if
Diane were still alive. He showed Randy the porch construction, then they went outside and walked the dog. He talked
about the grounds, how he'd planned to clear and landscape it,
and other plans for the farm.

Randy Wright considered all of this. Could Brad King have
killed anybody? Could he kill the woman he loved, the mother
of his children? Could he have shot her right in front of their
children?

It was unfathomable Randy Wright decided. Not Brad.

They spent time Sunday attending to the unavoidable,
mainly breaking the news to people by phone. The first call was

to Brad's mother, Marge Lundeen, in Kerrville, Texas. She said she would fly into Detroit Metro that night.

In the afternoon, they took clothes to the Elgutaas in Battle Creek. The couple offered to continue watching Marler and Kateri. Marler was playing, seemingly happy and unaffected. He didn't know his mother was dead, and nobody was eager to tell him just yet. Kateri was sick with a cold. They had dinner with the Elgutaas, then returned to the farmhouse to meet the local Catholic priest for a brief visit. Diane's mother Freida called and spoke to Brad briefly. Then they made and took more phone calls.

Late in the day, they just found themselves sitting in the living room, staring at each other, killing time until his family arrived.

Brad brought up the deer herd on the property. An incredibly large deer herd, he said.

"Do you want to see 'em? They come in around dusk."

"That's an idea," Randy said. "I think the air would do us both good."

Brad drove the Jeep Wagoneer, entering the back acreage from an access road on the west end of the farm. They crossed barren crop fields and fence lines, heading toward the lane that led south from the King barnyard.

About a half mile south of the farmhouse, Brad got the Jeep mired in a drift of wet snow. Randy tried to push, but it wouldn't budge, even in four-wheel drive. They were only a couple hundred yards from the hay bales where Brad said he was sitting the night of the murder. They both were wearing sneakers. They walked the vehicle lane at the fence line that had the bales, then north to the farmhouse, Brad leading the way.

On their way back, as Brad promised, they saw deer. Randy Wright, in all his years of hunting, had never seen so many deer. They crossed open fields and walked the tree and fence lines. Others explode out of the marsh near the stream, their white tails flashing as they leaped. Randy could see why Brad liked to walk the property at dusk. His jaunt before Diane came home Saturday made even more sense.

When they got back in the barnyard, the sun had set.

"Let's go up in the loft," Randy suggested.

He not only wanted to see what he'd read about in that search warrant, but the twilight was making him anxious, as was the imposing Victorian barn. Diane had been shot at twilight. He wanted to make sure that loft was empty.

Brad followed him up the stairs. Randy wandered over to the pile of straw near the door. It was still ajar. He looked down, into the driveway. You didn't have to be a cop or an infantryman, he decided, to appreciate the angle and the opportunity for cover. The door cast a dark shadow from the mercury vapor lamp. The elevation was high enough to be above eyesight. Low enough to shoot without adjusting the sights. Randy remembered where the Jeep was parked that morning. It was an ideal sniper's perch.

The view kindled something in him, something that reminded him of the men in his company and all the snipers in Vietnam. Randy Wright was alert once they returned inside the house, but it wasn't from the air. Yes, he decided, there was one sign of trouble in the living room. Those big front windows. White sheets had been neatly pinned and hung in the sashes. Diane had put them there because of that letter, he guessed. She didn't want anyone to be able to see in from the street.

Randy Wright decided he did not want to stand near any windows, sheet or no sheet, in the front of the house nor at the side. He avoided being backlit or standing motionless in any one spot.

He also became aware of sounds. Outside, he could hear the dog barking. Earlier the Doberman had barked at reporters that he had turned away. Now the dog seemed to be barking at nothing. Or, was he barking at somebody?

"Brad, why is that dog barking?" Randy asked.

"Oh, he just barks at animals," Brad said.

Brad seemed oblivious to any threat. Brad had been walking around, making a perfect target of himself. Grief and shock had put his old friend on another planet, he decided. Or maybe as a former cop, Brad knew killers only returned to the scene of the crime in movies.

Randy made himself busy with more phone calls. He took a few as well.

Later, family arrived in Marshall. Brad's mother Marge, her husband Cliff, his brother Scott and his wife. They met them at the Greek fountain in the middle of town and helped them check into a room at the Arborgate Motel. Diane's sister Darlene, brother Allen, his girlfriend Nancy Rapo, and cousin Elaine Wash also showed up at the farmhouse. They took the bedrooms upstairs. Brad took the couch. Randy Wright slept in the baby's room downstairs.

He slept very lightly that night.

Elaine Wash had arrived at the house on St. Joseph Street Sunday to find Freida Newton facedown on her bed in despair. It reminded Elaine of when her husband Bert Marler died. She'd lain on that same bed for days. Nancy Rapo said she'd found Freida hours after the murder scrubbing the white family poodle Pierre, seemingly disoriented with grief.

By Sunday, Allen Marler had shared some details provided by Brad at the motel about the shooting, but none of the family members sitting around the living room knew anything about funeral arrangements. Brad still hadn't called to talk to the family. This is ridiculous, Elaine Wash thought, marching into the bedroom.

"Aunt Freida, they're going to have her buried and nobody is even going to know it," she told her. "Why don't Darlene and I take a ride up there and find out what's going on?"

"Would you do that for me?"

Allen and Nancy had joined them. They drove first to the sheriff's department, asking for answers from a reluctant Jack Schoder and Jim Stadfeld.

"I've got an aunt who knows nothing," Elaine demanded. "People don't just die and then you hang them out on a clothesline."

They got some details of the shooting.

By mid-evening, they were at the farmhouse. Randy Wright seemed to be shadowing Brad.

"I mean, you couldn't ask Brad a question," she later recalled. "It was like you asked Randy a question, he answered, and then Brad verified. It was like, what is this? Your wife has died, what is going on?"

Elaine and Darlene looked at each other. The setting was so strange. Two men alone in that house. Where was the family? Why did Brad need the man he'd called "my friend and my attorney"?

"Both of us knew something was wrong," she later recalled. "You don't get our age and bury as many people as we have and not know something was wrong with the picture. Something was just very odd."

They took Brad up on an offer to sleep there.

At dawn on Monday, Elaine Wash heard a TV first, then a haunting whimpering as she descended the stairs. She walked into the living room where she found Brad sitting on the couch.

He was clutching a statue of Kateri Tekakwitha, the seventeenth century Mohawk maiden considered blessed by Catholic Iroquois and the namesake for the Kings' daughter. He was staring at a snowy TV and crying in the tones of a little child, pressing the statue to his chest.

"What's the matter, Brad?" Elaine asked. "Did you see something on the television? Did they have something on the news?"

It was near the time that Brad was accustomed to seeing Diane on TV.

Brad shook his head, and the tears stopped.

Elaine Wash heard somebody. She turned around and saw Randy Wright.

3

Jim Stadfeld and Calhoun County medical officials had ordered Diane Newton King's body transported from Kempf Funeral Home in Marshall to Blodgett Memorial Hospital in

Grand Rapids for a detailed forensic autopsy by respected Kent County pathologist Dr. Stephen Cohle.

Both Stadfeld and Jack Schoder drove up to the hospital for the postmortem late Sunday morning. By early afternoon, the autopsy was producing chilling results.

Dr. Cohle determined the gunshot to Diane Newton King's chest was from front to back, slightly from right to left and slightly from above downward. There were no signs of gunpowder on the clothes or skin. That meant the killer fired his weapon at a distance exceeding at least eight feet. The findings were consistent with a shot from the loft where the casing had been found.

That wasn't the half of it. The shooter, the autopsy appeared to show, had a deadly knowledge of human anatomy as well as a sharp eye and steady hand. Dr. Cohle found a .22 caliber bullet lodged in the soft tissue of Diane King's back. Before coming to rest there, the slug had passed through her chest between the third and fourth right ribs, cut through the upper lobe of her right lung, pierced her heart, continued through her aorta, and then grazed her spinal cord at the sixth thoracic vertebra. She had blood in the cavities surrounding each lung. She had blood in the sac around the heart.

It was the kind of kill shot that most likely had dropped her in her tracks. "She died on the ground within three minutes, if that," the pathologist said.

However, the abdominal bullet wound just above Diane King's pubic hairline made for a curious contrast. It was another .22 caliber wound, but nowhere near as precise. The slug had entered the abdominal cavity, passed twice through the small intestine, penetrated the diaphragm into the left lung, cut through the left fourth rib, and came to rest just below the skin of the left upper chest. The path appeared as though the shot was fired up from her feet, if she were standing, slightly right to left and slightly from front to back. If she'd already fallen, the gun would have had to be held almost parallel to the ground.

The pathologist turned over the spent bullets to Stadfeld. Both slugs were copper coated. Both slugs were deformed, the chest shot markedly. The detective placed them in a small manilla envelope for the crime lab.

When it was over, they hit the road for the two-hour trip back to Marshall. Jack Schoder's anxiety about a deadly stalker had been replaced by an entirely different worry. They'd been hashing over the case on the trip up and now on the way back.

Stadfeld's suspicions had been high since Schoder filled him in on the details of Brad King's statement the night before. He'd concluded that only with great difficulty could a stranger lie in waiting in the barn loft.

"Jack, you tell me how the fuck somebody's going to move in and out of there with King and that dog around all day," he said.

"Jim," Schoder said. "I hear ya."

They were thinking about the circular dog track and the .22 ammunition and cleaning rod in the attic of the farmhouse.

"But he says he's only got a shotgun," Schoder said. "I think I better ask him some shit about that."

Stadfeld nodded. "Whoever shot her was one deadly bastard."

"Yeah, like a fuckin' hunter, huh?"

"A hunter who likes to hang out in camo."

"Some fucker who knows how to shoot people. Kill people."

"Yeah, somebody like a cop."

Schoder lit a cigarette. The note with the cut-out letters. They could check into that later.

"Jesus Christ, Jim. Man, you know, we gotta get back out there to that property."

They had to get back out there in force.

The search party of a couple dozen men had taken a day to organize. Monday morning, a group of local volunteers—called the Sheriff's Posse—gathered at the Marshall headquarters, joined by anybody else in the department that was free to help. Outside, TV trucks were camped, staking out the entire department, waiting for somebody to make a move.

In the squad room, Jack Schoder was having his first face-to-face talk with the dog handler, State Police Trooper Gary Lisle.

Stadfeld was securing another search warrant, this one stating the investigators had probable cause to believe that somewhere on the farm acreage was a .22 caliber gun.

Schoder showed Brad King's boots to Gary Lisle. Earlier, he'd put them on the hood of his Grand Prix and photographed them, placing a ruler from heel to toe for the shot. Yes, Gary Lisle said, the sole pattern, particularly the heel, looked very similar to all the footprints he saw along the dog track Saturday night. But Gary Lisle also knew he was no expert in the forensic science of footwear impressions.

"Did you guys ever get a picture of that footprint way over there in the swamp . . . by the stream?" Lisle asked.

"By the bridge?"

"No. East of there. Way east."

Schoder was silent for a moment. "Man, Gary, what the fuck are you talking about?"

"About a hundred yards east of the bridge," he said again.

"Where east?"

Lisle explained again about the impression he found in the mud and slush. It was well to the east of the vehicle lane, he said, about twenty feet from the stream, just inside the marsh. Two days had passed since that information was supposed to be "passed along."

"You mean nobody told you about that?"

Jack Schoder looked extremely pissed.

They both knew that if that was Brad King's impression, it contradicted King's statement about where he had walked. It put him right on the dog track that came back to the farm. They also both knew that Sunday had been above freezing. In all likelihood, the impression now was nothing more than water and mud.

As if cued, the headquarters PA system made a page.

"Jack Schoder, Brad King in the lobby to see you."

"Gary, I want you in on this," Schoder said.

They borrowed a lieutenant's office. A few minutes later, Schoder returned with King, his friend Randy Wright in tow. They had been making funeral arrangements all morning. Brad wanted to know how the investigation was going. Did they have any new evidence? Did they have any more information?

"Nothing right now, Brad," Schoder said. "We're workin' on it, man."

Schoder told King they would be returning to the farm in a few minutes. They had another search warrant and wanted to explore the farm property. He introduced Gary Lisle as a tracking dog handler.

"Brad, this is the guy who is going to help us solve this case."

They shook hands.

"Brad, man. I need another favor from ya, okay? I need you to tell me again where you walked the other night."

Schoder handed King a piece of scrap paper and a pen. "In fact, you can show us, alright?"

King drew a cryptic map, showing the barn, the vehicle lane running due south to the creek and the hay bales beyond that. He said he'd walked to and from the hay bales.

"Let me get this straight," Schoder said. "You went straight down to these bales of hay and came straight back?"

Yes, King said.

"Now you haven't been over here at all, have you?" Schoder asked, pointing well east of the southward vehicle lane.

"No," King said. "Not since it's snowed."

It hadn't snowed for weeks.

Jack Schoder wasn't running tape, but he had two witnesses in the room. Schoder mentioned the .22 caliber ammunition they had found in the attic during the search early Sunday morning.

"Brad, you got a .22, man?" he asked.

"I used to," King said. "I sold it in Denver."

"When would that have been?" Schoder asked.

"In 1984."

Schoder wanted to know the make or model.

King said it was an old gun. He said he couldn't remember the make or the model.

King had a question for the detective. "Can I have my boots back?"

The request, Schoder later admitted, threw him. He handed King the boots.

"I wish I hadn't," he would later recall. "I guess I gave them back because . . . I had them on his consent. I felt that because I didn't have them on a search warrant, I had legal responsibility to give him those boots back. I also didn't want to freak him out."

King and Wright said they were heading back to the farmhouse.

"I'll see ya over there," Schoder said.

He showed them through the garage to avoid the pack of reporters that had gathered at the front of the department. He met them in the driveway of the farmhouse at 16240 Division Drive several minutes later.

Jack Schoder decided to start working him a little.

"Brad, there's just a lot of things about this that just don't add up," Schoder said. He eyed the horizon.

King nodded.

Schoder lit a Winston. "I mean, Brad, you told me no one was around here."

Schoder motioned toward the leafless trees and surrounding flat terrain. "Look around here, man. It's all wide fuckin' open. There's no traffic. You told me you were in the yard all day. I'm having a hard time understanding how a guy gets into this barn."

Randy Wright agreed. He had a hard time understanding that too, he said.

King shrugged.

"Brad, you're the only one who knew she was coming home. I have some real concerns about that, too."

Brad King said he understood that he was concerned. If he was in his situation, he would be concerned as well, he said.

"Brad, it just don't add up. Not what you're telling me, man. I gotta get this worked out."

Brad King offered no excuses. He did not complain. He was not shy about looking Jack Schoder directly in the eyes.

The posse began arriving in the driveway, car by car. Reporters and TV trucks parked along Division Drive. They posted a cruiser at the foot of the driveway to keep the press back.

King complained about the media. He didn't want to stick around with cameras staked out up and down the road. He told Schoder that he and Randy Wright had a lot of errands to run anyway.

Schoder planned to get the search started, then head back to the department to return a stack of phone messages. As he watched King and Wright drive off, Jack Schoder decided he'd already accomplished what he had set out to do when he asked King to meet him at the farmhouse.

"I wanted Mr. King to know this small-town detective was not buying this whole scenario," Jack Schoder later said. "I was sure of it. I was thinking, yeah, Brad, he's my man."

Deputy Guy Picketts and Trooper Gary Lisle knew the stream as Talmadge Creek. It ran the width of the old Zinn farm, flowing to the northwest before emptying into the Kalamazoo River near the Marshall city limits.

Picketts, Lisle, and a DNR officer named Michael Shay had been assigned the creek in the briefing back at the department. The rest of the volunteers would search all five hundred acres of the farm in grids. Lisle and his dog Travis would rework the original track, crossing the creek twice. Picketts and Shay would work the stream from west to east.

It was bright and sunny on February 11. When they reached the footbridge, both Picketts and Lisle noted Talmadge Creek was running much lower than the night they were out there in the fog. The boot prints were gone. What the sun hadn't accomplished, the deer herd had. Dozens of hooves had obliterated the impressions in the snow on the south side of the creek. Further east, the slush print was history as well.

When they approached the stream in the swamp crossing, Travis circled, putting his head down near the water. His ears and tail went up.

"What's that, boy? Thatta boy."

Lisle looked into the creek, but found nothing but glare cut by dark shadows near the bank.

Gary Lisle pulled out a small roll of toilet paper. He found it worked as well as anything, the way it clung to the brush and trees. He strung some in a sapling on the bank of Talmadge Creek, then got on the radio to Picketts and Shay who were approaching somewhere downstream.

"Hey, when you get up here, I've got some toilet paper strung," he told them. "Travis is really interested in this spot, but I can't see anything. You might get a better angle and check it out."

Lisle turned southwest, in the direction of the hay bales Brad King told him about back at the department. Near them, he found the Jeep Wagoneer stuck in the snowdrift. The lane was still snow covered. He saw two sets of footprints heading north from the Jeep back to the farm. They appeared to be running shoes. He looked, but found no boot prints heading south.

Guy Picketts, meanwhile, had a theory, based on the time he'd spent on that farm, based on what he knew about the land. If somebody wanted to hide a gun on the old Zinn place, somebody would put it in one of two places: in the culvert by the makeshift bridge or somewhere in the marsh.

Picketts and Shay checked inside the culvert. They found only red tile, fieldstone, and rushing water.

Just after the town siren marked noon, they headed upstream into the marsh. Shay had on a pair of hip waders. Picketts walked just ahead of him on the south bank. Picketts stepped on the mounds of swamp grass, checking the bank. Shay slowly waded forward, the silt flowing behind his heels like dark exhaust.

Deep in the swamp they saw Gary Lisle's foot-long strip of white toilet paper, fluttering in the wind.

Picketts chuckled. "With Lisle's paper around, we better look real good where we're stepping," he quipped.

Picketts looked along the bank. The marsh grass was tall and thick right to the bank. Except for one spot. The bank had deteriorated there from the hooves of stream-leaping deer.

Something unnatural caught Picketts's eye, as the casing in

the loft had two days earlier. It was the flat surface of molded material. Guy Picketts saw the heads of two screws. He saw black plastic.

"Damn, here it is!"

A butt plate. A gun stock. The dark wood stock was sticking out of the water not two inches. Somebody had shoved a rifle barrel-first, straight down into the black mud bottom of Talmadge Creek.

Jack Schoder was doing the best he could to explain the investigation was continuing to Diane King's cousin Elaine Wash and other family members when he heard the excited tone in Guy Picketts's voice on his police scanner.

"Get 401 and 402 and the undersheriff here immediately," he was saying to the dispatcher.

The numbers were codes for Schoder and Stadfeld.

"Excuse me, folks," he said. "I gotta go."

Schoder and the undersheriff ran out of the department and sped south in the detective's Grand Prix. Stadfeld followed in his car. Schoder cut in front of a speeding train at a closed gate crossing. Stadfeld waited for the train.

"Jesus, Jack," the undersheriff complained.

Jack Schoder was convinced something horrible had happened.

"Shit, I thought Brad may have killed himself or something," he later recalled.

They found Guy Picketts, Gary Lisle, Travis, and DNR Officer Mike Shay back at the creek. Shay was standing motionless, the water rushing around his hip waders. Picketts had asked him to freeze. Picketts had not only found a gun, he'd found a handful of .22 caliber shell casings nearby on the stream bottom. Shay was trying not to disturb the silt.

"The motherfucker did it," Jack Schoder said.

He wasn't talking about Guy Picketts or his dog, Travis. He was talking about Brad King.

A few minutes later, Mike Shay methodically slid a small reed into each shell casing in the water, picking them up and dropping them into yellow evidence envelopes Schoder held open.

There were seven casings in all. Schoder handed the package to Stadfeld.

"I'll bet they match the barn," Stadfeld said.

The gun wasn't going to be so easy. Everyone figured it would be nearly impossible to get latent prints off the weapon, but nobody wanted to rule it out. They needed something to pull it out.

Schoder cut a two-foot piece off his leather bootlace.

"Here," Shay said. He handed Schoder a small utility knife with a screwdriver blade. "Use this and unscrew the butt plate a little. Tie it around that."

Schoder threaded the leather under the plastic plate and tied it. Then, he began to pull.

The plate snapped, breaking in half. The gun had hardly moved out of the muck.

Someone suggested tying a slipknot on one of the screws.

Schoder pulled. The stream bottom refused to let go of the gun around the area of the trigger, so when it came out a ball of black mud came with the weapon, clinging to the bolt mechanism.

Everyone was looking at the slim barrel.

"It's a goddamn .22, alright," Stadfeld said.

A .22 caliber Model 511 Remington Scoremaster, to be exact.

Minutes later, Schoder posed as Stadfeld took an evidence picture near the bank of Talmadge Creek. He held the weapon up in front of him by his bootlace. He tried hard not to smile.

The bright sun was warm, the clean country air soothing. He was trying not to look like some kind of fisherman who had taken a trophy from the stream.

4

The Darling & Sons True Value Hardware was part of Main Street Marshall, one in a long procession of nineteenth Century storefronts that lined Michigan Avenue east of the Brooks Memorial Fountain.

As Tom Darling opened Monday morning, he still felt guilty about rushing to judgement about his neighbor the night before. Maybe it was the stress of the weekend. Maybe it was the timing. Certainly there was no way he could have prepared for that kind of news literally greeting him at the door.

Tom Darling and his wife Susan had just returned Sunday evening from a weekend with two hundred fifty teens at a Christian retreat. The "snow camp" had thawed into two days of sermons, rain, and mud. The telephone was ringing when Sue opened the door. He was pulling suitcases from the trunk when his wife yelled to the garage.

"Tom, Brad's on the phone. I don't know what he wants."

He knew his wife was irritated. They saw their share of Brad King, usually when he wanted something. A tool. A favor. A hand. Sue thought Brad treated their garage like it was the hardware annex. Tom didn't really mind. Brad always returned everything, but he knew it bothered Sue. It started bothering her when she found Brad helping himself in the garage when Tom wasn't home.

"What's up, Brad?" Tom Darling said, cradling the phone on his shoulder.

It wasn't Brad. It was a man who introduced himself as Randy Wright.

"Brad is too upset to talk to you," he said. "Mr. Darling, Diane was killed this weekend."

He moved the phone in his hand. "Killed? What do you mean, a car accident?"

"No. She was murdered."

It took a few minutes to get the details. It took a few more to tell Sue and his stepson, Sly.

Tom Darling sighed, looking at them both.

"You know," he said, "I'll betcha Brad did it."

Sue was angry, despite her feelings about Brad King. "Tom, you spend a weekend at a church retreat, and you come back and say something like *that* about somebody?"

He wished he hadn't thought it. He wished he hadn't said it. But he had. It was a gut feeling. That's all it was.

By Monday, other words were troubling him. Words from the speaker at the camp. Everyone was saying the ground war was coming in Iraq. Christians were talking about Armageddon. The speaker had seized the moment. He'd talked about being ready.

"Is your life in order?" he'd asked.

Yes, Tom Darling thought, my life is in order. But he wondered about his heart. He knew he had no justification to judge his neighbor that way. Neither Brad nor Diane had ever done anything to deserve it. Brad had some quirks. He was a bit of a pain, too, sometimes. But Brad and Diane were good neighbors, and exceptional customers on top of that.

The Darlings first saw their neighbors' names in the neighborhood newsletter. Another neighbor published the *Zinnland Recorder,* who used it to report about area people and wildlife, like the big deer herd everybody liked to watch in the local woods and marsh. "Zinnland" was the nickname for the farmland along Division Drive, all of it originally owned by an old Battle Creek family, who made a mint in the dog food business.

The *Zinnland Reporter* noted that Brad, Diane, and Marler King were moving into "Thunderspirit," the name given the farmhouse and grounds by its former tenants, Bob Randal and his partner, Ginger Hentz. Diane later told them they'd learned about the vacancy from Bob, who was the director of the food bank Diane served on as a board member. Ginger named the farm for inspiration.

"I figured if we named the home something powerful," she once said, "then anyone living there would one day become like it."

Diane was thrilled with the name. She kept the farm's phone number listed that way in the directory. It gave her the privacy she needed, but allowed her to pass her number to friends.

"Just look for Thunderspirit in the book," she'd say.

The Kings were different. They didn't look or act like most folks in Marshall. Brad had his shiny white, shaved head. Diane had big-city sophistication. The boy was dark skinned, like her. Some folks thought she was black at first. Some heads turned. There just weren't any mixed couples in town.

They guessed the Kings were looking for what the Darlings found in Marshall: a place to make a living among decent folks. A place to raise kids without urban hassles and threats. Sue grew up in nearby Athens, a smaller town. The entire Darling family moved to Marshall from Port Richey, Florida, when Tom's father bought the local hardware in 1975. The hardware was so run-down, the True Value rep said it just needed "somebody to bury it." Tom. His dad. His brother, Mike. Later, his sister, Janice. They made it work, then prosper. By the time his father retired in 1986, Janice was opening Darling and Daughter Variety up the street.

Still, they knew they were not true Marshall folks, even though their name covered two storefronts. That's just the way some people in the town thought. At least a generation or two had to pass before you were a "Marshall family."

Tom contributed anyway. He helped customers with plumbing and wiring jobs. He'd open up the store in the middle of the night to help someone in an emergency. He'd led a Cub Scout troop, served on the Downtown Development Authority, and raised funds for the annual home tour. He avoided politics and controversy. You avoided politics and controversy in a small town if you wanted to do business on the main street.

In fact, he liked living outside the limits, near Zinnland. They liked the privacy there. He and Sue had been married eight years. It was their second marriage. They had Chris Sly, fourteen, from her first. Daughter Lindsay, five, was their own.

They all got to know the Kings over a bonfire at Thunderspirit one night. Tom, Sue, and the kids walked down the road to chat when they saw the flames. Diane had big dreams for the farm. Brad seemed dedicated to making them come true. They bought a Jeep Wagoneer for her just after they moved in last April. Before they had only one car.

The house had come a long way. They painted and papered and refinished the floors down to hardwood. They installed new tile and stripped the antique oak cupboards. They lined the closets with cedar and repaired doors and locks. When Diane learned Sue had a machine sitting idle, she borrowed it to sew curtains. She made valances in Southwestern patterns. The inside went from old and ordinary to bright and earthy.

What Brad couldn't do himself, he convinced neighbors, friends, and students to do. Brad had a little Tom Sawyer in him, Tom Darling had decided. He found himself at Thunderspirit more than once when Brad ran into a difficult job. Eventually he found out the renovation was paying their rent.

Tom Darling figured it came back around. The landlord, a Detroit attorney named Frank Zinn, kept an open account at the hardware for tenant repairs. Brad filled card after card with charges. Sometimes Tom felt guilty selling him what he did. Brad pushed the definition of repair work to the limit. He bought top-grade rawhide gloves. He charged tools he'd likely take with him one day. New hammers and the like. But every month he'd send the itemized bills off to Frank Zinn in Detroit. Every month Zinn would send a check back.

There was other reciprocation. Tom stored his tractor in the King barn. In return, he kept the King driveway plowed. Sue sometimes watched the King kids. Diane helped teach Lindsay to read. Tom helped Brad rewire the basement in the farmhouse. Brad once helped Tom shingle his porch roof.

They seemed like genuine people. When the Kings came back from a vacation to Colorado last year, they stopped at their house to talk for an hour before they even went home. They had played Yahtzee and Euchre together. Tom and Brad hunted rabbit once. Brad joined him for a couple nickel–dime poker games. Brad was a quiet gambler. You asked him a question; he gave you an answer. He was quiet about most things, in fact.

Just at Christmas, the Kings had impressed everyone with a

little neighborhood party. Not a month from Kateri's cesarian delivery, Diane had decorated the house beautifully. The tree was stunning, the house trimmings done with a Native American flair. Diane was artistic and creative, right down to the surprise gifts she produced. She gave Sue a Christmas mug. She gave Tom three Jamaican cigars. Tom had told Diane once that he craved Macanudo Portofinos "just about three times a year." She'd remembered both the brand and the number. Diane impressed people with little details like that.

Both of them had never met anyone quite like Diane Newton King. They liked Diane a lot. They watched her every morning. Tom often complimented Diane or Brad on how good she looked on TV. Tom enjoyed knowing someone who was in her business, someone who did something different from most folks.

Something about Brad was different, Tom decided early on. His eyes, probably. When their eyes met, Brad's never glanced away first. He never yielded the psychological right of way. He reminded Tom of Jack Nicholson before he flipped out in *The Shining*. The wry smile. The penetrating gaze under expressionless eyebrows. The eyes, the bald head, and the silence made Tom uneasy sometimes. Sue maintained Brad was "a user."

"He's using you, Tom," she would sometimes say.

Maybe, Tom told himself, but did that make him a killer? Now he was a widower, with two small kids. He'd gone over to Thunderspirit on Sunday night shortly after getting the call and was moved by what he found. Brad met him at the door. They embraced. Brad wept, his shoulders shaking, his tears falling on Tom Darling's shirt.

"This is my friend, Randy," Brad said, stepping back, wiping an eye.

"Where are the kids?" Tom asked.

"They're in Battle Creek," Brad said, nodding. "They're okay."

"Brad, what happened?"

"She was shot from the loft of the barn as she got out of her car." She was returning home from Detroit, he said. He was looking at deer out back.

Tom knew all about the crazy letter. He'd sold the Kings the motion security lights for the house. In the weeks after she received the note, Brad called him several times, asking him to swing by and check on Diane when he was delayed at the university. Once, Tom and Susan both went down to check the farmhouse together. They found Diane hiding behind the door. She was poised to attack with a pair of deer antlers wedged between her fingers.

Tom felt uncomfortable Sunday night with him, partly because he'd judged him. When he returned home, he called his pastor at the Calvary Baptist for some counseling.

Now, on Monday morning, Tom knew he'd be seeing Brad later that evening. Brad had said that he and his friend Randy had stuck the Wagoneer in a drift while back on the property, looking for deer.

"Can you pull it out with the tractor?" Brad had asked.

"I'll come over after work," he'd said.

As the day wore on, Tom got to thinking about it. That farm was a crime scene out there, he told himself. Maybe first he better check with the police. In fact, he wondered why Brad would even go out there and drive around.

5

By late Monday afternoon, Jack Schoder and Jim Stadfeld were favoring bringing Bradford J. King in for more questioning, and bringing him in real soon.

Outside, neither detective had seen anything like it in all their years in Marshall. Reporters were everywhere. The sheriff couldn't walk into the building in the morning without microphones being thrust in his face. Robin Ivey, his administrative assistant, would work five double shifts that week trying to handle them. She was keeping a list. She was averaging more than two hundred calls a day.

It had not been a good year for Sheriff Jon Olson, who'd been sheriff since 1979. The past ten hadn't been good for most sheriff's departments around the state. Their rural patrols were disappearing with new suburbs and federal budget cuts. Sheriff departments were doing more jailing and less police work. Politicians were centralizing more power in the big cities like Battle Creek.

Marshall folks didn't go for that. County folks didn't go for talk about a new county jail being planned for Marshall moving to Battle Creek, instead. Olson thought that would make better logistical sense, considering all the crime in the city. But Jim Stadfeld had advised Olson, whom he considered a friend, that he ought to take a low profile on that issue. He was facing election in 1992.

The department could use some good news, like a bust. They could do it fast if Brad King copped.

Schoder and Stadfeld also faced a quandary. It would be a calculated gamble. King would find out they had discovered the gun and the shells when he read a copy of the search warrant. Law required they leave him a copy that day.

On the plus side, they decided another taped interview would create an official record of what they now believed were lies. King might clam up and hire a defense attorney when he found out about the gun. Right now, Schoder believed he had the element of surprise.

"I had to evaluate really quickly what I was going to do, knowing I don't know this guy as well as I'd like to know him," Schoder later recalled. "With that search warrant, I was forced to bring this interrogation on now. It was time to get it on."

"In retrospect," Jim Stadfeld would explain later, "I think we were hoping we could close this thing right there."

King actually forced the issue. Late Monday afternoon, as they were debating what to do, he called Jack Schoder.

"How's it going?" he asked.

"We've had some interesting developments, Brad. Could you come by?"

"Sure."

Brad King showed up at 6 P.M. in the lobby. He had his

brother Scott with him. Randy Wright had gone back to the Detroit area. Schoder took them back to the break room, offering them coffee. Then he asked King for his prints.

"Brad, man, you been a cop for a lot of years. You understand the need for elimination prints, don't you?"

Sure, King said, he understood all about those.

Afterwards, Schoder showed Scott King a seat in the lobby. He asked Brad King to walk with him to the detective bureau office in the county annex building a block away on Grand Street.

"Brad, man, we need to get some privacy. There's no goddamn place to talk around here."

Schoder sucked on a Winston as they walked. "I knew going into that meeting with Brad King that that was going to be one of the biggest interviews I'd ever do in my life," he later would recall. "I knew, obviously, that the media had been all over this thing like stink on shit. I knew that we didn't have any eyewitnesses. And I just knew it was going to be a major accomplishment if I could cop him out."

Jack Schoder would do the interview alone. He and Stadfeld had already discussed what buttons he might push. That was where the calculated gamble came in. They knew virtually nothing about the criminal justice instructor and his anchorwoman wife. Schoder had a long talk Sunday with Channel 41 Vice President Mark Crawford. The couple apparently had some financial trouble, he said. The IRS had tried to garnishee some $5,000 of Diane King's pay.

Other than that morsel of intelligence, Schoder would largely be winging it. He'd have to bullshit King on the rest.

Jack Schoder had never been formally trained at a police academy, but he'd tried to make up for that with street experience and seminars when the opportunity presented itself. One of his favorites had been schooling in an interrogation method called the Reid Technique. He'd attended a Reid seminar in Chicago a few years back.

The Reid method called for the interrogator to confront the subject with seemingly unrefutable evidence of his guilt, then study the nature of his denials closely. Were they qualified?

Strong? Weak? He then supplied the subject with excuses that might help him mitigate his crime. Consequences of confessing were minimized. The idea was to make confession personal and cathartic.

Some cop shops called it "running the religion angle." Others said it was just a fancy way of helping a guy get something off his chest. To work it relied on some important variables. The subject had to have a shred of conscience. He had to have some anxiety. He also had to be ignorant of the fact that the questioner was actually running a line of shit.

The two detectives had decided they would not read King his Miranda rights first. The legal standard in Michigan was custody. Only once a person was in custody he had to be given his rights. That's why Schoder had suggested the annex office. He and King walked there, not drove. King would be free to go any time. If King started confessing, Schoder would stop and read him his rights. If Brad King began to confess, then he would not be free to go.

The detective bureau office shared the small brick building with the city health department. Schoder's desk faced the south wall and a window. Schoder asked Brad King to sit in a chair off to the side of the desk, so that he was facing a windowless wall.

Schoder moved his chair over so he was almost knee to knee with King. There was an open door that led to the health department to Schoder's left, behind him. Jim Stadfeld was sitting in there, listening, just in case things got out of hand.

On the street outside, a car or two passed as Marshall folk headed home for dinner with the coming of another winter twilight.

Schoder told King he wanted to tape this. He said he needed to get all the detail he could.

"What do you need?" Bradford J. King asked.

"I've asked you to come over here and talk about a couple things. I just wanna go through, keeping in mind that you're the one person who was there."

"You ask a question," the criminal justice instructor said.

"Well, why don't we start. Let's go back to Saturday. Ah,

maybe I'll just summarize things a little bit, in brief, and we'll see if . . . basically that, ah, Diane has taken off and went to visit family in the Detroit area."

"Yes."

They went over when she left. Thursday morning, around 9:30 A.M., King said, after she returned from work.

"She was gonna . . . she had to pack her clothes when she got home," King explained. "Had the kids all ready. I loaded the car for her. Uhm, got my stuff together, and she said, 'I'm set. I'm just gonna pack my clothes. You go on and get to the university so you can get some work done before class.' "

King added he was teaching that Thursday morning. "And I said okay. And I gave everybody a kiss. 'Drive careful. And I'll call you.' "

They made arrangements for him to call her at her mom's later that day, he said.

Schoder covered what cars they normally drove. King said Diane took the Jeep Wagoneer. He drove the station wagon, the Dodge Aries. That's usually the way it was unless they were together, then they took the Wagoneer.

Schoder wondered about Diane's expected time of return on Saturday. "The arrangements were sometime Saturday, is that accurate? Or early in the afternoon?"

King stayed with Friday. "Well, I talked to her on Friday. I don't know. I called her around five, I guess. Maybe before. They arrived safe. She said she would call me Saturday morning and tell me what the plans were of coming home."

"So then, all right, so Friday goes by."

"Talked to her on the phone on Friday, you know."

"What are you doing Friday? Are you out and around the yard, dinking around with that porch?"

"I was all over the place Friday. I was in the barn goofing around. I was upstairs in the barn Friday."

This caught Schoder's attention. "What was going on up there?"

King explained he had been preparing an area on the opposite side of the loft, away from the door over the stable, for a workshop to refinish antiques. It was Diane's idea.

Diane, King said, planned the space for him. "She's a planner . . . I know you knew her, but I don't know how well."

"Not well."

"Everything to her you plan it out. . . . Even to the extent of
setting up my workshop."

They talked more about Friday. King said he let the dog run
loose all day while he worked on the porch. He talked to Diane
on the phone. He didn't know exactly when.

"I played around with my bird feeder. I went rabbit hunting
Friday, across the street. With my shotgun."

"I noticed you had your shotgun broken down by the washer,
or the hot water heater. That is a helluva place to set a shotgun,
get all moist and rusty."

"I know, that is where Diane put it. . . . She didn't want the
kids to see it."

Schoder moved to the subject of Saturday, summarizing
King's morning as he told him in the previous interview. He
was up at 8 A.M. and out working on the porch by 10 A.M. He
received a morning call from Diane that her cousin Elaine was
coming to her mother's and she was going to visit a while.
Diane called again at about 12:30 P.M., saying her cousin had
arrived later than expected and that she wanted to see her sister
before she left for Marshall.

King said, "I said, 'Okay, so just let me know when you leave
so I know when to expect you.' And she said, 'I will.' And I said,
'Have a good time. Love you.' "

"Okay," Schoder said.

" 'Hug the kids for me,' " King added.

Then, King said, he hooked the dog on its chain and headed
for McDonald's in Marshall.

"Okay," Schoder said, "You went into Marshall, made a
drive-thru at McDonald's and came directly back, and went in
the house and ate it? Is that accurate?"

No, King said. He stopped and got a movie at the local video
store.

"Oh, did you?"

"Yeah. I was gonna watch a movie."

"That evening?"

"I was bored. No, while I ate lunch."

"Oh, okay."

"I was bored," King repeated.

"What movie did you get?"

"*Next of Kin*. That's what it was called. With Patrick Swayze. It's a nice violent cop movie."

"Nice violent cop movie?" For Schoder that was an odd way to describe it.

"Diane says, 'Don't you ever get tired of watching cop movies? And I say, I don't think so. I guess I haven't got it out of my blood.' So I, you know, ate lunch and watched it. You know I think I watched it all, now that I remember, you know, about ninety minutes."

"Okay."

"Something like that."

"You still got the movie."

"No, I took it back."

Schoder wondered where he got it.

A video store near a Shell gas station in town, King said.

"When did you drop that off?"

Sunday, King said.

He was trying to make King account for every minute of Saturday. He was watching to see if he could fill up the time he may have been setting up the cold-blooded ambush of his wife.

"Okay," he asked. "You *think* you watched that. I want to get clear on this."

King backed off the movie. "I know I had it, but did I watch it? Maybe I didn't even watch it."

"Maybe you didn't?"

"It was in the case."

Schoder was not ready yet to sound accusatory, especially on a seemingly minor point. "What I'm trying to do is, you know, see when you're outside and when you're inside, and what motions and actions are going on around the house. The other day you didn't mention that."

"I didn't even remember."

"Yeah, I mean that you would have watched it. I mean, that is an hour and a half."

"Yeah. I bet I didn't watch it."

"You didn't?"

"Bought the movie and set it down and was gonna wait till later. Come to think of it, I'm sure I didn't."

"That's okay. We'll just move on."

King didn't want to move on. "That bothers me though, Jack," he said. "I don't remember stuff. I had the damn movie."

Schoder wanted to know if he did some more outdoor work.

Yes, King said, he worked on the porch. He had to correct a mistake he'd made in the construction. In fact, he'd told Diane about that when she called at 12:30 P.M. Then, King said, he came in because he was cold.

"Hold on," Schoder said. "I'm gonna test this tape." Schoder stopped the interview. The interview was eating too much tape. He switched the Microcassette to a slower speed.

King continued. He became cold because he couldn't do that kind of work with gloves on, he said. His hands were cold.

"I was also getting tired of doing it by myself," he added. "Lonely."

"Sure."

"I'm not away from my family much."

"So you go back in and—"

"Took a nap."

"About what time?"

King didn't know. The next time he remembered was 4:30 P.M., when his mother-in-law Freida Newton called. As with the first interview, he remembered the time on the VCR. "Yeah, well I remember I looked at it, because she said Diane and the children had left."

"So you tried to formulate in your mind an estimate when they would get home."

"Yeah."

"How long does that trip take?"

"Two fifteen, roughly."

"Two and a quarter hours?"

King nodded.

"All right, after the phone call, you figure you got about two hours and fifteen minutes before the family is coming home?"

Yes, King said. Then he went out on the porch to do some more work. He added, "Then I thought, well I better fix dinner, had that thought, too." But he decided they'd just order pizza, because it would be less trouble.

"So I did go back out," King finally said.

Schoder thought this didn't sit with what King had said in the first interview. "Okay, did you . . . after you talked to your mother-in-law, did you go back and, uh, nap out a little bit? I wasn't exactly clear on what we talked about the other day. I'm just trying to put you back outside and, you know, as far as how long you were in the house."

"Laid down again, but I didn't go to sleep."

"Okay."

"I laid down again. That's when I was thinking about, you know, dinner and all that stuff. And then I went back out, but I didn't do any work. I picked up wood scraps."

"Oh, okay. And then at some point you went for a walk?"

"That was when I went for my walk. I didn't come back in—"

"Yeah."

"After picking up wood scraps. I came in and went to the bathroom. Then I went for my walk."

"It's about this time, about six, right? I know you don't have a watch, but we gotta try to pin this down. So when you take off and you walk straight down the lane, across the bridge, continue straight south. We are going south, right?"

"Yes, we are."

"You find these big rolls of hay where the deer lay, and you sit there for a few minutes."

"Well, I stand around. Sit. Look. I thought I'd seen some deer so I just—"

"How long do you think you were there?"

"Oh, man. Maybe ten minutes."

"Okay, so you're gone ten."

"Yeah. Nothing was moving. It was starting to kinda dusk up more. . . ."

"Time to go back," Schoder offered.

They discussed the distance back to the hay bales, but King

was unsure how far it was. King volunteered to help nail it down.

"If you want, I'll go out there and walk it tonight and—"

"No, it's not important," Schoder said. "Let's go back to sitting there on your walk. Did you hear any noises? I'm talking about gunshots."

"I heard what I thought was a gunshot."

"One?"

Yes, King indicated.

"And where were you?"

"I was at the hay."

"You had not started back yet?"

"No."

"Okay. Let me ask you how long does it—you give me an estimate—how long does it take to get from the barn to the hay?"

King thought about it momentarily. "Whew. I don't know, depends on how fast you were walking again."

"How long would it have taken you?"

"Fifteen minutes, at the max."

"At the max?"

"I move."

"Okay."

"You know, nice brisk walk." King added he walked in the winter to get his exercise. Diane insisted on it.

"Okay," Schoder continued. "So fifteen minutes to get there, and you're sitting there for ten minutes, and the whole time you were gone you heard one gunshot?"

"I heard that. I hadn't been at the hay very long."

They rehashed where and when he heard the gunshot for a couple minutes, then Schoder asked, "Okay, and then you come up. And on your way up, you don't hear any cars leaving?"

"All I can hear is the traffic on the expressway." I-69 ran north and south about a half mile to the east.

"You don't hear any gunshots?" Schoder asked.

"No."

"You don't hear any car doors slam?"

"No."

"Obviously you don't hear anybody running through the swamp back there?"

King complied without hesitation. "No, and you certainly would hear them. You hear when you go through there."

They talked a little more about the freeway noise.

King added, "I don't think you would hear a car door slam, unless maybe you were closer to the house. . . . Certainly not from the bale of hay."

"You wouldn't have heard her car pull up in the driveway, I'm sure?"

"No," King said. "I've actually been walking back, seeing the car coming up—the lights coming up before and not heard anything."

They talked about her headlights, then Schoder asked one more time. "I guess the important thing here is that you did hear a gun—one gunshot."

King clarified. "Heard one, I *thought*. You know, I didn't pay any attention to it. I couldn't tell where it came from."

"Okay."

"And I'd been hearing gunshots periodically all day anyway."

"Okay, while you were working on the porch?"

"Yeah, when I was outside I heard gunshots."

"But around this time period?"

"That was the only one."

King's story was remaining consistent with his Saturday statement, but soon it became very clear to Jack Schoder that Brad King was quite aware that what he was saying was inconsistent with the evidence. The criminal justice instructor would even cite his sources.

"Well, I know there were two bullets in her body, you know," he said.

"Yeah," Schoder said.

King pointed out he'd read the search warrant. "I read all the stuff, and you told me that."

"Right."

"And that is what perplexes me, why didn't I hear the other

shot? And maybe did it happen so close to the other one that I couldn't."

"Yeah."

"But, you know it was like . . . why didn't I hear two?"

Schoder added that the timing didn't make sense, even on the one shot Brad King maintained he'd heard. If Diane left the Detroit area at around 4:30 P.M. and it took her at least two hours and fifteen minutes to get home, something was off.

"If you heard one gunshot when you got there . . . you heard that gunshot in the area of 6:15 P.M., 6:20 P.M., by our calculations here."

"Yeah," King said.

"Diane couldn't have been home yet."

"That's right."

They'd been at it a good half hour. Jack Schoder figured it was time to move in now, push the interview into a more accusatory mode. He moved closer to King on the corner of the desk.

"See that's where I'm getting messed up," he began. "I tell you, Brad, I'm getting messed up. And I've analyzed this shit, man. I've looked at this up one side and down the other—"

"I can tell you're frustrated," King said, eyeing him.

"I'm frustrated as hell."

"*I'm* frustrated," King agreed. "I know I'm in the area and I can't help you."

"Brad, I'm going to be real truthful with you."

"Okay," King said calmly.

"Okay, I've been in this twenty-one years. You were in it twelve. I'm being real truthful with you. With the information that we have there, I can't eliminate you as being a suspect."

King was calm, accepting. "I understand."

Schoder moved into what the Reid Technique called "relating," putting the suspect and his questioner on even ground.

"And I'm gonna tell you another thing, Brad, and it's man to man here, and I'm not gonna pull any punches with you—"

"I know. I don't expect you to. I just want the truth—"

"Based on the information I've got here, I believe you're

involved. I believe, Brad, that you're responsible for this. I've worked on this for two days. I can't explain away a number of things. It does not follow logic, your explanation of things. This is what I'm looking at. Number one: Most important, there is no one else that I've been able to uncover. We've talked to the relatives in Detroit. We talked to a lot of other people. And no one explains that anyone other than you and the family in Detroit knew when she was coming home."

Schoder was bluffing. He'd talked to very few people, in fact.

Brad King was calm. "I know," he said quietly.

"You and you alone knew she was coming home. Second of all, you're out there all day, Brad. Twenty years in this business, man. A person who is going to sneak or stalk, to whatever, is scared of being detected. Similar to a burglary. Lights and sound scare them. Man, you were there all day, Brad."

"I know."

"No one else was there. I'm telling you if somebody was running surveillance, from where I don't know, because cars aren't running by your house all day, and it's a lonely road. There is no one in the area that can see, that can't get themselves. I've tried to put your account of things together and make it convince me—"

"Yeah."

"But it ain't. There is no place somebody could have a vehicle, and there are no neighbors around there, okay? I can't understand for the life of me, Brad, how somebody could get into that barn and go in there without . . . with the dog being there. Now you say your dog is a friendly dog, and I observed that it's quiet. But a person is not to confine themselves to a building where they can only get out via the front door, with you being there all day, Brad. Diane's car is gone during the entire goddamned day. If somebody is stalking Diane, Brad, then what's happened, man, is they know you're there and she ain't. And they're not gonna go sneak in your barn while you're there and when she's not there if she's the object of some unknown stalker."

King agreed, with far less words. "That's what I would say." He was not rattled.

Schoder pressed on. "Okay. I cannot for the life of me explain away how you did not hear gunshots. I been out there. I been listening to voices and noises as they travel. I was out there at night. You would have heard gunshots. There were two distinct gunshots." Actually, the department had done no sound tests. Schoder was bluffing again.

"I . . . I—"

Schoder cut him off. Now he wanted to mitigate the crime. "Let me tell you a couple things, Brad. I been married for a few years and everything has not always been perfect."

"True," King agreed. "Ours has not been perfect either."

Schoder made a wild guess. "And you guys been receiving counseling?"

Yes, King said.

"For your marriage?"

"Yeah, we thought we needed some help. To get back on track."

"And, I tell you, Brad, and you know this as well as I do. We're both adult men here. You know as well as I do that there is a very fine line . . . and sometimes you can cross over that line. You add up the pressures of life. You've got your part-time job. You've recently lost your job at the probation department. Some other things aren't going quite well for you, Brad. I understand why things can fall apart and your wheels can come tumbling off, and I think that you probably need some counseling yourself. 'Cause I think what has happened in your life, as a person, Brad, is the fact that the wheels have come off and you're kinda skidding along. And you've reached a point of total frustration. And you couldn't handle it. And I think you went for a long walk to kinda sort things out for yourself. And I think that you had enough psychological and mental pressure that for just a minute, just a couple minutes, you snapped. You broke. And you lost your head, Brad, and I'm really sorry about that."

"No." King seemed to counsel Schoder back. "I understand how you feel," he said.

"Brad, *that's* what I think happened."

"I understand that."

"Brad, listen to me, man. You cannot go on with what happened there in your life without getting some help."

"Well, I know I have to see somebody," King said, sadly.

"I'm talking about your involvement with *this,*" Schoder said firmly, his voice rising. "Okay, I'm convinced, *I am convinced* that you're responsible for this. *I am.* I'm convinced to the point of proving that in court. Let me tell you something else, Brad, and you can handle this anyway you want. And I'll tell you something, man, there comes a time when the pressures add up and the wheels fucking fall off, that you gotta reach out and you gotta grab someone, man, and you gotta hang on."

"I was trying to grab my wife and hang on with her."

"I'm not talking about that. I'm talking about *you.* I'm talking about since this incident. You're gonna have to hang on to something."

Schoder paused, then continued matter of factly. It was time to drop his big surprise.

"We were out there this afternoon, Brad. We found the murder weapon. And we have other evidence of your involvement in this. Believe me, Brad."

King mumbled something about Diane.

"Brad, listen, man. Listen."

"I didn't do anything to my wife," King said, louder now.

Schoder continued, trying to minimize the crime. "Brad, what happened? If you're a good person, all I'm saying is that good people in today's society sometimes face stresses that they can't handle."

"I know that."

"And they break—"

"That's why we were seeing a counselor."

"Just a minute, just a minute, man. I'm talking about you. And you broke down for a few minutes, and I know that you did something that you would never again even consider. But you broke down and you lost control for a few minutes. I don't know whether they call it insanity, or whatever, you just broke down and you lost control. And I, I feel bad for you. But what we have to do is come to grips with it, Brad. It's important to you. You know as well as I know, that for you to go to this point forward with that on your head, without getting some kind of help, is gonna break you down, and it's gonna shatter your total insides."

King's voice lowered. "You don't know," he mumbled.

"Just a minute, Brad. You understand what I'm saying? We found the murder weapon in the creek. And we have more evidence, Brad. Okay? Everything doesn't happen in a vacuum. We have *evidence*. That convinces me, and it's gonna convince other people, Brad, that you're responsible for this. Okay?"

King said something inaudible.

"The gun is in the crime lab right now," Schoder said firmly.

"I didn't do it," King said, clearly now.

"Okay, I want to talk to you about this, Brad, because there is nothing that you have told me that does anything but implicate you."

King mumbled something inaudible again.

"There is no other explanation. And when I add the other evidence that I have, and I'm not gonna tell you all the evidence that I have, and all the witnesses that I have. You'll see it in the court, Brad, 'cause we're gonna be going to court."

"I hear," King said. "I hear that."

"And we're gonna tie that weapon directly into you. It's over, okay? I want you to begin to accept that: It's over."

King mumbled something again.

Schoder kept pushing. He left no silence. "Brad, believe me, I'm not asking you about it. I'm telling you I'm convinced to the point that we've got the evidence. And what I'm talking to you about is how are you gonna handle it? How are you going to deal with it?"

"I didn't kill my wife," King said flatly. "Why would I kill the woman I love?"

"Not everything runs smooth as it seems."

"I know that. But that doesn't make somebody kill their wife."

Now, Schoder mumbled inaudibly.

"Come on, Jack," King said. He'd switched the roles momentarily. "I can't believe this." King sounded irritated.

Schoder tried to regroup, but ended up revealing the weakness of an investigation only three days old.

"Based on what you told me, based on other evidence that I've got, my concern is with you," the detective said. "I don't at this time purport to know everything that was going on in your life, in your relationship with your wife, your family, and with you. But I do know enough to be able to recreate what happened out there. And I guess, what I want to do, Brad, is I want to sit down with you, as we are, and I just want to understand how this happened and what other things are going on in your life, that causes you all this stress. There are a number of things, I'm sure. *Not working?*"

"Of course, it is."

"Causing problems?"

"Yes."

"Financial?"

"Not dire financial problems."

"Okay."

"But it doesn't have you killing somebody." King was steady now, in control of himself, perhaps in control of the interview itself.

"What I'm saying, Brad, is that—"

"I didn't kill my wife."

"It's okay. Explain to me any other scenario that might fit."

"I—" King started to say.

Schoder kept going. "Please explain it to me Brad."

"I'd like to know," King said.

Schoder paused, then said, "We've got the gun."

"But—" King began.

Schoder cut him off. "You have any idea where we found that gun?"

"No."

"Okay. We have it. Remington bolt-action .22. Scope, what is it? Scopemaster?"

"I don't know what you're talking about."

"*Scoremaster*, Model 511. Bolt action. The clip missing. Brad, *please*. Help me out. I live with these cases."

"I know. I lived with them, too."

"I mean—sure. And I take this stuff obviously real serious. Help me out Brad. Give me—"

"That's part of the job."

"Give me something to hang my hat on. Give me someplace else to go look, Brad."

King sighed. "I wish I could. I mean, for my own benefit I've been trying to explain to myself how this all happened. I knew we had problems. We were doing what we thought we could do to try and straighten them out. 'Cause we cared very much for each other. And it wasn't worth giving up."

"Okay."

"There is so much stuff that is unanswerable about this. I know that. Does that mean, then, since it's unanswerable that I personally did it?"

"The reason that I'm bringing this up to you, man, is because based on the evidence of this case right here, I'm convinced, Brad, that you're responsible for this. I'm convinced of that. This incident happened as a result of your having too much pressure on you to the point where you cracked. You made a bad decision. That's where I'm coming from."

"I know that's where you're coming from."

"I don't want to be coming from there, Brad. But that's where the facts lead me. I have come to that conclusion in my mind. *You're* responsible."

"I did not kill my wife. It is the last thing in the world I would want to do."

Schoder tried one more time. He seemed to be going after him in crescendos, but he couldn't get the theme to resolve itself.

"Yeah, well, let's go through this again, okay? You came down the track. There was nobody else down the track. You go over to where we found the gun. No one else has been over there. There is one person, one person that went from that barn to where we found the gun. There are no other people that did that. We can show that. No one else is in the area . . . except you."

"Yes, I was there."

"That's right."

"You really think that we're gonna believe, Brad, that some-body else got in there within a short period of time when her car is not even home, and got themselves trapped in a barn where they gotta come out the front door, knowing that you're in the area. Absolutely not."

"It's not highly logical, no."

"No, not at all. And then we take other evidence into ac-count, and we add that to those things, and I think we can convince some people that you're responsible for this. I'm sure. And I want to get down inside of you and find out what's been going on with you."

"Not killing my wife, that's for sure."

"Okay, let me ask you this. Would you agree to a polygraph test? I gotta have some answers. I gotta have some logic in this thing. Something has got to make some sense to me. This doesn't."

King ignored the polygraph question. He said, "Doesn't make sense to me either, Jack, and it's coming out of my mouth. . . . But it's what transpired for me. Randy and I sat and talked and talked and talked, you know. Why would? What would? Why would a guy sit and wait?"

"Yeah."

"And you know, I don't have an answer to that."

"Okay. Let me ask you—"

"I mean, well . . . well, do we have someone that saw it happen?"

"Pardon?" Schoder said.

King was probing for information now.

"I mean, if we had somebody that saw it happen. You know."

Jack Schoder wasn't going to answer any of his goddamn questions.

"We'll see," Schoder said. "Okay. I think we'll wrap this up for now, okay?"

After he turned off the tape recorder, Jim Stadfeld came in from the other room.

Schoder was pissed. "Jim, this dumb fucker wants me to believe he didn't do it and won't even take a polygraph test."

They talked about it some more, then King got up.

"You're doing a good job, Jack," they later quoted Brad as saying.

Bradford King was holding out his hand. He wanted to shake the hands of Jim Stadfeld and Jack Schoder.

"I knew right then it was a fucking game," Stadfeld later said. "I could see it written all over him."

They ignored his outstretched hand.

With that, the instructor of criminal justice calmly walked out their door.

6

Cindy Biggs Acosta wept when she heard from her family her former colleague had been murdered. Then, she did what most reporters do when tipped to major news. She picked up the phone and asked questions. She made an international call on Tuesday, February 12, from her new home in Caracas, Venezuela, to Marshall, Michigan. She expected a friend or family member would answer the phone.

She didn't expect to reach the grieving spouse.

"Brad, it's Cindy."

"Oh, Cindy. Cindy, I'm so glad you called."

Brad King sounded so relieved, Cindy Acosta suspected he thought she was somebody else. She mentioned Venezuela, so he'd remember her from her days at Channel 41 as Diane's backup. She had no idea that only twenty hours earlier Brad King had been interrogated and accused by Jack Schoder.

"Oh, Brad, I just can't believe it." She rambled on with questions. How did it happen? How was she killed?

"I guess she was shot," he said.

You *guess* she was shot, Cindy thought. My God, your wife

has been murdered, her funeral is tomorrow, and *you guess she was shot?*

The reporter in Cindy Acosta wanted to ask a dozen questions. She kept it to a few. How about the kids? Are the kids okay?

"The kids are fine."

He sounded like he was alone in the house.

"Brad, I can't come for the funeral," she said, apologetically. "If I flew out of here right now, I couldn't get there in time." She was worried he had no support.

"Brad, are there people there?"

He went from glum to a state of excitement. "Oh yeah, there are people from all over. People are coming from all over."

She couldn't remember Brad ever getting excited about anything. He seemed proud Diane's funeral was drawing a crowd.

"Brad, she was so special. Diane was *so* special. And Brad, Diane loved you so much. She really did."

"I know."

He said it so flatly she was left momentarily speechless.

"How are Juan and the kids?" he asked, matter-of-factly.

She remained perplexed. She thought, what does he want me to say? That the big move back to South America was coming along just fine. That Juan was settled into his new job with an international restaurant chain. That he didn't miss his twelve years at Kellogg's? That she was going to be the Venezuela correspondent for ABC. That most of their stuff hadn't arrived yet from the States?

The tone of his question seemed so inappropriate, disconnected from the tragic circumstances about which she was calling.

She wanted off the phone.

"Brad, hang in there, okay? You're going to have to take it day by day."

"We love you."

"We love you, too."

She'd only said it because he had. She didn't love Brad, she loved his wife as a dear friend. Cindy Acosta hung up and

turned to her husband, who had been watching and listening.
"Oh my God, Juan," she said. "He did it."

His voice alone convinced her. He'd always been strange, she
thought. He was stranger in times of crisis.

She remembered the day Diane found the threatening note.
Diane had dropped by her house in Marshall that afternoon,
just after picking up Marler from day care. Diane was eight
months pregnant, but looking like she was carrying overdue
triplets. Diane was already at wits' end trying to finish a docu-
mentary so she could begin her maternity leave. She remembered the bright red dress she wore that day, the way it seemed
to accent her swollen joints and very pregnant face. She looked
utterly defenseless.

Diane left for home. Not a half hour later she was back at
Cindy's door, hysterical. She handed Cindy the note she'd
found in her mailbox:

you Should Have Gone to Lunch WITH me

"When I read the letter I was almost sick to my stomach,"
Cindy later recalled.

Cindy called the Calhoun County Sheriff's Department.
Diane called Brad's number at the university at 6 P.M., leaving
a message with his voice mail. He had a 6:30 night class scheduled. A sheriff's deputy came to take the letter and make a
report. The deputy and Diane went to the house to check for
intruders, while Cindy watched Marler. When she returned,
she wanted to wait at Cindy's for Brad.

It was October 30, the night before Halloween, the evening
everyone called Devil's Night, a night of pranks and vandalism.
In Detroit, the devils burnt houses down for laughs.

Brad seemed to take forever. They showed the letter to her
husband, Juan. He paced the floor. He was very concerned. It
was as if she were suddenly in the company of a friend who'd
just gotten the news about a family car accident. Pretense and
social grace gave way to vulnerability. There was something
very anxious and mortal and intimate about that night.

The clock was heading for 10 P.M. when Brad knocked on the door.

Cindy answered.

He said few words. He was aloof, like a specter coming through the door. She showed him to a room downstairs where Diane was resting. Cindy Acosta let them have their privacy.

"Well, let's see how the station is going to handle this," he said when they returned upstairs.

Did nothing faze him? she thought. Her husband was more upset. Cindy offered to sub for Diane the next day at the station.

"Oh, Cindy, yes," she said.

A few days later they talked on the phone. Diane couldn't understand how anyone could have found her mailbox. She said she was always aware of any cars behind her. Their number was listed under Thunderspirit, she said. Diane also was troubled by Brad's reaction.

"Cindy, he just isn't there for me on this like the way he's been on other things in the past," she said. "I guess I'm just going to have to handle this problem on my own."

Indeed, Diane and Brad King had always come as a package. Brad was either tagging along, or Diane was making plans to include him. Other than work, Cindy found it difficult to ever see her alone. One time, they agreed to meet at Schuler's for lunch, a girls' outing, just the two of them. Halfway through the meal, Brad appeared in the restaurant, saying he'd just thought he'd stop by.

He wasn't blatantly possessive or domineering. "It was like he was lost without her," Cindy would later explain. "She couldn't possibly have a life of her own because he was always present."

Cindy Biggs Acosta was thirty-four years old and blessed with a combination of education, good diction, and the All-American good looks of a blue-eyed blonde. "A gracefully aging homecoming queen," she'd quip. The combination landed her the job at Channel 41 in early 1990 as Diane King's sub.

She remembered her first day. "The first morning Diane King came into the newsroom was like a tornado had blown into the room. She was marching around at five in her bare feet, full of energy and spit and vinegar."

Diane slapped into her hand a pile of notes she'd kept about her morning routine.

"I'm gonna train you," she said.

Pull her, was more like it. The walking and talking tour was nonstop. The news wire machine. The editing room. Makeup. Lights. How to wake up. The TelePrompTer. Boy, it had its quirks.

"Cindy, let me tell ya. You just fake it till you make it."

It was her favorite expression. People approached Diane King in department stores, assuming she was a salesperson. Always, she was moving and looked like she knew what she was doing.

Diane idled in motion. As she filed papers or did other busywork at her desk, she sang in a celestial soprano. She sang in Native American melodies that reverberated hauntingly off the newsroom's high concrete ceiling and walls.

It was an unpretentious little station, Cindy thought. The studio was in the basement. Everyone drifted around the building. Somebody in the promotion department with some on-air background was just as likely to be called to sub for a sick weatherman as anyone. It was an electronic version of the small-town paper, where a reporter collected the news, set the type, and threw the papers off the truck if the operation was in a pinch.

Despite the humble surroundings, Diane King wrestled with the nuances of her job as if she were covering the White House. She was a perfectionist, and that cut both ways. She corrected mistakes in the next newscast. She threw away press releases and dug for news. She also rode her photographers, sometimes treating them like toady technicians, ordering them what to shoot. She expected instant results, but sometimes made instant enemies.

Diane was a walking journalism forum. She talked about ethics and advocacy and, most of all, compassion. "You have to have compassion," she said of reporting. "You have to have a feel for people."

Diane Newton King was just what Cindy Acosta needed after a ten-year sabbatical from the TV business. She'd raised two kids to school age while her husband worked his way up the international ladder at Kellogg's. They spent the eighties in South America. She was raised in Michigan, but coming back to Marshall was culture shock after the slow and balmy southern tropics. Diane King was a booster shot of full-tilt American hustle.

And, Lord, that woman seemed driven by some kind of destiny. "She felt she was placed on this earth for a special reason," Acosta later tried to explain. "You know, as parents, it's up to us to instill that. But not everybody believes that. Not everybody receives the message, and not everybody believes that message if they do. But Diane believed it beyond a shadow of a doubt. She felt like she was on this mission in her life and that made her feel good about herself."

She was fired up about being Native American. Its spirituality. The advancement of her people. Her burgeoning family was involved, she said. Brad was going to take classes in Mohawk so he could one day teach the language to Marler. The boy was going to grow his hair like her ancestors. And she had her Two Worlds Productions.

The first week, they covered a local story together at a Bob Evan's restaurant. Diane turned heads when she breezed into the place. She didn't need a photographer in tow to do that, she later learned. The story was about a man with Down's Syndrome overcoming his disability with a job there. The theme must have struck something in Diane as they talked over coffee between themselves.

She said she was her father's favorite. "He told me, you'll go to college one day."

His death when she was ten devastated her, as did her mother's marriage to her stepfather a couple years later. He drank excessively when they were young. There were vicious fights between her stepfather and her mother. Police cars in the driveway, officers inside breaking up the battles.

School wasn't always the place to escape. She'd been called

"a nigger." She was tubby. Her siblings called her "Chubby Checker" or "chunk of chocolate." She said her mother didn't foster their Mohawk heritage. Trips back to the reservation in Quebec reinforced that. She saw mostly poverty and alcoholism and dependency there.

"But I'm a survivor," she said.

No, an achiever, Cindy quickly decided when she learned all the details.

Diane knew all about bootstraps. She became the first member of her family to graduate from high school. She became the first to go to college. She started at Western Michigan University, then transferred to Mount Ida Junior College in Boston. She lived with the college president and his wife. She learned how to speak and hold her fork and set a table there. After graduating from Wayne State in Detroit, she was commissioned as an officer in the Army. She told Cindy about breaking into the business. Back then, she was shooting for a job in a top-twenty market.

The woman was a realist, a pragmatist. She made no apologies about working the minority angle in college, in the military, in urban markets always looking for minority on-air talent.

"It's God's gift," she said. "God gave you a beautiful face. God gave me the fact that I'm Native American."

Cindy found plenty to admire about her on the home front. At first, Brad appeared the epitome of the devoted, contemporary husband. He cooked. He baked. He washed and watched the children. He ironed and laid out her clothes for her every day. When they first moved to Battle Creek, she said, he took her and picked her up for work every single day. Cindy stopped by a couple times to pick her up at 4:30 A.M. Brad was up, shaved and dressed, helping her carry things to the car.

Cindy Acosta's early admiration bordered on envy. She was trying to get her bearings in the working world. She wanted to look like she knew exactly what she was doing and where she was going. She wanted to be on the earth for a purpose. Diane Newton King was her hero in the little station with the red brick and white sashes.

Maybe her disillusionment began when she heard Diane

humiliate a source on deadline, when a little schmoozing would have done just fine. Diane, she began to discover, picked fights with station staff when a little understanding or restraint would be in order. She watched her develop an ongoing battle with a female photographer, who one day blew up and called Diane a "neurotic bitch."

On the home front, she began to hear from Diane about financial trouble. That didn't surprise her with Brad working only part-time at the university. But Diane complained about money one day, then picked out thirty outfits for Kateri on the next.

She wondered if the woman understood balance.

There was trouble in her extended families. Brad's folks, now in Texas, were "wealthy," but a source of conflict. Diane also complained about her family's dislike of Brad. She said she penned an angry letter to her mother saying they would no longer stay at their home in Sterling Heights because of this. Yet, when her mother wrote her back that she was joining a convoy to supply food to Mohawks staging a revolt in Quebec, Diane was ecstatic.

There were other inconsonant extremes, Cindy decided, and most of them involved Brad. She first saw him walking around downtown Marshall, before she knew Diane. Nobody missed him. It wasn't just the shaved head. He wore a metallic-blue jacket with the ABC network logo. Across the back was the network slogan: "The One To Watch!"

After Diane's rave reviews of her husband, Cindy was miffed when he finally showed up at the station one day. Like the ABC jacket, his appearance demanded the eye, but once captured, he offered little else. He was void of personality, she decided. He didn't have much to say about anything. She felt like she was trying to coax a shadow into talking.

Cindy figured somebody like Diane would have needed someone with dynamics, just to keep up. But in Diane's presence, Brad couldn't even tell a good joke. He tried once for Cindy, but the results were pathetic.

"Oh, Brad, you don't know how to tell jokes," Diane said, shaking her head.

Cindy even felt sorry for him that day.

He showed no sign of an entire range of emotions. Anger. Frustration. Fear. Concern. She couldn't remember seeing any evidence of these, especially during one frightening situation she found herself in with him.

In the summer of 1990, she, Diane, and a dozen other TV staffers worked the Battle Creek International Hot Air Balloon Championship, a big yearly event that draws hundreds of balloonists from around the world. The weather service posted a tornado watch in the last hours, just when the station was doing a live broadcast of the closing day. Diane and a cohost decided to go ahead with the show.

The horizon was black, the heavy air charged and still.

Diane was three months pregnant, but an optimist. "Cindy, I want you to go with Brad and Marler back to the station. "You'll be plenty safe there. We're gonna take our chances and try to finish this thing up."

Brad drove. Marler was crying in the toddler seat, as if he'd tapped into the anxiety at the airfield. Cindy tried to pacify the boy in the back and reassure the man behind the wheel.

"I just know she's going to be fine, Brad. I don't see any funnel clouds. You know, she's really such a special person, Brad. You're lucky to be married to such a special woman."

"Yeah. I am." He sounded bored.

At the station, they spent the duration of the afternoon watching the broadcast in the green room. He seemed oblivious to the danger and the daring of his pregnant wife.

Cindy never quite understood Diane's attraction to Brad. She wondered about Brad's role. What first appeared as a supportive nature began to look more like servitude. Diane gave the commands: "Brad, get the baby's bottle." "Brad, get me a glass of water, will you?" "Brad, go get the car." "Brad see to Marler, will you?" Brad endured her orders without complaint or protest. He never lost his temper. He never raised his voice. He was so quiet. The only hints of deeper stirrings were in his penetrating eyes.

His passive nature even irritated Diane. Cindy saw signs of growing tension in the late summer and early fall, before and after the stalker letter. She was sitting at a desk right next to Diane.

"Well, *Brad,*" she heard Diane say one day, her words acidic with sarcasm. "I'm *glad* to hear that you went to the cleaners. I'm *glad* to hear that you got the house cleaned up. But, I would just like to know what you did for *yourself* today."

Then she slammed down the phone.

There was something quite unsettling about Brad and Diane King, Cindy decided. It wasn't about traditional male or female roles or who was dominant or who wore the pants. Something was amiss in their bond.

The wounds over her real father's loss gave Cindy a theory. "She married a father figure," Acosta later told a friend. "Here was a man who was going to take care of her. He was going to make everything all right and attend to her every need. He was going to worship her. If he didn't, it would disappoint her just like her dad did when he died."

That was her armchair analysis, at least, something to put them in perspective, when she found the couple a little too strange. But Cindy's theory fell far short of explaining why Brad would have killed the woman he seemed to need. He needed her company. He needed her money. She seemed to be everything to him.

The mystery was something for the police two thousand miles away in Marshall, Michigan, she told herself. And there were the fingerprints. She and Diane went to the sheriff's department in January before she left to let them take their fingerprints to compare with the stalker letter. Juan was supposed to come, too, but got snowed in at O'Hare. They were leaving for South America. The detective suggested he have the Venezuelan police do the prints and mail them. But you just didn't waltz into a Third World cop station and ask to be printed, she and Juan decided.

So, that would be the next step. They should get the prints, someway. It was some evidence. She had only hunches and observations. But maybe she knew a few things about Brad and

Diane King that detectives needed
also had a contact or two at the
Department.

Maybe she could help them out.

7

The funeral Mass was February 13, Ash Wednesday. It was cold, and the sky was the color of the burnt remnants for which the day was named.

More than three hundred fifty people filed into St. Mary Catholic Church in Marshall for the late morning liturgy. Near the steps, five members of the White Thunder Singers circled a large ceremonial drum, singing in unison as they beat out a mesmeric rhythm. They sang honor songs and sprinkled tobacco on the drum skin, a symbol of prayers to the Great Spirit.

The Indian rituals were not the doing of Diane Newton King's family, as some assumed they would be for a daughter of the tribe of the Iroquois Five Nations. In fact, Brad and Diane King's local Native American friends had planned the funeral. All week, one of them had been tutoring Brad King in Native American mourning customs.

Not two miles away, a fire burnt down slowly at Thunderspirit. On Tuesday night, Stella ("Bea") Pamp, a Potawatomi elder and friend of Diane's, had directed Allen Marler to light the funeral fire, a practice intended to help light the deceased spirit's journey to the afterlife. Later, at the farmhouse, another friend would conduct a sacred pipe ceremony for Brad King.

Inside the church, the service was eclectic. Brad King's Presbyterian pastor assisted and more Native American customs were included in the Mass said by the local Catholic priest. Participants burned the four sacred medicines of tobacco, sage, sweet grass, and cedar as incense. There was a reading of the

...rican version of the Twenty-Third Psalm. Some
...ers wore traditional costumes.

Some wore invisible masks.

"There was a vague, unexplained and somewhat angry look on many faces," a *People* magazine stringer jotted in her notes.

All week Diane King's family found reasons for further suspicion. They felt Brad was avoiding them. He grieved at the funeral fire or up in his room in bed.

On Monday, cousin Elaine Wash and Allen stayed again at the farmhouse. Brad's mother was at the farmhouse in the evening. Elaine overheard her tell her husband, "They think my son is a suspect." She didn't know if she meant the family or the police.

Elaine Wash noticed the woman had an odd effect on her son. "Mother is leaving now." "Mother is going to the motel." She talked in the third person to him and gingerly kissed him on the cheek. He seemed to cower around her. She was very dominant, Elaine thought, and he subservient.

Denise Verrier saw the first major confrontation between their family and Brad develop over the plans for her sister's body. On Monday, everyone found out that Brad was going to have Diane cremated. Brad maintained they had recently talked about what she wanted when she died.

"She wanted to be cremated and have a twenty-one gun salute," he said.

Nobody in the family had ever heard Diane talk about cremation. Diane was a Catholic, as was Freida. Elder Stella Pamp and Sister Anne Jeffery, a nun who had a Native American ministry in western Michigan, approached him. They said cremation was not consistent with either Catholic or Native American beliefs. Brad acquiesced.

The Newtons were not consulted on the funeral and felt like Brad had designed it for expediency rather than grief. The funeral home told callers visitation was only for family. Friends ignored that and came anyway. The parlor room was cramped and had only a few chairs. There was only one day of visitation, despite arriving out-of-town relatives. On Tuesday, the visiting

Diane King that detectives needed to know. Cindy Biggs Acosta also had a contact or two at the Calhoun County Sheriff's Department.

Maybe she could help them out.

7

The funeral Mass was February 13, Ash Wednesday. It was cold, and the sky was the color of the burnt remnants for which the day was named.

More than three hundred fifty people filed into St. Mary Catholic Church in Marshall for the late morning liturgy. Near the steps, five members of the White Thunder Singers circled a large ceremonial drum, singing in unison as they beat out a mesmeric rhythm. They sang honor songs and sprinkled tobacco on the drum skin, a symbol of prayers to the Great Spirit.

The Indian rituals were not the doing of Diane Newton King's family, as some assumed they would be for a daughter of the tribe of the Iroquois Five Nations. In fact, Brad and Diane King's local Native American friends had planned the funeral. All week, one of them had been tutoring Brad King in Native American mourning customs.

Not two miles away, a fire burnt down slowly at Thunderspirit. On Tuesday night, Stella ("Bea") Pamp, a Potawatomi elder and friend of Diane's, had directed Allen Marler to light the funeral fire, a practice intended to help light the deceased spirit's journey to the afterlife. Later, at the farmhouse, another friend would conduct a sacred pipe ceremony for Brad King.

Inside the church, the service was eclectic. Brad King's Presbyterian pastor assisted and more Native American customs were included in the Mass said by the local Catholic priest. Participants burned the four sacred medicines of tobacco, sage, sweet grass, and cedar as incense. There was a reading of the

Native American version of the Twenty-Third Psalm. Some mourners wore traditional costumes.

Some wore invisible masks.

"There was a vague, unexplained and somewhat angry look on many faces," a *People* magazine stringer jotted in her notes.

All week Diane King's family found reasons for further suspicion. They felt Brad was avoiding them. He grieved at the funeral fire or up in his room in bed.

On Monday, cousin Elaine Wash and Allen stayed again at the farmhouse. Brad's mother was at the farmhouse in the evening. Elaine overheard her tell her husband, "They think my son is a suspect." She didn't know if she meant the family or the police.

Elaine Wash noticed the woman had an odd effect on her son. "Mother is leaving now." "Mother is going to the motel." She talked in the third person to him and gingerly kissed him on the cheek. He seemed to cower around her. She was very dominant, Elaine thought, and he subservient.

Denise Verrier saw the first major confrontation between their family and Brad develop over the plans for her sister's body. On Monday, everyone found out that Brad was going to have Diane cremated. Brad maintained they had recently talked about what she wanted when she died.

"She wanted to be cremated and have a twenty-one gun salute," he said.

Nobody in the family had ever heard Diane talk about cremation. Diane was a Catholic, as was Freida. Elder Stella Pamp and Sister Anne Jeffery, a nun who had a Native American ministry in western Michigan, approached him. They said cremation was not consistent with either Catholic or Native American beliefs. Brad acquiesced.

The Newtons were not consulted on the funeral and felt like Brad had designed it for expediency rather than grief. The funeral home told callers visitation was only for family. Friends ignored that and came anyway. The parlor room was cramped and had only a few chairs. There was only one day of visitation, despite arriving out-of-town relatives. On Tuesday, the visiting day, Brad left after lunch and never came back. The Newtons convinced the funeral director to keep the home open until ten Tuesday night so an uncle arriving from California could pay his last respects.

There were whispers about the children. Denise Verrier worried Brad would move immediately back to Colorado. In the months before her death, when Diane was considering trying for a better paying job in the Detroit market, she'd said Brad wanted badly to move back out West. Denise told Julie D'Artagnan, one of Diane's local friends, "All I've got to say is he better not be leaving the state with those kids." Diane's sister disappeared into the crowd. A minute later Brad put his arm around her.

"Don't you worry, Denise," he said. "I'm not going to take the kids and leave the state. I'm going to stay right here and do just what Diane wanted me to do. Get my doctorate degree."

Later, Freida Newton played Brad much more coyly. "Brad, could I keep the kids a while?" she asked. "I know you're going to need to get your life in order. This will give you some time, some time to think."

He agreed.

Meanwhile, Denise's brother Allen shadowed Brad. Denise and Darlene thought he was lending support. Later he claimed to be doing surveillance. "Maybe he'd say something incriminating," Allen said.

Others watched Brad closely, his demeanor, and then they compared notes. They asked among themselves, what about Randy Wright? Why was the first person Brad called after the murder an attorney? Had he called him for support or legal advice?

Around dinnertime on Tuesday, when a report came across the TV that they'd found a weapon on the property, Brad was sitting in the living room with some family members.

"I sold all my guns in 1985," he said.

Nobody had asked him about his guns.

"When do you think the police will arrest him?" a neighbor, Joanne Karaba, asked a family member outright at the funeral home.

Denise and Don Verrier were staying at a motel thirty miles from Marshall. She wouldn't stay at the farmhouse with her mother and others. The entire situation had her spooked.

In fact, on Wednesday, anxiety tainted the entire funeral Mass for Denise. She was worried her sister's burial would be made even more of a media spectacle. She was worried police might drag Brad King off in handcuffs at any moment.

It wasn't an unreasonable fear. Rumor and innuendo that Brad King was the case's main suspect were spreading, not only at the funeral, but in coffee shops and bars all over Marshall.

"We have targeted no one and have eliminated no one," Sheriff Jon Olson said at the press conference on Monday, February 11. "Everyone is a suspect and no one is a suspect more than anyone else."

By Tuesday, the sheriff's theme had changed dramatically.

"We have the murder weapon," he announced.

Olson also specified that seven shell casings were found at the farm. There was "a single male suspect," he said. The stalker threat, he postulated, was a red herring.

"In my opinion," the sheriff said, "the person has said things or done things to divert attention from himself."

Darlene, Diane's eldest sister, didn't need to watch the newscasts. On Monday night, she and a cousin had paid a visit to Detective Jim Stadfeld at the Marshall Township Fire Hall. It was located just behind the motel where they were staying. Darlene had requested the meeting. Stadfeld, also the township treasurer, was working on property tax bills.

Darlene wanted to know if the detectives had a suspect.

"Don't ask the question, unless you want the honest answer," he cautioned her.

She wanted a goddamn answer.

"We believe Brad killed Diane and ditched the gun on the property."

He had something to add to that. "We're going to arrest him probably right after the funeral," he told her.

They'd probably do it right during the dinner at the hall, he said.

*   *   *

Marge Lundeen had read the newspapers. She knew her son would be scrutinized. She knew it the moment he called her with the news about Diane. She was not naive. She knew that's just the way it was in cases like this. She confronted him on Sunday when they first talked.

"Brad, have you and Diane been having trouble?"

"No," he said.

With that, Marge Lundeen decided once and for all that her son had not killed his wife.

However, the murder, the funeral, Brad's troubles with the Newton family, the squabbling, the entire mess—*they* were parts of a long continuum, part of a string of misfortunes all begun years ago when Brad left his first wife, Gail. Marge dearly loved Gail. And, Marge would never understand why Brad ever married into a family like Diane's in the first place. He'd made so many costly mistakes over the last ten years, she thought.

She would say it more than once. "I don't know how anybody raised in our family could make as many wrong decisions as Brad has made."

Marge Lundeen carried herself with more poise than most women nearing their seventh decade. She wore her pure white hair in a smart french twist. She could have balanced a book on her head when she walked into St. Mary Catholic Church.

When she and Cliff arrived, the only space left was halfway back in the church. Marge felt crowded out, pushed back by the flood of Diane's friends and family. Scott, her younger son, and his wife Lois joined them. She watched some of Brad's old school classmates from Croswell, their old town, find seats. She saw Gail arrive with Brad's daughter, Alissa. She saw Gail go somewhere near the back of the church.

Brad had not accompanied Marge into the church, but that wasn't necessarily out of character. In fact, Marge felt that Brad had only done two odd things since he'd called her with news of Diane's death.

When they talked the first time on the phone he wept. He kept saying, "Mother, I *need* you, I *need* you."

That was out of character. "He tells me he loves me, but he never tells me he *needs* me," she would later say.

When they met at the fountain in the center of town he wept again, this time in her arms. He was awfully glad to see her, she thought. Brad was not usually glad to see her in such an overt way.

They had never been emotionally close, not like she and Scott. Marge and young Scott talked and shared and played together. Brad had always been a loner. Sometimes she thought he even preferred "quiet time," the punishment of being confined to his room. Sometimes she thought he relished being alone and away from the family as a boy.

Brad did have some of the hallmarks of his father's personality. Yes, he was handling this funeral the way Willis would have, Marge thought.

"Brad is quiet," she'd later say, explaining him. "If he feels it's important enough to him, he'll do something about it. That's just the way his father was. If someone just wants to carry on and talk, he'd just sit there and let them. If he had something to say, he'd say it."

However, Brad was not stoic. Brad cried, just like Willis cried. Openly. King men taught other King men that they could cry. She remembered Brad breaking down a couple years back during a visit. They all attended a Presbyterian service together in Battle Creek. She guessed Brad was thinking about his late father that day. Then he became very still.

"He was like that as a boy, too," she would later say. "He'd cry, then get a hold of himself and shut it completely off."

Brad endured pain like his father, Marge decided. Willis paid dearly for his two Purple Hearts, his Silver Star, and his Bronze Star. He paid for them long after the bombs hit his company on a narrow road in France. The shell hit as he stood urging his 80th Division company out of a ditch where they would surely have died under artillery fire. He carried fragments in both legs for years, then lost one of the legs late in life. He had thirty-seven surgeries between the war and his death in 1986. She doubted there was a night that Willis went to bed without some kind of discomfort.

Marge Lundeen wondered about Diane's funeral. In the Presbyterian church we don't make such a big spectacle of it, nor of ourselves, she thought. At the funeral home, she was shocked when Freida Newton placed Kateri in the arms of her dead mother as Marler hung onto the edge of the casket. In Marge's family, they didn't believe in open caskets, let alone that sort of thing. Neither did they plan banquets after services nor parties after burial.

At the funeral home, Marge stood near the man she called "our pastor" for support. He was actually Brad's pastor. But if he was Presbyterian and a family member went to his church, that was good enough.

"When we get in trouble, we call our church," she liked to say.

Marge Lundeen did not like her late daughter-in-law's family. Certainly, their loss was a horrible thing and Diane's death was a tragedy. That notwithstanding, Marge had never really liked the family or Diane. She and Cliff made lunch for the Newton clan back at the farmhouse on Tuesday.

"We made coffee and lunch and cleaned up after them and they treated us like a bunch of servants," she would later say.

Baby Kateri was congested, but they passed her around the living room from person to person, chattering and puffing on cigarettes. She asked Barbara Elgutaa, Diane's friend who had been watching the kids, if she might take Kateri home, away from the smoke and cold breezes every time one of them burst through the door.

"You don't have anything to say about this," Barbara snapped.

No, Marge Lundeen thought, I guess I don't. Nor was I raised with those kind of manners, young lady.

Marge's father was a small-town banker in Luther, Michigan. Willis opened a bank in Croswell for her father and ran a couple of his branches before that. They counted doctors and lawyers and ministers among their friends. They were respected, but on merit as well as title.

"In a small town if you run a bank and you're the head of it and you're a decent person, you're respected," Marge would say.

Respect was earned by action and demeanor, and that was

one of her problems with Diane. They visited a half-dozen times in Texas, Colorado, and Michigan over the years. Marge had seen enough to know what she didn't like.

"I don't like people who are playing to the public all the time," she would say.

Diane was always talking about big projects and important friends she was making. She felt she exploited people of lesser station.

"We noticed that she always had these higher-level friends, people she thought she should know," Marge would explain. "Then she would have people who were down here that she always was telling her tales to. The people down here would do the baby-sitting for her, thinking it wonderful to be with her."

Privately, Diane had wide mood swings. They'd had a couple of arguments. Diane exploded at her in her home in Texas once over a discussion about her career plans. She yelled and used excessive profanity, announced they were going home in the morning, then promptly stormed right out of the house. Brad calmly drove off and found her. The next morning Marge found her sitting in her kitchen. Diane was singing and chatting away like nothing happened, her plans to leave cancelled.

Marge hung up on her on one long-distance phone call when she called to rant and rave about some issue. Brad called back, saying, "Mom, you don't understand, you can't hang up on Diane."

Marge said, "Oh yes I can." Then she hung up on Brad.

Maybe he preferred it that way.

"And it was his fault," she would later say. "The only time he was close to the family was when he was married to Gail, and that was because of Gail."

Marge and Gail were still close, in fact. Gail still came down to Texas to visit. Marge's second husband, Helmut, was an absolute gentleman.

Yes, she decided, Brad had made many mistakes. But, she also knew her religion taught that *all* were sinners.

"I still love Brad," she would say. "He is my son."

And, she would support him in his time of need, she'd decided, no matter what happened. As for criminal involvement, she categorically believed in his innocence.

The reason was simple.

"I just can't believe that anyone raised in our family would be capable of doing something like that."

8

Many eyes were on him at the funeral. He wore a sharply tailored charcoal suit and a full-length tan trench coat, its belt tied, not buckled. In his right hand, he carried the feather of a bald eagle, the most sacred of Native American symbols. The eagle exalted above the mountaintops. The eagle feather symbolized honor and strength.

Even those in the back pews could see him lifting the black-and-white feather up over his shaved head during the Mass. He sat with Freida Newton in the front, having made a beeline to his old nemesis when he stepped out of the car with his own mother. He wept, and cried out, sometimes quite loudly. When there was silence, people could hear the steam radiator vents in the church hiss.

The priest announced from the pulpit that burial would follow the next day in Detroit's Mt. Olivet Cemetery, not at Fort Custer National Cemetery as originally planned. Privately, the reason kindled old resentments among the Newtons. Despite a plea to a Michigan U.S. Senator, the government refused her body. Diane Newton King's military record was not quite as sterling as advertised. With some controversy, she'd resigned her Army commission in 1983 after less than a year of active duty, a decision that upset the Newtons. She'd left the Army to marry Brad.

Afterwards they filed out together, Brad and Freida arm and arm as they left the double front doors of the church. A swarm

of video and still cameramen who'd been detained outside, now
shot away at will.

Waiting over at the church gymnasium was a traditional
dinner of Native American foods such as corn, fried bread, and
sweetmeats. There, a long line formed to pay their respect to
Brad King and the Newtons.

If Brad King was worried that he'd be arrested, he never
showed it. In fact, his demeanor throughout the three days of
the funeral would later be subject to much observation and later
documentation. Most of it was subjective interpretation, perhaps influenced by suspicion, talk of an impending arrest, and
personal agenda.

However, several relatively neutral observers detected one
consistent behavior. They saw it when Brad King walked into
the church to the beat of the drums and when he emerged
before the slew of cameras outside. They saw it when he greeted
those waiting in the long line to give him condolences.

Gina Zapinski, a friend of Diane's since childhood, later
described it.

"He was looking around to see who was watching. It was just
too weird. It just wasn't natural. And, he walked very tall. You
know, and Brad *never* walked tall before. Everything changed
about him. It was like he was on camera. He was like he was
out there for show, walking around with that eagle feather in his
hand."

They would bury Diane the next day in the silky red dress
with the white lace trim, the one she was supposed to wear to
Gordy's wedding. Red and white lace on Valentine's Day.

"This was the dress Diane was going to wear to your wedding," Brad told Mary Kozak. "I thought it would be appropriate to bury her in it."

Love, marriage, and death.

Mary thought it was an odd thing to say.

Not fifteen miles away, in a small home with pristine alumi-
num siding and lawn, a young black man named James Wickware, Jr., was spending another day with his newspapers and
TV shows. The death of Diane Newton King generated a lot of

stories. James Wickware, Jr., had been hearing and reading about it all week.

Wickware remembered when he met Diane Newton King in person six months ago. He was waiting for a paper off the presses at the Battle Creek *Enquirer*. She was doing a story on a mental health center located nearby. She asked him what he thought of the "mental health crisis."

He thought she was very nice.

James Wickware, Jr., was twenty-two years old and lived with his parents in a house in "The Heights," the black section on Battle Creek's near west side. His father, James Wickware, Sr., didn't like his habits, that he didn't date or go out with other guys. His dad let him work for a while in his business when it was going. But now they just paid him to take care of his grandmother, a job that kept him home through most of the day.

Most folks wouldn't have guessed James Wickware, Jr. was called a slow learner. He soaked up information. This began every morning when he went out to get his papers. *The New York Times*. *The Chicago Tribune*. *USA Today*. *The Detroit Free Press*. *The Detroit News*. He spent the morning with his papers and "Good Morning America" and talk shows like "Sally Jessy Raphael."

Then, there were the radio stations. He listened to all the radio stations, and he called them regularly. He sat next to the phone and tried to be the first caller or the fifth caller or the seventh caller in the call-in contests. After a while, the local DJs learned to recognize his voice and name.

Most of all, he liked the women on television. The news-women. They were smart and pretty, and they looked you right in the eyes. He'd written some, asking for advice, asking for autographs and pictures. Some ignored him, but most responded. He kept the growing collection in a plain, manilla envelope. Later, he would have to get a box, as the collection would grow to more than 225 media personalities. But in mid-February 1991, he had only a handful. He'd started locally, with a Detroit TV station, then WUHQ-Channel 41.

On July 13, 1990, James Wickware, Jr., had written Diane Newton King a two-page letter. It was the letter now on the desk of Jack Schoder, the letter Brad King had given the deputy the day of the break-in at Thunderspirit.

In it, Wickware identified himself to Diane King as "one of your local viewers from Battle Creek" who hadn't "missed an edition of the news since you joined TV41 News." He called her the "best journalist" in the country, "certainly one of the most beautiful looking."

"I believe you have the prettiest color of hair I have ever seen," he wrote. "Also a pretty color of eyes, beautiful face, beautiful voice, and a nice looking body figure with beautiful wardrobe fashions."

He closed by wondering how much it would cost him for an autographed photo of the anchor. He signed his full name.

He got a response of only five lines. It was written in the large sanserif type that fed the station's TelePrompTers. The letter did not come from Diane Newton King, but from Vice President Mark Crawford. There was no autographed glossy photo from Diane Newton King. In fact, there wasn't a photograph at all.

In the response letter, dated August 24, Vice President Mark Crawford had told James Wickware, Jr.,: "Unfortunately we do not have photographs of our staff."

James Wickware, Sr., had opinions about newscasters and the issues they covered. His son had listened many times to his anger when his father told him about the system, how the system ignored regular people. How it ignored honest, legitimate people like them.

Later, James Wickware, Sr., frustrated by his own efforts to access the system, would say: "The only way a black man can get justice is at the end of the gun."

For years, James Wickware, Jr., had heard his father's story about his own fight with powers in high places. He told him how crooked interests cheated his small railroad construction company and exploited him as a minority partner in an affirmative action bid. He told him how he'd gone to the FBI and the Ohio attorney general and The United States Congress and the Department of Justice.

They had done nothing, he said.

He would say of the principals in that business deal: "If I could get all three of the ones together that gave me the fucking, I'd just take shit and wipe it in their faces. . . . I would shoot them and cut off their heads and take them to the attorney general."

James Wickware, Sr., was an angry man.

"If I had the atomic bomb, you know what I would do with the United States and all of the people that I have loved—other than my son and my wife, I'd get them out of this son of a bitch—when I got done leveling this corrupt no good son of a bitch. . . . The people left behind in what we call the good ole United States of America, I wouldn't leave a motherfucker living. I'm telling you I'd level this son of a bitch like we did in Hiroshima and Nagasaki."

James knew his father did not like him buying newspapers every day. He didn't like him keeping track of the careers of the women reporters or watching them on TV.

"What causes this shit in the first place?" his father would ask.

"Well, just from watching television," James Wickware, Jr., would say.

"Millions of people watch TV, but how many people do you think sit down and spend the twenty-nine cent stamp to correspond with somebody they see on television and wait for a response?"

He'd later try to explain, "I like looking at the women. I don't go out with nobody. I don't want to be bothering nobody."

His father didn't think the people on TV should be writing his son back or sending those pictures.

"These kind of people add gasoline to the fire. Shit, I could care less about any of them that I see on TV, men, women, any of them. Most of it's a bunch of bullshit. They're like the politicians and the lawyers."

As far as his father was concerned, the women on TV were part of the same system that should be nuked.

"Whatya doin' wastin' your time writing those cunts and white bitches on TV?" he would ask.

But James Wickware, Jr., wouldn't be writing his local favorite anymore.

His local favorite was dead.

There was no arrest in the hours after the funeral, but the expectations of the Marshall rumor mill were not lessened. Word continued to spread around town about who would soon pay the price for the local anchorwoman's murder.

Sue Darling had not heard those rumors. But on Wednesday night, after attending the funeral dinner, she went down to the Marshall Township Hall to pay her property taxes. She knew Jim Stadfeld, detective and township treasurer, would be there to take her check.

Sue Darling's week had been nerve-racking. As far as she knew, a psychotic killer was stalking the neighborhood. She and the kids were scared to walk the hundred feet to their small barn to feed their horses. She'd decided maybe their local detective ought to know about the teenagers they suspected of stealing things in the neighborhood. Maybe they were connected to the gun she'd just read about in the newspaper.

"My family is worried," she told Stadfeld as he prepared her receipt.

He told her not to be concerned. "We know who did it. We think Brad King did it." He quickly added, "But you didn't hear that from me."

She thought the revelation unprofessional, especially with no charges filed. She wondered how they could have ruled out the stalker already. She wondered why there hadn't been an arrest.

"We're going to make our arrest tomorrow," Stadfeld said.

"He's going to be in Detroit tomorrow," she said. "The burial is tomorrow."

"He may make it into Detroit," Stadfeld said. "But he'll never make it back."

Sue Darling wondered about evidence.

Stadfeld was nonspecific, but confident.

"We have so much evidence," he said. "There's not a jury in this world that won't put him away."

9

Police called the new prosecutor of Calhoun County to Marshall on the night of the murder, but it wasn't for the murder of Diane Newton King. Marshall city cops had woken Jon Sahli at 2:30 A.M., February 10, asking for a search warrant. They were sorry to bother him at such an hour, they said, but they couldn't find Sahli's assistant, who was tied up with the King homicide.

Without asking the nature of the case, Sahli drove the fifteen minutes to Marshall from his home in Battle Creek. At the police station, the prosecutor looked over the paperwork, then asked, "Well, what are you searching for?"

"Beer," an officer said.

"Beer?"

"Yeah, beer. We've got some kids in a house over here on North Kalamazoo drinking beer. They got away from us last night, but they're not getting away tonight."

After suggesting a couple more reasonable alternatives, Sahli left the station, perturbed and wide-awake in the town where he was born and raised. He decided to salvage the trip by dropping by 16240 Division. He'd talked with the sheriff's department detectives earlier. He figured he might as well see how their search warrant was going.

The prosecutor found no one was posted at the end of the driveway. He parked his car and walked quietly up to the farmhouse. He could hear yelling and profanity within.

Inside, he saw deputies wandering from room to room, conducting what appeared to be a haphazard search. A deputy was in the kitchen, glaring into an empty refrigerator. The deputy was the source of all the swearing. He was cursing that the goddamn King family hadn't left him any fucking thing to eat.

"It was at that point," Jon Sahli would later recall, "that I knew this case had lots of problems."

*   *   *

Jon Sahli had been county prosecutor only a month, but he'd seen plenty of search warrants executed over the years. He'd been appointed to the top spot after his former boss was elected a judge. At forty-six, Sahli was as ready for the top job as he would ever be. He'd served twelve years in the Battle Creek office, six of them as chief assistant. He'd tried more than two hundred felony jury trials. Balding. Mustached. Quiet. Republican. Mostly, he was known for his methodical closing arguments.

Jon Sahli believed good closings were crafted not by stylish verbiage, but spun out of the drudgery of investigative preparation. Throughout the week of Diane King's funeral, Sahli had decided that the detectives of Calhoun County were not only unprepared for court, they weren't ready for an arrest warrant, though they'd been seeking one on a daily basis.

Conflict between police who investigate cases and attorneys who must prosecute them was as old as American law enforcement. Detectives who thought they were ready for an arrest before all the evidence was gathered weren't unique. It happened in prosecutor's offices all over the state.

However, the two detectives seeking the warrant from Jon Sahli were at a disadvantage. Jack Schoder and Jim Stadfeld were not seasoned homicide detectives. Sahli later recalled that as far as he knew Schoder and Stadfeld had a half-dozen open homicides on their books. (Stadfeld later put the number at four, saying the bureau had solved a half dozen.) Sahli believed they had only solved one case in the last seven years, and that had been closed by a tip.

The prosecutor got his first look at their progress in the King case when the two detectives met with him on Tuesday, February 12, at a place called the Country Corner. They laid out the evidence over lunch. They had a dead body. They had a gun. They had the casings from the barn and creek. They had two statements from Brad King. He hadn't admitted anything, they said, but his story was inconsistent with evidence. They had the dog track, which Sahli knew wasn't always admitted as evidence. However, they said they had impressions on the track that appeared to be from King's boots.

"Great," Sahli said. "You got his boots?"

"Well, we had them," Schoder said. "But we gave them back."

Sahli's eyebrows converged. "Why in the world would you do that? I need those boots to match to the photographs and plaster impressions to see if it's him or not him."

"Well," Schoder said, hesitating. "There aren't any photographs."

"No photographs?"

"Well, no."

"Well, you got the casts?"

"Well, no."

Sahli wanted an explanation.

"You have to understand," Schoder said, apologetically. "I just left the party and didn't have the proper footwear to go out and look at those footprints."

They said Gary Lisle, the K-9 trooper, could testify that the boot prints were similar.

Similar meant nothing, Sahli complained to himself. He knew about footwear impression evidence presented in a local bank case. An FBI lab had made 156 points of comparison from a guy's shoe print he left when he jumped over the teller cage.

There was another matter the detectives thought the prosecutor should know about. They saved it for last.

"We have this letter," Jack Schoder said.

They told him about the note with the cut-out letters.

The stalker. They had not eliminated the stalker, Sahli decided. They might as well turn the stalker letter right over to a defense attorney, he complained, as a gift called reasonable doubt.

"All you have here is a circumstantial case," Sahli said. "And, I don't like circumstantial cases."

"You have to admit it's a strong circumstantial case," Stadfeld offered.

Sahli disagreed.

He suggested they formalize their reports. They could talk more later in the week.

* * *

Jon Sahli's downtown Battle Creek office was in the part of the county's Human Services Building where there were no windows and the top lawyer's office was not any larger than the ten-by-ten enclosures of his assistants. The basement wasn't a bad spot. It put some distance between the welfare and social services offices above. Sahli's staff of twelve attorneys didn't need any spillover from society's safety net. They already had their hands full with its guardrails.

Later on Tuesday, Sahli and his investigator Gerry Woods lit a couple of cigarettes and talked about the case. Woods said he'd been in Marshall himself the night of the murder. He was pulling a couple of twenties out of a bank machine when he heard the tone in Guy Picketts's voice. He was just getting ready to make the scene, when a blue state police car flew by running code and breaking eighty in downtown Marshall.

"Not going was the biggest mistake I ever made in my life," he later said.

Jon Sahli mused about the gun. He thought hit men used large-caliber weapons for that kind of work. "Well, it doesn't seem to me to be a professional, Gerry. I don't think a professional would use a .22."

Woods corrected him. "No, sir, Jon, that is not correct."

Like a lot of cops, he mixed slang and formal courtroom terms.

The .22 slug, Woods explained, was made of soft lead. There was no hard metal casing. It deformed on impact, making it impossible to link to any one weapon in ballistic tests.

"That's why they like it," Woods said. "Two kinds of professionals know that. Hit men and cops."

Gerry Woods also talked in a pretty deep Southern twang. He'd been hired five years ago by Sahli's predecessor to assist on difficult cases. An Eaton County detective for a dozen years, he'd left law enforcement to own his own bar, but the work had lured him back. He'd grown up in Mississippi River country, in Illinois near the Missouri border. The prosecutor's office had given him a car seized in a drug raid, a black 1987 Chevy Caprice with black tinted windows. Everyone called it "The

Batmobile." His son even put a Batman sticker in the middle of the back window.

Woods also had a wife, three daughters, and twelve coats of acrylic lacquer on a 1940 Cadillac La Salle he'd restored. He saw them on occasion. His old man, who worked in an Owens Illinois glass factory, once told him not to worry about impressing people. Just work hard, ask for help when you needed it, don't take any shit, and life would take care of the rest. The old man died at forty-six of hard work and hard arteries. Woods also was a tireless worker who liked his draft beer served in thirty-two-ounce glasses down at a bar called The Winner's Circle. Grey was starting to streak his red beard.

"Gerry Woods gives you one hundred ten percent," Jim Stadfeld would say of him, and Jim Stadfeld was no Gerry Woods fan. "He gives one hundred ten percent—a fact that will probably kill him at an early age."

Woods never expected to make a lot of friends second-guessing other cops for the prosecutor, and some said he was doing more second-guessing under the new prosecutor. "You step on a few eggs," he would admit. "And I've stepped on a couple and I paid hell for it. It's like: You don't get into another detective's case. Well, that's taboo. Well, that's *bullshit*. If they're not getting the job done and the boss tells you to do it, it's as simple as that."

Woods didn't always need an order. And on that Tuesday afternoon after the King murder, he went stomping through the metaphorical chicken coop. Woods and Sahli drove over to Channel 41. Woods wanted to read Diane Newton King's personnel file. They were hoping to find some kind of big life insurance policy.

They found no end of trouble instead.

Early Thursday morning, Jack Schoder and Jim Stadfeld met with Jon Sahli again, this time in the prosecutor's small, smokey office, again seeking a warrant for Brad King's arrest.

When they sat down, Sahli had somebody bring in a copy of *The Detroit Free Press*.

"The sheriff here says you have the murder weapon," Sahli

said coldly. "You don't know that you have the murder weapon."

Schoder and Stadfeld glanced at each other. The Michigan State Police Crime Lab had confirmed by telephone that the Remington rifle *could* be the murder weapon. The casing in the loft had firing pin markings consistent with the Remington Model 511 Scoremaster, but final ballistic reports weren't expected until the following week.

"You don't try cases with telephone confirmations," Sahli later said.

Jack Schoder thought the prosecutor might be angry because he hadn't been included in several press conferences held by Jon Olson that week. Sahli later recalled the opposite was true. He wanted the goddamn sheriff to back off on public statements. They were needlessly divulging the details of the case, he'd decided. Olson had revealed the gun, the caliber, the casings, the weapon's general location on the property, and hinted at the identity of the suspect. Eventually he found out that the detectives had named Brad King outright to Sue Darling and Sister Darlene Goins, both potential witnesses. The sheriff's department hadn't even canvassed King's neighborhood yet. Potentially solid testimony could be tainted with loose talk and publicity, he thought.

There was another objection, a strategic one. "My whole theory, as well as my predecessor's, was that you may say a few things, but you don't put your whole case out in the press. All you're doing is tipping your hand so that they can come up with a story to counter it. It was too early to have any kind of news conference at all. Anything more than the fact that she had been murdered or shot was beyond the scope of what we knew."

And they knew so little, Sahli argued to the two detectives, even about the gun found in the Talmadge Creek mud.

"Contact Remington," Sahli said. "See what they can tell you about this gun. If they know where or when it might have been sold. Contact dealers. Do they have any record of a gun like that being sold at a gun show, or do they keep those kinds of records? Go back to where he was when he was young."

They knew nothing of the nature of the murder, he complained. They knew nothing of its logistics. They knew nothing about the Kings.

Well, they did have some more, the two detectives said. Diane King's family members were saying Brad King should have been home to greet his wife on Saturday. She was afraid to come home alone since the threatening letter. They also had a tip from the local video store. King had returned the movie he rented Saturday on early Sunday morning.

"Does a guy who's just lost his wife worry about getting a movie back?" Schoder asked. Maybe it was involved in some kind of alibi.

The detectives presented two new arguments for a warrant.

"In order to protect those children, you have got to issue the warrant to get them out of his custody," Jim Stadfeld argued. "They're in grave danger. He killed his wife. He may kill his children."

"I don't think so," Sahli said. "If he wanted to kill them, he would have that night."

What if he flees the state? they argued.

"I don't care if he takes off," Sahli said. "We'll go find him when we get the proof to prosecute him."

"Whatya need?" one of the detectives asked.

They went down to the law library. Sahli brought Woods along as well as a chief assistant, John Hallacy. They began putting together a list, itemizing areas as Jack Schoder scrawled it upon a yellow pad:

- Talk to Diane's mother. What happened during her three-day visit?
- Who was the operator that handled Brad King's call to the police department? What did he tell her?
- What were the exact times of various department responses to the incident?
- Could they get a release from King for marriage counseling records?
- Somebody needed to talk to King's friend Randy Wright.
- Somebody needed to talk to Tom and Sue Darling. They

knew the Kings. Another neighbor had called the sheriff's department. She said she was Diane's friend. Talk to her.

- Get a copy of the lease on the farm. How much were they paying?
- Get the receipt for the video return.
- Time the trip from Diane's mother's house in Sterling Heights to the farmhouse.
- Check Denver records to find out when the Kings were married.
- Check Colorado gun laws. Was there a record of Brad King selling his gun?
- Interview all of Diane's family members.
- Interview the couple's coworkers.
- Use a laser scope to determine the angle of a shot from the loft. See if it is consistent with the autopsy.
- Get Brad King's work record at Pontiac Police Department.
- Check the lot numbers of the .22 shells taken into evidence. What year were they purchased?
- Check local gun shops to see if King purchased guns or ammo.
- Determine if Diane King had life insurance and how much.

"And, what about this letter?" Sahli asked.

The original stalker letter was still in the property room. They were waiting for an elimination print from Juan Acosta. Maybe the FBI crime lab could identify the paper or match the cut marks, Sahli suggested. That brought up another big hole.

"No one had thought of searching Brad's office at Western to see what was there," the prosecutor later recalled. "I didn't know that the FBI could match paper, could look at a pair of scissors and say those scissors made those cuts. I didn't know if they could do that. But I knew you could identify paper."

While the detectives went to lunch, Sahli wrote up a search warrant for Brad King's office at 2513 Sangren Hall at Western Michigan University. He wanted scissors, cutting instruments, glue, tape, paste, magazines—"Anything I could think of that could match."

The warrant was broad enough that it allowed Schoder, Stadfeld, and John Hallacy to take most anything else that might shed light on the affairs of the quiet criminal justice instructor. In effect, cleaning out Brad King's desk. Among the items were scissors, razor blades, publications, bank statements, a slew of bills, class schedules, correspondences from the IRS, Teke business, and a general accumulation of paperwork and junk.

They found no publications with cut-out letters, but they did find some interesting business cards. They were from the Oakridge Counseling Center in Battle Creek, marriage counselors. An appointment for Brad King was noted on February 7, two days before the murder. There were also appointments noted on February 5 and January 31.

On Friday, February 15, the day after Diane King's burial, representatives from the Calhoun County Sheriff's Department returned to see Jon Sahli for a warrant, but they weren't from the two-man detective bureau. They were Sheriff Jon Olson and undersheriff James McDonagh. The detectives, they said, were out working on the case.

Jon Olson had been the sheriff a dozen years, as long as Sahli had been with the prosecutor's office. They shared tenure and the spelling of their first names, but neither had spawned mutual admiration nor endorsements in local party politics. Olson still remembered a county drunk driving case Sahli had lost years ago as an assistant. He failed to support Sahli for appointment to two district judgeships. Sahli hadn't openly campaigned for Olson as sheriff. Olson hadn't supported Sahli for appointment to county prosecutor as well.

Both men would later provide somewhat different versions of what transpired at the meeting. Sahli would say the sheriff was angry and misinformed about the extent of the case's progress. Olson would say he couldn't get any straight answers.

Olson wanted to know why the prosecutor and his investigator were at Channel 41 going through Diane King's personnel file earlier in the week. "What are you and Gerry doing involved in our case?"

Sahli responded with few words. Work was piling up. More investigation needed to be done.

Olson demanded to know, why was the prosecutor's office refusing to issue a warrant? What was wrong?

"I can't tell you what's wrong, Jon," Sahli said.

Sahli saw no reason to rehash the mistakes made on the night of the murder. Olson later acknowledged there had been some problems, but blamed Gary Lisle for the fact that the detectives weren't told about the boot print Lisle found near the creek.

"He didn't communicate that the footprint was vulnerable to the sun," Olson later said. The undersheriff wanted to wait until daylight, he said. That still didn't explain why Jack Schoder didn't find out about the bootprint until two days later.

"I could have gotten them an arrest warrant," Jon Sahli would later say. "But that's all we would have had." Then he would have had to lay out the state's case in a preliminary exam before a judge would grant a full trial. A defense attorney could force an exam in twelve days. "There might even have been enough circumstances to bind him over," Sahli explained later. "But I've worked with police officers to know there aren't that many who continue to work after they get their arrest warrant. That ultimately would have been all I went to trial with."

The prosecutor offered a suggestion. "Why don't we put together a task force?" He would provide Gerry Woods, his investigator. They could also bring in the Battle Creek Post of the Michigan State Police.

Jon Olson didn't like that idea.

They were all dealing with a suspect who knew the system, Sahli argued. If Brad King had killed his wife, they were all going to be matching wits with a criminal justice instructor and a former cop. They needed manpower.

"I think this is far bigger than you recognize," Sahli said.

"It's nothing our department can't handle," Olson said.

In fact, the department was so sure of their progress, the sheriff said he planned to give Jack Schoder and Jim Stadfeld the weekend off. They were burnt-out.

"Jack and Jim have been working far too hard on this case," he said.

* * *

The same day, some sixty miles away, another meeting was underway with attorneys, but it wasn't in a cramped basement office.

The law offices of Miller, Johnson, Snell & Cummiskey took up the entire eighth floor of the Calder Plaza Building in downtown Grand Rapids, western Michigan's largest city. The firm not only covered a floor of Calder Plaza, it owned the building. One of western Michigan's premiere law firms, Miller, Johnson, Snell & Cummiskey had satellite offices in three other Michigan cities. Its letterhead listed seventy-six lawyers, including three former partners honored there posthumously.

One lawyer, James S. Brady, had been a partner since 1981. He'd come there after serving a five-year appointment by Jimmy Carter as the U.S. Attorney for the Western Judicial District of Michigan. Brady was a veteran of a number of sensational criminal trials. He'd been recognized in *The Best Lawyers in America* for his business law. He represented the *Grand Rapids Press* in media disputes. The governor of the state of Michigan had also appointed him in 1987 to the board of trustees of Western Michigan University. His law degree came from Notre Dame, but Brady had been an undergraduate at Western, where he pledged a fraternity called Tau Kappa Epsilon.

James Brady was a Teke. Another Teke, Randy Wright, had referred him to his old friend and frat brother, Bradford J. King.

On February 15, King met with James Brady in his Grand Rapids office. Brady exuded well-tailored confidence, especially for a man in his mid-forties. His round tortoiseshell glasses imparted a sense of studious prosperity, as did the understated patterns in his classic wool suit. A client who retained him not only got his services, the lawyer could remind any prospective client, he could access support staff and the accumulated experience of the entire firm.

The retainer was $25,000, just to get things started. A full trial, if it came to that, could easily push the total into the six figures.

A few days later, James Brady dispatched a letter to Detective

Jack Schoder at the Calhoun County Sheriff's Department, advising him if police wanted information or contact with King, they should notify the law firm.

Brad King's mother, Marge Lundeen, wrote the check.

From the View of

BRADFORD KING

Randy had talked about her. He talked about how "dynamic" and "vivacious" she was, just how "committed" to things she was. These words were always attached to Diane.

I wanted to meet this woman because he had talked about her so much. She had brought a lot of military people into est and professional guest seminars. But every time I went, she was never there. So I kept positioning myself, and it finally happened.

I remember the first time I saw her. It was at an est guest seminar, held in a hall in Bloomfield Hills. I was there as an assistant that night to enroll people in the training. Given that I was a guest seminar leader, that was my job. I saw her out of the corner of my eye. She was wearing navy blue wool slacks, little low-heel Ferragamo slip-ons, and a silk blouse. I think it was like a fuchsia—bright pink. Her hair was short. She had this smile that never disappeared. But I had things to do and I couldn't even get near her to talk to her.

Later, I was sitting, looking at her. The guy sitting next to me said, "What are you staring at?"

I said, "I'm staring at Diane."

"I'll fix you up," he said.

"No, don't," I said. "You just stay out of this."

She sat there with dignity, just proud of who she was, knowing who she was. To me she was the most beautiful woman in the room. And if you looked around, a lot of people would turn when they noticed her.

In the middle of the seminar, when we took a break, I walked right up and introduced myself. I wanted her to go out for coffee afterwards. She said she had other plans, but I got her phone number. She was warm, without letting me too close. I respected her for that. She wasn't aloof or cold. And, I had a reputation for sleeping around with anybody that would sleep with me. At that time I was single. I left guest seminars all the time with somebody to sleep with, and she knew it.

I called her five times to set up a date, but we never could come up with a day that worked. Finally, I thought, this has got to stop. This is driving me nuts.

I called her up and said, "Look, do you want to go out with me or don't you?"

"Yeah, I do," she said.

"Well damn it, clear your schedule," I said, "because I've cleared mine for a week."

Our first date was what they called "Graduation of The Training." That was the only time we could get together. We went to Greektown afterward, had a little bit to eat, and went back to her place. She lived in a big, mostly restored house near Wayne State. She poured some wine. We sat in a big bay window, over the porch, looking out over the street.

I remember I was nervous. I really was. I didn't want to blow it, you know. I didn't know a lot about her personally, I just knew what I felt when I saw her. I was awestruck. It's like I would start a conversation and I'd lose it in the middle of it. All night long, I sounded like one of the most unintelligent human beings. And all I could do is just look at her.

I'd never been struck by a woman like I was with her. Several glasses of wine. Several kisses. I avoided making any statement about sex at all. Do you want to have sex? she said. She actually asked me. And I said, yes.

I spent most of the night there. I had to work the next day, so I left between five or six in the morning. She wanted to make me breakfast, but I said I didn't have time. I could have made time, but I was scared. I was scared when I left there. I knew that I was attracted to her in a way I'd never been attracted to a woman before. Life had changed for me, and that scared me. I drove very slowly back to my place.

Well, by the time I got to my office, I realized that maybe this is what being in love is. Maybe this is how it starts. So, I called her.

"I know that you probably think I'm probably one of the stupidest people in the world after last night," I said. "Because I didn't talk about anything worth talking about and I must have sounded like a fool."

She started to laugh.

"What are you laughing about?" I said.

"I had a nice time," she said. "And, I thought you were wonderful."

"You know, I think I love you."

She said, "You *think?*" Because with Diane you don't get to *think* with her. Either you are or you aren't.

I said, "I've been putting a lot of thought into the fact that I love you. Maybe that's a more accurate way to put it."

"Well, if this will help you," she said. "I don't want to date anybody but you."

What made me fall in love with Diane? What made her fall in love with me? I'm going to answer this one backwards for you. What did we see in each other? I'll answer first what she saw in me. She saw an image of her father who died—her real father. She said I reminded her a lot of him. When we met I was about the age he was when he died.

She liked that I was strong-willed, determined, my level of commitment to things in life. I guess she must have thought I was, you know, nice to look at. I am kind of a handsome guy. I'm also quite conceited and vain.

She always said that my sense of humor was something that she liked. Diane always felt that she didn't have one and she really loved it. I had, to her, one of the best she'd ever encountered. Sarcastic. In fact, she would compare me to Jack Nicholson.

I think those are the things that attracted her to me. Well, I don't *think,* I *know.* She told me.

What attracted me to her was her obvious beauty, for one thing. And her beauty was more than just how she looked. She was an open book. She was energetic. She didn't keep secrets from anybody. Well, I shouldn't say that. I'm sure she kept secrets, but she was open. When you met Diane, you met somebody that was open to meeting you. She wasn't guarded. I think that's a more accurate statement. She had a level of energy that you rarely find in people, and that attracted me.

Early on, we talked about our families. She said, "I don't know if you'll like my family. They're not like yours."

She was making excuses. She was preparing me. I don't think there was a thing she didn't tell me. She told me that her mother and stepfather used to drink when she was a kid. On weekends they would fight. The police would be called to break things up. She told me that they didn't drink anymore, but that her stepfather was an SOB and probably wouldn't talk much. He was self-centered.

"I don't know how that's affected me, growing up with my parents fighting, but I know it has," she said. "I know that it has affected my family." She was crying. She cried through most of it.

And I said, "Why are you crying?"

" 'Cause I'm afraid you're going to go away."

"Well forget it," I said. "I'm not in love with your family, I'm in love with you. And it's obvious to me you're different than they are. Because if you were like them I couldn't be in love with you. You wouldn't be attractive."

It's not something that I grew up with, so it's hard for me

to relate to it, though I've dealt with those situations as a police officer, who knows how many times? But I could walk out the door with those people and they wouldn't mean a thing to me because that was part of my job. But, I had to get empathetic to what kind of condition Diane grew up in so that I could support her going through hard times.

I think that childhood created in Diane the unyielding perfectionist. Things were clean. I liked that. I grew up in a house like that. But her perfection was in everything, her job, everything, and she was very hard on herself. It was my job to temper that. That could be difficult sometimes, because she could get condescending. But it wasn't me she was upset with, it was what she was discovering.

She was very apprehensive about taking me to meet her mother and stepfather. She was embarrassed because she held me as being someone from a different world.

The night I met them, Diane planned something afterwards so there would be an excuse to leave. She's a smart woman, because if Diane and I hadn't done a lot of talking there wouldn't have been any talking to speak of. I shook hands, said hello.

I said, "I've heard a lot about you. It's nice to meet you."

And, that was about the end of it. The first night, I believed that Freida did not like me. She was as warm as cold toast.

Royal said, "I heard you play golf."

I said I played. "Diane tells me you play. Maybe you and I could go out and play a few holes."

And Royal said, "Oh, I don't play much anymore."

And that's kind of like he was.

He said, "You like being a cop?"

I said, "Yeah, I do."

I figured that might have something to do with it. Look at what they lived with for how many years, their experience with cops. Maybe I represented that. They were cautious about what they wanted to do around me.

I was thinking, if they're going to be like this, why am I even carrying on this conversation? Diane would look at me. She knew I was losing my patience. I'd been there for a half hour and I felt like I was lecturing, just saying something so that language was going on.

In time, it didn't get much better. Freida never said, "I don't like you." I don't think she would have the guts to do that. Not to my face. See, life would have been easier if she'd have done that. I spent a few years trying to get to know her family, because Diane asked me to. She wanted them to like me. I wrote letters. I had to force myself to talk. I didn't want to carry on a conversation with Freida. I mean, it was an exercise in futility. But if by some miracle forcing myself to do that, this woman would turn around and become human, I would do that for Diane. Left to my own devices, I'd have ignored the whole lot of them. I could have had a perfectly fine relationship with Diane and ignored them.

They were close minded people. Whatever they saw or read in the media was true. That's how they viewed the news. I remember sitting in that house and it was on the news that somebody had been arrested and released on bond. It was a Detroit cop who had been arrested, a corruption case back in 1983, if I'm not mistaken.

Both Freida and Royal said, "That son of a bitch is guilty or they wouldn't have arrested him."

I looked at them and said, "He's not guilty until a jury says he is. And then, he's not necessarily guilty."

And they said, "What are you, one of those fucking liberals?"

"I guess I am," I said.

They said, "You're just sticking up for him because he's a cop and you're a cop."

"No," I said. "I don't care who he is. I don't care if he's murdered fifty people. He's innocent until a judge or a jury are shown that he's guilty and they say he's guilty. That's what this country is founded on, and it can't be any other way. Now, if you want to sit here and say because the cops arrest somebody that they're guilty, God help him if you ever get on a jury."

I did make efforts to get to know everybody, to become a part of the family. I got along with Allen and Denise to a point. But becoming part of the family was like running into the proverbial brick wall.

I tried. Finally, that summer, shortly after we moved into the farmhouse, Diane said, "You don't have to do it anymore. You've given it your best and it's not working. You don't need to keep doing that to yourself, or to us."

Diane's family thinking I was calling my "attorney" after the murder was laughable. Randy never tried a criminal case in his life. I would never even think of asking him for that kind of advice. But why wouldn't I call my best friend? We're talking about a man who is my longest living friend. Who else would you call if you had no family to call?

A lot of what I went through during the weekend of the murder and at the funeral came from being a cop. There are just times when you have to be in control of yourself. You have to be on top of it. You can't afford to get emotional. When it's over, you can laugh, cry, swear, scream, yell, kick, go get drunk, or whatever. But right now, you have to maintain.

It was like the letter from the stalker, the obsessed fan. Somebody needed to remain objective.

Diane first told me about the phone calls. They started shortly after we moved to the farm. We moved in May 1, 1991. I don't recall how many there were, but they concerned her. What concerned her was that he kept calling.

We were having lunch together and she said, "This guy has been calling." That's how she put it. "He wants, you know, information about breaking into the media and I told him what he needed to do, but he keeps calling."

He didn't give a name. Not that I'm aware of.

I said, "Well you need to tell Rita Gillson, the receptionist, not to give you those calls anymore. If they can't give a name, don't connect them to you. The other thing you can do is tell him to put it where the sun don't shine."

"Well, I can't do that," she said. "I have a reputation. The station has a reputation."

She did think he was "strange." That was one word she used. She equated him to somebody who was using Lithium because we've known people who were on Lithium. Your speech gets weird. Slurry, slow, deliberate.

I said I thought the station manager and her boss should be made aware of this, then allow them to do it their way. But, I said, insist a screening situation be set up. And, that's what she did.

Then a letter came asking, "I want a picture from you." That came to the station in the mail with an envelope and a return address. That was the one from James Wickware, Jr.

"I wonder if this is the same guy who has been calling?" she said.

I said, "Well, I don't know."

She said, "I'm now a little concerned."

I said, "If you're concerned, I'm concerned, but let's not overreact. Let's not get crazed over this."

I saw that there'd be a potential for that.

I said, "You know we need to not allow this stuff to interfere with our life, our private life."

And she agreed. So she gave it to Mark Crawford to answer, which I thought was a good idea instead of Diane answering. She was taking herself out of the picture and if it was the same guy who was calling, maybe that would handle it. It seemed to, I guess. She never got another letter from him.

But, I thought, once somebody had written a physical letter then the station management needed to be more concerned about Diane's safety. And they weren't. I was getting pissed at the TV station.

Shortly after that, there was the invitation to lunch. I think this was in September. She said he called again. I don't know how he got through the screening. There could have been a relief person on the phone. He could have dialed direct into the newsroom. That may have been what happened.

She said, "He wanted to go to lunch with me. I told him I couldn't. You know, and I was polite about declining."

"It's too bad you didn't set the date up for a week later, and we could have found out who the guy was," I said.

"How?" she said.

I said, "We'll get the police involved and put a microphone in the car and on you, and when the guy shows up the cops are right behind you. And we find out what the guy's problem is."

The night she got the letter in the mailbox, I was teaching. It was Halloween night, I think, or Devil's Night. One or the other. I had gone back to my office and we had a voice mail system. So I called my number to see if I had any messages and there was one from Diane. She was hysterically upset, I guess is the best way to put it. So I immediately called Cindy's house. I said that as soon as I could get back to the classroom I would break class and come home.

Diane said, "I want you home."

"Well, I'm coming home," I said. "Just sit tight there."

I went back and broke class and left.

By the time I got to Cindy's it was probably nine or nine-thirty. Cindy met me at the door and said, "She's really upset. She's downstairs."

And I said, "Okay."

I'm trying to remain as calm as I can so that somebody can remain objective. At least I see that's what I'm supposed to do at the moment. And she's down there with Marler. And I went down there and hugged her and kissed her and said, "It'll be okay." Just talked to her. Said it's now time that the TV station take some measures here.

The letter had already been taken by the police. When I learned about the cut-out letters, I thought this is somebody who watches too many crime movies. Scriptwriters do it all the time. As an investigator, that's how I would look at it. This person is a TV nut.

Diane said how scared she really was.

I told her, "Diane, I know it scares you. I'm scared for you, but we can't let this run our lives. We have private lives and I'm not saying we aren't going to be cautious, but we aren't going to allow this to have us become paranoid."

We didn't sleep much that night. We spent a lot of time talking. She was concerned that I wasn't concerned because I was being objective. She wanted to make sure I wasn't going to blow this off. And I wasn't. But I didn't want to get out of hand with it because I knew if I got out of hand I'd be in her boss's office screaming and yelling and making a fool out of myself, creating problems for her at work. I knew if I let myself, I would. If they didn't do what I thought they should do, I'd be in there. They'd be calling the cops to get me out of the TV station and she didn't need *that* with this.

So, I was having to be a cop. I was having to be calm in the face of fear.

I never thought Jack Schoder was zeroing in on me as a suspect during the first interview. It didn't even cross my mind. He didn't approach it that way. He said, "The sooner the better," all that apology stuff.

"I *know*," I told him. "I've been through this on the other side of the coin, so to speak."

And we did it. Between cops there's a level of relationship that you wouldn't have if it was just somebody off the street. At that point, I didn't have any impressions of anybody.

By the second interview, I was able to form some impressions. I thought Jack Schoder was a jerk. First, I was convinced they were in the wrong because they accused me. Second, I started looking back at everything that was being done, and there was this mistake, this mistake, this mistake and, *this* mistake.

I only saw Jack Schoder and Jim Stadfeld together

once, and that was briefly during my second interview. If they were such a complement to each other, why weren't they both interviewing me? That's my question. When I worked with a partner, we both did the interview together. We double-teamed them. That says to me they don't get along, or they would have double-teamed me.

Stadfeld was in the back, then he would come in the room and Schoder would turn the tape off. If they were doing a professional homicide interview they would never turn the tape off. Stadfeld would never ask me any questions, but he'd come into the room to get something. They'd make a few snide comments to each other.

One was, "Hey, he doesn't want to take a polygraph. What do you think of that?"

This was not on tape. The tape was off.

And Stadfeld said, "What, are you afraid of them?"

"They're unreliable," I said. "Why the fuck should I do one?" That's just what I said to him. And I didn't do anything that would warrant me needing to take one.

Then they ran this old dodge on me, saying, "Well, you know, we were accused of stealing money. Some money turned up missing and we took polygraphs to prove we didn't do it."

That works on some people. But if you know about polygraphs, it doesn't work. Polygraphs are not lie detectors. They're nothing more than interrogation devices. That's all they are.

I looked at him and said, "Well, you were stupid to take one. If you didn't do it, you were stupid to take one."

See, if you did do the crime, take one. I've watched criminal after criminal do that: Take the polygraph, pass the sucker, yet you know every piece of tangible evidence says he did it. And he takes the damn polygraph and looks like the Virgin Mary.

So I didn't do it.

As for Schoder's interview itself, you know, when I was a cop, I never ran that on anybody: the get-it-off-your-chest-and-get-some-help confession deal. *Never.* That's stupid. I just kept asking them questions until they got tired of talking to me. They either got up and left or they confessed.

They did it all wrong. I mean, you want to run that on somebody who is a professional witness? I'm a professional witness. I haven't done it in over ten years, but I'm a professional witness. You don't forget that. And even if you assumed I was guilty, *assumed,* they did it all wrong. They didn't play the game. They forgot all the rules. They ran a number on me that you might try on some drug addict.

He might as well have announced it to me first. I call that the bumbling detective approach. You know, I was thinking about that interview, and one night it hit me. I was watching "Law and Order." The cops would ask a question and wait for an answer. That's when it hit me. Jack Schoder spent the whole time talking.

I just let Jack Schoder play it out. I let him make a fool out of himself, and I probably shouldn't have. I probably should have got up and walked out. But my whole reason for sticking with any talking at that point was that I wanted the crime *solved.*

PART THREE

The Cruelest Lies

The cruelest lies are often told in silence.
                    —Robert Louis Stevenson

1

Jack Schoder's weekend off ended promptly on Sunday night at 10 P.M. when the department reached the detective at home. A friend of the Kings was desperately trying to contact him, a county dispatcher said. Her name was Barbara Elgutaa, the woman who took care of the King children in the days after Diane Newton King's death.

The detective called her. The stalker wasn't the only trouble bothering Diane King, Elgutaa told the detective. There had been big trouble in the King marriage, she said.

A counselor at Kellogg Community College, Elgutaa said she'd met Diane King nine months ago at a powwow. They went to Native American events and visited each other now and then. By late summer, Diane had confided in her that her marriage was deteriorating. And three months ago, on the evening of November 20, she found herself alone with her new friend in the maternity ward at Oaklawn Hospital. Kateri was born that morning. Brad was at the university teaching class.

"Diane told me that the weekend before they'd had the biggest fight they ever had," Elgutaa said. "Diane said, 'I could walk out of this marriage right now.'"

Jack Schoder started taking notes.

Diane also complained that Brad seemed unconcerned about the stalker letter, Elgutaa continued. Her sister Darlene gave them the Doberman for protection, but Brad insisted it stay outside, complaining it bothered his allergies. In December, Brad was alarmed enough to call Diane in Detroit about the break-in at the farmhouse, Elgutaa said, but not concerned enough to put in a dead bolt lock right away.

Diane was planning changes, she told the detective. She wanted to leave the TV station in June to stay at home with her children and work on Two Worlds Productions.

"She said that Brad was going to have to go back to work full-time," she added.

Schoder wondered if she'd ever been in the King farmhouse.

"Quite a few times," she said.

"Did you ever see any guns there?" Schoder was thinking about the .22 caliber Remington Model 511 Scoremaster.

Elgutaa said she was at the farmhouse around Thanksgiving and that Brad had come in carrying a gun. Diane teased him about not getting a deer.

"He had a gun, like a deer hunting rifle," she said.

Schoder knew that only shotguns could be used to hunt deer in the lower part of Michigan. It must have been the Winchester shotgun. Elgutaa admitted she didn't have a very good knowledge of weapons.

Schoder wanted to know about February 9.

Elgutaa said she'd talked to Brad King the day of the murder. She'd called to invite the Kings over for dinner. He was noncommittal. Brad told her Diane had left for the Detroit area that morning to see her mother.

"He said she left on Saturday?" Schoder asked. "But, she left for Detroit on Thursday."

"I know, but he said she left that morning. I'm sure of it."

Elgutaa asked him to have Diane call her when she got home, then tried to end that phone chat with a pleasantry.

"How are the kids?" she asked.

There was some acrimony in his voice, she said. Marler was being disrespectful to him, he said. "And Diane never spends any time with the kids," he added.

Jack Schoder wondered about Marler King. "Have you talked to the boy? Has he said anything about this?"

Barbara Elgutaa said she hadn't asked the three-year-old anything, but he'd mentioned something when he was staying with her.

"He told me that he saw his mother fall," she said. "He told me that his mother got hurt."

Before she hung up, she gave Jack Schoder a list of contacts, though she only had first names for some. She suggested the detective call a woman named Cindy who moved to South America, an old friend named Regina in Detroit, a neighbor named Joanne, and an Indian elder named Bea Pamp.

Minutes after Jack Schoder ended that conversation, the dispatcher called again. Allen Marler was trying to reach him, he said. When he connected with Diane King's brother, Marler told him Brad King was planning an Indian observance for his late wife at a friend's apartment in Kalamazoo, something called "a ten-day feast."

Schoder wanted directions, but not to Kalamazoo. He wanted to know how to get to the Newtons' house in Sterling Heights.

"Man, do me a favor, would you?" he told Marler. "Tell your folks to stay put tomorrow morning. Tell them that Jim Stadfeld and I are on our way out."

The detectives were on the King homicide full-time now. Lesser transgressions against the people of Calhoun County (the B&Es, the armed robberies, the auto theft) would be handled by department deputies from now on.

"I want you on nothing but the King case," the sheriff had said.

No matter how long it took.

Family pictures greeted the two detectives inside the small ranch house on St. Joseph Street late Monday morning. Pictures covered the entire dining room wall. There were graduation photos of Gordon, Darlene, Denise, Allen, and Diane, plus maternity ward photos of a dozen grandchildren propped on a shelf of knickknacks. A ten-by-fourteen of newlyweds Freida and Royal Newton hung above the dining room archway.

In her youth, Freida Newton was strikingly similar to her middle daughter. Her bright eyes and white teeth. The raven hair. Even now Freida Newton's face was smoother than most women in their fifties. It was a face not easily given to expression among strangers. She had a silent demeanor that some interpreted as guarded mistrust, others as resilient inner strength.

Freida Newton still had the King children. Marler was moving from room to room, entertaining relatives and other visitors at the house. On Friday morning, the day after the burial, Freida had given Marler his own, small photo album. She'd been adding pictures of his mother to it for the boy. On the front she would eventually place a beaming shot of his mother.

"This is my mommy," Marler would say to visitors.

In the snapshot, Diane King was standing in her snowy driveway of Thunderspirit, her smile broad, her arms outstretched—as if to say *it's all ours*. Behind her loomed the red Victorian barn, the place where Jack Schoder and James Stadfeld now firmly believed Bradford J. King lay in waiting to kill his wife of seven years in cold blood.

They found privacy in Freida Newton's home beauty shop, among more family pictures. She detailed Diane King's last weekend, the last Saturday. Diane must have left between 4:15 and 4:30 P.M. on February 9, she estimated.

"It's no secret that I never cared for Brad," Freida Newton eventually got around to saying. "And I don't think he cared for us."

He wasn't sociable in her house, she explained. He wasn't sociable in *his* house as well. She stayed with him in the farmhouse while Diane was in the hospital having her c-section for Kateri in November. Brad spent the time in his bedroom. He left all the housework and care of Marler to her, she said.

When Brad and Diane visited, her daughter couldn't shake him, Freida said. "He followed Diane around wherever she went. We could never have a private conversation. He'd never let her out of his sight for more than a few moments."

The two detectives wanted to know about marital turmoil.

"Well, she was planning to quit her job in June," she said. "She wanted to spend more time with her kids, and she told me that had upset Brad." Brad wanted to go to school and get his PhD, she said. That's what Diane had said.

They wondered how that would stop him.

"If she stayed home he wouldn't be able to do that," Freida

Newton said. "Then Brad would have to hold down a full-time job. For as long as I've known him, that's something he's never been able to do."

Freida Newton told the detectives that Brad's alibi that he was out walking troubled her. "He was supposed to know when she left," she told them. "That was so Brad knew when she would be home. My Diane was so concerned because of the threats she was getting, she wanted him to know when she got there. That's why I don't understand when he says he was taking a walk."

She explained how her daughter's plans to leave the children changed. "I don't think Brad knew they were coming home," she added. "At least, I didn't tell him that. I just told him, 'Diane is on her way.' "

Freida Newton was adamant about it. She did not tell Brad: "Diane and the kids are on their way home."

They wondered, had Diane called Brad and told him the change in plans? Freida Newton was unsure about that.

Freida Newton wondered out loud if her son-in-law wasn't trying to scare her daughter. She wondered if he was behind the obsessed fan. She talked about the B&E Brad had reported at their house back in December. Diane was on another three-day visit to Sterling Heights that week as well, she said. Brad called to tell Diane all about it.

"She was really upset. I thought it was a bit strange that he called here to tell her. I don't know why he didn't just wait till she got back."

The B&E. The stalker letter. That's why they had all the security precautions, Freida explained, like the Doberman and the routine when she got home. That's why they had certain routines.

The detectives wanted to know about the routines. They wanted more detail.

As far as Freida Newton knew, when Brad was home Diane would pull into the driveway, honk the horn, and wait for her husband to come out and escort her inside. If Brad was not at home, she would get a neighbor to accompany her as she entered the farmhouse. Sometimes, Diane even drove around the house, across the yard, to look for tampering on the windows and doors. She'd seen some of this herself on visits.

"That's what I mean about Brad being out for a walk," she said. "See what I mean. My Diane wouldn't even get out of her car unless she saw Brad there."

Later, Jim Stadfeld said out loud what everyone was thinking.

"Maybe on the day she was shot she did."

Regina Zapinski didn't hesitate when police called and asked if they could talk to her about her friend's visit to her house the night before her murder. The thirty-four-year-old Native American culture teacher just hoped she could hold herself together long enough to talk.

Not only had the death of her oldest and best friend devastated her, all the whispers about her own husband being the killer had compounded the tragedy. Brad King couldn't have killed Diane, Gina kept telling herself. That just wasn't like the man she knew.

If anyone asked she would say it. "I liked Brad. He just seemed like a big, sweet guy."

The big, sweet guy always hugged her, sometimes a little too long, she thought. And now that was one of the things bothering her. They'd embraced the day before the funeral when she arrived at the farmhouse. He cried out her name loudly in front of everyone, but his hug was short and mechanical, his eyes tearless. Now, as she talked to the two detectives from Calhoun County, Gina Zapinksi didn't know what to think.

They'd met in the eighth grade, she told them. Two working-class kids, but a little different. Gina was part Apache and Mexican, Diane half Mohawk. Macomb County was white and blue-collar conservative, the demographic home of what would be known as Reagan Democrats, but neither of them would be denied.

Diane dated the jocks; Gina cheered them from the sidelines. They went off to Western Michigan University together. Diane made the cheerleading squad. Gina was a team ball girl. After one semester, Diane wanted new beginnings, and she found them at preppy Mount Ida in Boston, no-nonsense Wayne State in Detroit, the discipline of the U.S. Army in Georgia, and in New Age Colorado with Brad King. Gina zigzagged her way through Western, finally graduating after a half-dozen years.

They were opposites in many ways: Gina quiet; Diane the incessant talker. Gina didn't look for attention. Diane hugged and cried and made big public displays. Gina guarded most of her problems. For years, Diane talked about the loss of her real father as the missing piece in her life. Gina fancied herself the artistic type, an eccentric, a wanderer. Diane was "Yuppie before there were Yuppies," as one friend had put it.

"She always expressed what she liked and what she didn't like," Gina would explain. "I want to do this. I want to do that. I have to do this. I have to do that. I need to do this. I need to do that. She wanted to be the *best* wife. The *best* mother. The *best* marriage. She was always trying to be the *best* person she could be."

Her advocacy of est almost ended their friendship. Diane conned Gina into going to a guest seminar, saying it was a college class. After enduring a high-pressure sales pitch, Gina was livid. Diane began crying in the car. The Training literally saved her life, she said.

"She told me all kinds of things that I never knew," Gina recalled. "She said that she was so ashamed of her family because of their drinking and everything. It was such a big deal in her life that had made her so miserable. She hadn't been happy being Indian. She said that if it hadn't been for this program, she was going to kill herself. She said she'd actually considered killing herself at one point."

Then, Diane lured her to a second est meeting, saying it was a "world hunger" meeting. Gina stormed out of the seminar. They argued afterwards at a local restaurant. They didn't speak for months.

They met again a couple years later in Colorado in 1985 when Gina flew out to attend the Denver Powwow, one of the biggest in the United States. That's where Gina first met Brad. They all went to dinner, but what she learned about Brad came from Diane, though he was sitting right at her side.

"Diane did all the talking," she later recalled. "I don't remember Brad saying a word. She told me what Brad said, what Brad thought. She told me what Brad did. Brad, meanwhile, never said a word."

There was no more talk of est, only of Native American culture. Diane had discovered her culture in the West. They danced at the powwow together. Her Indian awakening was what Gina liked to call another one of Diane's "Big Events." There had been a half-dozen Big Events through the years: The Training. Her culture. The TV business. Having, baptizing, and raising Marler. Changing her middle name to Newton.

Diane couldn't have a simple birth or a simple job or a simple baptism or a simple name change. The birth had to be by midwife, the job had to be a pipeline to the networks, the baptism had to be multicultural, and the name change was a statement of reconciliation with her stepfather.

Kateri's pending christening was the next Big Event. In fact, Gina was helping Diane design a white buckskin outfit for the baby. Diane had come over to work on it the Friday night before she was shot.

Diane, Gina speculated, was probably motivated by an effort to please her family, an effort that Diane often complained fell short. The Newtons or her siblings weren't especially interested in the rigors of her career or the details of her climb to the top. They weren't subscribers to the Big Event. They even teased her when she named her son Marler Robert Tekanatensere King. One of her siblings scoffed, "Well, you know Diane. She has to do something crazy."

"Diane was looking for love and acceptance from her family," Gina explained. *"All* of them. She needed that and looked for that her entire life. And she cried all the time about it. She never felt like they took her seriously. She didn't think the family cared about her education and all the things she was doing. She was definitely a middle child. Everybody fit somewhere in the family, but her. She was the oddball out."

That hunger, Gina thought, gave Diane a certain naivete. It propelled her to superficiality and Me Decade fads like est. But, to her betterment, it also allowed her to tackle the TV business where many people's fears would have prevented them from even making the attempt.

Gina also knew that Brad truly worshipped her. She seemed to get from him what she couldn't get from her own. She genuinely loved the man, although at times he did perplex her. Diane was baffled why he couldn't hold down a full-time job. She found it mystifying, but minimized it. Gina knew Diane's mother Freida had been making an issue out of it for years.

Besides, Gina knew Brad was a regular "Mr. Mom." He wasn't a slob, parked in front of the TV with a beer and the sports page. He warmed bottles, changed diapers, and watched the children without complaint. He was impeccably groomed. Some men might even have considered him henpecked, but Brad never showed any signs of irritation. He wanted to be with her all the time.

Alone, Diane was more open. Gina detected trouble in the weeks before the birth of Kateri. She'd gone out to Marshall to visit, and Brad went out to rent some videos. Diane began crying. Brad wasn't making love to her anymore, she said.

"You're just feeling insecure 'cause you're pregnant," Gina said.

"Yeah, hormones, I guess," Diane said.

"Was he cheating on her?" one of the detectives asked.

"Not that she knew," Gina said.

The detectives wanted to know more about marital turmoil.

Gina offered the details she could. They had talked, in fact, the night before her death. Brad was not happy with her long-range plans to leave the TV business and become a home-maker, she said. He wanted to attend graduate school and finish his PhD. They were trying to work it out. They were seeing a marriage counselor, Diane said.

"But he has some real problems," Diane had told her. "The therapist told me he's happy being Mr. Diane King."

Brad, she said, liked the notoriety of being married to some-one well-known. He liked the recognition. He liked the special access they got at events. He liked the little perks that went with her job.

There were more problems, she said. Their sex life was nonexistent, Diane complained again on Friday.

"I should be so happy," Diane told her, crying again. "I have a beautiful daughter and a wonderful son. But I could walk out of this marriage right now."

Gina didn't take the words or tears as seriously as she might have with other friends. Diane King could be downright histrionic. She'd essentially said the same thing in the fall.

The detectives asked her about the stalker letter.

"It scared her," she said. "And she didn't think he took it seriously enough." As a former police officer he should have had more ideas to assure her security, Diane said.

But something about the stalker didn't sit right with Gina. If the threat was so real, she thought, why were they living in such isolation in the country? Why didn't they move back to Battle Creek?

She covered other subjects with the detectives. Yes, as far as she knew, Diane seemed to get along with her coworkers. No, Gina hadn't seen any of Brad's guns. Yes, Brad's demeanor was odd at the funeral.

After Jack Schoder and Jim Stadfeld left, the questions about infidelity inspired more thinking by Diane King's old friend. Yes, Gina thought, Diane was worried about other women. She remembered when Diane mentioned that Brad was in the company of young, attractive coeds at Western a few days a week. They had talked about it during one of her Marshall visits, or perhaps another time.

"Diane did tell me that one night she decided she was going to stay up, because she always went to bed so very early," she later recalled. "He was supposed to be coming home from school and he came in late and was walking up the stairs very slowly and got into bed. She asked him why he was sneaking up the stairs.

"And he said, 'Oh, I was trying not to wake you.' "

Diane also asked why he was so late. Brad said he'd run out of gas.

Then Diane asked him, "Brad, are you having an affair?"

"Diane, I would never do a thing like that," he supposedly said. "You and Marler are my life."

2

On Tuesday afternoon, February 19, Jack Schoder, Jim Stadfeld, and a half-dozen more police made use of another search warrant at 16240 Division Drive. It was the third warrant authorized by a local judge, and the most extensive to date. No one was home when they arrived.

Working from prosecutor Jon Sahli's check list and their own theories, the detectives wanted to eliminate as many crime scene variables as they could. Sergeant Robert Cilwa, the Michigan State Police Crime Lab ballistics expert who had been analyzing the Remington Model 511 Scoremaster, set up for several on-site tests. As Gerry Woods predicted back at the prosecutor's office, Cilwa could not say with certainty that the Scoremaster was the actual murder weapon because the soft lead slugs deformed on impact and obliterated rifling characteristics. However, Cilwa had been building an impressive circumstantial argument linking the shots with the gun found in the stream. He'd determined microscopically that certain firing pin and ejector markings from the Remington did match those on the shell casings found in the loft and in the seven casings taken from Talmadge Creek.

To strengthen the case, Jon Sahli had suggested the investigation try to match the angles of the shot with autopsy results. Cilwa brought a laser device to measure the angles of trajectory of shots fired from the loft and other locations. The loft measured seven degrees. It was the identical angle as the wound to Diane King's chest.

Cilwa also brought the Scoremaster itself. The detectives sent Deputy Guy Picketts back to the hay bales, where King said he'd been sitting. There were two sets of bales in fact, one a quarter mile beyond the first set. Picketts went to the farthest, almost a half mile from the barnyard. Cilwa fired a test shot from the loft.

Everyone waited a few seconds. Then Picketts reported by radio.

"Yeah, I heard it," he said.

They documented lighting, time, and distance. They made a video of the barnyard and back acreage and measured distances again. Dog handler Gary Lisle marked the dog track with toilet paper. They sent Picketts out to walk it twice at a brisk pace, timing him at seven minutes and five minutes to cover the course. Schoder and Picketts explored the spot where the gun was found with an underwater metal detector. They were looking for the missing rifle magazine. They picked up faint signals in the mud, dug up the creek bottom with a post hole digger, but couldn't locate the missing clip.

Back at the farmhouse, a department lieutenant busted down the front door. The warrant gave them permission to search for Brad King's boots, weapons evidence, and materials that might shed light on the couple's personal lives. They didn't find boots or significant gun evidence, but they left with all the film, video, and paperwork in the house. They emptied a camera of one roll and took another they found in the refrigerator. They emptied a two-drawer filing cabinet, filled with documents and family memoirs.

They logged the accumulation under only a dozen broadly worded descriptions, though the written materials filled several large boxes. The documents numbered into the thousands. Diane was a compulsive saver. They had seized college, Army, marriage, and children records. They had bills, financial statements, and cancelled checks. There were letters and brochures and poetry and even a file of Diane's favorite jokes.

Among the materials investigators would eventually discover were signs of ongoing financial difficulties. Not counting car loans, the Kings had arrived in Michigan $15,000 in debt, mostly to charge cards and clothing stores. This included a $5,006 federal tax bill from 1986 and 1987. The couple apparently had taken too many exemptions. They were paying it back in installments.

The total debt might have been insignificant for many in the television business. But, before he even knew their debt load,

Jim Stadfeld already was astonished at the family's financial affairs. It didn't take a township treasurer's eye to figure out that the Kings' tastes well exceeded their income.

The detective had learned that Diane Newton King was making only $22,000 a year, a take-home pay of hardly $1,900 a month. She'd hired in at only $19,000. It didn't surprise him to see the book *101 Ways to Get Money from the Government* in the seized material.

"I was appalled, and Jack was, too, by how little she actually made at the TV station," he later said. "Somehow they were living on it, too."

Meanwhile, Brad King's contribution was elusive. Various versions of Brad King's resume in the seized material showed he had held up to a half-dozen jobs. Missing from all his job entries was the length of tenure. Western Michigan University was paying him $1,800 per class per term. He'd taught three classes in the fall, but was teaching only one class in February.

Not three months after Diane, Brad, Marler, and their standard poodle Rasta moved to Battle Creek, the couple had sought the services of American Debt Counseling, a consolidation agency in Kalamazoo. The poodle mysteriously died, the police later learned. Some family members suspected it was poisoned. However, a mass mailing Diane King sent to friends back in Colorado, painted an optimistic picture about the couple's new life in Battle Creek. She bragged for three pages about their new apartment, her "fabulous" new job, the city's symphony and shopping malls and, of course, Brad's seemingly unlimited career "options," including "PR director for the city, assistant court administrator, and various mental health positions."

The letter was in the material seized with the February 19 warrant. After he read it, considering everything they'd been discovering, Jim Stadfeld decided Bradford King may not have been the only one in the family skilled in the use of smoke and mirrors.

Late in the afternoon, Allen Marler and his girlfriend Nancy Rapo stopped by the farmhouse, finding police there searching and conducting their tests. Brad King must be in Kalamazoo preparing for the Ten Day Feast, they told Jack Schoder. Allen Marler was on his way there as well, the only immediate family member who would answer the invitation to attend.

Allen and his brother Gordy had found Brad King hardly any more accessible than the women of the family. Allen had made a half-dozen trips out to the farm to pitch in on projects like the porch. So had Gordy. They both thought he was a little odd.

More than once, Gordy told the story about the time he and two friends joined King in some bow hunting near Thunderspirit last fall. They arrived on a Friday night, and Brad took them out under a full moon to show them spots to hunt in the morning, well west of the Zinn acreage. Brad said he'd be hunting north across Division Drive.

The next morning, when Gordon Marler and his friend were returning from the fields, they noticed movement just inside a tree and brush line a couple hundred feet away. It was Brad, standing motionless in his camouflage, watching them. He was a good half mile from where he said he was going to hunt.

"Look at Brad over there," Gordy said. "He thinks we can't see him."

Like some kind of invisible warrior, Gordy chuckled to himself. He couldn't resist waving at him, just to yank his string.

Allen Marler, meanwhile, had kept his thoughts about Brad King and his sister's murder to himself, not joining in the chorus of other family members who were convinced of King's guilt.

"I'm not going to influence the system," he said. "I'm not going to convict him. Either the evidence is there or it isn't."

On the way back from Kalamazoo, after the feast, Marler stopped at the sheriff's department to talk more with Jack Schoder. The detective detailed some of the evidence against his brother-in-law.

"We're going to nail the bastard," he told Allen Marler.

On the way back to Detroit, his girlfriend Nancy noticed his knuckles turned white from his grip upon the wheel.

*   *   *

On the matters of funerals and mourning, The Great Law of Peace, the constitution of the Iroquois Confederacy, states:

> Hearken you who are here, this body is to be covered. Assemble in the place again in ten days hence, for it is the decree of the Creator that mourning shall cease when ten days have expired. Then a feast shall be made.
>
> Then at the expiration of ten days, the Speaker shall say: "Continue to listen you who are here. The ten days of mourning have expired and your mind must now be freed of sorrow as before the loss of your relative. The relatives have decided to make a little compensation to those who have assisted at the funeral. It is a mere expression of thanks."

Brad King applied it literally, holding the Ten Day Feast, or "ghost feast," as Michigan tribes knew it. Twenty or so folks attended, including Gina Zapinski, Allen Marler, and Native American friends from the west side of the state.

The house belonged to Andre and Julie D'Artagnan, a Native American couple who befriended the Kings at Michigan powwows. The D'Artagnans had advised Diane on her Two Worlds Productions project.

After a meal of traditional foods, King stood before the group and ceremoniously gave away some of Diane's possessions. Earrings. Necklaces. Bracelets. Silver and turquoise jewelry. A leather headband. Baskets. Dishes. As people came forward, he embraced them. Some later forwarded their gifts to Freida Newton. It was not an entirely comfortable ceremony for some, most who already knew Brad King was the prime murder suspect in the case.

After the feast, the couple decided Brad was too upset to return to the farmhouse, so they asked him to spend the night on the couch. King said he had plans to look for an apartment in Kalamazoo the next day, complaining he was no longer comfortable at the home where his wife was murdered.

In the morning, the couple told him to look no farther. They had an apartment in their basement. They invited Brad King and the children to move in.

It would be a productive setting and an enlightening one for the widower. The D'Artagnans had arranged for the drum ceremony outside the church. Andre D'Artagnan had conducted the pipe ceremony at the farmhouse and given Brad King the eagle feather he carried at the Mass.

Brad King's interest in Native American culture seemed to be escalating since his wife's death, but the metamorphosis had only just begun.

3

The tip came late in the week of the funeral: An attractive college-age girl checked into the Arborgate Motel the day after the murder, made one phone call to Thunderspirit, then abruptly checked out. She told motel staff she was a "close friend" of Brad King's, but wanted no contact with his family staying in other rooms.

Jack Schoder and Jim Stadfeld found her at her apartment on the north campus of Western Michigan University. *Cathy Anson* was twenty-one, slender, and had dark blond hair that cascaded to her shoulders. She was a former criminal justice student of Brad King's.

"I guess I just went to Marshall on an impulse," she told the detectives, adding she'd left after finding out he had plenty of family around.

"I just considered him a friend," she said. "I figured he needed support."

"This friendship, does that mean you had sex with him?" Jim Stadfeld got around to asking.

"No," she said adamantly. "We're just good friends."

Brad King listened to her problems, she added, and gave her rides home from class when her car broke down. He'd dropped by her apartment to just chat and kill time before class a couple of times. In fact, Cathy Anson recalled, Brad King had gone out with her and two other of his students on February 7, two days before his wife's murder. They'd gone drinking at Claire's Pub in Kalamazoo after his class until about midnight.

"He seemed a little down," she said. "He said things were a little more complicated in his life than he wished them to be."

The detectives wondered why an instructor might go out drinking with his students.

"Well, he said his kids were at their grandmother's and he didn't have to get home at any particular time," she said. "He didn't have to get back early so his wife could go home."

Go home? the detectives wondered.

Yes, she explained, Brad King said his wife watched their children at his house when he taught.

"He told me they were separated," she said. "He told me that early on, right after we met."

On February 19, another anonymous phone caller sounded a similar theme. Somebody ought to have a chat with a couple of Western Michigan roommates, the tipster said, providing their name and address. They seemed to know all about an affair Brad King was having with a student.

Jim Stadfeld found one of the coeds at home on Wednesday afternoon. Yes, she said, she knew all about the affair. Her roommate was best friends with the student. From what she understood, they'd been seeing each other since the fall term.

"The way she told it to me, it wasn't really serious, just sexual," she said.

Kelly Clark was stirring rice on the stove, trying to boil up a quick dinner before her six o'clock class when she heard one of her five roommates say somebody was asking for her at the door.

The man identified himself as Calhoun County Sheriff's Department Detective Jim Stadfeld.

"I'd like to talk to you," he said.

"About what?"

"I believe you know about what."

Kelly Clark had been dreading this moment for days, and now it had come. She invited the detective into the kitchen, out of earshot of her roommates. She wanted to keep an eye on that rice.

"Isn't there any place we can go more private?" he asked.

No, she shrugged. Not in this house.

He didn't waste time with pleasantries. "I'm here investigating the homicide of Diane Newton King. It's my understanding that you were having a relationship with Bradford King."

"Well. . . ."

"Look, you might as well be straight about this, because we're going to find out anyway."

He made her nervous. Who is this hard-ass cop? she thought.

"Miss Clark, you're going to get drawn into this whether you like it or not. I've already talked to your friends."

All right, she thought.

"Did you sleep with him?"

"Well. . . ."

"Look, we're going to find out."

"Yes."

"How many times?"

"Twice."

Kelly Clark was a criminal justice student who knew just a little about police work, a little bit about interrogation, and she didn't like this man. He was treating her like an accessory, she decided. She was offended by his approach.

"Can you tell me about it?" he asked.

Yes, she thought, she'd tell him, but she'd keep it short. She'd made an adult decision when she got involved with her instructor, and now she was going to pay some adult consequences. She just didn't want to involve her friends or her family. *This* was not what she had in mind when she told them she was going to learn about police work.

They all were connected with the justice system, her brother, her sister, and her father. Her father's law practice had made a pretty swank life for them off Lakeshore Drive, not far from the Grosse Pointe Yacht Club and the other trappings that came with growing up in the Pointes.

But by her senior year at Western, Kelly Clark knew a few things about herself. Unlike her siblings, she was too undisciplined for law school, but she wanted to do something in law enforcement. She liked studying criminals. She liked studying the sociology and psychology of their behavior.

Secondly, at nearly twenty-two, Kelly Clark had come to accept she had an affinity for older men. In high school, she dated guys in their late twenties. In college, she dated men in their thirties and early forties. No, she told the curious, she wasn't looking for someone to take care of her or a father figure. She had a fantastic father, thank you. Just put her in a room full of guys, and she'd end up with somebody older.

Kelly Clark was not one to advertise. She wore her dark brown hair in a conservative wave and wore makeup of earthy colors. Years of school athletics had left her body more firm than classically feminine. When she wanted to flaunt herself, she did it in a tight bikini or tank top. Most of the time, she concealed her full breasts in oversized sweatshirts and sweaters.

She'd quit fighting her preference a couple of years ago. "I finally said I'm just not going to worry about it anymore," she told a friend. "I'm just gonna date whoever I want to date."

Kelly Clark knew who she wanted to date the first day of class in Sociology 464, The Sociology of Law Enforcement. Brad King sauntered to the amphitheater-like lecture hall, carrying a can of Coke in one hand, his books in the other. He wore a jean jacket and blue jeans, held up by a big silver belt buckle, and a tuft of light blond hair poked out above the top button of his red flannel shirt.

When he turned around, she was taken by his eyes. His deep blue, penetrating eyes. They looked heartless. Then he cracked a smile. It was boyish and mischievous.

She turned to her friend Shelly. "My God, Shelly," she whispered. "He's got killer eyes and a killer smile."

She remembered the "killer" line when the news stories about Diane King's death broke. Now, students in Sangren Hall were placing bets. Did he do it, or didn't he? Even odds.

Kelly Clark was betting that he did.

She'd gone to the funeral in Marshall. Brad King's loud sobbing in the church moved her at first, but the walk back to the car in the cold air cleared her head. She turned to another student who'd accompanied her.

"Well, I gotta give him an A-plus for acting," she said.

Actually, she thought Brad King fit both the criteria: He was the most likely suspect. He was the least likely as well.

As a teacher, he was a huggy liberal. He condemned macho cops and called for more women in police work. He told stories from personal experience, mostly aimed at shattering what he saw as the facades of honor and duty. He lectured on corruption and mismanagement. He argued for departments to reward creativity and problem solving, rather than single heroic acts in the face of danger.

Brad King's favorite whipping post was fatal force. She once brought him a local newspaper supplement that cited the policemen of the year. He lectured angrily that their bravery had been measured by their involvement in fatal shootings. He wrote down the magazine's address and promised to write them in protest.

"Look, this one killed someone, and this one," he said. "Is that what you have to do to be a good cop? Shoot somebody?"

Yet, privately, he bragged about his hunting prowess. He preferred bow hunting, he said. He maintained that he was so good with a rifle, there was no sport left for him with firearms.

But in class, he was a big softy. He encouraged everyone to call him Brad. He seemed exceptionally easygoing. He gave students pats on the back and hugged others. Students brought him tapes and books and snacks.

"Brad. Yeah, what a nice guy," some would say.

He had a genuine following, many of them women. A half-dozen female students were always following him back to his office, a fact that didn't go unnoticed by some of the men, many of whom were the ones now placing the guilty bets. Other male students raved about him, some of the frats he'd hang out with after class.

Brad King was a well-practiced, certified charmer, Kelly

Clark decided early on. He cracked jokes to draw people out. He punctuated one-liners with that Jack Nicholson grin of his. Or, he could get downright vulnerable if he wanted. In the first class, he confessed he was "working on my second divorce." She noticed a silver ring on his left hand that night, but then never saw it after that.

As they got to know him, they learned his marital troubles had not hampered his devotion to his son. He talked of wanting to take his son Marler hunting, but said his estranged wife complained that was no place for a three-year-old. He talked a lot about Marler, how bright the boy was. In fact, the way he talked, the kid was some kind of genius.

However, Brad King was not the fatherly type, Kelly Clark decided. He liked to hit the bars after class, hang out with the Teke boys. And, in November, when he revealed to her that his estranged wife had given birth to their daughter, Kelly and her friend Shelly asked him about the baby girl a couple of times in his office. They wanted to see a picture. He was indifferent and cold about the new child.

Instructor and class had the perfect setup, Kelly began to believe. The class that started at twilight was a walk, an ace. Booked for two and a half hours, it never lasted much longer than one. The pop quizzes were brainless. Once, he said his boy Marler had ripped up their quizzes, so everybody got a ten.

"All seventy of them?" Kelly cracked to Shelly. "I guess he didn't want to grade them, did he?"

Brad King lectured right out of the book or told stories, lots and lots of war stories. The midterm was a multiple-choice. The final was open-book, open-note, but not take home, meaning you could keep it nice and short. She wrote a half-dozen pages, one paragraph answers right out of the textbook. She scored a ninety-five.

Kelly Clark thought Brad King was teaching not out of any particular dedication or mission. She thought he was doing it for attention and spare change.

In the afternoons before his classes, King spent a lot of time in his office. He kept the door open and sat back deeply in his chair, his feet propped on his desk, his hands cradled behind his head. He always faced out, watching everyone who passed in the hall.

Inside, hypnotic flute and drum music played. The tape was Carlos Nakai, the Hopi flutist. He kept braided sweet grass on his desk, which he handed out to favorites. He kept a big photograph of the Native American actor Graham Greene, who played Kicking Bird in *Dances With Wolves*. One night, he told the class that he was a quarter Indian.

Kelly Clark looked at his blond chest hair and said, "I wonder which quarter that is?"

There was also a big jar of butterscotch candies in the office. Kelly Clark stopped by to munch on them as often as she could. She came up with a variety of justifications, both legitimate and contrived. Her attraction to Brad King was purely physical, she told herself. They had so little in common.

This notion was confirmed two months into the term when he invited himself to Pizza Hut with her and Shelly after class. He talked about repairs on his house, a porch he was building. He complained he didn't like his mother-in-law.

Kelly told him she was dating a guy in his early forties. "I don't like a lot of bullshit," she said. "Most guys my age are into a lot of bullshit."

She saw his eyes quickly scan all of her.

Kelly insisted on writing a check to pay for her share of the beer and pizza. She didn't want to look presumptuous. But when he asked her out to lunch alone the following week, she knew she'd read him correctly.

They went to a place called Schlotzsky's, his favorite place, he said, way off-campus. It was sometime in December. They ordered sandwiches and chili, but she was so nervous she could hardly eat. They shared some of their pasts, but they hardly connected. She told him about being the only girl all-star in boy's Little League baseball. He told her about his early days at Western and doing duty in Vietnam.

The next night, he asked her out to see *Dances With Wolves*. He picked her up, but made a call from her house, telling somebody he'd be late getting home. She guessed it was his sitter. He also called a friend for the movie's starting time.

He talked a lot through the film about the white soldier who finds his true identity in the wilderness by adopting Indian ways, instructing her. He explained what the eagle feathers meant and why the horses were painted. He delighted in showing off his knowledge of Native American culture. Well into the movie, he put his hand on her knee.

They walked out of the theater holding hands. She couldn't believe his blatancy. Students filled the theater lobby. They necked in the parking lot, then steamed up his car windows in front of her house. When he asked to come inside, she complained she had an exam the next morning in another class.

She wasn't making an excuse. She scored her only D of the fall term the next day, a few hours before Brad King called her with an invitation. He asked her to come out and visit him in Marshall. That was forty-five minutes away, too far to drive, she complained. He offered to come over instead.

They went almost directly to her bedroom. He grabbed the back of her neck and gently pulled her closer. When they fell onto the bed, she decided to ask him straight-out.

"Aren't you married?"

He looked into her eyes, pausing.

"Technically, yes."

"Oh."

Then, he amplified. "You see, she moved out in mid-November. The last time I saw her was three days ago when she picked up some of her stuff."

He paused, then asked, "Do you want to stop?"

"Have you, you know, ever done this before?" she asked back.

"No, I've never been this close to a student before."

No, Kelly Clark thought. She'd dated older divorcés. He should be much more nervous, especially with a student. He was too calm. He was too smooth.

"I don't believe you," she said.

"You're not required to believe me," he said. He cracked that Jack Nicholson smile.

She considered him the best she'd ever had. She struggled to keep herself quiet so her roommates didn't hear them.

"Is this okay?" he kept asking. "Is this alright?"

He was eager to please. Almost timid.

His lovemaking was more bashful than his anatomy. They did it twice in two hours, but he was perpetually erect. There was only one other oddity. Unlike most men, he paid absolutely no attention to her large, breasts.

Afterward, she ran her fingers through the blond hair on his chest.

"I like doing this," she said.

"I'm glad somebody does," he complained. "Both my wives wanted me to shave it."

She felt sorry for him. He sounded almost pathetic.

He noticed a book she had on her night table. It was about *Dances With Wolves*. He began flipping through it.

"This is nice," he said. "I'd sure like something like this."

Later, he mentioned his birthday was coming up in January. He's fishing, she thought. In time, she would notice a pattern. He had a way of moping when he was trying to get something he wanted. It reminded her of a little kid.

She offered him a Miller Lite from her compact refrigerator.

"I only drink imported beer," he said. He'd settle for a wine cooler.

Okay "Mr. Worldly," she thought.

He left sometime in the early morning hours. They waited until the voices of her roommates stilled downstairs. When they got to the bottom of the stairs, they were surprised by a voice in the living room.

"Hi, Mr. King."

A male student from his Tuesday class was on the couch, visiting a roommate. My God he must be dying with embarrassment, Kelly thought. But Brad King very calmly said hello, then poked his head into the stairway vestibule and kissed her good night.

"I didn't expect to see one of my students in your living room," he said when she saw him in Sangren Hall the next day.

He was smirking, and he was dressed in a three-piece suit, a gold pocket watch chain hanging smartly from his vest. He was going to a Christmas party that night, he later said.

A few days later, she ran into the male student in her living room. He said Brad King had walked forward and stood over his desk in class, looking down at him. King also shook his hand.

"He was as cool as a cucumber about it," he said.

Brad King was a study in contrasts, Kelly Clark thought. He seemed perfectly content to drive a nondescript station wagon, but wore snappy, crisply ironed clothes that always drew the eye. Emotionally, nothing seemed to rattle him. Yet he could appear vulnerable, evoking someone's sympathy at will. He seemed timid, but was undeterred if he wanted something. He was physically affectionate, but emotionally distant.

Brad King was outright coy, Kelly Clark decided. That was the word. Coy. And he had her absolutely intrigued.

They had hardly any contact through the balance of the term. It was as if nothing had happened between them. She dropped by his office to make small talk, but largely kept her distance. She decided it was probably better for them both that way. The term ended mid-December, and the campus closed for Christmas break.

When they returned for winter term, she borrowed some books from him for a project. A couple days before his wife's murder she stopped by his office to return one. The weather was damp. It was the mid-afternoon. Not looking for anything more than a lift, she asked him for a ride home.

When they pulled up in her driveway, he turned off the car and followed her inside. He said hello to one of her roommates, then followed her up to her bedroom.

"What makes you so sure that I'm going to sleep with you?" she asked.

He grinned. "Well if you weren't, you would have kicked me out by now."

Boy, she thought. He's got me down. She asked him to shut the blinds.

He got up slowly. It was a second-floor window. He walked over and made a comment. "Why? Teachers don't get fired for stuff like this anymore."

They made love twice.

Afterwards he didn't say much, certainly not as much as he

did the first time, and that wasn't a lot. He complained, really
He said he didn't want to go back to his office to give a makeup
test. He didn't want to go to Sangren Hall.

"I don't want to teach tonight."

He seemed depressed. Maybe he's coming down with something, she decided. He seemed distant, even preoccupied.

When he left, it was about twenty minutes to six.

Kelly Clark gave a brief sketch of the two liaisons to the
detective.

"Was he kinky?" Jim Stadfeld asked.

"It depends what you define as kinky," she snapped back.

She thought he had a lot of nerve. Kelly Clark didn't like the
detective's questions any more than his demeanor.

"You know he's dangerous," the detective added. "You really ought to steer clear of him."

As he left, the detective asked if she would come to the police
station so he could take a written statement.

"I have classes," she said.

"Will you call us when you can?"

"Yeah, I can do that."

"Call us in three or four days and let us know when you can
come in."

"Sure."

She was being less than honest. She was just trying to pacify
him so she could get him out the door.

4

The same day he found Kelly Clark, Jim Stadfeld dropped in
on the neighbor Barbara Elgutaa had identified only as
"Joanne." Jim Stadfeld knew Joanne Karaba, and the Karaba
farmhouse, located not a mile west of the King place on Divi-

sion Drive. Joanne and her husband Mark were separated, but still friendly. Stadfeld knew Mark. There were few people Jim Stadfeld didn't know around Marshall, Michigan.

Joanne Karaba was a wistful, creative, young woman. She filled her house with primitive antiques and a wide array of her crafts. She'd framed mirrors with woodlawn moss, blue salvia, and white delphinium. She made settings of bird nests and crafted hearts out of antique barbwire. Lilac, sea lavender, and other dried flowers were everywhere. Her farmhouse smelled of the potpourri she sold at craft shows.

They struck up a friendship in the late summer, Joanne said. She suggested Diane might try a home craft business and a herb farm if she left the TV station. They talked of going into business together. Joanne liked Diane's enthusiasm, her creative eye.

"Something between us just clicked," she said. "I'd felt like I'd found a soul mate."

The Karabas had done nothing together with the Kings as couples, though Brad once asked her if she and Mark would like to see *Dances With Wolves* with them.

Joanne Karaba, Jim Stadfeld soon learned, had more contact with Diane King in the last days of her life than anyone they'd talked to locally. After Christmas, Diane invited her and her son to see *Disney on Ice* at Wings Arena in Kalamazoo. Joanne watched Marler as Diane emceed the show. Diane drove. Karaba parked her car at the farmhouse.

When they returned to 16240 Division, Joanne reached for her car door, but Diane grabbed her arm.

"No, don't get out!" Diane said. "Wait."

The newswoman sounded the horn, and they waited. They waited until the porch lights came on and Brad King came out the door. Diane explained that they had developed that system ever since she'd received the threatening letter.

"She didn't want me to get out of the car because she was scared," Joanne Karaba said.

On Sunday, February 3, six days before the murder, they were together again. They went to a surplus food auction in Battle Creek, returning to the farmhouse around 6 P.M. Again,

Diane drove. When they pulled up in the driveway, Joanne reached for the door.

"No, wait," Diane said. Again, they waited for Brad.

Jim Stadfeld had heard Freida Newton's story about the security measures. Now they had it in place days before the murder, and at twilight at that.

Joanne Karaba reinforced other reports. The Kings were in counseling. It had become a sexless marriage. Diane said Brad was upset that he'd have to get a full-time job and wouldn't be able to get his PhD.

On February 4, five days before the murder, she'd seen both of them, Joanne continued. She baby-sat Marler while the couple attended a planning meeting for Kateri's christening. Returning, they both looked upset, as if they had been crying. Joanne felt uneasy about Brad, the way he was walking around her house looking at things as she talked with Diane in the living room.

"It was like he was snooping," she said.

Joanne also saw Diane on that Wednesday, the day before she left for Sterling Heights. She dropped by the farmhouse to help her with a basket she was making. Diane was sitting at the dining room table. Brad was sitting in the living room, holding Kateri over his shoulder. The baby was crying. Loudly.

Diane never stopped talking.

Brad was bouncing the child, glaring at her over Kateri's shoulder, she said.

"If looks could kill," she would say later. "I would have had it. He just didn't want me there. I knew there were things going on because it was just thick in there. That house. Very thick. I mean you could just feel it. The tension."

Unnerved, she had looked for a graceful exit.

"Let's get together on Friday," Joanne had suggested. "We're making Valentine's Day cookies."

Brad had walked in from the living room.

"We're not going to be here," he'd said, coldly.

In light of his seeming dislike of her, Joanne considered his behavior after the funeral Mass quite odd. He gave her a big warm hug in the receiving line.

When they finished the interview, they walked out through an enclosed side porch. Jim Stadfeld happened to turn to his right, noticing an open door in an antique cabinet. A clear blue plastic box sat at eye-level on the edge of its shelf. It was a plastic box of .22 ammunition. They were CCI Stingers.

"Are these Mark's shells?" Stadfeld asked.

Joanne nodded.

"Kind of a funny place to leave them, in the open here, isn't it?"

"Oh, that latch is broken. It always swings open."

They looked at each other momentarily.

"Any of them missing?" he asked.

Channel 41 bookkeeper Nancy Gwynn knew she had to do something. She knew Mark Crawford was right when he suggested she really ought to contact the police. She was interviewed by Jack Schoder on February 21.

Since the funeral, she'd cried every day at 8:40 A.M., the time Diane King always dropped by her office, the time she took her break over coffee and cookies Nancy baked. Nancy knew she'd become Diane's surrogate mother at the station. After seventeen years with WUHQ, she ought to be somebody's mother there.

"Diane wasn't what people thought she was," she'd later recall. "Diane was really a scared little girl. And all she wanted was for people to accept her. She wanted her family to accept her, and she wanted to be good at what she did."

Recent months had brought uncertainty for everyone. The station was going to be sold in June, executives were saying. Everyone was considering other jobs, but Diane seemed to have more troubles than most.

"She was having an awful tough time making ends meet," Nancy would explain. "And, Brad just didn't seem to understand. Brad just wanted more and more and more. He wanted money to do this and money to do that. He wanted money for clothes. He wanted money to go back to school."

Twice the IRS had started garnishment. Twice Diane had called the revenuers and promised payments to stop it. She told

Nancy she'd given Brad money for installments, but he'd failed to send it in.

They talked a lot about her marriage. She guessed Diane opened up because Nancy told her how her own husband left for work one day years ago and never came back. He walked out on twenty years of marriage and three children. She found him living in Otsego eight years later when her lawyer filed to have him declared legally dead.

She'd seen Diane the Thursday morning before her murder.

"You know I love you," Diane told her. "You're so special to me."

Nancy started to cry. "Oh, Diane, don't do that to me. That's just what my husband said before he left."

Diane had done her share of bawling in her office, week after week, it seemed, ever since she became pregnant with Kateri. Brad wanted her to abort the baby, Diane said. He never really wanted Marler, either, she added. Their marriage seemed to take a turn for the worse with the introduction of kids.

No, the man didn't like children, Nancy decided. She remembered when Brad dropped off Marler and Kateri at her house to baby-sit on Saturday night so he and Diane could see *Dances With Wolves*. He just laid the baby on the floor. Marler ran to Nancy crying.

Diane told her recently that Brad was losing his temper with Marler, slapping him around some. She knew he'd lost his temper with Diane. She showed Nancy bruise marks shaped like his fingers on her arms.

"He shook me so hard it rattled my teeth," Diane said.

Brad had hit her in the stomach days before Kateri was born, Diane also said. He knew not to hit her where anyone could see, she said. She reported he'd say to her when he got so out of sorts: "I'm going to kill you. I swear to God."

Brad King was a man who fed on attention, Nancy Gwynn decided. "He wanted her to pay attention to him all the time," she'd later say. "At parties, or get-togethers, or anything, he wanted to be the center of attention. And of course he wasn't. Diane was. Diane told me they argued about this all the time."

That was his problem with kids, Nancy figured. Kids required attention, just to get along from day to day. That was attention Brad wasn't getting.

"Diane told me he always wanted the kids in bed, away from them," she would later recall. "He wanted to be able to have a dinner in front of the fireplace. Or a candlelight dinner. He wanted to be able to make love to her in that way. 'I tried it,' Diane said. 'But Kateri cries. Marler needs attention.'"

And when they got down to it, Brad didn't want to make love, anyway, Diane kept saying week after week.

But Diane appeared to keep trying. They went into counseling. She tried to find more time alone for them. She proposed a number of different career changes. She thought she could work it out by staying home with the kids, but he didn't want that, she said.

"No matter what I try, it's not good enough," she said.

Nancy decided he was just plain possessive. He didn't like her friends. She knew she wasn't liked. When she called during Diane's two-month maternity leave, he always said she was busy.

That summer, everyone noticed Brad's behavior at Nancy's daughter's pool party. He retired to the background, as Diane entertained people in the center of things.

"He constantly was watching her," she later recalled. "My brother-in-law tried to talk to him and he didn't even answer. He just sat there and stared at her."

When Diane returned to work at the station in January, she told Nancy Gwynn that she suspected Brad was the letter writer. She suspected he'd faked the break-in at the farmhouse as well.

"I know it's Brad, he's trying to scare me," Diane said. "He's trying to get me in line."

The week before her death, Diane was talking about attending a party that Virginia Colvin, the general manager's wife, was throwing at the Colvins' house. She'd leave the kids at her mother's, she said.

The Thursday before the killing, their last morning break together, Diane had an especially hard cry.

"I just can't do it anymore, Nancy," Diane told her. "I'm done. I've tried everything I could try. I've tried to talk to him. I've tried to make him understand that the children are part of our lives. I've tried counseling. I can't live this way. I can't live in a closet. I can't live in a glass house."

Diane King told her she was going to contact an attorney. She wanted to get a divorce. But Nancy Gwynn had heard about lawyers and divorce back in December as well.

"I think you're going to have to do something," Nancy Gwynn told her back then.

"I know, Nancy, because, you know, I really think he wants to kill me," she said.

They seized more material with search warrants, talked to more people who knew the couple, and found more evidence of trouble at the place called Thunderspirit.

After interviewing Nancy Gwynn, Jack Schoder reached Diane's balloonist friend, Theresa Nisley, in Grand Junction. Nisley said she was Diane's labor coach for Marler's birth. They'd spent twelve hours huffing and puffing, only to have the baby be taken by cesarian at seven in the morning. Brad, she said, slept in a nearby chair.

"He didn't seem to give a damn that she was miserable," she told Schoder. "It just didn't seem right. It didn't seem what a husband should be doing."

Theresa had talked to Diane three weeks before her murder. Diane also reported to Nisley she'd been hit in the stomach. She'd also given Brad an ultimatum: "Get a full-time job, Brad, or get out of the house." She'd heard essentially the same thing during a call from Diane in December. Diane King was threatening to leave her husband.

But then Theresa offered some perspective, some context. Diane was threatening to leave Brad years ago when they lived in Grand Junction. It was the job issue then, too.

"She could be very difficult to live with, especially when she was pregnant," Nisley said. "She could drive a person crazy, in fact."

* * *

On February 22, the detectives secured the telephone records for 16240 Division Drive and for the Newtons' home on St. Joseph Street in Sterling Heights. The same day, Jim Stadfeld served a search warrant at the Pontiac Police Department for King's personnel file.

Schoder continued interviewing people who worked with Diane King at the TV station. A director named Larry Mahana said Brad King had been in the station on February 19, cleaning out Diane's desk. The director said he brought up the subject of Diane's life insurance, but Brad seemed disinterested, he said. Mahana asked King if he'd had much contact with police. King said no.

"They have a job to do," King said. "I hope they do it."

Schoder interviewed a station receptionist named Rita Gillson, who handled Diane King's phone calls. She remembered the persistent caller. She described his voice as that of a white male who talked in emotionless, quiet tones. She said she knew Brad King's voice. It was dissimilar, she said.

Schoder also interviewed an eighteen-year-old former intern named Kristina Mony. She said she'd developed a close friendship with Diane King and done some baby-sitting for her. She, too, spoke of marital conflict, Diane worrying about Brad's sexual apathy, his failure to stay gainfully employed.

Kristina Mony said she sensed conflict around a book she'd loaned the anchor: *Secrets About Men Every Woman Should Know*, a self-help best-seller by Barbara DeAngelis. Kristina had called Diane the week before her murder, asking for it. Brad had hidden it in the attic, she said.

Kristina also knew about the caller. She said Diane had told her they were keeping a "loaded gun" in the house, something that bothered her because of the children.

Kristina Mony added that Diane had told her that the stalker wasn't the first time she ever felt threatened as a TV reporter. She was worried about professional killers in Colorado, to the point of once planning to send Marler home to her mother's, Diane had told her.

"Why would someone want to kill her in Colorado?" Schoder asked.

Mony had only heard sketchy details. "She said it was ove a story on drug dealers she was going to do."

5

Later that day, Jack Schoder drove to a Holiday Inn nea Detroit Metropolitan Airport to interview Randy Wright Wright was cooperative and straightforward, but also suppor ive of his old friend.

They had a wide-ranging discussion. Wright gave the detec tive a detailed summary of what they had done in the hours an days after the murder. Schoder asked Wright about thei whereabouts on the property that weekend, about getting th Jeep Wagoneer stuck. Wright said they had not walked nea where the gun was found.

Wright talked about their long friendship, Brad's quiet per sonality, the various members of his family. They discusse guns. Wright hadn't been to the farmhouse until the murder, s he hadn't seen any guns there. He remembered an old gu cabinet Brad's father gave him fifteen years ago. He though Brad had several guns back then.

Randy Wright said he knew of some marital tension, but h felt it was nothing the couple couldn't handle. He certainl hadn't heard anything about a divorce, he said. Brad ha always subjugated his career plans to Diane's. Brad had alway been supportive of what she wanted to do. But Brad did lov teaching at Western, he added, and wanted to do it one da full-time.

"Did he share with you how they were doing financially?" Schoder asked.

"No, but I guessed they had some difficulty," Wright said. "But it was nothing obvious."

Brad losing his job at the probation department had probably caused some strain, Wright offered. In fact, Wright had referred the matter to his friend, an attorney in Kalamazoo.

"I think he's talking some legal action," he said.

Randy Wright wasn't the only one who heard Brad King was suing the Tenth District Court. Diane King had told quite a few people about it at the TV station, including Larry Mahana. Later, Mahana detailed what he knew.

"She initially told me Brad had been fired unjustly. Some sort of conflict with personalities with his boss. She felt that was completely unjust. Because of that they were going to put together this enormous package and sue them.

"I don't know the particulars as far as the lawsuit goes. All I know is they did get a lot of paperwork together because she went through volumes and volumes of stuff and Xeroxed it at the station. Some of it was sent in from other places. She was actually compiling this stuff for him. Evidence for some sort of lawsuit. I'm not sure what the hell she was compiling.

"In any case, she seemed to think they had a real good case. She thought there was no question at all that they would sue these people and this would be their lucky break. They wouldn't need the fellowship after all (for Two Worlds Productions) because they're going to get the money from the county.

"She was obviously calling around to get copies of whatever information she was piling up. She was doing a fair amount of legwork. She was consumed by it. There were things that really needed to be done around the newsroom, but this other little project came first. It went on fairly hot and heavy for a few weeks in the summer, then seemed to drop off."

Larry Mahana talked to Brad King about the lawsuit a week prior to Diane's death.

"I asked him every time I saw him, practically, at that point, when he came into the office. I knew he was involved in it. I knew he certainly wasn't employed, so I figured maybe this was his main thing. I asked him what's going on, if he was making any headway . . . he said things were going fine."

On Monday, February 25, Jack Schoder served another search warrant, this one at the Hall of Justice in Battle Creek. The two-story building across from the Battle Creek Police Department was the home of circuit and district benches and the home of King's former employer, the Probation Department for the Tenth District Court.

Schoder talked to Billy Joe Patterson, the chief probation officer. Patterson and King's work records obtained under the warrant told a story of squandered opportunity and outright fraud.

Brad King joined the department in October of 1989 after working six months at the Calhoun County Mental Health Department where he monitored foster homes for developmentally disabled clients. Program Administrator John R. Seita gave him a "satisfactory" review there. King fell in the middle of a five-category rating system that ranged from unsatisfactory to outstanding. Seita wrote:

"Brad's strengths include client advocacy, organizational activities, following through on assignments and sound clinical judgement. There are no major areas of concern with Brad's performance."

When the Tenth District Court created an intensive probation program for drunk drivers, it hired King, based on his police background and mental health experience in Colorado. King's job was to make unannounced visits to sentenced drunk drivers, giving them Breathalyzer tests and checking they were honoring court-imposed curfews. The program provided King with a Ford Tempo and a cellular phone.

On January 9, 1990, after King had been on the job only nine weeks, Michelle Hill, another probation officer, reported to Patterson that she'd received a call from one of King's probationers. The probationer said he hadn't seen King since before Christmas and was worried he'd be violated if he didn't see a probation officer soon.

Patterson checked a contact log probation officers submitted to document their work. King's log showed he'd been visiting the probationer "on a regular basis," Patterson wrote in his own report. Patterson asked another officer to get King's most recent contact log from his desk. The sheets showed seven contacts with the probationer, including curfew checks and Breathalyzer tests. King even put in for two-hours overtime for one visit.

Billy Joe Patterson decided to call the probationer himself.

The probationer reported he'd only received a phone call from King, who said he planned on stopping by, but might not because he had a cold.

"He never showed up," he said.

Later, Patterson asked another probation officer, Bruce Mueller, a former police officer, to investigate King's caseload and interview his clients. Mueller's report was also in King's personnel file. It showed King had only four clients. Three of them reported discrepancies with King's contact log.

Mueller also looked into King's time sheets and travels. Despite the small caseload and questionable schedule, King was billing the county thirteen hours a week in overtime, the maximum allowed. He'd put more than five thousand miles on the car in two months.

Court officials later barred probation department employees from talking publicly about Bradford King. But among themselves, they found much to talk about. They remembered him announcing that he was selling his own car when he got the county Tempo. He talked about the personal trips he made with the work car to Detroit. He arrived at work with a baby seat in the back.

"You don't get into this business to make a killing," one probation officer later recalled. "But with him you would have thought he'd landed a big executive's job. He had no idea what he was doing there, nor did he ask any questions. He was just a wild cannon on the loose, and he had an insatiable appetite for bucks."

Some officials suspected outright theft. After he was hired, $500 turned up missing from probation officer Michelle Hill's desk. She'd been saving money out of each pay check for a

Chicago shopping spree and putting it in an unmarked white envelope. She'd concealed the cash envelope in a package of fifty unmarked white envelopes in her desk.

Hill knew of only two people who'd seen her do this, she later told fellow workers, Brad King and a longtime, trusted employee.

One morning, staff found a half dozen of their desks jimmied open. Hill's money was missing out of one desk, a jar of pennies out of another. Money hidden in other desks was left behind. It was as if somebody hit the other desks to camouflage the core crime. King had been issued a passkey to the building and court offices. Police believed the theft occurred in the evening hours.

"He was the one who had the opportunity and the foreknowledge," one court worker later recalled. "In fact, the factors somewhat parallel the murder of his own wife."

On the morning of January 11, 1990, the court administrator confronted Brad King with the log discrepancies, then promptly fired him. A couple days later, King appealed to the judge who had hired him, but to no avail. After he was dismissed, one probationer complained that King had tried to shake him down.

"I want to see $20 in my hand every time you see me," he reported King saying.

One fellow staffer later remembered Brad King cleaning out his desk minutes after his dismissal. "You know, Brad never got upset over anything, over life events, over problems. You'd think getting fired would be a big event, wouldn't you? Nothing, man. It was just like it was any other day."

By the end of February, the Calhoun County detectives were wondering what it was going to take to get an arrest warrant from prosecutor Jon Sahli. They felt they already had put together a compelling circumstantial case. They'd firmed up the crime scene with the laser work and field tests.

As for motive, the detectives offered a couple of possibilities. They'd found a company life insurance policy on Diane King at the TV station. The payoff, with double indemnity, would have been $54,000. Clearly, there was trouble in the King marriage. After finding student Kelly Clark, both detectives figured the prosecutor would favor an arrest.

Jon Sahli was unmoved. He didn't think a jury would consider $54,000 a high enough motivation for murder. He argued that Kelly Clark could be considered a fling. Obviously, she wasn't in love with him. She wasn't demanding he leave Diane.

"Just because somebody is cheating," Sahli said, "doesn't mean they're guilty of murder. Hell, we'd have to arrest a good number of the people in Calhoun County if that were the case."

"Jon, what do you need?" Stadfeld said. "Just tell us what we need to get a warrant."

"Just keep going," Sahli said. "I'll know when you get it."

It became a regular exchange. They would hear it again and again in the days ahead.

They never expected the weeks to turn into months.

6

When Freida Newton heard her son-in-law was ceremoniously giving away Diane's personal belongings she was upset, but she still counted her blessings as the family waited for an arrest they expected any day now. She had Diane's most prized possessions. She had Marler and Kateri, and she was looking for ways to keep the kids.

Three days after the ten-day feast, Brad King had shown up at the Newtons' door to pick up the children. Freida began crying. Royal Newton made a plea.

"Brad, you know those kids are all she's got of Diane now. Why don't you let them stay another week, just to help Ma along, okay?"

King agreed. He visited for an hour with the kids, then left.

Later that week, the Newtons met with an attorney named Rudolph A. Wartella, a Native American lawyer familiar with the federal legislation called the Indian Child Welfare Act. The Newtons told him they were desperate. Detectives were promising an arrest, they told Wartella, but they were worried about the children's safety should King get them before he was jailed. They were considering fleeing with the children to the Mohawk reservation at Kahnawake. Royal Newton still had his Canadian citizenship. Brad King would have to run a gamut of international law to get them back.

Wartella suggested trying for temporary guardianship. The Indian Child Welfare Act called for Indian children subject to foster care or adoption to be placed with members of the extended family, particularly those of the child's tribe. But the Michigan law also was clear, he said. Brad King's guardianship couldn't be terminated just because he was a suspect. He had to be arrested.

The attorney spoke several times with the Calhoun County Sheriff's Department.

"I was led to believe an arrest was imminent," Wartella later said.

Wartella prepared a petition to the Macomb County Probate Court. He asked the family be named temporary guardians and conservators, which would also give the Newtons control over the small trust established at Channel 41. Wartella was trying to buy the family time. He decided that if he could get a temporary guardianship order, King would probably be behind bars by the time a full hearing was held.

On February 28, the court granted temporary guardianship based on Wartella's paperwork and set a full hearing for April 10.

Brad King found out about the move when he called to say he'd be picking up the children. Royal Newton told him he couldn't have them, and he had the paperwork to back it up.

"You son of a bitch," King said.

They had six weeks until the full hearing, but Wartella's plan was based on one important assumption.

"I figured by the time he was given notice and prepared a response they'd have from one to two months," Wartella later recalled. "I figured it would take him some time to find a good attorney to do that."

Denise Verrier didn't feel her niece and nephew were in any danger with her brother-in-law. "I really wasn't worried about him hurting the kids," she later said. "I figured he had already accomplished what he wanted to do."

Brad King had killed her sister, she now believed. As for why, she dared not guess. If Brad wanted to harm the children, she decided, he would have done it at twilight on Saturday, February 9.

As she learned sketchy details of the police investigation, Denise became suspicious of everything her brother-in-law had done in recent months and curious about everything Diane had said. Diane visited her several times alone with the kids in recent months, but she also knew her sister always put the best face she could on her life.

It was an odd estrangement, considering what they'd been through together. They shared painful family secrets, back when they were kids, back when Royal was drinking. They could predict the night when the folks came home past bar closing. They lay side by side at the top of the stairs, listening to the escalating voices, then the fighting. The confrontations were often violent. They shared the memories of the police cars that idled in their driveway in the darkest hours of the night.

Together, they begged their mother to leave him.

"He's as good as gold when he's not drinking," she would always say.

No wonder Diane clamored for knowledge of her real father, Denise thought. No wonder she worked to be so different from what they had. And of all people, Diane had married a policeman. She'd married one of the saviors of the night.

Denise Verrier had found her savior in the Lord. Unlike Diane, she did not suffer from crying spells and fits of deep depression. Unlike Diane, she did not imagine the family persecuting her. She didn't need all the attention Diane did.

But her sister had also changed since she'd returned from Denver. They used to argue; Diane for the right to choose,

Denise for the right to life. Diane used to tout her career, Denise her children. But recently, they'd become closer in motherhood.

"You know, I never appreciated what you do until I had Marler," Diane had told her. "You know, you've really become one of my heroes."

In recent months Diane was spending more time with her, visiting more often alone. Without Brad, they had more time to talk, more time to explore old memories and work on creating new ones. Together, they were beginning to understand. Denise had learned about co-dependency on Christian radio stations. Diane was reading books, and talked about Adult Children of Alcoholics and the Cinderella complex, the craving to transform a girl of ashes into a princess.

They were becoming real sisters again. It wasn't all serious, either. They chattered mindlessly and did crafts together, laughing at good times and the bad. One night they laughed themselves silly at the absurdity of their complaints about weight gain as they stuffed themselves with a big bag of M&Ms.

Diane was spending more time with the entire family, in fact, accepting all of them more for what they were. Together, they may argue and have their problems and not be Yuppie perfect, but they were a *family*. They were there for each other when they needed to be. Judging from what she saw and knew of Brad King's family, they were there for each other more than his family ever had been.

Still, Diane wanted everyone to think her life was perfect. She glossed over financial problems Denise suspected. She stuffed her frustrations with Brad. She wanted the family so much to like him. Diane had only said she wished her husband would grow up.

She complained she was jealous of his first wife. "I'm jealous," she once said. "Gail got all his responsible years."

The only real trouble they heard about came after the children were born. "You know, sometimes I feel just like taking Marler and raising him on my own," she told their mother days after his birth. "The last thing I want is a divorce, but that's exactly what I feel like doing."

Denise suspected trouble after Kateri's birth. She remembered when Diane spent the night in December, around the eleventh or twelfth, she thought. She remembered Brad phoning to say somebody had been prowling around the house. He suggested she spend another night with Denise.

His behavior just didn't make sense. Brad told Diane he'd heard footsteps on the porch in the middle of the night and patrolled the property with a gun. Yet, Diane had called him a couple of times in the early morning, but got only their answering machine. He said he was there, but hadn't heard the call.

"He can't hear the phone, but he hears footsteps?" Denise later confided in her husband. "I'm thinking, affair."

She never voiced her suspicions to her sister, though. Infidelity. Abuse. Deceit. Denise knew Diane would never talk about things like that.

Diane always talked about plans. On the Thursday before she was killed, she told Denise she was going to quit Channel 41 in June to stay home with the kids.

"What does Brad think about that?" Denise asked.

"He's not too happy," she said. "He likes being a celebrity."

On February 22, Detective Jim Stadfeld came to see her to interview her formally for the first time. She tried to remember the dates her sister visited, the day of the break-in. Everything was very fresh in her mind. She felt like she talked forever.

"I told him tons of stuff," she later said.

On a cold evening in early March, Brad King stopped by to see Allen Marler and his girlfriend Nancy Rapo at her home in one of Detroit's northern suburbs. He wanted to give her boxes of Diane's clothes.

Rapo, a mortgage banker, and Diane had been friends. She'd noticed a major change in Diane before her death. "I'd really become part of the family," she later explained. "Diane was ecstatic because there was going to be another professional woman in the family. She felt she was looked upon negatively by her mother because she chose a career and not to be a full-time mother like Denise. It was very difficult for her. She'd told me that her mother and her did not have the best relationship. Toward the end, though, Diane had tried to become a lot more like Denise with the home things, the farmhouse, the crafts. I think that was a part of her wanting to fulfill that connection with her mother. Diane was trying to find her place in life, to fit in, to have a purpose, to be the right one in everybody's eyes."

And it didn't take long before Frieda's name came up during Brad's visit. The next day, Nancy booted up her PC and composed an account of what happened. She sent it to Jack Schoder, telling him in the cover letter, "I hope the attached information helps in some way, even if it is minute."

It read:

Brad came by around 6:15 from Randy (Wright's) place in Birmingham. When he came, Allen asked him how he was doing and Brad started right away about Freida taking those kids. You could tell he was agitated about the situation. He said, "I'll get those kids back. There isn't a judge around who won't give me custody of those kids. The courts want them to be with their father. I'm not worried. I'll get those kids back." He said he was very upset and mad . . . Brad and Allen talked a bit about Freida and the kids. Allen was trying to play along with Brad and told him he was surprised his mom did what she did, that sometimes she pulls weird stuff on him, too.

I think Brad was really trying to get a feel for how Al and I were reacting to the situation over the custody. He insisted if he knew Freida was going to do this custody thing he would have taken the kids back the first Friday he came down and that he didn't trust Freida anymore (he said he promised her the kids would not be kept from their grandma and knowing who their aunts and uncles were).

I really got the feeling the whole custody thing was more of a nuisance to Brad then just a matter of a father being upset and hurt his kids were being "taken away" from him. Brad acts so strange, almost robotic. I definitely *did not* get the feeling of genuine concern for those kids.

Allen changed the subject by saying, "hopefully things will calm down once the police catch the person and we can go on." This was where Brad's mannerisms changed. He became very smug and said:

"They won't catch him. It's been four weeks and they have nothing. They won't catch him. I wouldn't be surprised if these guys have never investigated a murder before, they are just small time police. They won't catch him, only if he kills again or gets drunk and shoots off at the mouth."

Brad was very smug when he said that, especially when he said only if he kills again. His words hit like a brick wall. It was a very eerie feeling. There was a definite smugness about him, almost a smirk to his face and *proud*. Yes, that's a good word to describe how Brad was acting when he was talking about them never catching the guy. There was no mistaking, he was not acting like a man whose wife was just murdered, and he was torn because there are no leads and the murderer is still running loose. It was like a game to him.

I carried on and said, "Yes, it's not like the city of Detroit, where they have murders going on all the time. Small towns don't have these things very often. In Detroit, you don't even hear about half the murders that go on."

Brad went on to say, "When I was with the Pontiac force, I investigated about seven homicides. These guys don't know what they are doing. They aren't really interviewing people. They only talked to me once that following Monday."

I said, "You mean they only talked to you that first week and after that they stopped?"

Brad replied, "No, they talked to me one time, the Monday after the murder and haven't talked to me since."

I asked about his brother, Scott, and said how much I liked him. Brad mentioned he and Scott had never been close growing up. Then somehow we got on the subject of Mackinac Island and how pretty it was. Al said he'd never been there before and Brad talked about how he used to go up there all the time when he was growing up. The mood became much lighter and it was as if we were just getting together to sit and talk about pleasant things. Brad was much more relaxed and we were even laughing.

It was about 7:10 when Brad said he'd better get going. We went outside to help him with the boxes of Diane's things. He said her coats were packed away behind boxes and that he would get to them soon, that this was temporary until he could get a place on his own. We said goodbye and he left.

It was much easier for me to hide my feelings then [sic] for

Allen. At first Al was having a hard time sitting there with Brad. Brad looked at me probably ninety percent of the time and I really got the impression he was trying to get a feel for the situation. His actions and mannerisms did not come across in any way as someone who had just suffered a loss. He seems very calculating and smug about the whole situation. I have to tell you though, there are times when it seems like he has you fooled, like you have to say, could he really have done this? But then his smugness and coldness shows through and I have to believe that no man who had nothing to do with the death of his wife could be so stone cold.

More than a month after the murder, and still unable to secure an arrest warrant, Jack Schoder and Jim Stadfeld needed some kind of motivation, some kind of lift.

Schoder showed Nancy Rapo's letter to Jim Stadfeld.

"He's saying we're small-time," Schoder said.

Jim Stadfeld addressed King's personage.

"Okay, asshole," he said. "We'll just see about that."

7

Like others, Joanne Karaba had based Bradford King's guilt solely on his demeanor. The Monday morning after the murder, she'd dropped by Thunderspirit to drop off food.

She broke into tears when she first saw him. "Oh, Brad, is there anything I can do?"

He stood slump shouldered, shaking his head.

"You know, I talked to the police," she said.

"Oh, what did you tell them?" he asked.

She had been looking out her window late in the day of the murder, she said. She saw an old cream-colored Oldsmobile parked on the other side of I-69, near the long driveway that led to a pipeline pumping station and a couple of fishing and swimming holes called Zinn and Crystal lakes, a half mile from the King farmhouse.

"I told them about that car," she said. "I'd never seen it before."

Joanne Karaba later described what happened. "Brad's posture and everything changed. When I described the car he got all chipper. A smile came on his face.

"He said, 'Oh, yeah? Really? Oh, they didn't tell me about *that*.'

"I knew he did it right then. I knew he did it because he was so relieved. It wasn't the kind of excitement where he was saying, *good maybe they're gonna get this guy*. It was like, *good, they're going to be thrown off*. When I walked out of there, I was so upset I could hardly walk."

She was no less disturbed when Jim Stadfeld had asked her about the ammunition in the cabinet on her porch. My God, she thought, my girlfriend may have been killed with bullets stolen from my house.

When the detective left, she sped up to K mart where her husband Mark worked and told him all about the detective's visit.

"He wanted to know about your .22s," she told him.

"Why?" Mark Karaba asked.

"Well, he wanted to know if you had any shells missing or anything."

The coincidence stunned him momentarily.

"As a matter of fact, I do," he said.

On March 8, Jack Schoder met Mark Karaba to take his statement. Karaba said he'd used some of the CCI Stingers for rabbit hunting a month before Diane's death, then left the remainder in the cabinet with the broken latch. On February 17, he said, he picked up the shells again to go hunting and noticed he was missing some bullets, though he couldn't specify how many. He asked his son, Josh, wondering if he'd been using his bullets. Josh said he had not. He had no reason to disbelieve the boy. Josh had standing permission to use the gun and ammunition any time he wanted.

Nineteen days had passed since Jim Stadfeld noticed the blue box, deciding that day to leave it where it sat. Now, Jack Schoder took it into evidence and printed Mark Karaba for elimination prints. He sent the box and the prints to a Battle Creek crime lab.

He also sent Brad King's.

That same week, Jon Olson produced the Model 511 Remington Scoremaster for the newspapers and TV cameras. Posing with the gun, the sheriff asked for the public's help for information about the weapon and its possible sale to a suspect.

"Identifying the purchaser is a critical part of our investigation," he told reporters.

Olson's tune had changed. No longer was he promising an arrest. He put the matter squarely into Jon Sahli's court. A warrant would be issued, he said, only when the prosecutor was comfortable with the evidence.

Olson dispensed details about the gun, but only those that might help trace it. He "believed" it was the murder weapon, he said, but wouldn't pinpoint where it was found. He pointed out the rifle had no serial numbers. Remington didn't stamp on serial numbers on the Model 511 until 1968, which meant the gun was at least that old. Olson also said he believed the weapon was obtained outside of Michigan, but asked anyone who sold that type of rifle in recent years to contact investigators.

"What about a suspect?" one reporter asked. "Do you still have a suspect?"

Yes, the department had a suspect, he said.

"Aren't you worried he might flee?" another asked.

No, Olson said.

"The suspect is closely tied to the community," the sheriff added. "I feel this will be enough to keep him from running."

One Channel 41 staffer following the coverage on TV and in the papers was a promotion assistant and part-time news director named Steve Callens. The sheriff's comments made him recall a conversation he had with Diane Newton King in the cut room in October. He and Diane were putting together a news report about an estranged husband who stalked his wife, shot her to death, then committed suicide in a bank parking lot in Battle Creek. Callens, a former Arizona resident, mentioned to Diane that in Arizona anyone could carry a weapon in plain view.

"And there's less violent crime there," he said. "But it's a good thing I don't have a gun in my house. My wife would have used it on me a long time ago."

He remembered Diane King's reply. He remembered it very clearly now.

She said, "Well, the only weapon we have in our house is an old gun that Brad's father gave him."

"You mean like an old double-barrel shotgun?" he asked.

"No," she said. "Just an old .22 rifle."

Steve Callens figured he'd better tell the story to the police.

Their winter cruise through the Panama Canal couldn't have come at a better time, Tom Darling decided. They left for Jamaica on February 22, the day before the ground war started in the Gulf and just as reporters started calling the house. When they returned a week later, the war was over. They were surprised the same couldn't be said for the King case. Based on Jim Stadfeld's comments to Sue about an imminent arrest, they figured something must have gone seriously wrong.

Tom Darling had not seen Brad King since he asked him to plow snow from his driveway the week of the funeral. Darling's tractor wouldn't start. He had to drag a 150-pound diesel battery from the barn for recharging.

Tom Darling soon would find himself carrying far heavier loads.

On March 4, Jim Stadfeld interviewed both Tom and Sue in the loft office of the Darling & Sons True Value Hardware. They detailed their friendship with the Kings. They detailed their trip to the church camp the weekend of the murder. Tom told the detective how he pulled Brad's Wagoneer out of the field on the Monday following the murder.

"Did he ever purchase any .22 caliber ammunition here?" Stadfeld asked.

"Not that I can recall."

Stadfeld mentioned the CCI Stinger brand.

"We don't even carry those," Darling said.

A few days after that interview, Tom Darling saw a picture of Jon Olson and the Remington Model 511 Scoremaster in the news coverage somewhere. Something was familiar about that gun, he thought. How did he know Brad King had a .22? They went rabbit hunting in the fall together. As he recalled, they talked about whether Brad would use a shotgun or a .22.

No, Brad brought his shotgun. Then, Tom Darling remembered more.

"Three or four days had gone by," Darling would later recall, "and finally I just said, I think I have to call the police. I said, I can't be positive, but I think I've seen that gun in the King home."

On March 14, he called up Jim Stadfeld and told him just that, but he included an amendment. He told the detective, "But if you put me on the stand and say, 'Is that the gun you've seen in their house?' Jim, I'm gonna say I can't be positive."

However, Tom Darling was clear on one point. He recalled both Brad and Diane King coming into the store in the fall, wanting a live animal trap. Brad said they had a woodchuck rummaging through their garbage. Darling knew that landlord Frank Zinn didn't allow hunting on Thunderspirit, but he made a suggestion anyway.

"It would be very easy to take care of your woodchuck by shooting it with a .22," he told the Kings.

He offered Brad his own .22 rifle.

"No, I can't do that," Brad said. "If it comes to that, I'll just use my own."

"Tom, is there anybody else that heard that conversation?" Jim Stadfeld asked.

Tom Darling didn't know. He'd have to check around his store.

* * *

Through March and into April, the detectives worked the gun and the timing of the killing. Some advances came from legwork. Some came from just plain luck.

Zinnland neighbor Doug Nielsen called the Calhoun County Sheriff's Department. He'd let a month pass, but wanted to lodge a complaint about being misled by a deputy at the foot of the King driveway the night of the murder. He didn't think the deputy should have advised him he could leave his children home alone.

Jack Schoder got on the phone.

The deputy was irresponsible, Nielsen continued, considering the way he and others had been watching the neighborhood because of break-ins. In fact, he told Schoder, by watching he'd seen the silhouette of Diane King's Jeep Wagoneer parked in the driveway just after 6:40 P.M. He wouldn't have been able to see Diane King's body from his angle on Division Drive.

"How do you know that's what time it was?" Schoder asked.

"Well, you look at the clock when you order pizza," he said.

Now they had the car in the driveway at a definite time.

Yards west of Nielsen, another neighbor was watching her clock. Tonya Scott and her mother Elsie were moving the day of the murder. As she loaded a pickup, Tonya heard two shots. When news accounts made her realize she'd likely heard her neighbor being murdered, she spoke with her mother. Elsie Scott was in the house during the shooting and hadn't heard anything. But a few minutes afterwards she'd left for their new house on Old 27 and looked at her watch when she arrived there. They did some arithmetic and figured Tonya heard the shots between 6:30 and 6:35 P.M.

Brad King had called the dispatcher at 6:49 P.M. Now, investigators had an approximate twenty-minute window in which they theorized King had run the dog track and buried the gun.

Jack Schoder spent several days knocking on doors, talking to more neighbors. Neither Nielsen, the Scotts, or others had seen strange vehicles parked in the area, with one important exception. There was the cream-colored Oldsmobile Joanne Karaba had reported, the same car she said had perked up Brad King.

The detectives tried to eliminate problems, but found new

ones. The Battle Creek crime lab had dusted a fingerprint on the stalker letter, but couldn't identify it. By the end of March, they were still waiting for a set of prints from Cindy Acosta's husband, the only other person to handle the paper.

The Battle Creek PD crime lab also lifted two fingerprints from the plastic box of CCI Stingers, but blamed the sheriff's department for its failure to identify them. A technician called the prints the department supplied of Brad King and Mark Karaba inferior. "I was unable to make an identification, but would not rule out either subject, because of the poor quality of the submitted inked impressions of both subjects," his report stated.

The sheriff's news conference on the weapon generated twenty-one phone calls from people who had sold Remington Scoremasters. The detectives followed up every call, but struck out.

Jack Schoder phoned an expert at Remington Arms in Ilione, New York, seeking more information about the model. The Scoremaster Model 511 had a six-shot magazine, the expert said, plus it held one in the chamber. That was seven rounds in one loading, the same as the number of casings found in Talmadge Creek. Schoder mailed the expert a Polaroid of the gun's stampings. An "OB" on the barrel indicated the gun was made in July of 1955, the expert said. The company manufactured the rifle when Brad King was about eight and a half.

Schoder talked to a young Teke named Ken Kullman, who knew Brad King from Western. Kullman and three other brothers had helped the Kings clean Thunderspirit one weekend in January. As far as Kullman knew, no one had seen any guns.

Kullman did remember something about the week of the murder, however. Brad was at the Teke house around midnight on Thursday, February 7, he said.

That was two days before Diane King was killed.

On March 13, Jack Schoder interviewed Gail Hietzker, Brad King's first wife, who lived in a Pontiac suburb. They were married thirteen years, from 1968 until 1981. Unfamiliar with firearms, she could not put the Remington Model 511 Scoremaster into her ex-husband's possession. She only knew that Brad had "two hunting guns, maybe three." She wasn't aware that Willis King had given Brad any rifles.

Gail Hietzker did know that Willis King had kept his son well supplied in money and clothes. Gail, in fact, handled the finances when they were married, she said, because Brad King was not good with money. She also said that Brad had tapped his mother regularly for cash in recent years.

Their divorce had been largely amiable, she said. She'd asked for it, but made him file the divorce papers, she said. She didn't feel that he was capable of being fully committed to her and their daughter, Alissa. Brad was upset when she became pregnant, in fact, leaving her for six weeks. Three years after they were divorced, he went off on another odd emotional jag. He showed up at her door one day, saying he'd broken up with Diane and asked her to remarry him.

Gail Hietzker, however, said she didn't believe her ex-husband was capable of murder. He was an extremely "passive" partner, she said.

"He was never ever violent with me," she said.

While Jack Schoder worked Michigan, Jim Stadfeld flew out to Colorado, pursuing the couple's background. Former news director Mike Moran portrayed her as opinionated, aggressive, and cantankerous.

"I would think she'd be very difficult to live with," he said.

One staffer's husband recalled an elk hunting trip Brad King went on with him. King brought a high-powered rifle with a scope, but the man had no idea what other guns he owned. King dropped an elk with one shot at about one hundred yards. After the kill, he seemed cool and dispassionate.

"Most people get really excited after a kill," he said. "But that wasn't the case with Brad."

In Denver, Stadfeld interviewed people at Wackenhut Corporation, a security and private investigation firm where King worked for a year in 1985. Nobody remembered much about

King, but his handgun targets were still in his personnel file. At thirty yards, he'd put everything in a four-inch cluster.

"Man, that's damn good shooting," Stadfeld told Schoder when he got back.

In late March, Jack Schoder and Jim Stadfeld still seemed no closer to getting a warrant from Jon Sahli, so they hatched a plan. They'd ask the prosecutor for the help of his investigator, Gerry Woods. Maybe Woods had the key to Sahli's lockbox of arrest warrants.

In late March, Woods went up to the Croswell area to talk to Brad King's old high-school classmates in an effort to pin him down as the owner of the murder weapon. He came back only with stories about Brad being a teenage loner whose father lavished him with money and cars.

Still, they had tied a .22 rifle to Brad King with Steve Callens's statement, Jack Schoder figured. They had the new information from Tom Darling.

They pitched the prosecutor again.

The Callens story was inadmissible, Jon Sahli said. It would be considered hearsay under court rules. The reason: In most instances, the defense has to have the opportunity to cross-examine the source of information to determine its accuracy. Hearsay doesn't afford that opportunity.

The source, in this case, was Diane King.

"Keep going, I'll know when you get there," the prosecutor said.

It was never very clear where or how the idle talk started, but then again, the source of origin was never a requirement to run the Marshall rumor mill.

Somebody may have seen Jim Stadfeld in the loft at Darling & Sons True Value Hardware. Somebody may have noted that Tom Darling had played cards with Brad King, and that the Darlings and Kings sometimes got together for parlor games. Somebody may have heard Tom Darling complimenting Diane about her appearance on a newscast. Somebody may have wondered why Tom Darling stored his tractor in Thunderspirit's barn. Maybe that both Tom and Sue were in their second marriage inspired some of it. Maybe somebody remembered that Tom's first wife was a dark-haired Lebanese.

Some sources later would say the sheriff and the newspapers sparked the rumors, giving everyone opportunity to mull the words over in black-and-white.

The suspect "is closely tied to the community," the sheriff had said.

Some would say it was the combination of them all.

As the investigation dragged on from the chill of winter into a muddy Michigan spring, people in Marshall were talking less about Diane Newton King's widower as her killer.

They were talking about Tom Darling, the good citizen doing business on Main Street in the sweetest place on earth.

8

*N*ita Davis could hear her new classmate talking with friends halfway across the student lounge.

"And he said he was in Vietnam," Kelly Clark was saying. "But somebody's parents checked on that, and he'd never even been in the service, let alone the 82nd Airborne."

Nita Davis listened more closely, then interrupted a few seconds later.

"Excuse me. I couldn't help but overhear you. Did I hear you talking about Brad King?"

Yes, they both had him in the fall, Kelly on Thursdays for Sociology of Law Enforcement, Nita on Tuesdays for Criminology. For the winter term, Nita Davis and Kelly Clark were together in a criminal justice class taught by Thomas Edmunds, the sheriff of Kalamazoo County.

As Kelly shared more details, Nita Davis realized they had more in common than a class.

"Well, I was seeing him a little while, too," Nita admitted.

"Brad?" she asked, raising her eyebrows.

Nita nodded, embarrassed.

"Well, that doesn't surprise me," Kelly said, wryly.

Thank God, Nita Davis thought, I'm not the only one.

But, unlike young Kelly Clark, Nita Davis was thirty-two, divorced, and the mother of three. If the police wanted to stir up scandal, she had a hell of a lot more to lose.

Time and news coverage had only made everything worse. Brad King's version of his life just didn't match what the newspapers had reported. With each story she felt herself slipping deeper into some kind of sleazy police drama. Now, Nita Davis knew she was part of something much bigger than an unfortunate misjudgment of character. No matter what Brad King had said.

He had whispered in her ear when she greeted him in the receiving line after the funeral.

"We need to talk."

Instead, she avoided him when he returned to campus to teach. Then, he called her, saying he'd been urgently trying to reach her. She had unplugged her answering machine. She hadn't been home much. In fact, by then, she was contemplating leaving town.

Finally, they met among a sea of tables in the Student Center Building. Brad sat with his back to a pillar. He had a good view of everything. He thought he might be under surveillance, he said.

Right off he told Nita that he had reconciled with his wife, Diane, before her death, he said.

"We were trying to work things out."

This made no sense, Nita decided, considering what she knew. But she wasn't going to grill him about it. She was too scared for that.

She told him that she'd heard about some female students being questioned by the police.

Brad blew it off. They were unimportant.

"They don't know anything," he said.

Then, he asked, "Have the police contacted you?"

She shook her head. "And I have no desire to talk to them."

"I'd like to keep it that way," he said.

He said he was the victim of a police witch-hunt. They had singled him out because he had a lawsuit against the county. They were after him because he was married to an Indian.

"They've also come close to violating my Constitutional rights. But I'm making sure they won't do that."

There wasn't a word more about Diane. That he missed her. That her death was tragic. That he wondered who had killed her.

"They can't pin this on me," was all he said.

Back then, she was willing to go along with the silence. She didn't want to assume the role of the "Other Woman" in his sleazy drama.

"I didn't want somebody pointing the finger at me," she would later say. "I didn't do anything except make the mistake of briefly getting involved with this guy."

His clothes and authority struck Nita Davis at first. "The Emperor's New Clothes," she thought, the fable about superficiality and prestige. Brad King's twills and shirts and bulky sweaters were always color coordinated. She liked nice clothes, too. But her new instructor dressed as if his wife had read a *GQ* feature on how a college professor *should* look, a notion that made her think he was married at first.

Class opinions about him ran the gamut. Unconventional. Irreverent. A joke. A braggart. The best they ever had, some students said. The worst, said others.

Brad King went after the fatal force types, the guys who walked around with weapons magazines and military catalogues. He made them look naive with war stories from Pontiac PD, anecdotes that illustrated a hail of police gunfire never solved much of anything. But if a student wanted to learn about criminology, the sociological study of crime and criminals, a student had to read the textbook.

Brad King liked drawing attention, Nita Davis decided, and he liked shock value.

"How many people in here have ever been raped?" he asked the entire lecture hall one night.

She was one of the very few women who put up her hand. A stranger had fondled her when she was very young. But before he could get very far into the subject, she rose from her seat and left. She'd told him earlier that day she would be leaving class early that night.

"I'm a single parent," she'd explained. "One of my kids has an open house at school."

Nita Davis was in Sangren Hall two days later when she heard Brad's voice beckon her from his office.

"When you left, I almost came after you," he said. "I figured you were really upset because of the subject matter."

"No, that's not it."

He seemed compassionate, anyway. "You know you can talk to me. I know how this is. I've walked a lot of women through this."

She reminded him of the open house.

He smiled. "Oh yes, right. You know, I know what that's like, too. You see, I'm a single parent, too."

They began talking. About his son. About having custody. About his life and his farmhouse out in Marshall. Unlike Nita, who had only been divorced a year and a half, he seemed so at ease in the role.

She liked him. It was nice talking to someone with some miles. She'd not found many students her age pursuing pre-law and political science at Western Michigan. The university population was very young.

Nita Davis had a lot going for her. She was the daughter of professionals, her father a department chair at a major, prestigious university, her mother an accountant. She was an accomplished classical guitarist. She was a patient listener. She appeared more suited for an urban campus than Western. She had an affinity for the color black. The color complemented her shoulder-length, dark brown hair and her attractive, petite figure. She liked short black skirts and black nylons. Few would ever guess she had an eleven-year-old and nine-year-old twins at home.

Still, after a ten-year marriage, she was new to the world of divorcée dating. She'd heard too many jokes and horror stories about women trying to start again, especially with three children.

The next time she saw Brad King he asked her, "I was wondering if you'd maybe like to go out."

She thought about it for five seconds. They were adults.

"Sure," she said. "Why not?"

They went to Waldo's after class for a couple of beers. Canadian beer, he insisted. They talked about her music, about his years back in Pontiac. Somehow Spanish came up. He said he used to be very fluent in Spanish. He said he wasn't formally divorced yet. He was waiting for it to be finalized. She knew what those divorce delays were like.

As she got to know him, Brad King seemed like a Renaissance man. Sensitive. Liberal. Curious. He liked to cook. He knew about the rigors of homemaking. He talked about his son. How bright he was. How he verbalized way beyond his years. How he wasn't cutting his hair because he was rooting himself in his Native American culture. Brad said he, too, was part Native American.

She had no reason to doubt him. She knew that lineage didn't always show up in hair and skin color.

They were out only an hour. He didn't push himself on her. He didn't even kiss her. But he had eyes that were absolutely penetrating.

"Sometimes I feel like you're looking right through me," she would eventually tell him.

"Lots of people tell me that," he said.

The next week, he left a message with her baby-sitter. He must have found her number from his class list. He wanted to come over, he told the sitter. It was October 27, a Saturday. She remembered the date because she was out of town that day at a political science conference in Flint. He left his home number in Marshall.

She called him back, but they ended up going out during the week. He broke class early and they walked to the Knollwood Tavern, a bar that had been very popular when he was a student, he said. Unlike Waldo's, the Knollwood and its dart boards drew a focused, less raucous crowd.

On that and other meetings, he shared more interesting asides to his life. His interests seemed multicultural. He did a lot of police work in Hispanic neighborhoods, he said. That's where his Spanish came in handy. Graham Greene, the medicine man in *Dances with Wolves,* was a friend of his, he said.

He also listened. She liked that. She could talk about her kids and college and her struggle to keep some kind of balance. And, he seemed so interested in his own son's life, unlike so many other men she'd met. She felt comfortable talking about her own children, as though she was sharing stories with another mother.

Back at her car, inside, they began kissing. Making out. It reminded her of parking in high school. Then he pushed a little further.

"No," she said. "I don't want to do this so fast. Not in the car, like this."

He apologized. "Sorry, it's just that it's been a long time for me."

He said he wanted her to be happy. It was very important to him that he satisfy his lovemaking partner, he said.

"It's always foremost in my mind."

Nita Davis looked up through the windshield. They were parked at Sangren Hall. She pointed out that the second-floor window above them was brightly lit. It was the office of the sociology department chairman.

Brad chuckled. "That guy would shit in his pants if he knew what was going on down here."

Thank God, she thought, the car windows were all steamed up.

"How about up there?" Brad said, mischievously. "How about up in my office?"

She realized he was serious. He wanted to have sex in his office, on the same floor with the chairman. He was flippant about it.

"No," she said. "I don't think that would be a good idea."

It was nearing ten, she guessed, when he left.

A couple of days later, he laughed when they talked in the afternoon on campus. He was laughing at his estranged wife. He said she was mad that he'd returned from the university so late. She was watching his son the night they went out. He was laughing about the scolding she'd given him.

"She said, 'I'm not going to be your baby-sitter while you're out fucking every coed on campus,'" he said.

Nita couldn't help noticing his demeanor. "He thought it was something that she had the nerve to try to tell him what to do and he was extremely proud of the whole thing," she would later say. "It was like, *I'm grown up and she can't tell me what to do and she thinks this all went on and it didn't.*"

Later that day, they consummated their relationship, but in no less of a public setting than a campus parking lot. It was a bright Indian summer day, the fall colors past peak, but still glowing, the temperatures in the sixties. They went to Millen Park in the mid-afternoon. He laid a blanket in an area obscured by trees and bushes. They began kissing.

He kept saying: "Come on, lose your inhibitions. Have the guts to lose your inhibitions."

He rolled her over on top of him, pulling the blanket around them. They never undressed, really. He just pushed her underwear aside and entered her.

Then, it was over, just like that.

"I think ninety percent of the thrill for him was that it was in the open," she later recalled.

Afterwards, there was no intimacy. It was as though his personality switched channels. He was ready to leave. She thought it odd, considering what he'd said in the car about satisfying his lovemaking partner. She was more disappointed in her own behavior. She'd let him manipulate her, she decided. She wished she'd thought more of herself that day.

Nita Davis thought maybe that afternoon was an aberration, until a subsequent afternoon rendezvous in her apartment during November proved otherwise. Behind closed doors, he took longer, but she thought his lovemaking was self-serving. Sometimes he reminded her of a cocky, spoiled student half his age looking for a quick, straight lay.

Brad King's demeanor outside the bedroom changed as well. He no longer listened like he did when they first started talking. They still talked, but the subject was always himself.

In hunting season he bragged endlessly about his bow and rifle skills. He said he was tanning an accumulation of hides for a Native American dancing costume. His friends, however, were miserable hunters. He had to drop animals they'd wounded. He, however, had mastered the kill shot. He could drop an animal in its tracks with one bullet. That's why he bow hunted.

"With a gun, it's just no sport," he said.

Desert Shield was underway. One day, they talked about the subject of war. Nita had taken part in a peace demonstration. He talked about Vietnam. He said he was in the 82nd Airborne in some kind of command level. He saw a lot of carnage, he said. If someone died right in front of him, he added, it wouldn't bother him.

"I've become immune to it. I've seen lots and lots of death."

She didn't want to talk about death. She wanted to talk about life, *her* life, at least once in a while. He always found a way to shape the conversation back toward himself. She wondered what happened to her patient, listening friend.

"I was the audience and he was the actor, and I don't need that," she later confided in a friend. "I've got kids. I get enough of that with my children. I need adult interaction, not watching."

He acted strangely when she called him at his office. He'd say he was in the middle of something, promising to call back, but never would. She called him at home a couple times, just to talk. She felt like he was playing some kind of game. She confronted him about it in what she felt was an adult, rational manner.

"Why are you acting like such a complete stranger when I call you?" she asked.

"I'm not ready for a heavy relationship right now," he said, coldly. "And I don't think you are either."

"What heavy relationship are you talking about? I'm just talking about treating each other like friends."

She wasn't looking for torrid romance. In fact, he'd already defined what they were to one another. "Good friends who could give comfort to each other," he once said.

Then, came November 20. She remembered the date because it was right before Thanksgiving break. She showed up at his office before Tuesday class. He was supposed to call her that afternoon, but never did. He looked drawn and tired.

"There's something I haven't told you," he said. "My wife has been pregnant, and she had the baby today."

He broke class early, and they went to Waldo's. She listened in silent anger. She wasn't angry that his estranged wife was pregnant with his child, she felt he'd been dishonest by leaving out such a large detail.

Before long, he had her feeling sorry for him. He seemed depressed and angry. His wife was domineering and self-centered, he complained. There was going to be a big custody fight over the new child, he said.

He told her the baby's name, Kateri.

"It's an Indian name. I'm surprised my mother isn't more upset."

"Your mother?"

At forty-something he's concerned about his mother? she thought.

He launched into a story about his father being part Indian, an Indian who had denied his own heritage. He loved his father, but had lost respect for him for that. He'd denied his Indian heritage at the urging of his mother, he said. He sounded angry when he talked about her.

"This man has been denying his identity all his life," he said. "And *she* supported that."

That wasn't the half of it that night. Brad King said he was going to his in-laws house for Thanksgiving. He had to do it for the sake of the kids. His estranged wife's family also denied their heritage and carried on like a bunch of drunken Indians, he complained.

The conversation was interrupted briefly when someone at a nearby table sent over a beer, someone from his Thursday class. He slouched deep into his chair. She couldn't understand why he was so embarrassed.

Nita Davis thought, what more don't I know about him? Why is he being so strange?

That night she put an end to any thoughts of a serious relationship. She would listen to him, if it fit her schedule. Once, he called on the phone from his farmhouse. She was home studying. She could tell he had the baby on his lap. They had a fairly lengthy conversation. He'd never hung on the phone like that. But she felt he was showboating.

"It was like, *aren't I a wonderful guy sitting here taking care of my kid,*" she later said.

One day, she saw the three of them together in Sangren Hall. He was standing in the corridor holding the baby. The woman that she guessed was his wife was there by his side as well.

She saw a staffer approach them saying, "Well, are we going to see her again soon, now that she's had the baby. We miss waking up with her in the morning."

Later, she asked another teacher what that comment meant. That's when she learned his wife was a TV anchorwoman. She'd never watched Channel 41.

Nita Davis walked right past the two of them that day. Brad King made eye contact, smirked, then continued soaking up all the attention he was getting in the hall from other staffers and students over the baby.

"Yeah," he said loudly. "I finally did something right."

He called her that afternoon. She thought he was going to thank her for not complicating the situation.

"You should have stopped by and said hello," he said.

"I thought if you wanted to say hi, you would."

He seemed to be reveling in the notion that he could have introduced a lover to Diane without her knowing it. "I just think he thought it was a delicious moment," she would later say.

Not a week before Christmas, he called her again, inviting her to come out to his farmhouse in Marshall. She knew what that meant. Some quick intimacy was better than none at all, she decided. She rationalized, he'll be my placebo for the holidays.

When Brad King met her at the door, he talked briefly about

the Doberman chained out front, that it was an attack dog. Inside, she could see he'd been on the floor grading papers in front of a snowy TV and a lush Christmas tree done in big red bows. He was dressed in a green-and-red sweat outfit. He was quite cordial at first. He gave her a little tour of the first floor. She saw pictures of his wife all over, many of them taken in her twenties.

Maybe he's still obsessed with her, she thought.

Not ten minutes passed, and he had Nita Davis naked on the couch.

"I like this," he kept saying. "I like doing this."

He said nothing about her. He said nothing that made her feel special. Afterwards, he methodically put on his clothes.

"You want something to drink?" he asked, flatly.

She was shocked at his superficial comment. No, right now she wanted to use the bathroom. She wanted to clean up.

In the lavatory, she became curious. She saw a blow dryer and makeup brushes. He certainly doesn't need a blow dryer, she thought. Maybe they were not so estranged, she speculated. Maybe his wife stayed overnight at the farmhouse sometimes. Or, maybe the items were his older daughter's.

She poked her head out the door. "What do you want me to do with this washcloth?" She figured he'd tell her where the hamper was.

He was unconcerned. "Oh, just leave it on the towel rack."

When she returned to the living room, Brad King was back on the floor, grading papers.

"Here, what do you think of this one?" he asked, handing her a sheet.

The TV was tuned to the same snowy channel, and Brad had switched right back to the frequency he was on when she arrived. He'd done the same thing at the funeral, she decided. Changed channels effortlessly in that receiving line. Weep here. Laugh there. Be cordial a second later. It wasn't that grief was incompatible with such an emotional range. It was the way he so easily switched from one to another, seemingly commanding them for the benefit of his company.

That night at the farmhouse she decided never to sleep with

him again. He kept too many secrets. Hell, they never got to the sleeping part, anyway. And, she didn't drive all the way out to Marshall to watch him grade papers. She had a sitter at home. She'd rather spend the evening with her kids.

"Brad, I've got to go," she said.

She wasn't surprised that his goodbye kiss was passionless.

There were other encounters, but only on campus or the phone. He asked her to drop by his office one day in early January, a few weeks before Diane was killed. There, he told her that his estranged wife had tied up his money. Now, he'd have to cancel two classes he'd enrolled in at Western Michigan. Diane was screwing up his schooling, he said.

"She's frozen my checking account."

He got up from his desk, closed the office door, and embraced her. She didn't respond to his kiss.

"Come on," he said.

She was mad. "I don't see you or talk to you for three weeks and you just expect me to screw you right here in your office?"

"You're right," he said. "I guess I'm jumping the gun."

She agreed to a drink at the Knollwood. There, he could produce only a couple of singles. He was so broke he had to order Miller Lite instead of his Canadian brew.

By the time the beer came, he was entirely deflated. He confessed that it was his wife who had left him. She was the one wanting the divorce, he said. He looked like he was going to cry.

"I really want to be with my wife, but she doesn't want me."

Depression eventually transformed into anger. She saw a dark side of him, a darkness connected with women. He was angry with his mother. He was angry with his first wife. He talked with such anger about his mother-in-law it scared her. He said he'd seen her spank his son recently.

"It made me just want to break her arm," he said.

His eyes were black. He seemed to be staring at something three feet behind her.

When they left the bar, she dropped him off at Sangren Hall. She didn't want to spend any time with him alone.

A few days later, she noticed he seemed to pull out of his depression. She did him a few favors when he asked. She typed up his resume for some job applications. She typed his autobiography for PhD programs he was applying for at Western and Michigan State University. He seemed to be making plans, getting on with his life.

Then came what turned out to be the most disturbing phone call, though back then it seemed largely uneventful. Nita Davis had talked to Brad King on the telephone the day his wife was murdered. He'd left a message on her answering machine the night before.

She guessed police would want to know about that.

9

They had the children only three weeks in March, until a motion filed by Brad King's attorney prompted a Macomb County probate judge to order Freida and Royal Newton to give Marler and Kateri King back to their father. As long as Bradford King remained uncharged, the court ruled, the Newtons had no legal standing.

The Newtons felt humiliated and betrayed. Where was the arrest the police promised in the days after the funeral? What was taking so long? They began to suspect the investigation was seriously screwed-up.

The court had also ordered the children not be taken from the court's jurisdiction while they were in the Newtons' custody. Brad King still allowed his children to spend time at the small ranch house on St. Joseph Street, sometimes as long as an entire week, but only one at a time.

Denise Verrier or Darlene often accompanied Freida on the 140-mile drive to Kalamazoo for the exchanges. King also offered to meet them halfway, near Jackson. The meetings were brief, the conversation limited entirely to the children. They never talked about Diane or the investigation. Brad often wore sunglasses.

"It used to bug me," Denise later said. "I often wondered what was going on in those eyes."

Denise Verrier's husband Don was miffed. The exchanges only added to his suspicions. "After he has to go to court to get his kids back, he still lets the kids visit," he later said. "If I was innocent, and that happened to me, I'll tell you, these people would have never gotten my kids again."

Freida Newton worried about the children when they were with him. She thought her son-in-law had only become more bizarre since her daughter's death.

One day, they drove out to Kalamazoo for another children exchange at the D'Artagnans' house. Freida found King sitting alone in the darkened living room in front of a glowing television set. His eyes were riveted on the screen, its light dancing across his shaved forehead.

"He was in another world," she later said.

He had a Native American instructional tape playing. The video was about how to dance. The video was about how to put on war paint.

Jack Schoder was pumped when he finished his interview with Nita Davis on March 20. Not only did he have a twenty-eight page recorded statement, Nita Davis had Brad King on tape the day before the murder. When she heard about the killing, she pulled the Microcassette from her answering machine and saved it.

The Friday, February 8 tape went: "Nita, it's Brad. If you get in tonight, ah, give me a call at home. Ahm . . . I won't be home after tomorrow morning for the rest of the weekend, so, ah, but if you get in tonight, give me a call. Bye."

Nita Davis told Schoder that she called Brad King back anyway on Saturday morning, the day of the murder. He answered, saying he was just on his way out the door.

"I got your message," she told King. "What did you want?"

He said he was just calling to see if she wanted to do something with him on Friday night, but he couldn't do anything Saturday.

"He said he was going out of town," she told Schoder, "and that he didn't expect to be back until either really late Saturday night, or sometime Sunday."

After the interview, Schoder and Jim Stadfeld wondered, was King setting up some kind of alibi for the night of the murder? If he was, why would he use a woman like Nita Davis, someone who could only cast more dispersion on his character?

It wasn't the only thing about him they found curious.

"And these girls," Schoder said. "Just what in the hell does this guy got going for him?"

"Well, we know it isn't his looks," Stadfeld said.

That afternoon, a transmission came across the sheriff's fax machine. It was a Silent Observer tip, an anonymous phone call to the Western Michigan University police. The caller had something to say about another Western Michigan coed and Brad King.

Schoder read the fax.

"Jesus Christ, Jim," he said. "Man, it looks like we've got another one here."

The caller said they were having an affair.

Seven days later they were still trying to find a good address for the student in the fax when the twenty-one-year-old woman called on her own volition. Jack Schoder hung up and drove straight to where she worked, a pub in Kalamazoo called Chap's on Main.

Heather Taylor was an attractive blonde with brown eyes and a turned up nose, and she was another criminal justice major. Bradford King was her instructor in the fall for Sociology of Law Enforcement, the class held on Thursdays, the class also taken by Kelly Clark.

Jack Schoder listened to her story, but struggled to keep up. Heather Taylor talked in rapid quantums, like a teen who had guzzled too much Mountain Dew.

No, Taylor maintained steadfastly, she was not sleeping with Brad King. In fact, she was upset that rumors persisted to that effect. She was afraid of Brad King. It was one of the reasons she'd called them.

"But I do think he was hitting on me," she said. "It was really weird."

She first met King at a Teke party. She was a Chi Omega sister involved in a number of Teke functions. The night she met King, she'd been pouring Yugoslavian plum brandy down a Teke pledge's throat, and he was puking drunk in the third-floor bathroom of the Teke house. The house was dark for the party. She was helping him out of the lavatory, when Brad King approached her out of the deep shadows.

"Who is this?" he asked, glaring at her.

"Heather Taylor," she stammered.

When he saw she was scared, he began to laugh.

He introduced himself, then asked her about a candy bracelet she was wearing, part of the party nonsense that night. When she told him she was a criminal justice major, he told her that he would be her instructor. She didn't believe it, especially when he reached down and grabbed her wrist and began eating the candies off her arm.

"He's crunching down and signaling for my friend to come over and rescue me," she explained. "I raised my hand and left. In my mind, I keep picturing this old, perverted, bald man."

Months later, when he strolled into his Sangren Hall auditorium for her class, Brad King looked much less threatening. Not long into the term, she joined in with students who joked and chatted with him during breaks.

Back then, Taylor worked at a yogurt and sandwich shop called Garpikes. As part of a work promotion, she invited King to stop by for a bite to eat. He began showing up every Thursday, sometimes Tuesdays. Other workers teased her about it.

"Your boyfriend coming by today, Heather," they'd say.

He always stayed an hour, sometimes talking to her while she was working. He offered her rides to class. She politely declined. He talked about a lot of nonsense, she thought, some pretty strange subjects for a man his age. Often, he bragged about his college days. He told her how good-looking he was in college.

He said he dated scores of women, the best-looking women on campus, he said.

For weeks, she thought he was looking for an angle, but he never directly asked her out. He began calling her at home, leaving messages on her machine, mostly about class matters. She returned them, but only after-hours when she knew they would reach only his voice mail.

"I don't know, it made me uncomfortable," she said. "He didn't act like a man in his mid-forties. He acted like a young Greek."

On the last night of class, Brad King urged the entire class to meet him at Waldo's. The bar was a student hangout with director's chairs for seats and beer posters of half-naked models intermixed with vintage campus photographs from decades past. Most instructors preferred the Pilsen Klub downstairs, with its fireplace, tartan chairs, couches, and etchings of old breweries.

Brad King joined them upstairs, downing shots of tequila that students bought him. Half wasted, he took her aside and commented on the rumors about them.

"So, what's it like to have an affair with your professor?"

She blushed. He told her she was beautiful and reminded him of the first woman he had ever fallen in love with in college.

"Heather, I wish I would have met you twenty years ago," he added.

She told him that she had to leave, but would be back. She kept right on going. She was glad to get away from campus for Christmas break.

She saw him again in late January, sitting in his Sangren Hall office. She was with a male friend. Brad King asked her if she wanted to grab a sandwich with him before his evening class. She felt so awkward she said yes.

"Why didn't you just say no, if you didn't want to go?" her friend asked.

"He caught me off guard. I didn't know what to do."

She took another friend's car so she had an excuse to leave. They went to Schlotzsky's. She expected him to make a move on her, but his demeanor surprised her. He was hunched over in the car and in the restaurant.

"I don't know, Heather," he said. "I'm just so depressed. My wife and I aren't getting along."

He had a litany of resentments. He complained about his mother-in-law. She didn't approve of the way they were raising his children in the Indian way.

"I can't stand that bitch," he snapped.

He complained his wife wanted to retire, but he couldn't afford that. "I don't get paid for shit," he complained. He said he was happy back when he lived in Denver, but had been miserable since he'd come to Michigan for his wife's job.

Heather Taylor felt sorry for him.

"He seemed real sad," she said. "I thought my gosh, he just needs a friend to talk to. I wondered if maybe him hitting on me was all in my mind. I was thinking I'd been arrogant to think that."

On Thursday, February 7, two days before the murder, she saw him again on campus. She saw him being yelled at by a professionally dressed Native American woman in the student cafeteria. She thought it was Diane King, until Jack Schoder pointed out Diane was already in the Detroit area by then.

She ran into King later that day on campus. He said he wanted to talk to her again. She agreed to get a quick bite at Garpikes. She thought he needed to vent again, but he bored her with the same meaningless small talk about his prowess as a student lover.

As they walked back, she told him about a recent trip she'd taken to Chicago, how she liked the guys she met there.

"There's just no guys like that here in Kalamazoo," she said.

"What am I, chopped liver?" he said, coldly.

The way he said it frightened her. His looks frightened her. "He looked crazy in his eyes," she said.

That night, just after midnight, she dropped by the Teke house for a party. As she moved through the crowd, she noticed that Brad King was there. He was staring at her from a distance. She hustled out the front door.

The Kings, an all-American family, in a 1950s photo. (clockwise) Willis, Scott, Marge, and Brad.

They called him "Mr. America." Bradford King as the backup quarterback at his high school in Croswell, Michigan.

Brad King when he worked in a surveillance unit at the Pontiac Police Department in the early 70s.

Brad, his first wife Gail, and his daughter Alissa. His receding hairline earned him the under-cover nickname "Bozo."

King as an undercover cop in his early days at the Pontiac Police Department.

Diane King
in a junior
high school
photo.

Diane in her
twenties.

Diane King at Christmas. Friends said she "was full of life."

Diane King mugging in front of Thunderspirit's Victorian barn after she and Brad found their new home just outside Marshall.

The women of Diane's family: (left to right) her mother Freida Newton, her oldest sister Darlene, Diane, and her younger sister Denise.

Diane and Brad with his daughter Alissa.

Brad, Marler, and Diane King during happier days in Grand Junction, Colorado.

Brad King dances at a powwow in a coyote headdress that some thought was the skull of a wolf.

A family photo of Brad, Diane, and Marler King.

Marshall's main street decorated for the holidays. *The New York Times* called the town "the sweetest place on earth." (*Photo by Lowell Cauffiel*)

The King farm during a bleak Michigan winter. (*Photo by Lowell Cauffiel*)

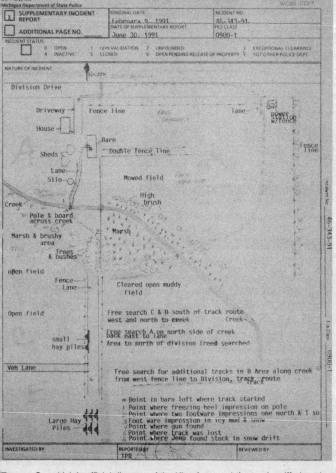

Trooper Gary Lisle's official diagram of the King farm and the track sniffed out by his dog Travis less than two hours after Diane King's murder.

Deputy Guy Picketts snapped this photograph of Diane King to document her exact position as he found her in her driveway.

With this photo Deputy Picketts recorded the effort by emergency medical technicians to save Diane King's life.

Minutes after their arrival, police found the loft door open seven inches, leading them to the sniper's nest.

Holding a sacred eagle feather, Brad King walks arm-in-arm with Diane's mother Freida at the funeral in a Marshall Catholic Church. (*Copyright 1992, Battle Creek Enquirer. Reprinted with permission.*)

The sniper's view from the barn loft (during a reenactment of the murder).

Minutes after fishing it from a stream on the King farm, Detective Jack Schoder holds the prize catch, a Remington Model 511 Scoremaster, believed to be the murder weapon. (right) Trooper Gary Lisle and his dog Travis marking the area nearby which the suspected murder weapon was found.

Almost a year after the killing, Detective Jim Stadfield (left) escorts Brad King from a plane to a waiting car after his arrest and extradition from Denver. (*Copyright 1992, Battle Creek Enquirer. Reprinted with permission.*)

The "Brad Busters": (left to right) State Police Detective Gary Hough, Prosecutor Jon Sahli, Investigator Gerry Woods, and Assistant Prosecutor Nancy Mullett.

Bradford King's first defense attorney James Brady, a former U.S. Attorney from Grand Rapids, Michigan. (*Courtesy of the Marshall Chronicle.*)

Former prosecutor, Judge Conrad Sindt presided over King's month-long trial through the sunless days of November, 1992. (*Courtesy of the Marshall Chronicle.*)

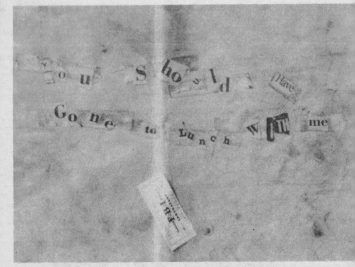

"You should have gone to lunch with me." The terrifying stalker letter Diane King received in her mailbox. The FBI examined it for fingerprints.

Weeks after the murder, Calhoun County Sheriff Jon Olson holds up the Remington Model 511 Scoremaster during a press conference, asking for the public's help in linking Diane King's killer to the gun. (*Copyright 1992, Battle Creek Enquirer. Reprinted with permission.*)

Young Christopher Sly testifying during King's trial. The defense could not shake his damning testimony. (*Copyright 1992, Battle Creek Enquirer. Reprinted with permission.*)

Brad King with his second lawyer, John Sims, and his assistant counsel, Virginia Cairns.

Bradford King in the attorney conference room of the Gus Harrison Correctional Facility. Known as a model prisoner, he works in the law library of the Michigan prison. (*Photo by Lowell Cauffiel*)

Two weeks after the murder, she ran into him again on campus between the Student Center and Sangren Hall.

"How are you doing?" she asked him.

He was angry and complaining. He talked about the murder investigation. She didn't know the police were focusing on him. He said they were harassing him.

"I've had to take an apartment in the city," he said.

He said he'd hired an old Teke as a lawyer.

"They don't have anything on me," he told her. "They can't prove a fucking thing. That's what fraternity brothers are for."

Heather Taylor told Jack Schoder, "You know, I thought it was an awfully strange comment to make."

By April, police weren't the only authorities who knew about Brad King's philandering. The chairman of the sociology department and the head of the criminal justice program interviewed Kelly Clark, Nita Davis, and several other female students.

With King, they handled the matter gingerly, suggesting to King that he needed some time off because of his grief. This was evident, program director Paul Friday said, because it had come to his attention King had been breaking classes early since his return to campus.

King agreed.

Kelly Clark was having a few beers at Waldo's on the last Saturday in April when one of her friends told her that Brad King was pounding down beers with a group of young Tekes at a nearby table. King was dressed in turquoise pants and a turquoise-and-white striped shirt, fresh from a golf outing.

It was the last Saturday in April, almost three months since his wife's murder.

She went over to say hi. Soon, he was rubbing her back. She put her arm around him. Brad King was feeling no pain. "He was talking to everybody, just Mr. Social Butterfly," she later recalled.

Kelly Clark was at a loss to explain the attraction, despite the

fact she knew he was a murder suspect. "Something drew me
to him. I can't explain it. I was intrigued."

"Can I call you later?" King asked her at the bar.

"Sure."

When she left the bar, she thought he meant a few days later.
Sometime between two and three in the morning, after the bar
closed, one of the other girls living in the house woke her up.

"Kelly, Brad King is at the door."

Her housemate was frightened. Kelly Clark knew no one in
the house wanted Brad King around.

A few minutes later, Brad was taking his clothes off at the foot
of her bed, drunk to the point of slurred words, but his sexual
readiness was not diminished one bit.

She said it obnoxiously. "Well, take off your clothes and stay
a while."

"You want me to leave?" He looked at her as though it didn't
make any difference.

She hesitated only briefly.

"No," she said.

They had sex three times.

As she lay with him there in bed afterwards she thought, God
this man killed his wife and here he is lying right here next to
me. He's in my bed.

It scared Kelly Clark. It mostly scared her that she *wasn't*
scared.

It had been one abomination after another, decided sixty-
two-year-old Stella Pamp, the Potawatomi elder everyone just
called Bea. Some thought the abomination started with the
murder of Diane, the young woman whom she had treated like
one of her five grown daughters, but she knew it started long
before that.

She remembered when Diane received the stalker letter,
about a year after they first met at the Burlington Powwow. It
was the powwow her husband Leonard had started years before
her people's ways became fashionable among white men and
women. Leonard Pamp was an activist. He'd been honored
with many eagle feathers in his travels.

Bea Pamp stayed with Diane on the Tuesday and Thursday right after Diane received the note with the cut-out letters, while Brad was teaching class at Western. She met Diane at the house at twilight. Diane was so scared she brought a neighbor girl with her when she drove up. The following Thursday she found her just sitting with Marler in the car, very pregnant and afraid to move.

After they checked the house, they went inside and made dinner. As they finished, Diane began to talk.

"You know, sometimes I think it's Brad that was calling," she said. "Because it sounds so much like his voice."

"You sure?" Bea said. "You're kidding."

"No. Because it sounds like him, and he's trying to disguise his voice."

"Why would he do something like that? He knows you're scared."

Diane shrugged.

"I would never do that to anybody," Bea said.

"There's all kinds of people out there," Diane said, befuddled. "You never know."

"No, Diane," Bea said. "It would take somebody sick."

The week before her friend was killed, she was in New Hampshire, visiting a daughter. Bea Pamp got a message from one of her daughters. Diane was urgently trying to reach her.

Bea called that Tuesday. Brad answered the phone.

"How's Diane?" she asked.

"Oh, she's depressed and down," Brad said.

When she got on the phone, she sounded full of life, like she always did.

"Oh, Bea, I need to talk to you."

But she didn't want to talk on the phone. They agreed to talk when Bea got back. When Bea Pamp got back to Michigan, Diane King was dead.

She had no idea where Diane had been killed or how she had been shot. On that Tuesday, she drove up to the farmhouse to direct the building of the funeral fire, as was the custom. When she walked across the driveway, where the Jeep Wagoneer had

been parked the day of the murder, she suddenly knew. It wa
an experience that could only be described as spiritual.

"I don't know why, but I knew," she said later. "When I go
up to the tree, where I later found out she'd fallen, I knew h
shot her. I can't tell you how, but I did."

When she saw Brad King carrying the eagle feather in th
church it was an abomination.

"We value the eagle feather more than gold," she alway
said.

Brad King had defiled it.

As she sat at powwows in South Bend, Indiana, then Mt
Pleasant, near the Isabella Indian Reservation where she wa
born and raised, she watched the man further defile her friend'
memory. The custom dictated that you did not dance for a
least a year after the death of a beloved, unless you had beer
given permission by the person before they were deceased.
That's the way she was taught.

She knew Diane had not given Brad permission, but Brad
King danced. He danced to the drum with Marler, who knew
no better. He danced in full Native American regalia. He had
buckskins and feathers and a bright crimson shirt. He painted
a circle around one of his eyes red with war paint, then circled
that in a border of black. From that, black lines streamed
straight down his cheek.

There was more dancing at other powwows into the early
summer. Brad King was covering his head with an animal pelt
as he danced, her friends were telling her.

Some said it was the skin and skull of a wolf.

10

When the detective from Michigan showed up unannounced in early April, flashing his badge at the door of her ranch home just outside Kerrville, Marge Lundeen invited him in for coffee. It was only basic courtesy.

"You have a very nice home," Jim Stadfeld said.

"What were you expecting it to look like?" she asked. "The Newtons?"

He had questions. About Brad. About his brother Scott, then Diane.

"Did you know Diane was planning on leaving her job and staying home?"

No, Marge Lundeen didn't know that.

They talked about Brad's life, growing up, marrying Gail, the divorce, the way he'd always been distant.

The detective wondered if she'd given Brad any money.

"I've given money to both of my sons," she said.

When Brad got into financial difficulty, which had been repeatedly, she would help him out. She couldn't readily give the detective the exact amounts.

The detective wanted to know about guns. She told him that she knew Brad had a family heirloom, her father's shotgun. There was another gun she believed he had, a rifle, a .22. They were living in Tustin, Michigan, when Willis bought it.

"His dad bought it because there was an accident in the community. A boy had shot out another boy's eye with a BB gun. So, Willis decided that he should get some kind of gun to teach Brad how to use it for safety. We had property just outside of town, and Willis had put up a little range there."

Marge Lundeen had some questions for the detective. Were they pursuing anybody else?

"Sort of," the detective said.

"Why would you think that Brad did it?" she asked. "I mean, he's certainly worse off monetarily now without her, isn't he?"

Yes, the detective had to agree with that.

Marge Lundeen had already heard from friends back in Croswell, the town where Brad had gone to high school, their last Michigan home. It was embarrassing, she thought, humiliating even. Someone connected with the investigation had been in Croswell. Old friends of the family had been asked questions by some kind of investigator with a thick Southern accent, very crude man, she would later decide.

Marge Lundeen suggested to the detective in her living room a change in focus. They ought to take a good look in Diane's past associations, she said. The woman had the kind of personality that could make enemies. Brad, after all, was the one who came from a good family.

"I don't think you could say the same thing for Diane," she said.

On April 20, Jim Stadfeld returned to Texas, this time to Longview, the home of Brad King's brother Scott. They had talked on the telephone earlier. Scott King remembered the rifle his father had bought when they were young. It was a .22 caliber, he said. He'd shot it himself back then.

Jim Stadfeld later recalled Scott King telling him: "If I saw the gun, and it's the gun, I'll be able to remember."

But arranging an interview had been difficult. Scott King worked for an oil equipment supply company and was always traveling. They finally agreed on a date and a time. King asked that they meet at a restaurant just outside of Longview.

Scott King was a tall, gaunt man. He looked old enough to be Brad King's father, rather than three years his junior. His hair was receding and silver well beyond his years.

They talked a little about his relationship with his brother. They were not close, Scott said. Before the funeral, they hadn't seen each other in something like eight years.

Jim Stadfeld had not told Scott he was bringing photographs of any weapons. The detective later described what happened next when he began producing them:

"We started getting down to the nitty-gritty of things. And I thought, this guy is going to tell me. I start out with the pictures f the grandfather's shotgun. He isn't hesitant at all about that ne. Yep, that's the shotgun. Then, I show him the .22. His mouth somewhat drops.

"He says, 'Well, I don't know.' "

Scott King complained about it being a long time since he'd een the .22. "It's been years," he said.

"I knew I could sit there for three hours and pump him, and hat's all I was going to get out of him," Stadfeld later recalled. "But I *knew*. I could tell by the expression on Scott King's face. *That* was the .22 in the family. And, then again, it would be a errible thing to have to do to your brother—put the murder weapon in his hand. I don't know if I can blame him. I really lon't."

They did only one interview the entire month of May. Jim Stadfeld complained the case could not be made any stronger. ack Schoder went to see Jon Sahli several times. He wondered whether the King case had become something personal. Maybe conflict over witnesses and evidence had created hard feelings.

"Let's bury the hatchet," Schoder told the prosecutor. "Let's get on with this thing."

There was nothing to bury, Sahli later maintained. Cases could not be won on a detective's impression of a key witness's acial expression, he argued. They didn't have a motive. They lidn't have that Remington Model 511 Scoremaster in Brad King's possession. They had one shot at Brad King, and if they ost in court, under the double jeopardy rule, it was all over, just ike that.

Publicly, Sheriff Jon Olson now was on the defensive. Critical reporters were questioning whether his department had the ability to solve the case. The tabloid TV shows had moved on o other stories, but the Battle Creek *Enquirer* was doing regular updates. One story pointed out that the county had yet to solve he burnt schoolhouse homicide, either. In Marshall, people vere posting news clippings on local company bulletin boards, highlighting the sheriff's quotes and penning acidic comments.

Privately, the conflict was ugly. Sheriff's department deputies and command officers were sniping. Sahli was gutless, some said. He feared trying the case because he had to face election in November of 1992. Others pointed out that Jon Olson was up for reelection on the same Republican ballot. If Sahli won the King case, the reasoning went, the sheriff would get the credit. If he lost, the prosecutor would shoulder the blame.

Publicly, the prosecutor's office supported the investigation. Privately, Sahli was telling his staff he was dissatisfied with the detective work. Basic scientific evidence, like fingerprint and paper analysis, had not been completed. The possible stalker scenario had not been thoroughly investigated and eliminated. Times, distances, and sometimes police reports didn't fit logistics. Important people hadn't been interviewed. The detectives procrastinated on evidentiary requests.

The prosecutor saw a repeating pattern of near-misses, in keeping with the theme of the first night on the scene. They followed King's trail to the edge of the creek, but only one deputy crossed it. They called for a tracking dog, but didn't debrief the handler. They made crime scene measurements, but could not fit them into any particular scenario or scheme. They interviewed the suspect, but didn't ask the right questions. They found women sleeping with Brad King, but couldn't link them to a murder motive. They found what appeared to be the murder weapon, but hadn't put it in the killer's hands.

Jon Sahli didn't know whether it was a testimony to Brad King's cunning or the limitations of the sheriff's detective bureau..But by late spring, the prosecutor was losing his patience with protocol. He called up the county's state representative in Lansing.

"Do I have the backing if I take this one away from the sheriff?" he asked him.

Indeed, it had gotten down to politics. The prosecutor was seeking the blessings of the most powerful Republican in Calhoun County that he could find.

In the trenches of the investigation, Gerry Woods expended as much energy bickering with the two detectives as working with them. Woods spent less time driving to interviews in his Batmobile, and more time confined to the cramped backseat of

Jack Schoder's Grand Prix. Woods would make suggestions from the back. The detectives in front would shoot them down.

"I'm tellin' ya fellas, we need more help on this case," Woods kept saying. "We just need some more help."

The sheriff's detectives had distanced him from the core interviews. It didn't take long for Woods to tune in the picture.

"Shit, I knew they were just using me," he later said. "They were just using me to try to get to Jon Sahli. They didn't give a shit what I could offer to the case."

But Gerry Woods had a strategy of his own.

Woods had decided that if Brad King had killed his wife, he might be a lot more clever than even the crime scene indicated. It was as if he had expected foul-ups in the investigation. They knew for a fact that King himself was boasting about the probe's shortcomings. He seemed to have decided that before ever giving the investigation a chance. Now Woods had heard that King was saying that "hick" and "hillbilly" cops were working the case.

Gerry Woods only let his friends call him that.

There wasn't going to be any conclusive evidence, Woods predicted. If King were the killer, he was too smart for that. King's own statements to Jack Schoder were telling. The man offered little or nothing, even in the face of contradictions, like hearing one gunshot back at the bales instead of two. He thought like a cop. Cops knew that you strung a suspect up with his own words, his own information. Brad King knew that was how you played the game.

They had to operate on a much more subtle playing field, Woods believed, and that was the kind of case that required manpower.

"Jack, we need more help," Woods kept saying. He said that to Jack Schoder every time he had the chance. That was his strategy. If he could convince Schoder, he'd eventually bring along his partner.

As summer approached, the battle was over phone records. Woods volunteered to analyze the records obtained from the telephone company. Then he saw the Kings' $250 phone bills and hundreds of calls to scores of numbers. Woods suggested they send the statements from Thunderspirit and King's Sangren Hall office to analysts with the Michigan State Police in Lansing. Woods, in fact, had already made the call. The state police told him they'd have them processed by computer in a week, sorted by date, then by number called.

"Let the state police do the busywork," Woods said. "Then, when we get 'em back, we can get down to determining the nature of all those calls."

From the backseat, Woods could almost see the hair rise above their collars. *Michigan State Police.* Woods knew from his tenure in Eaton County, some cops resented state police, from their crisply dressed troopers on local highways to the department's intelligence groups in Lansing.

"Gerry, we don't want the goddamned state police involved," Stadfeld said.

Back at the department, Woods pulled Jack Schoder aside, showing him how it would take weeks to sort the records by hand.

"Look at these calls," he told Schoder. "Some of these may fit into that pile of statements we've got."

Schoder sucked on a Winston, half nodding.

"Jack, see what I mean," Woods said. "We need help. We can't do all this stuff ourselves."

A Michigan State Police detective sergeant named Gary Hough considered it quite an admission, coming from Gerry Woods. Woods was sucking on a cigarette, his face red, the lines in his forehead deep and thick.

"Gary, I can't complete this case," Woods said. "I don't have the ability to do it. I need help, man. I need your help."

They worked a couple of murder cases together in recent months, Hough assigned to the state post in Battle Creek. Woods soon learned to pronounce his last name with a hard "g." They'd become friends, in fact. After work, they liked to stop at the Winner's Circle, a bar across from the Post plant. The smell of various Post cereals wafted outside. Inside the bar, Hough watched Woods drain a couple of thirty-two-ounce glasses of draft and vent about the King case.

Gary Hough already admired Gerry Woods. He butchered the King's English, rarely wore a tie, and worried himself miserable half the time. But Hough also watched Gerry Woods identify a homicide suspect by logging four hundred miles in an eighteen-hour day. He admired Woods's tenacity.

"I'll say this about any detective," he would later say. "The good ones. They all have the same quality. When they lock onto something, they'll just follow it and go. No matter what the people over them say. No matter what other investigators say. They just won't stop. Gerry, when he gets connected with something, just won't stop, whether you ask him to or not."

Gary Hough could see that Gerry Woods had no plans of stopping on the King case. It was all he talked about anymore.

Freida Newton received the letter on June 10. It was postmarked in Illinois. Brad King was writing on new stationery, something he'd designed himself, something that appeared only after Diane's death. The top had an Indian ceremonial pipe, the bottom a Native American bead pattern.

Dear Freida:

   When you get this, the kids and I will be in the Denver area. I did not want to leave this way but you set the ground for it when you tried to take the children. I feel that I cannot trust you and had to leave this way to insure that you did not try something again. We moved to Denver because I have a job offer and I needed to take advantage of it, in that I can provide for my family. I will give you our address etc. when we are settled. Marler and Kateri send their love to grandma and grandpa.

                                                              Brad

The move pushed the family's frustration with the investigation to the brink of panic. Brad leaving the state with the children was everyone's worst fear. They complained to the state attorney general's office. Freida and Royal joined the support group, Parents of Murdered Children. Members of the Detroit chapter were making inquiries at the state level about the case.

Freida Newton sent King's letter to the detectives.

In the second week in June, Denise and Freida dropped in unannounced on the detectives in Marshall. They were on their way to Kalamazoo. They were running down a rumor that Brad King had left Kateri behind with the D'Artagnan family. Before they headed farther west to find Kateri, they wanted to see if they could get some answers.

"I can't say anything," Jack Schoder said.

"I want to see whoever is in charge," Freida demanded.

"Everybody is gone."

"I'm not leaving until I see somebody," she said.

She sat down in the lobby of the jail and wouldn't move.

Gerry Woods and Jon Sahli greeted Denise Verrier and Freida Newton in their smokey basement office in the Human Services Building in Battle Creek. Jack Schoder had sent them over. The two women were demanding to know about the arrest the detectives had promised them in the days after Diane's death.

"I don't care what the detectives told you," Sahli said. "There's too many parts missing."

"You know, really, I don't care if you ever find that man," Freida Newton said. She started to break down crying.

"I just want my grandchildren back."

Sahli stuck to the point. "Mrs. Newton, I don't want to arrest Brad King if I don't have a chance of convicting him. And, I don't think you want that either."

Denise Verrier wanted to know what they were going to do.

"We're starting over," Jon Sahli said. "The whole case needs to be redone."

They had only one shot at him, one shot on a very circumstantial case, Jon Sahli said.

"If he's acquitted," he continued, "Brad King could even confess to killing your daughter, and just laugh at all of us from now to doomsday."

Gerry Woods could almost hear him laughing now.

From the View of

BRADFORD KING

I t never changed. My job was to take care of her so she could do her job.

Diane wanted to have this career. I'd already had one. So, I felt she should have the experience if she wanted it. That was the choice I made. I will be the one who moves. I'll be the one who will look for a new job or stay home to care for the children. That was so Diane could do her job, and I had no qualms. I was perfectly happy doing that.

We had a beautiful life in Denver. After we were married, we moved into a house in an area called Washington Park, on 691 South York. We could walk up to the corner of University and Exposition, one block east of our house. There was a little corner bar that served great Mexican food. There were shops, a clothing store, a little Italian restaurant, an ice cream parlor. We could go down Gaylord Street six blocks to an area called Old South Gaylord. It was all restaurants and stores. Our favorite bar was down there, Hemingway's. There were boutique shops and a bookstore. We'd walk down there and hang out.

Diane was working for est. I was working for a jewelry manufacturer. I was an inventory control manager, responsible for gold and diamonds and semiprecious stones. At that time, our friends John and Susan Van Vleet came to us and said there's some irregularities here in the organization (est) and we think you should know about them. We want you to know we're now distancing ourselves and, as our friends, we recommend you do the same. We immediately did.

I was redefining my job at the jewelry manufacturer because I'd mastered it. I was bored to death. I basically had my work done before lunch. So I had some conversations with John Van Vleet. We put together this proposal to the owner of the company, asking for more responsibility and more work to do. I was telling him I was willing to give him more bang for his buck.

I said to John, "What do you think?"

He said, kidding, "Well, the worst that could happen is that they'll fire you."

I turn it in, and they fire me. I'm sure the guy who I was directly responsible to felt threatened by me.

Diane exploded. It's a wonder the walls didn't come down in the house. She was pissed. And she said, "Well, you gotta call John." So we went to their house that night for dinner. We laughed. I mean, after the emotion of it, all there was to do was laugh at how stupid these people were.

That night, my mother called and said that my dad had died. I knew he was supposed to have heart surgery, but I didn't know that he'd gone in yet. They hadn't told me. She just called, saying Dad had a heart attack during his operation. We went to Texas for the funeral.

Right after my dad died, I shaved my head. I was tired of paying to cut a half a head of hair. I wanted to see what it looked like. Diane loved it. My mother was appalled. She hated it. She said, "You look menacing to people."

Some people did perceive me differently. But even before that, I could intimidate people just by my presence. I guess it's the eye contact. I've always known there's power in that. I've used it to my advantage whenever I've needed to. My father always looked people in the eye. I began discovering it in college. Being a policeman fostered it. I look into your soul, and that bothers people.

We moved to downtown Denver, a high-rise on the fifth floor, right on Spear Boulevard and Cherry Creek. Oh, it was beautiful. We could see the capitol dome. We could walk to the grocery store. Walk to the theater. Walk downtown. Diane walked to work at the public broadcasting station. We loved it. I was working for John and Susan's consultants business and doing some work for a security company.

If you could have seen Diane's face when that guy called to offer her the job in Grand Junction. They hired her based on her tape alone. We went out that night and celebrated at Marlo's in downtown Denver, one of her favorite restaurants.

But, I don't think it really sank in. I remember when we were driving to Grand Junction. I was going to stay in Denver until she got settled at the station, so I took her there and she would keep the car. We crossed the Rockies and we were coming into Grand Junction on I-70. We could see the whole Grand Valley, all lit up. After dark, the lit houses look massive, but it's all these little communities, close to two hundred thousand people.

Diane said, "I'm scared. I'm gonna be on all of those TVs, and they're all gonna see me and know when I screw up."

I said, "Who says you're gonna screw up?"

But she was doing something she wanted to do, and that had her hooked. For me, I would be taking on a new role for the male in our society. We'd had conversations with John and Susan about this. We were really choosing these roles and not just making up some crap that sounded good.

I wasn't a talker until I met Diane. We spent hours talking. My parents never argued in front of us. There's a way to argue in a relationship. I didn't know how to do that. Diane taught me how to do that. You can argue to drive the relationship apart, or it can bring you closer together. Accomplish some things. That's what I didn't know how to do.

I ended up moving to Grand Junction within two weeks. Susan told me I needed to move.

She said, "You know that I know you and Diane as well as my own husband, so what's going on?"

I said, "I can't stand living apart."

She said, "I know that. You're fired. You're not really

fired, but you can't work here. Call up Diane and arrange it. Move your ass out there. That's where you belong. You're not equipped personally to live without her like this."

When I first called Diane, she was angry. I just said that I was moving and there wasn't a conversation about it. I'd made the decision without her, and I was crying.

Diane said, "You're intruding on my life."

I said, "Wait a minute. We're married."

She hung up the phone.

Susan said, "You didn't handle that very well."

I said, "I know."

So Susan called Diane. She said, "If you could see your husband the past few weeks, you'd know he doesn't belong here."

Diane apologized. She didn't mean it. Things got worked out.

We were in Grand Junction almost two years. It was a good place to live. We made a lot of friends, and the community just took us in. Diane was a celebrity. Everybody knew her, then me. But beyond the celebrity status, people also took us into their homes just because of who we were.

I remember this Halloween party. TV people and newspaper people and radio people. All media people. Diane was pregnant with Marler. She went as a nun. I went as a priest. The weatherman hosted this special Halloween movie, and we all went over there on his show. We were his guests. He introduced the pregnant nun and her husband priest. We had so much fun that night.

I remember when Marler was born. The community's response was incredible. The TV station came down and did a story. I'll bet she received fifty plants and flowers. She was just a reporter, not an anchor, but they loved her.

I never missed her stories. I never wanted to. I was proud of her. Pride would just well up in me. That's what would happen. It was like, she *can* do this and she *is* good, and she's my wife.

There were perks. We went on a raft trip on the Colorado River, and it didn't cost us a dime. We went to a bluegrass festival. We went to Salt Lake City for a weekend as part of a story. Sometimes I didn't go. The one time I really wanted to go, I didn't get to. She covered a celebrity hunt in western Colorado, where the meat went to soup kitchens. Kurt Russell, Billy Martin, and Ted Nugent were there. She spent three frigging days there. I was pissed. I could have gone up there, gone hunting and hung around with those guys.

I did meet Kurt Russell in Grand Junction, briefly. We met at the airport. He was just another person. I'm not taken by stars. I met Ted Nugent at his bow hunting shop in Jackson, Michigan, but not to really have any conversation with him as I did with Kurt Russell.

The soap stars would come to the mall in Kalamazoo, and Diane would host them. We all went; Marler, too. Sometimes she would pull him up on the stage and include him in the show. He sat there and just loved it. I liked to watch Diane doing what she did. I got to shake hands with the soap stars, and we went out to eat with them afterwards. They're just people. To me, they're just people.

Now, Tom Darling, he was very impressed with Diane. I could see it. He'd introduce me to somebody and then tell them who I was. I was *her* husband. That irritated me. It was like he was trying to impress the person rather than introduce one customer to another. I didn't care if people knew I was Diane's husband. That didn't matter one way or the other. But when she's not there and he made a point of it, that was irritating.

I never felt as if people were overlooking me because of her. With a bald head and sitting around confronting people eye to eye when I met them, they didn't have a chance to do that. Most people when they're introduced don't confront you eye to eye, and I do. People can't ignore you then. It makes them very uncomfortable and they can't overlook you.

I established my own credibility with people. They talked to me, not as Diane's husband, but to *me.* Diane didn't want some guy who sat in the corner. Diane wouldn't let me be that, because I can be shy if I don't know people. She worried I'd huddle off in the corner and ignore everybody. In fact, if I was going to be that way, she didn't want to take me.

We got in trouble with the charge cards. We just spent too much money. It came from a lot of different sources. We always had nice clothes. We didn't manage our money well.

My first full-time job in Grand Junction was at Community Mental Health. Eight hundred bucks a month. That's not much money. I worked with the developmentally disabled for seven months. The director was suspect in his ability. Diane jumped into a story while I was there and just tore the organization up. The staff director came in and told me I couldn't be in the staff meetings because I might divulge some things.

I said, "My wife doesn't get that from me. That would be unethical. She's got ethics."

He said, "Well, I'm not letting you in the meeting."

I said, "Well then I'm taking the day off. My contract says anytime I have a personal need I can take a day off." And I walked out the door.

Two days later, I interviewed with Western Slope Rehabilitation for almost three times the money, and I took it. I was managing a client base of workman's compensation cases for ten months.

We had Marler, and then Western Slope Rehab laid me off. Had I been using my head, I would have sued them. It wasn't a layoff in the legal sense because they had hired somebody after me and they didn't lay that person off. They had no grounds to fire me because I had just received a bonus for performance two months prior.

Diane said, "Well, if this is going to keep happening, maybe that's a sign that it's time I start looking for a better job."

That's what brought us to Battle Creek. I wanted to be close enough when Alissa graduated from high school, it wouldn't be a huge trek. Also, Diane wanted to spend some time with her family. We had decided when Marler was three that we were going to get pregnant with Kateri. So, we wanted the kids to develop some kind of relationship with Alissa and their grandparents, because developing a relationship with my mother would be difficult. My mother had even made the comment once: "Don't expect me to be the real grandmotherly type, I'm getting too old."

Well, at first we were happy, but then Diane found it really wasn't a smart career move. The TV station presented one picture, but, in reality, it was a little different. We weren't that familiar with western Michigan and we should have been making some phone calls. They lumped Grand Rapids, Kalamazoo, and Battle Creek as one TV market, but it really wasn't. Channel 41 barely covered Battle Creek and Diane brought them up a notch. Investigative reporting? Nobody even knew what the hell that was until she got there.

I started working for Community Mental Health, then transferred over to the court. I was setting up an intensive probation program for drunk drivers. Multiple offenders. There was a model for it, and they had a grant. I was putting together the program.

Well, they came in and fired me one day. They took me down to the court administrator's office and they showed me this document and said, "Did you prepare this?"

I said, "That's my weekly client contact log."

"Did you turn it in?"

I said, "No, I did not turn it in because it's not ready to be turned in. It's inaccurate."

What I did was make out my weekly log in advance for the week. If they weren't there when I visited, I had to adjust the log so it was accurate. I would turn the adjusted log in and throw the old one away, but I hadn't done that. Somebody had taken it off my desk and turned it in, and I got fired based on that.

I found out later why they really fired me. There had been a theft in the building, but they never questioned me about it. Never confronted me. The day the money was found missing I was in Holland, Michigan, observing a similar program. And, I had an alibi for the night before if they want to say anything. I was home with my wife, but, of course, right now I can't prove that. They interviewed everybody else, why didn't they interview me? My desk had been broken into also. So had a couple of other desks. They have a cleaning service that works in that building at night.

They thought I took it; they couldn't prove it. So, they fired me. I was the new guy in the office, I guess. They manufactured a reason to fire me because they knew how I did my log. Everybody in that office knew that I prepared a log on Monday for the week and then readjusted it on the following Monday for pay.

I called Diane from home. She said, "Get on the phone with Randy and get on the phone with John Van Vleet. Tell them the story. See what our next step is."

She was being logical. Both of them said well you've got an unlawful discharge. Sue the sons of bitches. So that's what we started to do.

We hired an attorney, a friend of Randy's out in Kalamazoo. I gave him two hundred dollars to put the paperwork together, the rest of it was going to be on contingency. I got busy with the farm. I figured the papers would be filed and at some point we'd be doing depositions within six to eight months. In fact, Diane and I had a conversation shortly before she died that we'd better check on that lawsuit.

All of it feeds right into the sheriff's department not taking care of Diane's complaints about the stalker, really. It just builds a whole scenario of malfeasance and incompetence.

It fits with my theory of why they were trying to frame me for the murder of my wife.

PART FOUR

The Point of Formlessness

Be extremely subtle, even to the point of formlessness. Be extremely mysterious, even to the point of soundlessness. Thereby you can be the director of the opponent's fate.

— Sun-tzu, Fourth Century, B.C.

1

State Police Detective Gary Hough expected some alienation when he agreed to head a task force on the murder of Diane Newton King, but he didn't expect it to show up in the decor. Jack Schoder and Jim Stadfeld had their desks waiting for them when everyone showed up for work on June 12 at the annex building office. Four task force desks were together on one side of the room. The county detectives' were on the opposite wall.

Hough couldn't blame them. "I knew they resented me being there," he said later. "Hey, I would resent it, too."

Gary Hough was thirty-seven, the youngest cop in the room. He'd spent seventeen years with the state, but only four as a detective. He'd worked only seven homicides, but he had three things going for him: Compulsive organization. A frequent, infectious laugh. And the substantial resources of the Michigan State Police. Already, Hough had been in Lansing researching successful strategies used by task forces around the state.

Sheriff Jon Olson first approached Hough in late April, asking him to read the investigation's file, asking for an outside opinion. Hough conferred with investigators in Lansing, then detailed obstacles he saw. First, most of the evidence of Brad King's character—his affairs and his probation department firing—would likely not be admissible in court. Second, any trial would require the testimony of at least fifty civilians and a half-dozen police officers. Managing that testimony would be difficult with the current file. It was riddled with unanswered questions that could only aid in Brad King's court defense.

Compiling a solid circumstantial case would take at least six months with five to six detectives working three days a week, he told the sheriff. If he wanted the state police involved, Hough told Olson, he would have to direct the investigation. The case needed a fresh eye and a neutral party in charge, Hough argued. If his department was going to put its reputation and resources on the line, then he would have to take responsibility. He'd report only to Jon Sahli and his own command.

The sheriff agreed to the terms in June, but outside help hadn't been easy to find. Battle Creek homicide detectives declined an offer. The King case was a loser, some said. Hough looked in his own department, recruiting a detective sergeant from the Coldwater post named Phil Mainstone, a twenty-year veteran known for his easygoing demeanor and the acreage he farmed in his off hours. He had to be easygoing, other troopers said, to sit on his tractor all those hours.

Gerry Woods found the other task force member on the east side of the county. Albion Detective Sergeant Lou Mueller was a twenty-five-year veteran and an Army Reserve CID officer. He'd just come back from seven months of active duty with Operation Desert Storm. He'd handled felonies in Saudi Arabia and helped guard General Norman Schwarzkopf in Dhahran. Tenacious and outspoken, Mueller had worked cases before with Schoder and Stadfeld.

Mueller got everyone's attention when he made the task force's first phone call. It was to an evasive Native American woman they suspected of sleeping with Brad King.

"Alright, I'll tell you what," Mueller told her. "This is a state police task force now. We'll just put you up in front of a grand jury and you can lie in front of them."

Hough laughed, but Jim Stadfeld didn't. Stadfeld and Schoder had just objected to the unit being called a "task force" in a previous meeting.

"Lou, we're not calling it a task force," Stadfeld said, after Mueller hung up.

"Jim, that's bullshit," Mueller said, scowling. "Call it what it is. I ain't pussy footin' around here, Jim. I'm over here to do a goddamn job. It's a *task force*. What the hell else do you call it when you put a bunch of departments together to work on a case?"

Hough would say later, "I had a room full of type A personalities, one hundred years experience total, who all believed in what they were doing. They all could sit there all day long and argue a point. Well, I was willing to accept somebody's brighter idea, but this was also where it had to be: You can resent the hell out of it, go have secret meetings, do whatever you want. But when you're here, this is the way it's got to go."

It had to go in two fundamental directions: They had to solidify the crime scene. They had to come up with a motive. "If we couldn't do both," Hough would say later, "in my mind, we were simply screwed."

Complicated investigations like the King case called for simplistic organization, Hough believed. He wanted the hundreds of pages of reports organized in a master file, arranged by date of occurrence. He put Gerry Woods to work filling out forms for every possible witness. The forms would be discussed every Wednesday morning. Detectives would assess each witness's possible contribution to the crime scene and/or motive. Then some would be interviewed again by a new detective to stimulate a fresh approach.

Hough wanted visuals. He wanted aerial photographs taken of the property. He asked dog handler Gary Lisle to come up with a detailed sketch of Travis's track on February 9. Hough had copies made of photographs of the Remington Model 511 Scoremaster and King's sixteen-gauge Winchester shotgun. He wanted the photos shown to people.

"I don't care who they are," Hough said. "If they had some sort of contact, have been in King's house, around his house, show them. Ask them if they were there, even if you don't think so."

Hough looked over the search warrants. They had sketchy descriptions, none listing any more than a dozen or so items. He wanted a master list compiled of the seized materials. He asked the county detectives to bring everything they had from the evidence room. Schoder and Stadfeld brought box after box of materials, much of it from King's Sangren Hall office and home file cabinet.

Hough was stunned. "I figured I was starting from scratch, but I never figured on that," he later said.

Hough assigned the job to Jack Schoder. It would take him three weeks to read and log the material. The master lists documented more than two hundred fifty items, some of those subdivided into dozens of individual pieces. A couple dozen categories turned into more than a thousand letters, documents, and other articles of potential evidence.

Other elements defied organization. As they began meeting weekly, nothing prompted more discussion than the question of what might have prompted Brad King to kill his wife.

They spent hours discussing motive. Diane King wants Brad to go to work. He doesn't want to work, so he kills her? It didn't make sense. Why would he kill the proverbial golden goose? Why would he make more work for himself as a single parent? Why didn't he kill the kids?

Some detectives argued that the $54,000 life insurance money from the TV station had to figure into the scenario. Others speculated there might be insurance money the investigation hadn't discovered.

They talked about the women he was seeing. Was there a mistress they didn't know about? Were the women they had talked to being truthful?

The more they talked, the more work they seemed to create. For Gary Hough, it was a practical matter. "It wasn't a matter of whether he was guilty or innocent for me," he later said. "For me, it was a matter of cleaning up the complaint. We needed to clean it up first, plug the holes, before we could see exactly what he'd done."

But the unanswered questions troubled Gerry Woods. He still wasn't convinced Bradford King was the killer, though he was leaning heavily in that direction. He still held out the possibility King was just an oddball who was in the wrong place at the wrong time.

Hough agreed he was odd, probably more than they possibly knew.

"Look, you know he's not of sound mind," Hough said one night at the Winner's Circle. "There's no reason for a husband to go to that extent to kill his wife like that. You don't hide out in the shed, shoot her right through the heart, then set up a story. You don't go through all this bullshit unless you got somebody who's not in a normal state of mind."

The Michigan State Police had a section in Lansing for guys like King, he said. The detective had already set up an appointment.

"I want to see what they think of this guy," he told Woods. "I'll bet they'll say King's goofy. I'll bet ya they'll say he's goofier than a shit house rat."

The offices of the Behavioral Science Section of the Michigan State Police were unlike any in the department. Soft chairs and plush carpet. Focused lighting rather than fluorescent, lighting that its director kept subdued. Troopers and detectives visited the director after shootings and other job stresses. They also sought out Dr. Gary Kaufmann when they were confronted with suspects who eluded conventional crime solving techniques.

Gary Hough sat at a circular table, telling everything he'd learned about Brad King from the case file. Listening were Dr. Kaufmann and David Minzy, a detective sergeant in the state investigative resources unit. Both men were purveyors of an eclectic investigative technique called crime scene profiling. Employing psychology, sociology, forensic pathology, criminology, and patterns evident in hundreds of homicides, Minzy had devised a popular service, formulating more than 150 profiles in four years. The basic theory of profiling was this: A perpetrator's personality was reflected in the crime scene.

Dr. Kaufmann found Hough's stories about the ostensibly mild-mannered criminal justice instructor quite telling. "Your man sounds like a passive-aggressive to me," he said. "That's why you're having trouble finding a motive. The passive-aggressive isn't likely to show motive. It's simply not in his nature to do something like that."

Hough wanted a definition of the term.

"A passive-aggressive is a person who doesn't assert himself directly, usually for fear of being punished," Kaufman said. "So, he does it in a backhanded way. A passive-aggressive would punish a punctual loved one by being late with a good excuse or scare somebody with a boogeyman completely distanced from himself. A passive-aggressive would be bemused if confronted, rather than launch into a spirited defense. A passive-aggressive would not quit a job he didn't like. He'd find a way to make a boss fire him and lay the blame on him."

Minzy said the crime scene reflected that passive-aggressive nature. The shooting was an aggressive act committed from the obscurity of the dark barn loft. No direct confrontation. No overt rage. Just precise shooting and instant death. "The crime scene is consistent with everything you're describing about your suspect," he said.

Minzy had more. "Look, the killer had to have substantial amounts of information to pull this crime off where he did. This shooting appears thoroughly planned. The location of the loft. The escape route. The location of the hidden gun. Usually, that kind of knowledge is not accessible to a stranger. It's usually a person right next to the victim."

"Then, where do we look for motive?" Hough asked.

"He's going to be a manipulator, a subtle manipulator," Dr. Kaufmann said. "You need to look for the places where he manipulates. For him, any aggression is going to be a game. You've got to figure out his game."

Dr. Kaufmann added that while the suspect's aggression may be subtle, his need for positive reinforcement (his need for attention) may be grand and insatiable. "He may very well have a lot of narcissistic qualities," the psychologist said.

Both Minzy and Dr. Kaufmann spent considerable time discussing the second gunshot. They decided the second shot, the one to Diane King's vaginal area, was significant.

"You see this kind of gunshot when men feel the woman has made some kind of sexual transgression," Minzy said.

"Or, I think this guy may very well have a problem with women," Dr. Kaufmann said. "I'd just be willing to bet about anything on that."

Interview King's ex-wife thoroughly, the psychologist suggested. Girlfriends. Women he worked with. Old partners at Pontiac PD. They should interview anyone they could find that knew Brad King.

"You need to get to know him if you want to know why he killed her," he said. "You need to get to know him better than he knows himself."

David Minzy could have told this to the investigation much earlier, Hough later learned. After seeing the case develop in the news, Minzy had offered his services to the Calhoun County Sheriff's Department.

They declined twice.

Gerry Woods drove his Batmobile to the task force's first interview on June 18, a follow-up with Kristina Mony, Diane King's intern at Channel 41. Mony had written Jack Schoder a letter, saying she'd seen King when she and her mother retrieved the book *Secrets About Men Every Woman Should Know* before he left the state.

She was an emotional, bright-eyed girl of eighteen. Her mother joined them to offer support. They went over Jack Schoder's previous interview. Then, Woods turned on his tape recorder. They talked about the book that appeared to upset King so much, but everyone was at a loss as to why it had.

Woods asked, "Was she a domineering-type person, in your opinion?"

"Yes," Mony said. "She was always in control of every situation. . . . To some men she could be very intimidating. Never in a mean way. That was just her personality . . . but always done with a lot of love. She might be a little snippy when she was trying to get you to do a job, but the next minute she'd be willing to help you."

"What did Brad feel about this? How did he act underneath her directions?"

"In my opinion Diane was also very intimidating to Brad, her strength and her independence suffocated his personality. . . . Even the way he walked, he was like a weak individual.

He walked with rounded shoulders, a tucked down head. Behind Diane. A puppy dog."

Once, she'd seen Diane work him over in the newsroom simply because he'd come to her workplace with some stubble showing on his head.

That was before the murder, Mony explained. But there had been a major transformation, she said. The meek man who used to give her hugs had become cold and defiant after the killing. She talked about their visit to pick up the book.

"It is almost like Diane never existed," she said. "He was very strong, almost like he'd broken out of his shell."

Brad King talked about getting his kids back after Freida Newton had taken them, she said.

"They might think they can walk over me," he'd told her. "But nobody will cross me."

He wasn't the same man, she said again. "A totally different personality. A totally different man. You're gonna expect a change, because he lost his wife. People change when they go through that type of tragedy, but it's more than that. It's a *totally* new person."

The interview was a good start, Gerry Woods decided when he got back behind the wheel of his Batmobile. So was the task force. He felt like a weight had been taken off his chest.

That weekend, Gary Hough received a call from Jon Sahli. Gerry Woods, he said, might not be in the task force office that week. He was admitted to a hospital, the prosecutor said.

"A hospital?"

"Yeah, he went in complaining about pain in his arm and back."

"That doesn't sound good."

"Yeah, they're running tests. I guess they think Gerry may have had a heart attack."

2

Brad King's arrival in Denver the day before the funeral was some kind of tragic timing. Another sudden, unexpected death. Another mother. This time the mother was Susan Van Vleet's own.

Susan and John Van Vleet had offered their basement apartment to Brad and his children, and he'd arrived as scheduled with the Jeep Wagoneer, towing a U-Haul trailer. He brought Marler, but left Kateri with the D'Artagnans in Kalamazoo. He was planning to return for her after he got settled.

Susan would have offered the apartment to both Brad and Diane King, but Diane never gave her the chance. She'd found out about the stalker letter only after the murder. Diane had come to Susan before in a crisis. She could only guess why Diane hadn't told her about the threat.

"Maybe she knew what I would say, which would have been stop what you're doing. Get off the station. If they're not protecting you, demand protection. If they won't, come back here. Drag Brad and the kids with you. Come stay in the basement apartment until we figure out what to do next."

Find solutions. Susan and John built a successful consulting business doing just that. They served Fortune 500 companies with training seminars on new challenges in the American workplace. Names like "Productive Relationships," "Managing Corporate Change," "Surviving a Dual-Career Marriage," "Gender Diversity," and "Women Moving Forward" filled their list of seminars. Susan's background was social work, family services, and effectiveness training. John's was clinical psychology and training at Adolph Coors. Together they were Susan Van Vleet Consultants, Inc.

The work and frequent flights to both coasts produced a satisfying life. A creek ran through their redwood office complex in Englewood, and their split-level and two young boys were less than a minute's drive away. Their home was loud and lived-in and well stocked, not all that different from what Susan remembered as a young Jewish girl growing up in New Jersey. You took care of friends and family. You took care of people the way you hoped they would one day take care of you.

Friendship was not something Susan Van Vleet dispensed carelessly, as Diane King found out when they first met. They'd met the Kings through est. Back then, Susan and John had noticed a pattern among the people they called "esties."

"We had this built in discrimination against some esties," she would later explain. "The hard core would leave important jobs to become waiters after the est training. Instead of empowering them, est became an excuse not to do anything for the rest of their lives."

In fact, Brad King had been on one of those mystic sojourns for years. When Diane sought Susan's friendship, she was blunt.

She told her, "Diane, people who are in relationships with me have purpose in their lives. And if you're not working toward your purpose and being successful doing that, which is code for, *unless you have a job and are really doing something in life,* I'm not going to be your friend, because I'm not going to do ad nauseam therapy with you in my off hours."

Diane took "Women Moving Forward." In the seminar, Susan found Diane's outpouring moving.

"She came from a massively dysfunctional family," she recalled. "She knew nothing about her real father. She had suffered once herself from alcohol and cocaine problems. It was a problem in her community and now she wanted to do something about it. She kept trying to have a relationship with her mother and she was concerned something was wrong. She was blaming herself. There was no hugging. No love. She had to learn how to dress on her own, use deodorant, all the things a young girl needed to learn. There was no time left for the kids because her mother was always dealing with Royal. He was a beast. As an adult, she was the only child not under her mother's thumb. She would not let her mother control her life."

Diane King also had dreams, and as they became friends she watched her realize many of them. She'd announced in the seminar that she wanted to contribute to her people, become a role model for Native Americans on television. When she came up with Two Worlds Productions, she wanted to tap Susan's heritage for guidance. Why did so many Jewish children grow up to succeed, despite, like Indians, being seen as different by so many? Diane King's best work was ahead of her, Susan thought.

Always in the background was her mother. At least that's the way Diane portrayed it. "Freida didn't like Marler's name," Susan would recall. "She hated Marler's name. She didn't like Diane going to powwows. She didn't like them committing themselves to the Indian culture. She outright meddled and argued. She wanted control over the grandchildren. What schools they would go to, how they would dress. She blamed Brad."

Freida hated Brad, Diane said, simply because she couldn't influence him like other sons-in-law. "Brad will do whatever *I* want him to do," she told Susan. "He's not somebody my mother can control."

However, there were aspects of Bradford King that even Diane couldn't control. One night later, Susan and John Van Vleet talked about his liabilities.

"Brad can be kind of a jerk," John said.

"He can be really stupid, a multiple jerk," Susan said.

"Finding himself all those years," John said. "Going from one job to another, and it was kind of never his fault, and he's got a family to support."

"And there's the way he has to handle himself, the way he had to dress," she said. "He had to be dressed to perfection, whether they had money or not. That's kind of jerky."

Diane had taken care of Brad, emotionally as well as financially. Susan remembered when she left for Grand Junction, leaving Brad behind. He was working for their agency. He outright cried every day at his desk.

"He really folded," she recalled. "That relationship was tantamount to his well-being. He could not continue without her."

She remembered sending him to Grand Junction, giving him his work to take with him. "I think that was kind of jerky, too. We sent him there and he wasn't really doing anything for us there, so we asked for all of our stuff back, and he got angry about that."

"Brad has never been financially responsible," Susan said.

"Brad has never been responsible for his own life," John added. "That's what always got to us."

In some ways, they were a perfect match, the Van Vleets decided. Diane complained about the father she never knew. Brad talked of the distance he had with his mother, Marge.

"She was the mother he never really had," Susan said. "He was the father she never had."

"They had symbiotic pathology," John said. "You know, they'd *feed* on each other that way."

That's why Brad King being a suspect in the murder of his wife made absolutely no sense to Susan and John Van Vleet. Brad was lost without her. They could see that when they flew him out in March for the Denver Powwow. They bought the ticket to boost his spirits, but he was stoop shouldered and drawn, barely functioning. Susan put a dinner gathering together for him, inviting old friends from the area. Brad hardly ate. Susan was shocked at the questions their guests asked him only a few months after the murder. They wanted details about the killing and the investigation.

"I'm very upset with what happened here last night with these people," Susan told him the next day.

"This is their way of relating to it," Brad said. "But there isn't a lot I can answer. My attorney had told me that since I'm a suspect I cannot tell anybody anything."

Susan had only one question. What about the investigation of the stalker?

"I don't know," he said. "I haven't spoken to them. They haven't talked to me since the murder. They haven't talked to my lawyer, either."

Susan and John had talked with Brad only once about the murder, and he had volunteered the information. It was during his visit to their motel room after the funeral in Marshall. They didn't think it was appropriate to ask someone who had just lost his wife what the crime scene looked like, but Brad did make a few comments.

"He said the children were screaming in the car," Susan would later recall. "The police wouldn't let him off the porch to get the children out of the car, he said. They didn't ask him for his boots, he said. He offered them. They trampled all over the crime scene. He could barely talk about what she looked like when he found her. He said there was blood all over."

At the Denver Powwow, the second largest in the country, organizers held a memorial dance for Diane, a testimony to her standing in the community, Susan believed. Brad joined in the dancing.

"For him, it was the same as my father going to services after my mother died. This man was dancing because he was dancing for his wife. This was the only thing that gave him any kind of connection with her."

Returning now in June, Brad looked and sounded better. Susan's own loss notwithstanding, she and John were eager to help their old friend get back on his feet. Those King kids needed their father, Susan had decided, not all the trauma and uncertainty in Michigan. She was especially alarmed at Freida Newton's attempt at guardianship. Not only was she outraged that the children would be taken away from their natural father, she was concerned about the Newton home itself.

Susan clearly remembered the phone call a few years back from Diane, the night she called in a panic. Diane said her sister Denise had called her from Michigan. She walked in on her stepfather alone with a neighborhood retarded woman in his living room. She suspected sexual abuse. Diane said the rest of the family wouldn't call authorities. Susan left a tip with a Michigan abuse hotline. Nothing ever came of it. Denise later backed off the story, saying there was nothing to it.

Knowing this, the idea of the Kings moving back to Michigan in the first place had disturbed Susan. Diane was ambivalent about the move. One day she was talking about building family ties with her mother for her children, the next day she was talking about her need to maintain her distance.

Susan suspected part of that was cultural. She remembered when the Kings visited for the Denver Powwow in 1990. During a large group dance, Diane talked with Indian leader Russell Means, who told her about the need for Native Americans to honor all their elders. The conversation seemed to deeply disturb Diane. The Mohawk culture was matriarchal. Women wielded the power in the old tribes. Susan guessed Diane was torn between her culture and her family's past.

The Kings' move to the remote farmhouse also disturbed her. Though Diane never mentioned being stalked, Susan suspected something was seriously amiss. They talked three or four times in the six months before her death.

"Diane, are you all right?" Susan had asked her several times.

Diane answered with silence. With silence there wasn't a lot that could be done.

So, now they had Brad King and Marler, but no place to put them. Susan's mother had died of a massive heart attack while Brad was en route. Susan and John had a house full of relatives and didn't know how long they'd stay.

They resolved the problem quickly. They decided they would find a furnished apartment for Brad and offered to pay three months' rent in advance. Brad didn't hit them up for the money. He knew Susan would never tolerate begging.

Susan also handed Brad King a check for $3,000.

"Here," she said. "Take this till you get on your feet."

A thirty-five-year-old physical therapist named Cindy Zedelman preferred listening to talking, even when only children were in the room. She'd gone to listen in the Van Vleets' lower-level family room, watching Charlie and Adam Van Vleet play with Marler King, as the Jewish wake called *shiva* was underway in the upper part of the house.

Marler was talking to the other boys, oblivious to her and everyone else but his playmates. When Brad King visited three months earlier, Cindy Zedelman had heard Marler speak briefly in the same room with the same boys on the same subject. Now he was going into more detail.

"You know, I know who killed my mommy," he said. "They were two men in black cowboy hats."

"They were?" one of the boys said.

"Yeah, and I was afraid they were going to kill me, too."

3

G erry Woods was sitting up in his bed with the thick spiral notebook of the King case on his lap, underlining sentences in some reports, drawing big stars in the margins of others, places he thought offered good leads. He'd had a heart attack, now the doctors were looking for the source.

A night-side nurse's aide showed up, making small talk.

"Yeah, brought the office with me," he said.

"So, where ya work?" she asked.

"The prosecutor's office. Calhoun County."

She knew the office. Her mother had been a murder victim.

Gerry Woods knew the case, so did John Sahli, Jim Stadfeld, and Jack Schoder. It was the woman who burned up in the old schoolhouse, the foundation where Schoder was digging on the day the King homicide came in to dispatch. Woods knew that case had problems, not the least of which were caused by the fact that the King case had the sheriff's department spread so thin.

"Do you know why they haven't solved my mom's case?" she asked.

Gerry Woods could see the pain lines in her face.

"Ma'am, I don't know why it's not solved, but I do know it's not solid."

"Tell me," she said. "How come there's all this work on the King case, but not my mother's?"

Gerry Woods didn't know what to say.

The following day he vetoed his doctor's suggestion he remain in the hospital for more testing. He was thinking about two homicides now.

Gerry Woods decided he had to get back to work.

Back at the task force, Jack Schoder's documentation of the search warrant materials was producing discoveries previously obscured by sheer volume. The documents told their own story about the couple.

Diane King had kept copies of revealing letters. Prior to marrying King, she'd had an abortion and had a preference for dating married men. Task force detectives wondered if an affair had prompted Brad King to kill her. They began questioning witnesses about Diane King's own fidelity.

Schoder logged a file folder of her poems. One was written to her stepfather, Royal Newton. She seemed to want to reconcile past troubles when the family moved to Battle Creek in 1989. Others were addressed to her late father, written more than twenty years after his death. She seemed psychologically fragile. She held little back in the poems.

Maybe Diane King wasn't as in charge of the relationship as everyone thought, detectives speculated. Maybe King pulled her strings. With her endless talking and histrionics, she certainly would have handed a clever manipulator enough of them to tug.

One poem written shortly after their marriage was particularly telling. It was called "Oh Dad, Oh Dad."

> Oh daddy I miss you so long.
> Oh daddy, there's so much for you to see.
> Miss so much that's happened to me.
> I'm married now and have one girl.
> Her name's Alissa, she's a joy.
> My husband Brad, is hardly a boy.
> He's 39 and tall and fine.
> Oh daddy, he's all mine.
> I suspect his love is strong, like yours.
> Yet from time to time he's very coy.
> Dear daddy, did you play such silly games?
> I'm sure you did. I'm dying to know . . .

Diane's Army career faltered only after Brad King came into the picture, other documents showed. In 1983, she received an Article 15 for going AWOL for a weekend while assigned to Army Signal School. She told the Army she'd flown home to her family under "extreme stress." Weeks later, she cited "academic difficulties" in her officers' training and an unwillingness to "compromise my relationship with my fiancé, Bradford J. King," as her reason for seeking discharge.

Task force detectives studied family photographs developed from seized film. They were hoping for a snapshot of one Remington Model 511 Scoremaster, but found clues of family trouble instead. The photos of Brad King holding Marler and Kateri as newborns seemed to confirm what they'd already been told. Brad King didn't adjust easily to children. He looked glum, even angry in many of the pictures.

The documents and interviews with people who knew the couple were producing a pattern. Two influences pulled at Diane King constantly, two influences which had always been at odds. One was family. The other was Bradford J. King.

The itemization also produced some background on Bradford King. There was an autobiography, one typed by Nita Davis for King's doctorate application at Michigan State University. The first paragraph seemed inappropriately flippant, especially considering its intended audience, a studious academic admissions panel.

> I was born to military parents of Major and Lt. King in 1947. My mother met my father in the hospital when he had his pants down. Shortly thereafter, my parents were discharged from the Army and we moved to Luther, Michigan. My father became a banker, my mother remained at home to take care of me and eventually my brother, four years my younger. We moved two more times, finally settling in Croswell, Michigan. My father was president of the bank and I completed my secondary education at Crosslex High School.

In the same document, King cited corruption in the Pontiac Police Department as his reason for leaving police work. He wrote of finding himself in teaching. Gary Hough found his choice of words telling, considering what the state police psychologist Gary Kaufmann had said about King's narcissistic potential.

"During my tenure as a trainer," King wrote, "I realized that

I loved being in front of the room and providing instruction in a learning situation."

In the hundreds of pages of material, another important, influential woman emerged in King's life, a woman that detectives guessed he also might have manipulated for years. Jack Schoder logged a 1990 letter from Marge Lundeen. It was addressed to no person in particular, but its intent was clear.

"The following is a list of amounts of money that has been given to my son Brad King," she wrote. "Documents are attached to verify transactions. The total amount given him is deducted from his/per my estate."

Marge Lundeen listed ten disbursements, a total of $13,530 she'd given her son. Most of the payments were in 1989 and 1990, dispensed in amounts ranging from $300 to $1,500.

As task force detectives sifted through all the past-due notices, Gary Hough secured another search warrant. This one was for American Debt Counseling, the bill consolidation agency the Kings had signed up with in Kalamazoo.

Jack Schoder interviewed one of the staffers at the agency, who said the Kings seemed eager to get out of debt as soon as possible. They were prompt with their payments, the staffer continued. Then after the murder, all contact stopped. Four weeks after the killing, Brad King contacted the agency, apologizing that he was having trouble coping with his wife's death. He made several appointments, but kept cancelling them. Then, in early June, he finally showed up, saying he was leaving on vacation for the summer. He brought his account up to date and then some. He gave the agency a payment of $2,000.

Marge Lundeen had signed the check.

Gerry Woods went right to work on a subject also covered in Schoder's inventory, Diane King's five-page grant proposal for Two Worlds Productions. It sought $470,000 for costs in the first year of the project, but promised an income of nearly $6 million by the third year. It cited Coors, Upjohn, Kellogg's, and the National Geographic Society as "targeted" corporations for support.

On June 26, two days after he was released from the hospital,

Woods drove to Michigan State University in East Lansing to talk to a source familiar with the proposal. Dr. George Cornell was director of the university's Native American Institute and a member of the Michigan Commission on Indian Affairs. Cornell also had a PhD in American Studies. Diane and Brad King had approached Cornell in September of 1990, seeking advice on where to find funding.

The director clearly remembered the meeting. Over the years, he said, he'd dealt with a parade of questionable people seeking sources of state and private money for minority projects, but even so, the Kings especially stood out. Their proposal and appearance were long on glitz and short on substance, he said.

"He was wearing a cashmere coat, and they were both dressed to the nines," Cornell later recalled. "In fact, I thought if they're doing this well, what do they need this money for?"

Woods ran tape as they talked.

"They came to this office with a business plan, primarily looking for resources tied to Indian status and Indian economic development," Cornell said. "Something to do with broadcasting, training, the production of audiovisual materials tied to American Indians in the United States."

"During the meeting, who was presenting this to you?" Woods asked. "Was it him or her?"

Cornell leaned back into his chair. Diane did most of the talking, he said, but checked in with Brad King frequently, as though she were asking, "How am I doing?" "They were looking for, pretty much, start-up capital. Basically, they were looking for free money."

Woods wondered if the proposal was realistic.

"I wasn't really helpful. I basically told them some sources that they could check into . . . but it was pretty obvious to me, because I've worked with a lot of Indian economic development, and economic development activities, that they were looking for free money tied to Indian status. I get those kind of phone calls every week, and it's very difficult for me to deal with them seriously . . . I pretty much look at that as a con. When you talk about individuals going into business trying to use public resources, it doesn't work that way. I mean who is it *really* going to benefit? It's going to benefit them. It's not going to benefit the Indian community. . . . You're attempting to use minority status to catapult you with free money into business."

"I mean a half million dollars with five pages?" Cornell said later. "You've got to be kidding me."

Cornell had other impressions. "Without being too prejudicial or too biased, I really didn't like Brad King very much," he said. "It was pretty obvious to me that this was a partnership, and I really had the idea *he* was really looking to benefit from her Indian status . . . without question he was a player. I would go a step further. I thought he was pretty good at, at kind of catering to her, and playing her in some respects."

"I use the term *manipulator*," Woods said. "Is that a correct term or not?"

"I think that would be a real accurate term."

By late June, the field corn appeared right on schedule. Knee-high by the Fourth of July, folks in the Midwest like to say. Before it got any taller, the King task force gathered at 16240 Division. Thursday, June 27, was sunny, hot, and humid, but Gary Hough arrived with a taxing list of chores at Thunderspirit that day.

Five detectives and thirteen members of a Battle Creek search and rescue team converged on the farm. They broke their first sweat looking for a location Brad King might have aligned the sights of the Remington Model 511 Scoremaster. In his police statements, King had hardly accounted for his time on Friday, the day before the murder. He said he'd gone rabbit hunting. Maybe he'd said that, detectives speculated, to cover for his own gunshots as he zeroed in his gun with the CCI Stingers somewhere in the area. Then he'd dumped the casings from the target practice when he'd shoved the gun in the creek.

Volunteers and detectives worked the dog track, then fanned out across the property on both sides of Division, studying trees, fence posts, and other objects for bullet holes. They found impressions in the cement silo and a shell casing, but neither could be tied to the gun.

That day, Gerry Woods was on a different kind of search. Woods still believed they hadn't eliminated the possibility that Brad King was the unfortunate victim of circumstance. He found himself on an investigative course without personal precedent.

"We were in the business of trying to prove the negative," he would later recall. "We were in the business of proving nobody *but* Bradford King could have killed Diane King. I'd heard about proving the negative. I'd heard about it from other detectives, and what they said was true. It was terribly hard to do."

Gary Hough's methodology for determining what *couldn't* have happened at twilight on February 9 involved working with known times and distances: Neighbor Tonya Scott hears shots fired at 6:30–6:35 P.M. Doug Nielsen sees the Wagoneer and nothing else in the driveway at 6:40 P.M. There are no cars parked near the road. Brad King calls the dispatcher at 6:49 P.M.

In the early afternoon heat of June 27, Hough added another factor into the mix. He wanted to experience firsthand the distance and the sight lines involved in Brad King's version of that night.

Jack Schoder positioned himself at the barn and was asked to briskly walk the dog track upon cue. Meanwhile, Hough walked back to the hay bales where Brad King said he was when he heard the gunshot. Just after Schoder began his jaunt, Hough began walking the 2,069 feet back to the barnyard.

Gerry Woods already was drawing his own conclusions about the route from the hay bales to the barn. He'd theorized that King would have had a clear view of the marsh where the gun was found on his trip back to the barnyard on February 9. More importantly, King would probably have had a view of the dog track along the edge of the marsh and through the bare field between the creek and Division Drive.

Schoder's run took nine minutes. It took Hough fifteen minutes to walk in from the hay bales. When they were done, Hough and Schoder stood perspiring in the barnyard, the tall Victorian barn behind them contrasted against the hazy summer sky.

"So what did you see?" Woods asked.

"Just our friend Mr. Schoder here comin' right along that swamp. It's physically impossible for King not to have seen something. He's got to see the shooter in the swamp, or in the field. He's got to see a car. He's got to see something."

"And King says he doesn't see shit," said Woods.

"And if he hides in the swamp, and waits for King to pass," Hough continued, "then everything is thrown off. A shooter can't get back to the car in time."

Gerry Woods lit a cigarette. "I think we may be on track here."

"You're damn straight we're on track. Ain't nobody else could have done it but old Bradley."

They had a bunch of times and distances. They had a swamp and some farm fields. Later they would do it all again at twilight with the same results. But Gerry Woods also knew they couldn't run a jury of twelve around that swamp with stopwatches.

"There's just one problem," Woods said, exhaling. "Now how the hell we gonna prove it, Gary? Will ya just tell me that?"

4

Freida Newton and Denise Verrier were sure Kateri King was still in Michigan. They drove up and down the streets of Kalamazoo, hoping to see someone with the little girl.

"If I saw her, I was just going to pull over the car and grab her," Freida Newton later admitted.

They went to the Department of Social Services, seeking protective custody. Instead they were cautioned. Brad King had the legal right to leave his child with whomever he wanted. King, in fact, had left documentation with the D'Artagnans, certifying their temporary guardianship in medical emergencies.

Freida then began calling the D'Artagnans' home, asking about Kateri, but getting no answers. On July 3, Diane's sister Darlene called Kalamazoo police, asking them to make a welfare check on the child at the Indian couple's home.

Andre D'Artagnan met police at the door, saying Brad King and the children had moved out. When police asked if they could look in the house to confirm the child's absence, he refused. Hours later, Julie D'Artagnan called Susan Van Vleet, telling her the police had shown up at the door. The consultant booked both of them on a Denver flight that night.

The day after Independence Day, Frieda Newton received another letter on the peace pipe stationery. Brad King provided a Denver phone number, but no address.

Dear Freida,

  We are moved into our own place now . . .

  I have heard through people in Michigan that you are concerned about the children's safety.

  This only further indicates that my concern regarding you and attempts to take the children are valid.

  There are two explanations you owe me and I will not stop asking for answers until you provide them.

  1. Why did you try to take the children from me?
  2. Why are you concerned for their safety?

  They are a product of the love and commitment that Diane and I had for each other. They are my responsibility until they are—well at least 18 and then I still feel that I have a continued responsibility at a different level.

  I will provide an address when I get some answers.

  Now, the last thing that I have to say is this—you cost me $1,700 over your trying to take the kids. That is money I can use. It was most of our savings. I expect to be paid back!

Sincerely,
Brad

While Jack Schoder and Jim Stadfeld argued that Brad King was now free to flee into obscurity, Gary Hough and Gerry Woods contended that Brad King's personality unwittingly would transform his own children into his tether.

Hough based this on Dr. Gary Kaufmann's psychological profile. Woods just felt like he was getting to know the man through his interviews. Brad King valued only people, places, and things that enhanced him, they both believed.

"Sure, he wants those kids, but he don't give a shit about 'em," Woods said. "He wants 'em because he can use 'em. He ain't goin' nowhere where we can't find him."

The children were worth at least $800 a month in Social Security benefits, Hough pointed out.

"He won't be hard to find," he added.

On July 8, Woods talked to Jerry Colvin, the general manager of WUHQ-Channel 41, and later his wife, Virginia. They contributed to King's emerging portrait of a man who seemed to take passivity to the extreme. Colvin told Gerry Woods that King had shown up at the station about two weeks after the funeral.

"We sat down and talked and he just said, 'Well, I wish she was here and I miss her,'" Colvin told Woods. "But there was no aggressiveness on his looking for a killer or reasons why someone would do that to his wife. I thought that was kind of strange."

His wife, Virginia, recalled the couple sitting with her at the TV station Christmas party and Diane talking about conflict between Brad and Freida Newton.

"She said to me, 'This marriage isn't everything I'd hoped it would be, but it is what it is, and my mother is just going to have to accept that.'"

"But Brad was there?" Woods asked.

"Brad was sitting right there and heard every word of it. And I was surprised at that. . . . No rolling of the eyes. No turning of the head. Just nothing."

Woods found more of the same as he learned everything he could from the priest and nun involved in the planning of Kateri's baptism. There had been no significant arguments at the meeting, Sister Josephine Karas told Woods at St. Mary Church. Diane had the baptism pretty thoroughly planned out already. She largely ignored Brad King's suggestions.

"As the meeting went on, he became very involved in what we were going to do and tried to assist Diane," she said.

"But still, she was the domineering force?" Woods asked. "Is that a fair statement?"

"Oh, yes. She, well . . . that's right. I would say it was a fair statement. She knew what she wanted, and she overrode him many times."

Sergeant Lou Mueller discovered another side to King when he interviewed the couple's baby-sitter, a sixteen-year-old neighbor named Kameron Kae Knowlton. She was the same neighbor girl Diane King would have walk in the house with her when Brad was not at home. She estimated she dropped by to just visit with the anchorwoman more than a dozen times.

"He was *really weird*," she said of Brad King.

He demanded she call him "Mr. King" and teased her about not believing in killing animals. He bragged of his latest hunts and seemed to say things just to scare her, she said.

Kameron painted a relationship between Brad and Marler far different from previous, superficial accounts. He yelled at the boy for trivial things, then Diane would intervene and caution him not to be so rough, she said.

The teenager also saw no sign of the contemporary husband Diane King puffed about to people she was trying to impress at work. He was unmotivated and irresponsible, the girl said. He didn't finish projects he started, like his remodeling of the porch. The house was often in disarray, though he was home all day. Diane usually had to clean it when she returned from work.

Like Cindy Acosta, Gina Zapinski, and others, Kam Knowlton said, Brad King never gave them any privacy. Brad seemed obsessed with Diane. Photographs in the home only reinforced this for the teenager. All the portraits on the walls were professionally done. They were all of Diane. There were no pictures of him.

"Even wedding pictures," she said.

On July 10, Woods sat down with Joanne Karaba, Diane King's artistic neighbor. Earlier that afternoon, Woods had interviewed her husband, Mark, committing his story of the missing .22 CCI Stinger shells to tape. Karaba said he had as many as a dozen shells missing. He was certain his son hadn't taken them. He hadn't raised his boy, Josh, that way. He pointed out, why would Josh sneak them when he could shoot the gun any time he wanted?

Now, Woods ran his tape recorder with Joanne. They had a wide-ranging discussion about her friendship with Diane and the tension she saw between the Kings in the days and weeks before the murder. Joanne talked about what she knew about the break-in before Christmas and the trips to *Disney on Ice* and the food show. She told Woods that Diane had told her about the mysterious caller.

"She goes, 'I thought for a minute it was just Brad playin' a sick joke on me,' and kinda laughed it off," she said.

Woods explored the Kings' visit to the Karaba home on February 4, the day the couple appeared to be upset coming back from Kateri's baptism meeting, the day Joanne was watching Marler. Woods wanted to account for the entire visit, to see if King might have had an opportunity to see the blue box of CCI Stingers on the porch.

"How long did they stay?"

"Probably, I'm gonna say they sat in the living room and talked for about five minutes, maybe seven minutes, eight, not quite ten, when Diane looked at Brad and said, 'Kateri's out in the car, oh my God! We forgot Kateri's out there.' So then she asked Brad to go get Kateri, and Brad went out and got Kateri, came back in, and she had messed her pants, and she was crying."

But Diane, Joanne Karaba also said, asked Brad to go outside to the car and get the diaper bag. He left out the door of the side porch.

"So, we're right there at the changin' table," she continued. "I mean, your daughter is cryin' and messy, and it seems like he would have zipped back in."

Instead they waited. So long, she said, Joanne offered Diane a diaper. "It was in the back room. I got that. Came back. And gave her a pair of rubber pants, and then Brad came in."

"How long a period would you say?" Woods asked.

"About three minutes. 'Cause by that time Kateri was cleaned up, I mean we had her all wiped up before he came back with the diaper."

"So Brad was out of your sight for at least three minutes in your opinion?"

"Yeah, that's why it stands out in my mind, because it was like, *where did he go?*"

Maybe out to the porch to "borrow" a half-dozen .22 caliber CCI Stinger bullets, Woods thought.

The task force spent July and early August solidifying the crime scene and covering old ground with new tools.

Gary Hough wanted key people who responded to the call at 16240 Division interviewed. He wanted detectives to talk to paramedics and sheriff's department personnel who came into contact with Brad King in the minutes after the shooting. He wanted King's demeanor documented.

Gerry Woods interviewed the clerk who rented King the video the day of the murder, the store receipt obtained by search warrant. He also interviewed her husband as well. It turned out he was cutting wood across Division Drive the day of the killing. Woods watched the rented movie, *Next of Kin.* He could see no connection to the case. It was about a hillbilly cop who goes to the big city to help his brother solve a big case.

The computer sorting of phone records from Thunderspirit and King's Sangren Hall office came back from the State Police Intelligence Unit in Lansing. Sergeant Phil Mainstone taped detailed interviews with Gina Zapinski and Denise Verrier, discussing calls made to their homes in the months, days, and hours before the murder, pinning down what happened when and where. Gerry Woods would reinterview Freida Newton, probing the final days and hours before Diane's death.

Later, Jack Schoder and Jim Stadfeld complained between themselves that the task force was not producing anything new. Bitterness over the involvement of the state police continued. At the top, Jon Olson would wonder for months if Jon Sahli had insisted on a task force just as some kind of political payback.

"I've said this to anybody who wants to listen," Stadfeld would later maintain many months later. "That anything done by the task force made no difference. I think it was already there."

Other detectives could argue otherwise. But soon, all that was about to change.

The detectives discussed Barbara Elgutaa when her name came up on the profile sheets. She'd picked up the King children on February 9. She'd phoned the sheriff's department a week after the murder, eager to cooperate. She knew all about the stalker and the Kings' security measures. Jack Schoder's report of their phone conversation also noted she'd seen Brad King come in from a walk with a gun last November. No one had yet talked to the woman face-to-face.

"I think we better have a talk with the young lady," Gary Hough said.

On July 11, Sergeant Lou Mueller met Barbara Elgutaa in her office at Kellogg Community College. Mueller turned on his tape recorder.

"Apparently you knew Diane King," he began. "How long did you know her?"

"Around nine months," she said.

Elgutaa described their relationship in a wide-ranging discussion. They both were professionals with Native American backgrounds. She visited Diane frequently. Their children played together. She didn't know Brad well, she admitted. He was always at the house, but rarely took part in discussions.

"He was different," she said. "I felt something strange about him."

Elgutaa discussed conflict between the Kings over the stalker letter. "He thought she was overreacting. That's what she said."

"Was there a time where she asked him to beef up the security systems in the house?" Mueller asked.

"She asked him to change the lock, and she said that she was angry because it took him a week. . . . He had just made a comment like 'I don't know what you're worrying about. Nothing's going to happen to you. . . .' she said, 'You do it today,' and he did."

A week and a half before Kateri was born, Diane called her crying, saying she feared for her life. She visited Diane in the hospital the day her daughter was born.

"I said, 'How are things going with you and Brad?' And she said things weren't getting any better, that they had just had a big fight that weekend, the biggest fight they had ever had.' I asked her if she was going to go into counseling, and she said that she would think about it . . . but that things had to change, and that Brad was going to have to make some changes."

Diane was adamant about this, Elgutaa said. "It seemed that she was gonna put her foot down. That's what it seemed like. Enough is enough. 'You're going to have to go to work. I am going to stay home with the kids, and that's the way it's going to be.' "

Mueller wondered if she'd noticed any changes in their relationship after this.

Elgutaa remembered running into the couple at a Christmas concert. "He never said a word the entire time. I held the baby, he got up. In fact he got up and walked away and stood by the wall."

Elgutaa told Mueller how angry King sounded when she called him around noon the day of the murder. "He mentioned that Marler was being sassy, and being disrespectful to him, and that he was very angry about that. And he had said, 'Diane never spends any time with the kids.' And he was angry."

Elgutaa said she asked him when Diane and the children would be back. King said early that evening.

"I said, be sure to tell her that I want her and the kids to come over tonight, I'm gonna come pick her up."

Mueller needed to pin down King's exact response. The task force's working theory was that King didn't expect the children to be in his wife's car the night of the murder. They speculated he probably planned to drive off to ditch the gun and secure an alibi, leaving his dead wife to be discovered later. When he saw the children were in the car, probably after shooting her, he decided to hide the gun on the property and call the police.

Even King, they decided, wasn't insensitive enough to leave his kids alone in the cold.

"You were under the impression those children were coming back from Detroit, or you just didn't know?" Mueller asked Elgutaa.

"I would, just knowing Diane, I wouldn't see why she would leave her kids there, but I had the impression that the kids were coming back."

"But Brad never said, 'The children are going to stay in Detroit,' or—"

"No."

" 'Okay, we may come over with the children?' "

"No."

"He never said one way or the other?"

"And I didn't make the invitation to him either. I said specifically, 'I'd like Diane and the kids to come over.' So he knew I wasn't inviting him."

Mueller wondered about King's indulgence in Native American culture. "Is Brad an Indian?"

"No, he's not. He's not an Indian. He seemed to be fascinated, very fascinated with Indian ways. He seemed to want to get his hands on everything he could that had to do with Indians."

This was evident before Diane's death, she said. "I watched him watch the way the men act, the way they move, the way they wear their clothes, the way they talk. He was an observer. He sat back and observed everything around him."

"That observance, was it more in awe, or he appreciated it?"

"It didn't feel like appreciation. It seemed as if he wanted to be Indian himself, and he, if he could do anything to make himself an Indian, he would."

Mueller ended the interview with a question that had become a task force standard. "Barbara, at any time that you were out at the King residence, did you see any type of firearms?"

Elgutaa answered matter-of-factly. "In November, before the baby was born, that same time, we were in the house, and Brad and Nuri had gone for a walk, and he had come in, and he had a gun in his hand. He stood between the utility room and the kitchen, he stood there, and he held it in his right hand. All I noticed about the gun was the long barrel. How long and skinny it was."

She relayed their conversation. "I just said to him, 'Did you get anything?' Jokingly. And he didn't say anything.

"And Diane said, 'Well, he can't hunt for deer.' This was deer season. 'Because our landlords want the deer to be here, so there's no hunting deer.'

"And he stood there for a moment, and he was digging in his pockets, or whatever."

Mueller was digging in his pockets, for pictures.

Elgutaa continued, "My father has rifles and he used to go deer hunting, and I just noticed how different it looked compared to the rifles I seen my father (use), when he goes deer hunting."

"Okay, Barbara, I'm gonna show you a photograph of a gun, and I want you to look at it, and tell me if you recognize this gun."

With that, Mueller dropped a photo of the Remington Model 511 Scoremaster on her desk.

5

Gerry Woods and Jon Sahli were smoking cigarettes on the front porch of the Hall of Justice during a recess for a murder trial when Sergeant Lou Mueller's car came squealing into the traffic circle.

"She identified the goddamn gun," the detective said as he climbed the steps. "It looks like the gun, she said."

Gary Hough was just coming out of the courthouse doors.

"I knew he had something," Hough later said, "because that hard, old, stubborn bastard just don't get excited."

"What are we going to do next?" Woods asked.

"Screw the pictures," Hough said.

The next day Mueller and Woods both drove to the campus of Kellogg Community College for another appointment with Barbara Elgutaa.

"My first question is, what is your basic knowledge of long guns, or any type of weapons?" Mueller asked. "Do you know the difference between say a small gun and a deer gun?"

"I know the guns that my father would use when he would go deer hunting, and how big and heavy, and how long they were. I know that there's different kinds of guns used for different kinds of things: small game, large game, handguns, bear and deer guns. And that's the knowledge that I know of guns and how to hold them. . . ."

They talked about the difference in actions. She had brought up the day before that she knew what a bolt action was.

"Okay, so think back to the day of November of 1990, what is your estimation of the type of gun Brad had when he came in from hunting?"

"Okay, the gun that he was holding had a very long, skinny barrel. He had his hand over where the trigger is, and if there was a bolt, that's where his hand was, so I wouldn't see if there was a bolt or not. I was curious about it because it looked different from the guns my dad had used, because they were big, heavy guns, and he was using one hand to hold his gun, and I noticed he could hold it in one hand comfortably."

Barbara Elgutaa knew the difference between guns, Mueller and Woods decided. She just didn't have the proper vocabulary to articulate it. She saw handguns and "long guns." She noticed differences in the barrel sizes and action. Mueller wanted to know if she knew the difference between a rifle and a shotgun. Mueller had shown her pictures of both the rifle and King's Winchester shotgun the day before.

"I know by looking at it, but I don't know the names of the guns," she said.

Mueller pulled out the photograph of the Winchester shotgun. "I showed you a picture yesterday of a rifle, or a long gun, and you said that definitely was not the gun."

She pointed to the shotgun. "This one, no."

"Which I am now showing you, that definitely wasn't a gun like that?"

"No, because I . . . no."

They asked her to follow them to the parking lot. Waiting in the trunk of their car was the Winchester shotgun and the Remington Model 511 Scoremaster. They wrote up her response in a formal report:

> After the taped interview with Barbara Elgutaa at Kellogg Community College on this date the following inquiries and questions were made which would not reflect on the transcribed portion of the interview.
>
> When asked her feelings toward Brad King at this time Elgutaa stated that she held no animosities toward him nor did she hold a vendetta toward him. Elgutaa advised that the only thing she felt toward him was sorrow . . .
>
> At 1:10 P.M., 12 July 1991, Barbara Elgutaa was shown the .22 caliber rifle which was being held in evidence by the Calhoun County Sheriff's Department as the one they believed killed Diane King . . . Elgutaa after viewing the .22 rifle stated that it was "very similar" to the one she had seen in Brad King's hands at his residence in mid-November but could not be absolutely sure.

Six days later, in the loft office of Darling & Sons True Value Hardware, another witness was struggling with what he might or might not have seen.

They called Phil Mainstone the "farm detective" on the task force. It was unclear whether that was because of his acreage, or because he just liked to visit a spell before running tape.

"This is a tape recording, an interview with Mr. Tom Darling," Mainstone began, noting the date, time, and their location. "I believe we're on the second level?"

Darling nodded.

"Second level at the office of Mr. Darling. Present, obviously, during this interview is Mr. Darling. Mr. Darling, you and I have sat here and talked for approximately an hour now.

"And there was a particular section of our interview that

concerns the use of a .22, and also comments that were made by Mr. King in regards to the use of the .22." Mainstone noted Tom Darling had talked to Jim Stadfeld back in March.

"Yes," Darling said. "I called his office."

Darling told the story about Brad King saying he'd use his own .22 if necessary for the troublesome woodchuck. He explained how King had brought his grandfather's Winchester shotgun on a rabbit hunt. Later, Darling would remember discussing with King whether King might want to use a .22, a gun some top marksmen preferred because it added a challenge to the hunt.

"Earlier in our conversation I showed you a picture of a shotgun . . . and you identified that."

"Yes, that's the gun."

"Okay."

"Yeah, Brad told me it was his grandfather's gun."

"And I also showed you another photograph, and that is of the .22 rifle."

"Yes."

"And then you made some remark about that. If you'd restate that, please."

"In all the times I've been in Brad and Diane's home, I've been in upstairs, downstairs, in their attic, in the basement, and helped on many projects—"

An employee buzzed Darling with a business call. When Mainstone turned the tape back on, Darling continued.

"If it were . . . I guess, being that I've been around guns all my life, seeing a bolt-action .22 wouldn't have been a big thrill, and I look at that gun and something about it says 'I've seen that before,' and I'm sure I've seen it in their home. You know, if it were something really special, if it were a Target Master, you know, super deluxe gun, I would say, golly, that's quite some gun. But a bolt, an old bolt-action .22 didn't do anything for me."

"Okay."

"And so that's why I . . . I'm kinda vague on when, where, why, being in their home so many times. Yeah, that gun looks familiar."

Mainstone got right down to it. "It looks familiar and you recall seeing it in their home?"

"I'm . . . I'm sure I have."

"But you don't recall when or exactly where?"

"Right."

Thursday was "dog day" at the Copper Bar: Regular dogs forty cents. Chili dogs not even twice that. On Thursdays, fourteen-year-old Chris Sly and his folks always had dogs for lunch. The boy had worked all morning in the Darling & Sons True Value Hardware, now it was half past noon, and his stepdad was still talking to the detective in his upstairs office. He wondered what could be taking him so long.

Chris Sly knew a little bit about the King case, but a lot more about skateboards and arcade video games. For a long time, the name Brad King usually meant he had a yard to cut. He used to drive their lawn tractor all the way down to Thunderspirit, then spend a good couple of hours mowing the lawn. King usually came out on the porch to pay him. Sometimes he got a compliment. Sometimes he didn't. He always got five bucks. He never got a tip.

Brad King was okay, Chris Sly thought. He never said much, about sports or cars or music or anything. They never talked about hunting. He might have told Brad King he had hunted, and that his stepdad had let him use his shotgun, but he really didn't get into hunting much at all.

Finally, they crossed the street and ordered up their chili dogs. His stepdad was talking about Brad King to his mother. Finally, he turned to Chris.

"Chris, you ever seen anything unusual down at the Kings'?"

"Well, I just seen a gun on his porch."

Tom Darling stopped chewing. Chris Sly had told him that before, but he never seemed to show much interest. He didn't seem to really hear him, like parents sometimes do.

"When did you see a gun on the porch? I don't know of a gun that sits on his porch."

"When I was down there mowing the yard."

"Last summer?"

"Yeah, when he was paying me. It was laying on the freezer."

"There was a gun there?"

"Yeah. Like I said, there's a .22 that used to sit on his porch."

A week later, Jim Stadfeld laid out five photographs of the Winchester shotgun and the Remington Model 511 Scoremaster on Tom Darling's back porch for Chris Sly.

"This looks like the one I saw," he said.

He was pointing to the .22.

A week later, on July 30, Stadfeld committed the interview to tape. Chris Sly gave him three transcribed pages of one-word answers. Later, Stadfeld told other task force detectives he wasn't sure Chris Sly would make a good witness. He was the same age as the detective's daughter.

"He was awful quiet. I know if it was my daughter, and we put her on the stand, she'd probably freeze up and not be able to say a word."

Jim Stadfeld was concerned about the entire Darling family, in fact. Earlier in the summer, before the task force was formed, Tom Darling had called him, extremely upset.

"Jim, what's going on with this case?" Darling asked. "Have you heard the rumors about me that have been going around town?"

"Yeah, I've heard 'em." Stadfeld, and most everyone else, had heard quite a few.

First, the talk was that a Marshall businessman was the case's new suspect. Then, people got right down to using Tom Darling's name. Tom was having an affair with Diane King. Kateri was his child. Diane demanded Tom leave Susan, so Tom killed her. Or, perhaps Susan had shot her when she found out.

"It's just small-town bullshit," Stadfeld said.

But the bullshit could get downright creative, especially after some truth was thrown into the mix. The Darlings were at a church function the weekend of the murder, somebody pointed out. So, Tom's brother Mike was the triggerman, went the gossip. That's why Mike Darling had left town earlier in the year, everyone said. Some were now saying that Mike Darling was being kept in a faraway jail.

Tom Darling wanted help. "You know, this is hurting me, Jim. What can you guys do?"

Stadfeld was apologetic. "Absolutely nothing, Tom. There's a gag order on this case. You're just going to have to weather it, ignore it, if you can. We both know it's not true. It will eventually pass."

It had only worsened, in fact. Mike Darling had left Marshall not for jail, but to work for Wal-Mart in Iowa. Their family partnership altered, the Darlings had decided to put both the hardware and variety stores on the commercial real estate market.

This confirmed it, the gossip mongers said. Tom Darling was trying to escape. Tom Darling was trying to get out of town.

When Jim Stadfeld read the transcript of Phil Mainstone's interview with Tom Darling about seeing the .22, he became concerned. "I've known Tom to be the most honest person I know," Stadfeld would later say. "I just couldn't understand why all these things were popping up now. I felt like I had an obligation to flat-ass ask him if he was fabricating."

He called up Tom Darling.

"Tom, what do you mean you saw that gun in King's house? You didn't tell me this at first."

"Jim, I told you I can't testify that *that* is the gun," Darling said. "But I do believe I saw a gun that looked like that in the house."

They talked about the wording of their first interview. Darling maintained he thought Stadfeld was asking him to say without hesitation that he'd seen the Remington Model 511 Scoremaster.

"You know, Tom, it's going to sound like you're manufacturing evidence," Stadfeld said. "*I* know you're not. I know you're a deeply religious person who wouldn't do it on a bet. But that's what it's going to sound like."

Tom Darling knew all about it. He knew how things already sounded around Marshall.

Jim Stadfeld was worried what some crafty defense lawyer might do to Tom Darling and son on the stand.

6

Returning to Marshall to visit her parents in August, Cindy Acosta talked at length with Jim Stadfeld, telling him about Brad King's possessive obsession with his wife and the night the stalker's letter showed up in her mailbox.

Months earlier, she'd sent the detectives her husband Juan's fingerprints. They just went out and bought some ink and made the prints themselves. A month ago, the FBI crime lab had analyzed the stalker letter. The unidentified prints on the letter turned out to be her husband Juan's.

More memories surfaced in the seven months since her colleague's death. She remembered Christmas time, going over to Diane's the day she was decorating her tree. Diane was trying so hard to be like Martha Stewart with all the right trimmings. Carols played. Marler watched a Sesame Street Christmas show. But something about the scene was hollow, Cindy decided. Brad appeared to be just going through the motions. There was something counterfeit about Diane Newton King's little Christmas and her little farmhouse and her little family. Cindy found the scene jarring, but she could never pinpoint exactly why.

Cindy remembered Brad sulking at a Christmas party she and Juan threw just before they moved to Venezuela. Diane had a crowd of people around her minutes after she arrived. Brad stood off by himself, watching quietly and drinking too much.

Eventually, he came over to Cindy, draping his arm around

her and whining about how difficult Kateri was as a newborn. Cindy thought, *Diane* had the cesarian. *Diane* was breast-feeding and had to endure the sleepless nights.

Cindy Acosta felt very uncomfortable. She was uncomfortable with Brad King's behavior with his three-week-old infant when they arrived. He'd carried Kateri, wrapped in an Indian blanket, to a bedroom where nearly two dozen of their guests had put their winter coats on a double bed. Cindy walked in to a guest room, urging Brad to bring Kateri there where they had another bed. She set up pillows, but he insisted.

"No, I'll just put her here," he said. He placed her among all the coats.

"I felt very uncomfortable with this newborn in there and people literally throwing their coats on the bed," Cindy later explained. "I told people to be careful, because there was an infant there, but I couldn't always be there. One couple even came out saying, 'My God, there's a baby on that bed.' "

When Diane learned of Kateri's location, she tried to make light of it, blaming Brad in a joking tone. But Cindy could tell she was shocked and embarrassed.

At first, Cindy wondered where Brad's empathy was for the newborn. When she heard he was having trouble adjusting to the baby, she wondered if Brad King wasn't just very cleverly trying to smother the child to death.

Gail Hietzker didn't object when task force detectives called and asked her to meet them at a state police post in Ypsilanti on August 28 for more questioning about her ex-husband. She had no secrets. She had no real horror stories to tell.

Brad King most likely had not killed Diane, she'd already decided. Not only had Gail never sensed a violent streak in the man she lived with for thirteen years, there was another consideration. Killing Diane meant that Brad King would be stuck raising two toddlers.

That simply wasn't his style.

Months later, she explained it all again to another interviewer. "The children are the issue to me because I just couldn't see him willing to take on the responsibility of two children. I don't think he had anything to gain."

In fact, Gail Hietzker maintained that the unexpected introduction of their daughter caused the first breakdown in their relationship, a marriage that up until then had been very good. Doctors had told her she wouldn't be able to get pregnant. Four years into their marriage, morning sickness and an examination confirmed she was four months along.

"I really think he loved being the center of attention," she recalled. "He was like my main focus, and I think he really enjoyed that. Me getting pregnant was not what he wanted."

By their daughter's first birthday, they separated, Gail and the baby staying with her folks for six weeks. Finally, they worked out their differences on the phone. When she returned they did not go into counseling, but she made herself a promise: If he ever started acting that way again, she'd dump him.

A half-dozen years later, he came to her on a Sunday night and said, "I don't think I want to be married anymore." She gave him until Tuesday to get out of the house and told him he'd have to file the papers.

"I didn't want him to come back later and try to say that it was my fault," she explained. "I thought the guy was immature. Totally immature." Their daughter, Alissa, was eight. "He left when she was young, but emotionally he may have never been there."

Overall, for Gail Hietzker, falling in love with, marrying, and divorcing Bradford J. King was a civilized ride, with some inexplicable side trips along the way.

She first met him during her sophomore year when he held the door open for her at the library at Western Michigan University. All the girls in the dorm called him "Mr. America." He looked that good. She was bright, determined, and attractively blonde. They both liked to party and dance. They were pinned within a year and a half.

Brad had money, or at least his father did. She remembered the first time they went shopping. He went to Redwood & Ross and Brad bought sixteen sweaters. They went back to the dorm and he picked up the phone and asked his dad to put some more money in his account. Other times his father just stoked it with cash when it got low. One time she watched him ask for and get a $2,400 deposit. It was the sixties. She was in shock.

Gail learned Willis King wasn't the only one spoiling his eldest son. Apparently his grandparents also lavished him with attention and gifts as a boy. Brad took a summer full of lessons from a golf pro and played regularly with his grandfather and his dad.

She saw some curious family dynamics early on. Brad corresponded with his father privately, sending his letters to an address at his bank. Willis was a quiet, affable man. Gail thought he sometimes used his war wounds to avoid going places or not taking part in activities. He seemed to worship the two boys.

Brad's major conflict was with his mother, one that lingered many years after he'd left the nest. She appeared to favor the younger brother, Scott, and Brad made his younger brother pay for that favoritism. Scott seemed desperately to want an older brother to consult and look up to. Brad simply shut him out. Once, she saw them get into a fistfight over some nonsense. It was one of only two times she'd seen Brad react with violence. He seemed to really be trying to hurt Scott badly during the fight.

But Marge was the force to be reckoned with in the King family. Gail remembered the first time Brad took her to meet his mother. It was at Schuler's, in fact, in Marshall. They were chatting over lunch when all of a sudden Marge turned and began picking something off his blue blazer.

"Brad, where did you get all this blond hair on you?" she said.

Gail felt as if she'd been caught trespassing and she'd left trace evidence with the hair.

In time, Gail came to know the woman who placed much value on appearance, career status, and all the trappings of model citizenry. Marge's mother was a 1919 graduate of Western Michigan, she reminded everyone, and Marge herself was a graduate of Michigan State. Gail suspected she scored her first big points when Marge found out she was at Western Michigan on a scholarship.

"Well, what do you think she thought of me?" she asked Brad after their first lunch.

"Well, she thought you were a little on the chubby side," he said.

She lost eighteen pounds by their next visit. She figured she scored a few more points with the diet.

Brad, however, never showed up on the scoreboard. Marge didn't approve of his choice of universities. She wanted him in a Presbyterian school. Both her sons were major disappointments in her life, she said. She demeaned Brad's work as a police officer, until he received his master's degree. Then she told him she'd always approved of law enforcement.

"Mom, that's bullshit and you know it," Brad told her.

Ultimately, Gail and Marge became friends and remained so even after the divorce. It took some time and effort to get past the veneer. But if you invested the time, Marge could be just as mortal as the next person. When she got out of hand, Gail just spoke up and put her in her place.

Brad's sense of entitlement, Gail figured, came from his up-bringing. "All their wants were met and their decisions were made for them," she explained. "I don't think Brad ever got the chance to grow by making any mistakes."

Gail ran the finances of their home. Brad largely stuck with the program. But when Brad didn't get something he wanted, he would pout for days. He ruined one Christmas pouting about a pair of cross-country skies and another week pouting over a mountain bike.

He was a satisfactory lover, but distant outside the bedroom when it came to affection. Gail felt unconditional, spontaneous affection was missing in the entire King family. She always felt that the hugs and pecks on the cheek between Willis and Marge were more for show than anything.

Brad, however, was known to cry, sometimes over the oddest things. She saw him cry the first time when they were in college when he wasn't elected to a student office he badly wanted. One time, during an argument, she slapped him and he broke into tears.

They rarely argued, however, and he never raised a hand. Gail stressed this to the police.

Back then, she wished Brad would have argued, but there was never that level of commitment, that level of feeling. She'd only seen him get jealous a couple of times, and the most notable instance was pure chivalry. It was in Las Vegas, as they were stepping out of a car into Caesars Palace. A drunk who had been thrown out of the casino grabbed her breast. Brad intervened, the man pushing him several times. Brad exploded, swinging furiously. Then the man grabbed Brad's hair, but it came off. He was wearing a hairpiece. Brad reached for the drunk's and came away with a toupee as well. After the police took the man away, they couldn't help but laugh at the sight.

Brad King was the only man she'd been intimate with for the first dozen years of her adulthood. She just figured he was what they meant by the strong, silent type.

"Sometimes I would see feelings from him," she said. "But somehow I just didn't think they ran that deep."

Gail's parents were down-to-earth folks. Her mother worshipped Brad. "She was definitely a mother figure for him," she said. Two years into their marriage, her mother came down with what everyone thought was terminal cancer. One day, Gail was talking to her mother and she brought up Brad.

"You know there has to be something that a twenty-two or twenty-three-year-old man would rather do than spend his afternoons with an older lady who is dying," her mother told her.

"What do you mean?"

"Well, Brad's over here every day. Didn't you know that?"

He'd told Gail he'd been playing golf and offered other excuses. Secretly, he'd been over there every day for months.

"And that was probably the most sensitive or giving that I can really think of Brad ever being," Gail recalled. "My mother wrote Marge a letter after that and told her what a wonderful son she had, and I thought Marge would have been pleased. It made her *furious*. She said she was angry Brad had been so nice, when he treated them like dirt."

Something in Brad King's emotional growth was stunted, Gail decided. They had the best of times as long as they stuck to the party life like they had in college. That's why he chose law enforcement, she thought. They were driving in Pontiac one day when he spotted an old fraternity brother directing traffic. Brad began thinking about joining the department after they were invited to a cop party that weekend. With all the police parties, the golf outings, and hunting trips, Gail thought the whole fraternal experience might as well have been armed Tekes all dressed up in blue.

Brad also found his niche as a youth officer at the high school, where there were more kids and more outings with young schoolteachers. He seemed to find some satisfaction when he finally applied himself and earned a master's degree. But he became frustrated when he was passed over for promotions in the department.

"Most of their job promotions come through exams," she recalled. "I remember my father had to study his butt off. Brad just decided to go in there and wing it, and he couldn't."

At home, Gail provided the focus and the discipline, making major family decisions. She was pretty rigid back then, she thought, right down to her weekly cleaning schedules. In some ways, she wasn't all that different from Brad's mother, Marge.

In their interview, the detectives kept speculating whether Brad had undergone some kind of major breakdown after she left him, then taken on some kind of new persona. She doubted that. If anything, Brad had a new persona now, simply because he was taking care of those kids.

The detectives asked her again about Brad's guns or if she had any family pictures that might show them. She didn't know, she told them, she'd have to look. The detectives also wanted to know if she'd talked to her ex-husband since the murder. Yes, he'd stopped over on his way to Kalamazoo with Marler in the weeks before moving to Denver. It was the last time she'd seen him. He complained about being lonely.

"Were you having an affair?" she asked him.

He denied it.

Gail had never suspected him of cheating in their marriage. But after their divorce, she remembered the time he told her he'd been "unfaithful." It was part of an amends exercise in an est seminar on restitution he'd attended.

Brad said little about the investigation.

"He did ask me what were the police asking me. And, he told me he would be a likely suspect. The only thing I said to him though was, 'You were out walking in the woods, right?'

"And he said, Don't you think if I, as a police officer, was going to plan something I would have a damn better alibi than that?' "

Gail Hietzker was ambivalent about seeing him. Both he and Diane had created their share of trouble over the years. Brad had ignored child support payments and important events in Alissa's life. Gail paid Alissa's way to see her father in Colorado, but Diane turned into a meddlesome stepmother. She tried to take direct control of Alissa's upbringing. She began writing monthly letters to both Gail and her daughter, saying how spoiled the child was and in what areas she needed correction.

Finally, Gail called him. "Brad, you better muzzle this broad," she said.

Another trip to Colorado produced another disturbing incident. Alissa said that she, Diane, and her father had gone shopping together at a mall, where Brad lavished himself with new clothes.

"Would you go buy me a pop?" Diane asked Brad.

"Sure," Brad said.

"Dad, can I have one, too?" Alissa asked.

"Where's your dollar?" he asked. He was quite serious. He made her pay for her own.

Diane, too, had a real cruel streak. Marge told her that after Willis's funeral she and Diane argued. Diane backed her into a hallway and wouldn't let her into her own bedroom. "Her husband had just passed away," Gail recalled. "I mean, it didn't matter who people were, she would just attack them."

Finally, Gail made a deal with Brad's lawyer. She took his equity in their old house for back child support payments. Even then, when she sold it, he showed up, pouting that he deserved to be paid a share.

Brad and Diane made quite a team, Gail had decided. When Brad told her he handled the family's finances, it didn't surprise her when Marge Lundeen said she'd been sending her son money in $10,000 amounts.

She remembered an outright crazy interlude they had during their engagement. Alissa answered the doorbell on an October day, only to come running into the kitchen, crying, saying her father was weeping at the front door.

"He runs in sobbing and hugging me and telling me how much he had missed us," she recalled. "I mean, we were just starting to sit down for a meal. It was really bizarre."

They'd been separated for three years. She'd been dating her current husband Helmut for a year. He was there for dinner.

"It was very uncomfortable," she said.

Gail calmed Brad, telling him to sit down for dinner.

"I broke up with Diane," he said.

He appeared so emotionally unstable she put him up in a spare bedroom for the night. He stayed four days. He asked Gail to remarry him on the second day, then he called up Diane on the telephone that night.

"I'm at Gail's," he said. "I've asked her to remarry me."

Then he hung up.

On the fourth day, Gail told him, "You're going to have to leave here."

Weeks later, Diane came over and had a long talk with Gail. She said how much she loved him. She liked that he came from an upper-middle-class family and that they could communicate. Before Brad, she said, she preferred married men because that allowed her to define the terms of the relationship.

"Why did he break it off?" Gail asked.

"I don't know," she said. "He won't tell me that."

Diane said she had dated a guy in the Army while they were engaged. She seemed blind to her own behavior.

"And she couldn't understand why he would make such an issue out of it," Gail recalled. "She felt he should accept her apology."

Apparently one day he did. They were married the following July in Colorado.

However, Gail Hietzker told the police, she left Diane King with an important piece of advice.

"Just don't have any children with Brad," she told Diane. "Just don't have any children, Diane, and you'll be all right."

7

They thought it was over. "You know, you wanted a picture of Brad's guns," Gail Hietzker told Gerry Woods when she called the task force later in the afternoon. "Well, I have a picture of them in a gun case."

Woods and Lou Mueller sped east for the photograph. They could make out three guns standing in the cabinet, but a flash burst wiped out all the details of the weapons in the reflections in the glass. The two detectives sat for a couple of minutes passing the snapshot back and forth, as though looking at it repeatedly might somehow change it.

Later, they tried technology, sending it to the state police crime lab in Lansing, hoping for some kind of enhancement.

The tech laughed. "We can't do anything with this."

Further results from crime labs and other experts were equally disappointing. No prints were found on bullet casings found at the scene. A match had been made on the latent print off the CCI Stinger ammo box. It was the right forefinger of Joanne Karaba.

The Material Analysis Unit of the FBI crime lab in Washington, D.C., made an extensive comparison of the stalker letter and items seized from Brad King's Sangren Hall office. The lab checked the backside of tape that held down the letters of the note for prints, but produced nothing. The FBI tried to compare the cut marks on the dispenser with those fragments on the note. The latter, however, were distorted as though they'd been ripped by hand. Scissors, razor blades, and cut-out sections of a Tau Kappa Epsilon newsletter were compared for cut patterns on the type letters, but no comparison could be made.

Two materials *could* have come from King's office, results showed. The legal-size paper used for the note and legal paper from King's office had the "same observable physical characteristics," the FBI lab reported. The tape on the note and that from King's dispenser had the same "physical and chemical characteristics." But the same could be said for a lot of tape and paper on store shelves all around town.

As the task force labored on for the next three months, physical evidence in the King case was as elusive as the melting boot print in the swamp slush.

Gerry Woods talked to the retired owner of a hardware store in Tustin, asking him if he remembered selling a .22 to Willis King when the family lived in the small northern Michigan town.

"Can't remember ever sellin' him a gun," he said. "I don't even remember him buyin' one."

Woods spent the balance of the same day in the basement of the hardware store, reading thousands of sales slips, choking on the dust of old acid paper, hoping to read about one Remington Model 511 Scoremaster sold to Willis King.

"Gerry, you sure you went through all those records?" Gary Hough asked, when Woods reported in.

Woods was all stuffed-up and pissed. "Yeah, I went through all them fuckin' records."

"How far back, Ger?" Hough started laughing before he said it.

"How does goddamn 1927 sound?"

The task force talked to old neighbors in the towns of Tustin, Luther, and Croswell, all small towns where the Kings had lived. They talked to old hunting partners, more Channel 41 staff, and Sister Anne Jeffery, the Catholic nun who had counseled Brad King during the funeral. They talked to young Tekes at Western Michigan and a boyfriend of Alissa King who had talked hunting with Brad King.

Phil Mainstone and Lou Mueller spent a week talking to cops at Pontiac PD and teachers at Pontiac Central High School. "It was funny," Mueller said later. "Half the people were shocked, saying there was no way Brad King could have done it. The other half said it didn't surprise them a bit."

They interviewed more than one hundred people, but nobody could give the task force a definitive sighting of the Remington Model 511 Scoremaster. A new interview with Steve Callens at the station only reinforced their belief that King had not sold the gun in Colorado. Also, Lou Mueller came back with compelling information from an interview with Randy Wright. Wright couldn't identify the Scoremaster, but he said he'd received a call early in the investigation from someone who said he could. After the rifle had appeared in the newspapers, Scott King called saying he'd shot the rifle "plenty of times" and was sure he could identify it. He wanted to know what to do if police called on him. He had asked, how could he protect himself?

"Cooperate and tell them the truth," Wright told him.

Task force detectives began debating the use and disposal of the weapon itself in their weekly meetings. "Why the hell would he take a chance at using a gun that people might have seen, or might be in some family picture somewhere?" somebody proposed. "That's a pretty dumb move."

Jim Stadfeld had a theory. "Look, who has positively put it into his hands? Maybe he considered going out and buying another gun, but that was too easy. Maybe he knew he'd get a bunch of cops beating the pavement, hitting the stores, and they're gonna run across whoever sold him the gun. Maybe he's figuring no one will remember. His mother and brother haven't seen the gun in years. Maybe he's counting on family ties. Maybe it wasn't such a dumb move on his part."

"But why put it so close on the property, where it could be found?" somebody asked.

"Maybe that's not where he planned to put it," Woods said. "Look he's got that movie rented. Everything we've found out indicates he didn't expect the kids with her. Maybe he shoots Mamma, then plans to be somewhere else. When he sees the kids after he shoots her, then he's got to make an alternative plan. Hell, who'd ever find it in that swamp? I just don't think the man had thought about the possibility of a dog."

"He may have been surprised by the kids in the car, or he may not," Gary Hough offered. "I don't think he gives a shit about those kids one way or the other. Maybe there are *two* guns in this case."

Everyone paused.

"Maybe the Remington is a plant," Hough continued. "It's an awful tidy package out there in that little creek with the seven shells and all. Maybe he wants us to find the gun. Maybe we take him to trial and the goofy fucker produces *his* .22, one we don't know about, and we all look like assholes. He's supposed to be some kind of criminal justice genius. If I was some kind of devious bastard, that's exactly what I'd do."

The possibility would haunt Gary Hough for months.

By summer's end, the task force had exhausted all the Michigan connections to the weapon, firmed up the crime scene, and come up with a working model of what they believed Brad King's activities were on February 9.

The other key to the King case, Hough still believed, was in the larger picture, what Brad King had not only done the day of the murder, but what led him up to the crime in the days, weeks, and months before.

Hough had further meetings with Dr. Gary Kaufmann and David Minzy in the smartly appointed offices of the Behavioral Science Section. Minzy was working up a crime scene profile. He'd gone to the scene, seen the forensic evidence, but had not read any interviews dealing with Brad King's personality. He wanted to let the crime scene speak for itself.

Minzy applied basic analytical criteria to the homicide. Diane King was shot either by a stranger or an acquaintance. Stranger motivations included robbery, sexual assault, self-defense, a thrill kill, or obsession. Evidence at the crime scene ruled out the first two. Thrill kills, or random sniper shootings, were extremely rare, amounting to no more than twenty a year nationally. They were also committed from locations like freeway overpasses where risk of apprehension was low. Such wasn't the case at 16240 Division, Minzy said.

By fall, Minzy was discounting the obsessed fan motive, arguing it simply didn't fit many of the patterns evident in those kinds of homicides. However, they still had not ruled it out. Minzy formalized his analysis later in a report:

> The (obsessed fan) generally involves a one-way love affair where the offender is obsessed with the victim. . . . Generally, the obsessed fan is mentally ill, possibly delusional. Recent research indicates that the more dangerous individual may be the one who is perceived as a nuisance. . . . Most will identify themselves during their communication with their victim. Only a small percentage are violent. The fact that the caller requested a face to face meeting with the victim would seem to increase the risk potential somewhat. . . . However, as of this writing, there is not enough information to make an accurate assessment.

Minzy didn't like the stalker for the same reason that Jim Stadfeld hadn't.

"With the husband on the property most of the day," he said, "there was a low probability that a disturbed individual would have the opportunity to get set up for such a shooting."

No, Minzy decided, the murder of Diane King likely involved what he called "an acquaintance motive." He listed four: Self-defense. Financial attainment. Emotional and, Self-esteem. There were no signs of self-defense at the crime scene, Minzy argued. The financial attainment motivation depended upon what weight the task force put on the TV station's $54,-000 insurance policy. The emotional motivation usually was more impulsive, and the offender was usually upset or remorseful afterward. They often choked, shot, or slashed the victim in rage.

Minzy discussed the last motive in his report:

> The final scenario considered would be that of self-esteem. The victim in this scenario is viewed as a threat to the offender's ego. The offender feels that the victim is "winning." In fact, the

purpose of this type of homicide is to "win." These homicides are generally well planned and organized. The weapon used is one that the offender is comfortable with and is specifically chosen by the offender.

Minzy argued the final scenario fit. There was no sign of overt rage in Diane King's wounds, such as beating or mutilation, only precision marksmanship. He called the wound to her vaginal area a possible "insurance shot," but it still may have involved some "emotional action" by the shooter. The shooter likely suffered from low self-esteem. Something the victim may have done or said put the shooter's plans into motion, he predicted.

Minzy reiterated what he'd said in earlier meetings. "Offenders that kill like this don't have the ability to confront face-to-face. Because of this, they are dependent upon others."

In his formal profile of the crime scene, Minzy wrote:

> Individuals who commit these types of homicides, where the victim is viewed as threatening their ego, tend to be hedonistic. Everything revolves around him. This type of homicide reflects very little emotion. The offender will likely be described as having an anti-social personality. These individuals do not feel remorseful for what they have done, however are quite manipulative. Those who know this offender will describe him as being a notorious liar, manipulator, and back stabber. While he cannot confront someone face to face, he will sneak around their back and retaliate in more devious ways.
>
> Being manipulative, this offender will attempt to display the "appropriate" emotional response, however those around him will find that it does not seem natural. It is possible that the offender may date frequently. This is merely to satisfy his ego and these relationships are superficial and usually sexually oriented.

Hough left the Lansing meetings convinced that the trial vehicle for bringing out King's manipulative personality would be the coeds at Western Michigan. If they could show that, they had a chance at convicting him with what little physical evidence they had.

"It's a mental game with him," Hough later told Woods, Jon Sahli, and others. "No matter what it is, it's mental. So based on that, you want to go back and look at the girls. What we're looking for with the girls is that type of personality, where he is trying to manipulate them for whatever purpose. When you talk to them, look for him playing his game, using these people for his own gain. I'm telling you, this guy's mental."

"But Gary," Woods later asked, "how are we going to argue that in court?"

Everything had to be stitched together, he told the task force. Diane's travels. The phone calls. The meetings with coeds. The dates with the girls, he said, they had to be nailed down.

"You can't argue it," Hough said. "We're gonna have to show it."

Already, Gary Hough had something in mind.

8

Cathy Anson, the criminal justice student who'd shown up at the Arborgate Motel the day after the murder, sat across from Gerry Woods in her off-campus apartment, her legs crossed. She'd dressed for their scheduled interview in a skimpy nightgown and nothing else. Within two minutes, Woods found an excuse to leave.

The investigator returned the next day. This time he brought a secretary with him from the prosecutor's office as a witness to his professional conduct. This time, Cathy Anson was wearing blue jeans.

"I'm here to clarify some of those statements that you made to Detective Stadfeld," he began. "Apparently you had classes with Mr. King, is that correct?"

"Yes, I did."

They became friends in the fall of 1990, she said. King

offered her a ride home after she finished a makeup quiz in his Sangren Hall office, then asked her on the way to her apartment if she wanted to go for a drink.

"We went to the Left Bank on West Main, and were there for approximately an hour and a half. He told me about his involvement in the Vietnam War, that his marriage broke up as a result of him donating approximately $10,000 to the construction of the War Memorial in Washington, D.C."

The man didn't even serve, Woods thought.

"And that was the first marriage?"

"Yes."

"What was the situation with his current marriage as you know it?"

"He told me he was separated from his current wife."

He tried to kiss her at the door on their first outing, she said, but she pulled away and he only got a "peck on the cheek." He'd come over later in the fall term to see her, too, sometime before Thanksgiving. She told him she was going to "bust" him if he connected her grade to their relationship. She just wanted to be his friend, she said.

"In the kitchen he did make advances toward me," she said. "We kissed for a brief amount of time, and then I kinda shooed him out the door and he left."

Woods got right to it. "Did you back then, or had you ever had sexual relations with Brad?"

"No, I never, ever had a sexual relationship with him."

Woods moved on to February 7, two days before the murder. She said she'd gone out drinking with King and another student named Dan Smith at the Player's Pub that night. King had about four beers.

"What all happened?" Woods asked.

"Dan got up to go to the bathroom, and, ah, Brad said to me 'I want to screw or fuck your brains out.' And I just was, you know, I had been drinking and I just sort of laughed it off, and Dan came back, and that sort of opened the door to just more conversation, sexual innuendoes. The fact that I have a breast disease came up, that occasionally I get lumps in my breasts. He said something about 'I'll gladly feel those lumps.' "

Later, she said, they rose to leave, and Dan went off to the bathroom again. "He took me by the lapels of my coat and pulled me toward him and said, 'So are you gonna make love to me tonight?' "

In the parking lot, he asked if he could go home with her, she said, but she refused. Then, Brad King disappeared into the night.

Cathy Anson saw him again at school about a week after his wife's funeral. She was having a cigarette in the stairwell of Sangren Hall and told him she needed to talk to him.

"So we went down a flight of stairs and I told him the police had come and questioned me. I said, 'I don't understand, they told me you weren't separated, that you lied about being separated.' He admitted that he lied to me about being separated. He just figured it would be easier for me to want to have a relationship if he wasn't married. And, he did ask me not to mention the fact that he was an Indian."

"Why?" Woods asked.

"Well, he said in Calhoun County they don't like Indians."

"He made reference to you not to tell the police that he was Indian?"

"Right, yes."

Cathy Anson couldn't understand why it was such a big deal. It was something he'd told the entire class.

Three days later, Gerry Woods piloted his Batmobile down one of America's most exclusive stretches of road. Lakeshore Drive runs through Grosse Pointe Shores where estates like the old Edsel Ford mansion are walled, and the view is good of the boats as Grosse Pointe Yacht Club members set sail on the teal waters of Lake St. Clair.

Kelly Clark met him at the front door of her parents' home, a sweeping two-story with high white pillars. She was finished with her studies at Western, a criminal justice graduate now. They sat in the kitchen, drank coffee, and talked most of the morning. Woods liked her. She was practical and blunt. They hit it off well.

"She'd probably make a damn good cop," he later said.

Kelly Clark had more than a good memory about the instructor she'd slept with almost a half-dozen times. She confirmed dates and offered documentation. She had a cancelled check from their first meeting at Pizza Hut. The sorted phone records confirmed her memory that the lunch at Schlotzsky's and the *Dances With Wolves* date had taken place December 11, 12, and the early morning hours of the 13. An interesting twist showed up as well. The woman that Brad King called for times on his favorite movie about the solitary soldier who became like an Indian was none other than Nita Davis.

Kelly Clark also told Woods how King had shown up for class dressed for a Christmas party on December 13. Woods remembered bookkeeper Nancy Gwynn's comment about a fight between Brad and Diane at or before the Christmas party.

"Did he mention anything else about that Christmas party?" he asked.

"Nope, not a thing," she said.

Kelly Clark knew what day she'd had sex with him before the murder. It was the afternoon of February 7, the same day he'd made moves at the bar on Cathy Anson.

Woods and Kelly Clark discussed their contact after the murder, how she'd run into him at Waldo's and their middle-of-the-night sexual encounters in late April and May. King's campus persona became more machismo. He drove around in the silver Jeep Wagoneer, his eyes covered with a dark pair of fashionable Ray • Bans. Other students reported him showing them Indian medicine bags and an eagle feather.

Kelly Clark saw him one more time, she added, on June 1, a Saturday. They were taking entrance exams for graduate school. They went to lunch at a Wendy's. He kissed her in the parking lot. They went back to her house, but she decided they couldn't stay there. Her roommates had already told her they didn't want him around. She grabbed a blanket and left a note: "I went out with Brad, so if I don't turn up, you know who to blame."

They went to a park. Soon they were intertwined on the ground. He had his hands all over her, totally unconcerned that people were walking not ten feet from them. He wanted to have sex right there.

"Look, I'm not comfortable," she told him. "I've got an idea."

They left and checked into a motel called the Just Hol-Day Motel near the freeway. They made love for nearly three hours. The motel was the first time they had any real privacy. She made a lot of noise.

"I can't believe I made you feel that good," he kept telling her, seemingly surprised at his own prowess.

After the motel, she said, he dropped her off at her house just off-campus.

"And what was the conversation then?" Woods asked.

"I said, 'Goodbye, have a nice life,' and he said, 'What's that supposed to mean?' I told him I wasn't gonna see him again, because . . . I got the feeling he wasn't going to be staying around much longer. And that was the last time I saw or heard from him."

Never once during their encounters did he ever talk about Diane's murder, she said. She had no desire to bring the matter up.

Kelly Clark still had a matchbook she'd taken from the motel room. Woods asked her to sign and date it. He was thinking Kelly Clark might be a good witness to the extent of Brad King's grief about his dead wife.

Woods asked about King's demeanor.

The only time she saw him down was when they slept together two days before the murder.

"Were there any changes after the murder (when you saw him) in the bars?"

"Well," she said, "he was very, very carefree . . . as if he had no cares in the world."

All the elements together perplexed Gerry Woods: Kelly Clark. Her "mansion," as he described it to Gary Hough. The bald suspect who wasn't particularly good-looking.

He asked her why.

She really didn't know why, other than there never was an

iota of emotional commitment. There was never any strings, and she liked that.

"The odd thing is, and I know this sounds crazy," Kelly said. "If he showed up, I'd probably sleep with him again."

Gina Zapinski went over much of the same material with the task force detective, who'd come to her house for a second interview. This time, however, there were some letters and other documents involved.

Phil Mainstone wanted to know if Brad King's involvement in Indian affairs had changed since the murder.

"It increased dramatically," she said. "I really don't know why, either, unless it was the kids."

Earlier in the year, Brad responded to a letter Gina wrote. She wrote him that she had many questions about Diane's death. His response read:

> I too have many questions and have come to realize that there are some which may go unanswered. I do know that the Creator will reveal to us through time those answers we need to get through our life journey. I've found comfort in the powwow. It is a time that Diane is very present for me.

His change from a quiet, supportive spouse to a dancing Indian warrior was one reason Gina Zapinski now believed Brad King had killed her old friend. She told the detective how he'd taken charge of arranging Diane's funeral, a move completely out of character. But his grief seemed fabricated, as if he were acting how people thought he should act. She had another letter from Brad on the subject. There was a certain removed quality to his words:

> I've been seeing a grief counselor ever since the week after the funeral. I'm now in a grief support group. I'm going through a lot in dealing with my loss. But everything I read and hear says that it is painful and that is what allows us to heal the loss. There are days I hurt so much, but I keep going. Some say it may take up to two to three years to fully (heal) my loss.

They talked more about Diane's last night at her house, the Friday evening before the murder when she visited for three hours. They hardly worked on Kateri's baptism outfit as planned, she told the detective. Other visitors kept dropping by the house, then Diane was too upset.

The detective helped her pin down the exact order of events, using phone records from Diane's farm. He said there were two successive calls, the first at 7:25 P.M., lasting three minutes, the next right after it at 7:28 P.M., lasting five minutes. Kateri was sick with a cold and crying loudly, she said. She didn't listen to the calls. She couldn't remember two calls exactly, but she knew Diane talked to Brad and she knew right afterwards Diane was upset. It was after the call that Diane began crying and they talked about marital problems, her desire to quit work and stay home, Brad's plan to get his PhD and his need for attention as "Mr. Diane King."

Yes, she said, it was after the call that Diane said: "I could walk right out of this marriage right now."

Back at the task force, Gerry Woods and others discussed and reconstructed Bradford King's activities on February 7 and 8, the two days before the murder of his wife. Hundreds of pages of interviews, documents, and computer-sorted phone records told the story.

On Thursday, February 7, King appeared to have gone on some kind of campus bender after his wife left for Detroit that morning. At noon, he was on campus asking Heather Taylor to join him later for dinner. Around 2 P.M., Taylor saw him being scolded by the mysterious, well-dressed Native American woman. Investigators hadn't been able to prove her identity, for the record, at least. By 3 P.M., King was in bed with Kelly Clark, but appeared depressed afterwards. At 5 P.M., he ate with Heather Taylor at Garpike's, then frightened the coed with his remark about being "chopped liver." At 6 P.M., he taught. At 9:30 P.M., he was drinking at the Player's Pub and trying to seduce Cathy Anson. At 11:30 P.M., he asked to go to her apartment. At midnight, he was at the Teke house party, eyeing Heather Taylor.

At 9:56 A.M. the following morning, phone records showed a call made from King's Sangren Hall phone at Western. His office partner told police he didn't use the phone in the locked office. The task force speculated King had spent the night in Kalamazoo, perhaps, with the mysterious Indian woman. King had told Jack Schoder he was working on his porch on Friday at Thunderspirit and went rabbit hunting. With all their search warrants, detectives never found any live or spent shotgun ammunition.

The task force believed that, in fact, on Friday, February 8, Bradford King was zeroing in a .22 caliber Remington Model 511 Scoremaster with his stolen CCI Stingers and planning his wife's ambush murder. That evening, phone records showed he called Nita Davis just before 7 P.M. He made the two calls to Diane at Gina Zapinski's a half hour later. Then, right after hanging up on his wife, he called Nita Davis again, leaving the message on her machine.

"We know one thing about those last two days," Gary Hough said. "Old Bradley was one busy boy."

Jack Schoder was working on phone calls Brad King made after the death of his wife. One led him right to rock star Ted Nugent, the heavy-metal guitarist known for his hunting advocacy as well as his rock and roll.

On a Wednesday in September, Schoder stopped by Ted Nugent's Bow Hunter's World, the guitarist's archery shop near Jackson, Michigan. A media staffer told the detective that Diane King had interviewed Nugent at least twice in the past.

Nugent's big-game trophies hung all over the shop. He was a skilled archer, who promoted precision shooting, specifically the skill of bringing down a large animal with a single shot.

Schoder showed the staffer several numbers in the Jackson area code that came out of the computer sorting of King's phone records. The staffer identified one number as Ted and Shermane Nugent's former residence in February of 1991.

A minute later, Schoder was talking to Nugent himself on the phone.

"I don't ever remember talking to the guy," Nugent said.

"Understand though, I've met thousands of people backstage and it gets a little difficult to keep 'em all sorted out."

Schoder persisted. Somebody from Brad King's phone called the Nugent residence on February 11, he said, two days after the murder.

"I have no idea what that's all about," the rocker said.

He suggested the detective talk to his wife.

"She handles a lot of stuff," Nugent said. "Maybe Shermane knows something about that call."

9

As she had with Detective Lou Mueller, a thirty-three-year-old Kalamazoo hairstylist named Elise Renee Caporossi sat down one day to talk about the TV anchorwoman who'd come to her shop Charisma for two years.

A half-dozen employees and fifteen years of experience had taught Caporossi to just smile, listen, and keep cutting when customers began talking. With Diane Newton King she also found she had to hold her tongue frequently.

"She came to us because my shop and her station were associated with a barter club," Caporossi said. "She came once a month, but also liked to stop just to chat. At first, I thought she handled it real well that she was on TV. I thought she was really nice. I was surprised she wasn't stuck-up, until I got to know her better. Then, that all began to change.

"She said her husband was a former policeman. Mostly, she talked about all the money he came from, to be honest. It was a secure relationship, she said. He knew what he wanted. They were leading marriage classes to help other couples. Whatever she wanted, Brad was behind her, supporting her. That was a big thing with her, she said.

"I couldn't wait to meet him. The way she talked, I thought

he'd be this wonderful person. I expected this tall, dark, hand-some man with a great sense of humor. He was none of that. 'Oh, hi.' That was the most he ever said. He was so unfriendly, I thought can this be the same guy?

"When Brad lost his job, she said he was fired because he knew something that was going on there. She was going to get to the bottom of it and become famous. The investigation was going to do a lot for her career. She was going to crack this case, but she could never tell me what it was. Then she started getting into this thing that she was going to be a big media star, like Barbara Walters. It became nauseating after a while.

"She became very self-centered. We all noticed it. It was like a radical change. All she talked about was *me, me, me, me, me.* When she came in and little kids were here, she would say, 'Have you seen me on TV? Do you want my autograph?'

"I don't know how to put this, but she's no one I would choose as my best friend. She was so superficial. She wanted you to think she was really somebody special.

"She was so surprised once when one of the vice presidents of Upjohn came in here. He stopped in to make an appoint-ment one day when she was here. I always teased him.

"After he left she said, 'Why didn't you introduce me? I can't believe you're treating him like he's just anybody. You should treat him as somebody important.'

"I said, 'That's why he likes coming in here. I don't treat him like he's somebody important.'

"Then there was Marler. He was the *smartest* kid and *isn't he gorgeous.* It was nauseating. In a way, he was a brat. He tore the shop apart and was noisy.

"She'd say, 'You just have to let him do what he wants. I'm sorry he's making your shop a mess, but that's their way of learning.'

"I said, 'To be destructive to my place?' He'd take everything off my retail shelf and be opening bottles.

"I'd get other lectures. I have fourteen-year-old and nine-year-old daughters, and Diane was always telling me how to do this or that with them. She'd say, 'Well, if you would have gone to college, you would know what to do.'

"I thought, you don't have one kid past three, and your time with teenagers is coming, Diane. I learned to laugh at her to myself.

"The first conflict I heard about in her marriage was about finances. He wasn't working and they were getting deeper and deeper into debt. Then, she told me he was always mad because she was spending money they didn't have. Here she was just this newsperson, and he's an unemployed policeman, and she wants the best of everything. Now. Now. Now. Clothes. I went shopping with her once at the Battle Creek Center. She used to go in and say, 'I should get a discount. I'm going to be modeling your clothes on TV.' I was so embarrassed.

"She also said Brad didn't want to go to functions, the pow-wows she used to go to. I guess he wasn't fond of them. He didn't want to go to her family's either. Whenever there were social events at her business, he also didn't want to go.

"She also said Brad was jealous. He was becoming increasingly jealous of the men she worked with and was around all the time, while he was stuck in the background. He was stuck watching Marler. He was always complaining, but she didn't care because she wanted to make a name for herself, and he didn't understand what it took, she said. That was before the baby. She said she was considering splitting up because her career was more important than he was.

"But, you never knew who was going to walk in the door from week to week. All of a sudden, one day she comes in and she's obsessed about having a second baby. That's all we heard about. I'm thinking, you were just talking about leaving him to pursue your career.

"She wanted to get pregnant, but he didn't want to. She tried a new negligee. She tried taking him someplace for a romantic weekend without Marler. She asked me, 'What am I doing wrong?' She kept asking me that. She made it sound like he didn't want her to get pregnant. She told me he didn't want to have a second child.

"Well, when she did get pregnant she was so shocked. She said, 'Like they say, it only takes once. I guess he's finally seen it my way.' But, he was ticked that he'd slept with her. He was really mad. She said he was so mad he'd gone off and left her for the night.

"I thought that Diane brought a lot of her problems on herself. She showed no care to anyone else. She was capable of some real cut downs.

"When she found out my first husband was a dentist, she said, 'I'm surprised you were married to someone with such high education. I never would have pictured you with someone like that.'

"My (present) husband was in here once, and she said, 'Oh, he's really handsome. I'm surprised you found someone that cute.'

"I said, 'You're joking, right?'

" 'No, he's really, really handsome,' she said. 'I guess I just can't picture the two of you together.'

"I just thought, consider the source. Then, she asked me what he did. I said, 'Construction business.'

"She said, 'Well, that's more your caliber.'

"I didn't tell her that my husband and his brother owned the company and did two and a half million dollars in business last year.

"She put down her family, too. She told me that her mother was a hairdresser and her childhood hadn't been the best. She made it sound like she was better than them. She told me that if anything ever happened to her, she would never want her family to raise her children.

"I said, 'Do you have that in writing?'

"She said, 'I'm not going to die for a long time.'

"She didn't want her kids in that environment. These perfect little kids had to grow up in this perfect little environment so they could be somebody important. She talked about the competition with her sister, because her sister got pregnant easier. But Diane said her kids were special, because her sister didn't know how to be the right kind of parent.

"But when Diane became maternal, and things started getting bad with Brad, she began running to her mother's. Toward the end, she was spending a lot of time there. Some of it was that she needed to get away from Brad and have some time to herself so they could sort things out. Once, she mentioned to me that if they were ever going to split up, she needed to know what it was like to not have him around.

"Well, we both became pregnant around the same time. My son was born in September and her daughter was born in November. My son had to have open-heart surgery three weeks after he was born. And here she was telling me how beautiful her daughter was, and she was going to be the Gerber baby. She had taken her in for pictures. And she said it was such a shame that I had to have a son with a heart problem. She said, 'He's going to have scars and never be able to model or be much of anything.'

"I felt like shaving her head. I couldn't stand her. I thought she was a bitch. It wouldn't have bothered me if she would have gone somewhere else. I felt like telling her, well, at least my husband wanted my baby.

"I thought maybe it was all the problems she was going through, because this was at Christmas time and she was in a really bad mood. She wanted Brad to be part of the family, but he'd thrown the Christmas tree at her and thrown ornaments at her. There was a lot of conflict in the house. She made it sound like the conflict was because of the baby.

"She asked me if I thought he was running around on her. I reassured her that I thought he wasn't. I said, 'Maybe he's just concerned because you're the breadwinner. Maybe you should try and build his ego back up and gently push him into getting a job so you can stay home.'

"She was also working on the Indian project and planning to quit the TV station. She said, 'I don't know why he's so worried about money, I've already worked my salary into that.'

"She thought he was being selfish by being mad that she wanted to stay home.

" 'I don't see why he doesn't understand,' she said.

"I said, 'Diane, first you want to be this career woman, now you want to be this domestic person. The guy is probably confused.'

"She said, 'Don't you want to stay home with your kids?'

" 'Yeah, but I don't put that kind of pressure on my husband.'

"Well, the next time she came in (she was) wearing a big diamond ring and saying, 'Look, look, look. Can you believe he bought this for me with all we've been through? I guess he wants to try to work things out. He's going to let me stay home with the kids. We worked everything out. I don't know where he got the money for this.'

"Yet, she was crying before she left. She said Brad didn't want to have this baptism ceremony for the baby, make it this big of a deal. He just wanted to go do it and get it over with.

" 'This is his daughter,' she said. 'I just don't understand.'

"The last time I saw her, I cut her hair on a Thursday, a week before she was murdered. She was talking about going to a big party that next Saturday with people at work. We also were supposed to get together that Sunday, and she was going to show me about making baskets. I feel so funny, the last thing I ever said to her was if you ever die, make sure you will the ring to me.

"When I heard she was murdered, at first I thought somebody really was stalking her. Then, when I sat down and thought about it, I thought, I'll bet Brad did it. I wouldn't blame him if he did."

Working with charge card receipts, task force detectives eventually traced the source of the money for the diamond ring. King had borrowed a credit card from a neighbor to buy it, but never paid the neighbor back. A jeweler in Denver had done the work for Brad King. It was, in fact, one karat: one karat of pure carbon zirconium. The price: About $300. Her original wedding ring had been an imitation as well.

Diane Newton King had been passing both off as sparkling diamonds, knowing the whole time her most prized gems were fake.

10

Five months after the King task force was formed, Gary Hough sent Phil Mainstone and Lou Mueller back to their jurisdictions just in time for hunting season, an annual ritual when nearly three-quarter million hunters take to the Michigan woods and fringe lands to pursue the elusive whitetail.

Gerry Woods hit the road on a different kind of hunting trip, a six-day expedition to Texas, one of two final interstate journeys that would be the task force's last.

The Calhoun County Sheriff's Department loaned Woods a new Ford LTD for the trip. The Batmobile was pushing 150,-000 miles, but flying was out of the question. The "chain of evidence," as police call it, had to be intact. Gerry Woods needed to maintain possession of the evidence that he wrapped in a soft blanket and placed in the trunk of the Ford.

Woods first showed up unannounced in Longview, Texas, but had to push on another 260 miles to catch up with Scott King, who was on an assignment in Austin. On November 12, Woods met Scott King in a small room where the sounds of Interstate-35 penetrated the motel's walls.

As they started the interview, Woods laid out Marge Lundeen's letter showing the $13,500 she'd given Brad King, making sure it was in plain sight, making sure Scott King knew his brother had been regularly tapping his mom.

Scott King gave Woods a history of the guns in the King family. He remembered his grandfather's shotgun clearly, its unique markings and case. He'd shot the .22 as a boy, he said, and when he was older. As far as he knew, Brad got them both.

They talked about Brad as the family loner. Scott King, himself, struck Woods as quiet and withdrawn, until he brought up the subject of money.

"Apparently there was some type of estate set up after your father's death?" he asked King.

"Well, no. Not that I'm aware of. There was somewhat of an

estate, naturally when somebody dies. . . . All went over to my mother, that's it. There's nothing there that's mine. There's nothing there that's Brad's. But mother says that of any money left, she's deducting whatever she lends us and we don't pay back. She deducts it from whatever will be divvied up when she passes away. I really don't care about it."

"Right," Woods said, nodding.

King said maybe a half million dollars was involved. "I told her it's her money, go spend it. Have a good time. I can make it on my own."

Woods pointed out the letter.

"I had no idea about that," King told Woods.

With that Woods took him to his car to show him the contents of his trunk. Scott King would not say positively that the Remington Model 511 Scoremaster was the family gun, but he also would not say it was not.

"But is it similar to what you remember as a child?" Woods asked.

"Yes," Scott King said.

That night, Gerry Woods drove on another 120 miles to Kerrville and found a motel in Austin. The following day, he interviewed Marge Lundeen at her home. When they were done, she followed him outside, hanging on to the shoulder of her husband Cliff as she looked into the trunk of the LTD.

"I can't say if that's the gun," she told Woods. She also couldn't say it wasn't.

She began crying. "How will I know when you're going to arrest him?"

"I don't know, ma'am," Woods said. "That's just something I don't personally have a lot of say about."

A few days later back in Battle Creek, Gary Hough and Gerry Woods began putting the King case all together for the official who did have a lot of say. They had moved their operation to the basement offices of prosecutor Jon Sahli's office in Battle Creek. The two investigators were in the basement of the law library sorting through reports and raw notes, arranging them in order, when Gary pulled out a sheet of paper buried in the materials provided by the county detectives.

Gary Hough paused for a minute over a page of Jack Schoder's notes. Then he handed Woods a page.

"Shit, Gerry," he said. "Take a look at this."

They were raw notes about a young man named James Wickware, Jr., somebody the notes indicated who was infatuated with Diane Newton King, somebody who had written her at length. There hadn't been a hint of any such individual in their conversations with Jack Schoder or Jim Stadfeld. There hadn't been a hint of James Wickware, Jr., in the official reports they received.

Gerry Woods's face turned a dark red. "We're fucked, Gary. All this goddamn work, and we're fucked."

They called the sheriff's department. A few minutes later Wickware's letter to Diane King came over the fax. Then they received Deputy Al Lehmkul's report, documenting how Brad King had given him the letter back in December of 1991.

Woods himself called Schoder, who said Wickware had been eliminated as a suspect. He'd personally interviewed Wickware back in March, he said.

"Then where is the goddamn report, Jack?" Woods asked. "How come we don't have a goddamn report?"

"Gerry," Hough later said, "who's going to be the one to tell Jon Sahli about this?"

Jack Schoder couldn't understand why Woods and Hough were so rattled. He'd paid a visit to James Wickware, Jr., back in March. He'd checked the kid out. The guy seemed shy of his own shadow. He just didn't strike Schoder as the type to do any killing.

On November 21, he decided to pay a visit not only to young Wickware, but also to his father and mother. He wrote a formal report, including details of his first visit for the task force. It read in part:

R/O (Reporting Officer) made contact with Mr. James Wickware, Sr., 62 years of age and his wife, Eddie, age 66, at their residence in Battle Creek. R/O advised that I had, on March 4, been at their residence and had interviewed their son James Wickware, pertaining to a letter which he had written to Diane King prior to her death. R/O showed them a copy of the letter, and they read it. R/O indicated to them that I wanted to discuss with them the activities of their son, and his habits, in terms of information he had given me pertaining to his whereabouts on February 9th. I further indicated to them that this was a routine matter, in that we had to verify the information that he had given me in some manner.

I asked Mr. Wickware if he would have any recollection as to where his son may have been on a Saturday night, February 9th, and he indicated unequivocally, and without hesitation, that his son is home every evening, and that he goes to bed every night around 7:00 or 7:30 P.M. R/O inquired as to whether a Saturday night perhaps may have been any different, and he indicated to R/O that Saturday is no different than any other night to his son. . . .

He further offered to R/O that his son has never once, ever, fired a gun. In fact, Mr. Wickware, Sr., feels that his son wouldn't even know how it would work.

In the report, James Wickware, Sr., was at a loss to explain his son's penchant for soliciting letters and photographs from TV newswomen. He told Schoder he didn't date. He spent most of his hours reading newspapers, watching TV, and looking after his elderly grandmother, who also lived in the house.

Schoder also included a report on his second contact with James Wickware, Jr. He noted the extent of the collection of fan photographs from newswomen, which numbered more than two dozen and ranged from local female reporters to CBS's Paula Zahn. His report read in part:

R/O talked with James Wickware, Jr., and asked him if he recalled my being there to interview him back in March, and he indicated in fact that he did. R/O again asked him if he had written any other letters to Diane King, or called her. He indicated in fact that he had not, only the one letter. R/O again asked him if he remembered what he told me in terms of his whereabouts on Saturday, February 9th. He indicated he was home, and he always goes to bed early, and that night would have been no different.

Three days after he'd been called on the matter, Jack Schoder sent the report to the prosecutor's office, hoping it put the matter of the stalker to bed once and for all.

Gerry Woods was relieved to get some paperwork and see young Mr. Wickware had an alibi. At the time, he had no idea that the letter writer's father had an explosive personality. In fact, Schoder later said, the elder Wickware was furious about his son's penchant for writing TV newswomen. He hadn't characterized it that way in his report.

Still, the night of the murder, no one had sighted any black males near the crime scene. Black males would certainly be noticed in and around Marshall, Woods reasoned. Profiler Dave Minzy's propositions also applied. Only Freida Newton, Brad King, and a couple of relatives knew when Diane was due to arrive home.

Still, the report troubled Woods and Hough for months.

"Jesus, if they didn't tell us about this," Woods said, "what the hell else haven't they told us about in this case?"

On the first day of December, Hough and Woods flew to Colorado to try and eliminate any more surprises in the case.

"You watch," Hough predicted, "something will come up. He's had time now with those kids. I wouldn't be surprised if we run into some kind of story out here."

By December 2, they were in Grand Junction, talking to Diane King's friends, former fellow employees, and supervisors at KJCT-TV. They wanted to know more about what Kristina Mony had told the investigation, that Diane King had been threatened because of a drug story she was working on for the station. Nobody at the station could produce any documentation of such a threat.

By midweek, they were in Denver, where they'd met up with Jon Sahli, who'd flown out to Colorado to put together a search warrant. They were looking for a gun cabinet witnesses had told them King's grandfather had made. They were hoping there might be a record of a purchase of a Remington Model 511 Scoremaster tucked away in one of its drawers.

Just after sunrise on December 5, a Denver patrol car pulled Bradford King over just after he left his apartment complex at 3300 South Tamarac Drive. His two children were with him in his Jeep Wagoneer. Woods and Hough watched from another car as a Denver detective presented King with the papers.

"You have a choice, Mr. King," he said. "We can go back to your apartment and you can open it up. Or, we can kick down the door ourselves."

When they arrived at the apartment, King jumped out of the car and hustled into the apartment. Marler left the Jeep with him, but King left the back door open, leaving Kateri sitting out in the parking lot alone in her car seat.

He walked quickly inside the door, heading to his back bedroom, when one of the Denver police ordered him to halt. They never did figure out why he was in such a hurry.

Just inside the door, they found the rubber boots he was wearing on February 9. They found Indian costumes, medicine bags, and the animal skin headdress, but found no gun cabinet. They added the boots to the search warrant, and seized them before they left.

Brad King hung around for a few minutes, glaring in silent anger. It's the first time he'd seen Woods or Hough. They asked if they could talk with him.

"You talk to my attorney," he said.

They handed him the search warrant before he walked out, leaving them with the apartment. A Denver uniformed officer handed him something else. He'd written Brad King a ticket for expired plates.

Susan Van Vleet estimated the interview with the two detectives from Michigan in her office in Englewood couldn't have lasted more than fifteen minutes. They didn't seem eager to linger, and she had a luncheon to attend as well.

Susan Van Vleet told them as far as she'd been told the early murder investigation had been botched.

"We're here basically to clean up their mess," she later recalled one saying.

Near the end of the interview, one asked, "Has Marler said anything about the murder?"

"As a matter of fact, he has," said Susan Van Vleet.

She told the two detectives what her children had heard about two men in black cowboy hats.

"I invited them back to the house afterwards, and told them they could speak to me and my children," she later recalled. "We'd be happy to spend as much time as they wanted. They said they were terribly sorry, they had to leave on the next plane back to Michigan. I suspected they simply weren't interested in the information, and that became very clear."

The police asked about infidelity.

"If Brad was having an affair, and Diane knew about it, I think I'd be the first to know," she said. "I don't think she knew about anything like that."

"What makes you think so?" one of the detectives asked.

"If Brad did have an affair, and Diane found out, I think you'd be investigating a murder of an entirely different type."

Gerry Woods and Gary Hough never asked *the* question in the new year.

"I refused to ask Jon Sahli when he was going to issue," Woods later said.

The probe had involved four departments, more than a dozen uniformed officers, a half-dozen evidence specialists, and had been underway nearly a year. It was one of the most expensive investigations in the county's history, but the task force had managed to produce no publicity as investigators went about their work.

In the months ahead, both Jon Sahli and Jon Olson would be facing elections. It was hard to say who might have lost more: Jon Olson if he didn't get a warrant, or Jon Sahli if he refused to take the case to trial. Ostensibly, once the warrant was issued, the police would have finished their job and received some credit. The matter of Bradford J. King would then become the prosecutor's case to win or lose.

Hough and Woods spent weeks in the basement putting the thousands of pages of the case together. In meetings, they'd taken to talking in odds.

"I just don't think there's anything more we can get," Woods told Sahli in a meeting in January.

Sahli looked at Hough.

"Jon, he's right," Hough said. "I'm giving it fifty-fifty we can convict him."

"I think it's a little better than that," said Woods. "I think it's more like seventy-thirty. If King testifies and opens himself up for cross-examination, I'll go eighty-twenty."

"At best, fifty-fifty," Sahli said.

"He never believed in this case," Hough said later. "He hasn't been keen on it from the start."

One late January morning, a few days later, Gerry Woods was riding in his Batmobile when he got a call from the prosecutor. He wanted to be picked up for lunch. On the way out to a hideaway, a small bar out on the north side called the Robinhood Inn, where nobody knew them, Sahli kept asking questions.

"I felt like I was on the stand," Woods later said.

After burgers and a couple of beers, Jon Sahli reached for the Batmobile's car phone when they drove off. He put in a call to his secretary.

"Shirley, type me up a warrant for Bradford King," he said. "Type it up for open murder and leave it for me in your drawer."

The next call was the sheriff's department.

"Have Jim Stadfeld in my office at 8 A.M.," the prosecutor of Calhoun County said.

From the View of

BRADFORD KING

I just didn't love Gail. We got married because everybody got married. We didn't sit down and look at what that meant: To live with one person in a home and all the ramifications of that—two people working and having kids. I don't know if Gail's parents sat down with her, but they didn't sit down with the two of us. My parents sat down with the two of us, but it wasn't like a talk to wake us up. They said you're old enough to make your own choices and we'll back you. That kind of a talk. Had our parents sat down with us and said, "Look, this is what it's like to be married, you need to look at this," I think they'd have done us both a service.

I know Gail loved me a lot, but it just wasn't there for me. And after a while, it was a lie. I tried to make it happen and it just didn't. I tried for a three-year period, working on myself. It just wasn't there. But I respect her. She's a wonderful woman.

I told her I had an affair on her after we'd been divorced. She was just a girl, nobody I worked with. Just somebody I'd met in a bar. Nobody I was getting married to. I don't even remember how long it was. That's how much it didn't mean to me. I just felt I needed to tell her.

Getting married to Diane was different.

I remember tooling along, probably heading into Greektown in Detroit to eat, and Diane touched my hand and said, "We're gonna get married." Just out of the clear blue. She said, "We're gonna get married. I don't know when, but we are."

I damn near wrecked the car. I mean, she just shot that one at me.

I swerved and she said, "Calm down, we're not getting married tonight."

I personally hadn't thought about it. The relationship was so wonderful I wasn't even thinking about getting married. I think she just threw it out on purpose to see how I would react.

Finally I said, "I know, you're right. We will. When we're ready."

Well, she received her regular Army commission because she was the cadet commander. She was stationed in Savanna, Georgia. Our relationship was going to become long-distance. We knew it was coming.

So here was what happened. The est organization had this training, which I had done myself before I met Diane. It was six days in the Catskills of New York. You stay in cabins, six days of looking at yourself, discovering yourself. You get up every morning with calisthenics and a flat-out mile run, pushing yourself to your limits. There's classroom work, sex issues, and relationship issues. The entire gamut of life is looked at and discussed with a small group. Part of it is ropes, rappelling down a mountain and doing a zip line across a lake.

She wanted to do this training before she went into the military. I chose to be an assistant, so we got to have a cabin together. One of the things we did was something Werner Erhard had taken from Dale Carnegie, a breakthrough exercise. It's where you take a rolled-up newspaper and beat a pillow until you have no strength left, just to get out all your pent-up anger. For some reason, I was particularly good at being a facilitator for that. It required screaming. I got to be there for Diane. I'd never seen her let it all out. She was just drained completely. I think it was all the frustration of having to go through what she had to go through as a child.

That night we just laid in bed and hugged and cried. That week cemented our relationship together, completely bonded us.

After that she left for her Army training. And I eventually

was in Cincinnati working for est. She came up as many weekends as she could. She went back late one day. I said, Diane you're AWOL.

She said, "I'm spending another day with you. I don't give a shit."

That's when I knew something was going on about the military, because officers are committed for a career. They don't think like that. I told her, if she didn't want to be in the Army, she shouldn't be in the Army. Get out of it.

She said, "I can't."

"You can't?" I said. "You can get out of anything in this world. Just follow the rules and get out."

She told them military life was not suited for her and she was more committed to her relationship with me than the military. She jumped through every hoop they gave her. It's damn hard to resign a commission, but she did it. She got an honorable discharge, too.

Now, I have to tell this story because Diane would have made me tell it if she were here. She always made me tell it, and I hated telling it because it really revealed what an asshole I was. At a point in our relationship, I called off everything. Called off the wedding and the works. I got scared.

In fact, I told Gail that I wanted to have her back. I knew that it wasn't true about wanting Gail back, but I was so scared I didn't know which way to turn. I look back at that trying to figure out what the hell scared me, other than being married and making a wrong decision again. I had major cold feet.

She had gone out with a guy once at the military base, and then she called me up and told me about it. And she apologized in every which way a person can apologize for that. Maybe I didn't believe her. Maybe back in my mind that's why I had cold feet.

I went out to Colorado to work for est in Denver. Diane showed up out there at Christmas. She flew out to see a friend who lives in Boulder and showed up in my office. When she walked in the door, I thought, maybe she won't notice I'm here. She walked right over to my desk and sat down. And I wouldn't look up.

And she said, "I thought I'd stop by and see how you're doing."

Tears were running down. The paperwork was getting drenched.

She said, "Why are you crying?"

I said, "Because I love you."

I knew when she walked through that door that I was being stupid.

Now, Diane also threatened to leave me over the years, mostly around the birth of our children. When she was pregnant with Marler, she was like that. One time, before he was born, she just packed her bag and walked out. It was the night of her baby shower. She came back crying.

I looked at her and said, "Diane you know I'm not one to keep count of things, or hold them against you, or anybody, but did you know this is the seventh time you threatened to leave me since you've been pregnant? Frankly, if you do it again, I'll leave you. I've had it. It's bullshit. None of it is over anything. It's all over crap. I know women's emotions and hormones are bouncing all over the place when they're pregnant, but you don't need to threaten me, because it doesn't scare me. I'm tired of hearing it."

People say I got strange when we had children? Well, I'm sure it affects me. I'm not going to say it doesn't. It's a change in your life. And, it's an adjustment that you have to make. I don't know that I'm overly dramatic about how it affects me. I have my up and down days like everybody else. And I think the mood swings swing a little further when you're talking about adding to your family, for both of you.

But I never took it out on her—not directly, like threatening to leave her, refusing to go places, or do things. I guess I was taking it out on her if I was moody about it, but we would talk it out. And I think anybody who has kids goes through it. And if they deny it, they're full of shit.

That's the truth of the matter. You continue to adjust

until you die, or your child dies before you. They're a part of your life. So it creates a—problem is not the right word—but it describes it. Anyway, these people are a bunch of lay people saying this. I wouldn't listen to their advice if I had to. They don't know what they're talking about, for one.

Now, I *was* being stupid before Diane's death. What happened to us in the end was we stopped communicating.

We communicated when our relationship was healthy. I think the financial pressures had something to do with it. I think it was taking its toll on me more than her. I never experienced it, until I did it to myself. To some degree, Diane grew up having to pinch pennies.

Diane believed in family, strongly, even though her family is dysfunctional. Another trait of an adult child of an alcoholic: She's going to make a functional family, and she's going to do it by visiting, because when she visits, everybody comes together. Everybody goes to Freida's house when Diane visits. She has this myth or idea or belief that the family has got to be close. And once she had children, once Diane was a mother, she was more accepted by her family as a person.

And so now I'm over here and she's going this way, because she's given me permission to quit trying with her family. She said it that summer, shortly after we moved into the farmhouse. What kind of decision did I make? I made a decision that I then didn't have to communicate as much with my wife.

So, I went to somebody else. I made a mistake. Most of the world, if people are truthful with themselves, won't judge me for that. I just heard the infidelity statistic for couples. I think it's seventy-five percent.

And I was not going to divorce Diane to be with one of them. That was not it.

Nita Davis called me once at home, maybe twice, when I was being really stupid. That was on the edge of utter stupidity. That, and a lot of other things, told me *what the fuck are you doing?* The one time she came out to the house she had called before she left home. That was the wake-up call. I thought, what are you doing? *What are you doing?* And I was like, *I'm doing what I don't want to do.* And then the question was, *well, why are you doing it?*

I don't know why. No, that's a cop-out. I can tell you exactly why. I don't want to tell you this. I'm probably going to cry. But I felt like I was losing Diane to her family. I felt like they were becoming more important to her than me. And what's even more stupid is that I just didn't talk to her about it. What I was feeling. And for some reason I just couldn't.

But I was done playing around. It was like, *Brad, you're stupid.* You've got the best thing in the world right in the house with you and you're fucking around.

I called Nita Davis the Friday before Diane died because I wanted to solidify the fact that there was no more between us. Because it hadn't been done. And for me, it *had* to be done. I wanted to do it in person, and I wanted to do it with Diane gone. I told her I was going to be gone for the weekend because I didn't want her calling home when Diane got back. I didn't want that phone ringing and having her on the phone after Diane was home.

I was setting up what I needed to straighten the issues out, straighten my screw ups out for myself so that I could then go to Diane and make it right with her.

Diane had no idea I was screwing around. There would have been a point where she would have found out because as part of handling all of that I would have told her, "It's over. I did this, and if it affects you that much that you have to leave us, break up the relationship, I'll accept that."

I would have taken it like a man, and handled it. But we never got to do that. And part of me wishes I would have.

It just seems kind of undone for me. That I didn't get to set it right with her.

I miss her. I miss her a lot. I still cry at night.

PART FIVE

The Cause

I am the cause of my own world.
—est training slogan

1

Tom Darling's phone began ringing in the third week of January, the calls transparent queries to determine if he was at home or work or locked up in jail. The rumors had escalated to delusional proportions. Some people were saying they'd heard his arrest was on radio and TV. Calls also were coming into the Calhoun County Sheriff's Department about Tom Darling. The department logged forty-five calls in one day alone.

Tom Darling escaped to his monthly Thursday-night poker game at a friend's house, where he heard another ringing phone. When his friend picked up, he heard him say, "Well, no that's not true. Tom Darling is right here, would you like to talk to him?"

The voice on the other end was stammering. "Do you know what they're saying about you?" the caller asked.

"Yes, I do, but it's not true. Read about it in the paper tomorrow."

"Do you know who I am?"

"No."

"Good." And then she hung up the phone.

Darling had already documented the impact on Darling & Sons True Value Hardware. Business was down ten percent in December and sixteen percent in January, a loss of more than $15,000. His children were being confronted now in school with the idle talk. He wasn't sleeping well and he'd lost twenty pounds.

The next day, on January 24, a news release ran in the papers, one issued jointly the day before by the prosecutor and the sheriff.

"Prosecutor Jon Sahli and the sheriff's department indicated that as of Jan. 23, there has been absolutely no arrest made in connection with the ongoing King murder investigation," one story went.

The release further stated, "The suspect in this case is not a Marshall businessman."

Neither his name nor business appeared in print. But in the town of hospitality, hardly anyone had to guess.

One week later, on the morning of Friday, January 31, the real suspect in the case slipped on jeans, running shoes, and a gold sweatshirt emblazoned with "Western Michigan" and the university's seal.

For Bradford King the past six months in Colorado had been marked by cultural and spiritual pursuits, but continued personal setbacks. Indian elders invited him to sit in sweat lodges, but his applications to doctorate programs at various Colorado universities had been failures. He cochaired a parent's advisory committee of the preschool Marler attended at the Denver Indian Center, but folded his own house painting business after a dispute with a homeowner about payment. He was starting training as an insurance salesman with a Denver company, but largely had been living off $1,200 a month in Social Security death benefits.

Now, King was moving from the Tamarac Apartments to a smaller, cheaper complex. Three months behind on rent, he was facing eviction.

At 7:50 A.M., as he led his children out the apartment door, Denver plainclothes and uniformed officers were waiting just beyond the complex parking lot. Michigan police were not among them. Much to the protest of Jack Schoder and Jim Stadfeld, Denver police had insisted on making the arrest for reasons of liability and protocol.

King placed his children into their car seats in the Jeep

Wagoneer; Marler in the front, Kateri in the back. Marler would be four in March. Kateri was fourteen months old.

The two Denver police cars converged as King started out of the parking lot. In seconds, King was driven away, the children placed in a separate car.

Not a half hour later, Denver Detective Doug Jones, a twenty-year veteran who helped supervise the arrest, was on the phone with a social worker named Bea Marquez. He had an hysterical young boy on his hands, he told her. He needed help.

Jones felt no sympathy for Brad King. "But my heart was bleeding for that kid," he later said.

Jones picked up Marler King and carried him back into the spartan corridors of the Denver Police Department Headquarters, into the detention facility, past the felons, past the sex offenders unit, to Brad King's single lockup in the back. Jones later recalled Brad King looked stunned by his own arrest.

"I decided to let the boy say goodbye," Jones said. "It not only calmed him right down, I figured, hey, he might never see his dad again."

Both Colorado and Michigan news media found no shortage of people to comment on the arrest. The tabloid TV shows returned to Marshall, Michigan, as well.

James Brady, King's lawyer, called his client a "convenient scapegoat" for an unsolved crime. "He is absolutely innocent," Brady told the *Grand Rapids Press*. "We don't know what happened, and I don't think (police) know what happened. They've questioned him and harassed his family, and gone all over the country following him. They've turned members of his wife's family against him. They've done what they could to make his life miserable."

Brady also lashed out at the manner of King's arrest. "He has been cooperating with the investigation. The prosecutor and my office are in contact and they have known that we represent him. If they had called and said, 'Would Brad turn himself in?,' they know and I know that that would have happened."

Said Jon Sahli, "Brad King was not arrested any differently

than any other person charged with open murder in Calhoun County."

Reporters groped for motive. In Colorado, they found help from KJCT news director Mike Moran, who told the *Rocky Mountain News* he had "mixed feelings" about the latest development concerning the husband of the reporter he once supervised.

"He was a nice guy, always pleasant, in good humor," he said of Brad King, who he also noted had a "moody side."

"He was also dominated by Diane. Diane ran the family. He did whatever she said. If she wanted to go to a party, they went to a party. If she wanted to move to Michigan, they moved to Michigan. Her career and her life is what mattered."

The next day in the *Denver Post*, Moran went a step further. "If anyone could push you to the brink of doing something like that, it would be her. We didn't really get along, and I really didn't feel that badly (when I learned that she had died). She was really, really strong-willed and constantly was having personality conflicts with other people in the newsroom, including me."

Moran went over the top with "A Current Affair."

"It makes sense in a way for something like this to happen to Diane King because I don't think there was a person she was in contact with that she didn't aggravate. I talked to one of her best friends off and on this week. As she put it frankly, 'Can you imagine living with Diane King knowing what a b-i-t-c-h she can be?' She said, 'I don't know if I as a good friend wouldn't think about shooting her once in a while.' Who knows what goes through your mind when you face a person like this day after day? I could see the nicest, sweetest guy in the world just go crazy."

Back in Michigan, the Kalamazoo *Gazette* ran a picture of a woman sitting under a hair dryer in a Marshall beauty shop. "You just don't expect something like this to happen in Marshall," she said. The headline: QUESTIONS ABOUT THE KINGS. Was He Loving Husband or Angry Man?

Mike Moran was quoted in the *Gazette* story, as well as a

former WUHQ photographer named Jerry Martin who worked with King in Battle Creek. He recalled the time they were on assignment together in Bronson Methodist Hospital doing a story on new natural-born twins. The photographer and his wife had recently lost a son at birth. The assignment turned out to be in the same room where his child had died. Martin became ill, set down his equipment, and went down the hall for air.

"She chased me down the hall and said, 'What the hell are you doing? You're going to have to shoot this.' *That's* the kind of heartless person she was."

Martin sounded like Mike Moran and hairdresser Elise Renee Caporossi in her private statements, but with one important reservation.

"I think (Brad) had justified motivation, but I think he was smart enough where he didn't do it. If she treated him in their private life the way she treated everybody in her professional life . . . you can only take that for so long," Martin said.

The ruminations went on for days, Diane King's supporters saying she was a well-liked, charitable professional and that King was comfortable "living in her shadow." The coverage drew fire from feminists. Women deluged Moran's station with calls. Two women wrote the Battle Creek *Enquirer*.

When people read such statements as Diane was "up front, abrasive and pushy. Anything you could describe as a domineering person was Diane all the way," or statements such as Diane "wore the pants in the family," it conjures up views of a woman's tragic death as being deserved and justified.

Do we consider these utterances of an unenlightened male or do we judge a female who is attempting to rise in her broadcast journalism career and has future lofty goals, equivalent to a man who has the same ambitions? Why is it deemed appropriate for women to uproot their lives to follow their husband's career, yet a man who does the same is somehow viewed "as a man living in the shadow of an ambitious, career-minded wife?. . . . We are once again being force-fed the old standby of the double standard.

Back in Grand Junction, the owners of KJCT very publicly fired Mike Moran on February 5, saying he violated station policy of talking to other news media without management permission. Two days earlier, Moran had softened his comments by saying, "I would have taken a newsroom full of Diane Kings."

But ultimately, Moran remained unrepentant. "I'd say it all again," he said. "Someone needed to tell a little bit more of the truth."

2

They had been portrayed as contentious and estranged by Diane King herself, but no one could say the family didn't come together during a crisis. When Gerry Woods told the Newtons of the pending arrest, Denise Verrier sped over to the house on St. Joseph and made airline reservations to Denver with her mother.

Freida Newton packed. Allen Marler wasn't far behind.

"Now, we've got work to do," Royal Newton told everybody. "Our main concern is those kids."

On Friday evening, the day of the arrest, they arrived at Denver airport. TV cameras were waiting at the gate.

"I always believed it was him," Freida Newton told reporters. When a newspaper asked Royal Newton for his reaction, he said, "I'm as happy as a pig in shit."

After the arrest, the Denver Department of Social Services had placed the King children in a group shelter called the Family Crisis Center. A date was pending in Denver Probate Court to decide more long-term arrangements. Everyone expected a custody battle.

The Newtons, however, didn't need an attorney. Royal Newton had already hired a Colorado attorney before they caught the flight.

In her home in Englewood, Susan Van Vleet believed they had a full-blown emergency. They had to protect the only living witness to the crime.

By now, she had heard Marler's story from four sources: Her two children, Cindy Zedelman, and Tony Gallant, Brad's thirteen-year-old baby-sitter. Everybody heard pieces, but Van Vleet believed the pieces were consistent. Marler said two men in black cowboy hats and cowboy boots had killed his mother. They had a black car. Both had guns. One had a rifle. They came up to his car window. He thought they were going to kill him, too. Then they ran off in separate directions.

"He said his dad didn't get him out of the car," Tony Gallant recalled. "When the police came, they wouldn't let his dad get him out of the car. His dad was yelling and stuff, but the police wouldn't let him get him."

The boy often woke screaming in his bed. "He was always scared his grandmother was going to come and get him," she said. "He was always scared that the police were going to come and get him, too."

Weeks before Brad's arrest, Susan had made calls to the office of his attorney James Brady in Grand Rapids. She told his staff about Marler's story. She was frustrated by their response.

"We'll pass that along to Mr. Brady," they said.

When Brad King was arrested, Susan called up Brady's office again.

"Look, the only eyewitness is going to go bye-bye with somebody who hates his father," she told an assistant. "The only material witness is in danger of being brainwashed."

On the Friday Brad was jailed, James Brady arranged local counsel. A Denver attorney named Bernard Messer would handle extradition and the matter of the children.

On Monday, a juvenile magistrate gave the Department of Social Services a week to do background checks on potential custodians. Susan Van Vleet was no longer frustrated with lawyers. She was frustrated with Brad King.

She'd warned him months ago, "I know you think you're not going to be arrested, but what happens if you *are* arrested?" She'd asked him, "Where do you want the children to go?"

"Well, I want them to go to my brother," he said.

"Do you have that in writing, Brad?"

She complained later, "Well, it was *very* clear to me he hadn't talked to his brother. And, that's the kind of thing that always got to us. This guy showed up not responsible. He wasn't responsible if he got arrested. He had nothing together. He had a will, but the court had nothing to go on. Everything was left in a tizzy again."

In days, the tizzy included Scott King, then Marge and Cliff Lundeen, converging in Denver, each with shaky agendas. Scott King arrived first with a letter from his mother that pledged three things if he were awarded the children: A "wholesome Christian environment," a college education, and her unwavering financial support.

When Marge herself arrived, money was on her mind. She complained often about her son's legal bills. "You don't know how much this is costing me," she told Susan repeatedly.

Susan finally said, "Marge, you could just have a public defender."

"Oh no, I could not let *my* son have a public defender," she said.

They all tried to come up with a winning combination on the custody matter. Bernie Messer believed a judge would find it difficult to deny custody to the Lundeens. Denver law gave grandparents first priority over siblings.

Marge Lundeen, however, said it was too much for them. "A judge would be out of his mind," she later said. "I'm sixty-nine and Cliff is seventy."

It might be easier to secure guardianship if the children were kept in the Colorado jurisdiction, Messer suggested. Susan talked with John and they volunteered. They explained the option to Scott.

"But I have enough money," he complained. "My mother is going to be giving me the money."

"I thought, is money the only thing that drives these people?"

Susan later said. "They didn't seem to care about the children. They didn't seem to care about the ramifications of the children being with the Newtons."

Susan Van Vleet had come to believe it was a dangerous environment, considering the way Diane and Brad had talked about the suspected incident involving the retarded girl in the neighborhood. She called up a supervisor at social services, then the caseworker. When the caseworker came to her home to interview them as prospective custodians, Susan brought it up again.

"Denise says she jumped to conclusions," the caseworker said. "It's not a serious concern to her."

Denise told her mother, "I didn't want this to have to come out." It came out when the caseworker asked her.

This is how she now remembered the incident of a few years ago: She dropped by on a warm day at her parents. The front door was wide open. No one seemed to be trying to keep secrets. Royal was sitting on the couch, his back to her. The woman from the neighborhood was sitting in a love seat across from him, leaning forward. They were fully dressed.

"Where is everybody?" she asked.

Royal looked sleepy. "They're gone."

The woman was giggling.

"I had my suspicions," she admitted. "But I talked to my husband about it, and we decided you go through proper channels. You don't just fly off the handle and destroy somebody's life."

She talked to her minister.

The minister talked to her stepfather.

"Sir, I have never touched anyone like that in my life," he said.

Denise spoke with the girl's mother.

The mother said it was nothing. "She don't have a dad, you know," the mother said. "She just likes to hang around men."

Denise explained, "The more I thought about it, I decided this man had never, ever touched me as I was growing up."

But her sister Diane wouldn't let it go. She kept calling and writing, telling her to do this and that.

She finally told Diane, "Look, if I didn't do a good enough job, you come back here and tell Mom if you feel you need to tell Mom. You lower the bombshell."

And Diane did. But to what end? Denise thought.

Denise apologized again, saying, "Mom, if I didn't believe *my* children were safe there, they would never be at your house."

On February 7, the dim halls of the Denver City-County Building bleached bright with camera strobes as deputies took Brad King in handcuffs to the courtroom of Melvin Okamoto for the juvenile magistrate's last hearing of the day.

Okamoto was to determine where the children would be placed until a full custody hearing could be held a week later in district court. The Newtons had retained a popular, savvy Denver criminal attorney named Frank Moya, who came prepared to argue the King children should be turned over into the Newtons' care. Bernie Messer's plan was to argue that his client's parental rights hadn't even been legally terminated, and he wanted his children to go with the Van Vleets.

Right off, Messer was caught by surprise. The Department of Social Services was recommending the children go to the Newtons. The day before, caseworker Bea Marquez had told Messer her department would remain neutral. Now she'd come with an assistant city attorney to help argue her case.

The Newtons had won her over. "Their love for the children was wonderful," she later said. "They knew these children inside and out. These were people who were in-tune with the children."

King's attorney launched an attack on several fronts, beginning with the most newsworthy. "There is one argument I would like to make that overshadows all others that I'm about to make," he told the court. "Marler has given a statement as to who the assailants are in this matter and identified them in some detail. And he has clearly stated that the assailant is not his father.

"Furthermore, as many in this courtroom are aware that the maternal grandparents have made numerous statements in public that Brad King is guilty. Two issues arise. Would this be an adequate situation in which to place the children? If he is placed in a situation with relatives who believe (his father) is guilty, obviously they will attempt to manipulate this child to change his story.

"Secondly, how can you place children in a situation in which relatives think (the father) is responsible for their mother's death? How will he in turn relate to his children later on, and I think that's contrary to their best interest."

Messer said an adequate investigation hadn't been made. "I've been advised of information concerning an alleged sexual assault in the state of Michigan involving the grandfather. I understand the department tried to investigate that by interviewing Diane's sister. . . . I understand that there's been a long history of alcoholism regarding the family in Michigan, that there's been numerous police contacts."

Messer wondered why Brad King's wishes that the Van Vleet family care for his children was being ignored. "It's as if he has already been convicted of the crime. I submit pressure is being brought to bear by the maternal grandparents."

When he was done, Frank Moya rose and called Messer's argument "character assassination."

"Simply put, there's no truth to any of it," Moya told the court. "It's extremely unfortunate that he would make the kind of scurrilous arguments about my client without any basis in fact."

Moya argued they were not there to try a murder case. "All this discussion about the protection of witnesses, that's not what we're here about. What we're hear to determine is what's in the best interest of these children. We're not asking for permission to take a rubber hose to Marler King so that he will conform his story with that which might be argued by a prosecutor in Michigan.

"Mrs. Newton has no opinion whatever with regard to whether Mr. Bradford King killed her daughter, and that is an issue for the courts of Michigan to decide. She, in her wildest dreams, would not try to persuade the children that Bradford King murdered their mother. They have problems enough as it is."

Okamoto asked caseworker Bea Marquez to speak. She'd observed the children's interaction with the Van Vleets, the Lundeens, and the Newtons at the shelter.

"How are the children doing now?" Okamoto asked.

"I would tend to say they are confused. From a child's perspective, I don't think they're sure as to what's going on."

The social worker praised the Newtons' visits.

"How would you characterize their reaction to the Lundeen family, particularly Marler?" Okamoto asked.

"Overall, it went all right, *but* it just wasn't a real warm, not superwarm type of thing."

The magistrate wanted to know about signs of trauma.

Marquez explained the Denver detective's emergency call to her to comfort Marler King. By the time she got to the shelter, however, he'd regained his composure, she said.

"Losing his mother, now his father," she said. "He's clearly been through a lot."

Assistant City Attorney Chris Mootz rose to argue the statutory preference for grandparent placement, saying the Newtons seemed the most compatible couple. He called Bernard Messer's argument "smoke."

"It is not the purpose of this hearing or the purpose of this court to preserve Mr. King's defense," he told the court, adding influence could go both ways. "Who's to say Brad King is not the one who influenced Marler's statement? It's just as logical as any argument that the maternal grandparents would try to change it.

"Also, it defies reason that the maternal grandparents are interested in anything else than who truly killed their daughter. To argue that they want somebody falsely accused and imprisoned for that, defies logic."

Messer was incredulous, pointing out Freida Newton's comments at the airport in his final argument. "Either I have poor eyesight or I saw the maternal grandmother Friday night on television telling the entire world in effect that she thought that Brad was guilty."

Frank Moya left the court with a final image. He described Marler King running to the Newtons at their first shelter visit.

"Marler yelled, 'Gramma, Grandpa, when are we going home?' " Moya recalled. "I think that is about as good a summary as I can make."

After all the rhetorical fanfare, Melvin Okamoto's decision was anticlimactic. He ruled the Newtons and the Lundeens could take turns watching the children for the next week.

Bernie Messer asked Brad King and Marge Lundeen their wishes. Custody would be determined at the district hearing, but winning might be difficult considering the social services recommendation. However, Messer was willing to fight on if they wanted. His fee had only been $500 for the extradition and juvenile matters. He would need another $500 to argue the case in district court. It was a bargain compared to the nearly $8,000 the Newtons would pay for Moya.

Mother and son didn't want to spend the money.

On February 14, the Newtons returned to the City-County Building to appear before District Magistrate David Johnson. Messer recommended to the Van Vleets not to bother attending the hearing. Marge and Cliff Lundeen showed up. They had the care of the children in the last few days.

Brad King was not in the courtroom. He had a different kind of court date pending in another courtroom, in another state.

A child psychologist recommended the Newton home as well as the caseworker.

Freida Newton took the stand. She wore a sweatshirt with a large heart marked "Grandma's Lovables" surrounded by more hearts with the names of her eleven grandchildren. She talked about children's books and videotapes she had at home.

The judge wanted to know if she would allow visitation by other parties, members of King's family, or King himself.

"Absolutely," she said.

"Do you love these children?"

"Very much."

"Does your husband love these children?"

"Yes, he does."

Magistrate Johnson acknowledged a handwritten letter he'd received from Brad King. King stated he didn't want his children with the Newtons, but he hadn't indicated where he did want the children to go.

The judge asked if anybody was there to speak on behalf of Brad King.

Marge Lundeen rose from one of the seats, her voice shaking.

"I know that the Newtons love the children just as much as I do," she told the court. "My concern primarily is that the children be put in a situation that is less disruptive."

She said they would be best served staying in Colorado with the Van Vleets.

"Are they here?" the magistrate asked.

Several people in the courtroom shook their heads.

Marge Lundeen continued, "I think (the) father should have some say in where the children go. There have been public statements that my son is guilty of killing their daughter. This is fearful to me that it will be conveyed to the children. When you have that kind of hate in your heart, it shows. It consumes you."

It was a good lecture, but she was no advocate. The magistrate granted Freida and Royal Newton temporary custody of the children.

"I'm so happy," Freida Newton told the cameras. "This is the best Valentine's present I could have ever gotten."

Freida Newton had buried her daughter a year ago to the day.

Brad King had waived an extradition hearing, James Brady told reporters his client had "no desire to run from these charges." Jack Schoder and Jim Stadfeld picked King up in Denver, bringing him back to Marshall for arraignment. King said two sentences during the six-hour journey back. One about the Denver traffic, the other to the flight attendant.

"No, I don't want any more juice."

He stepped off a plane at Kalamazoo-Battle Creek International Airport wearing his golden Western Michigan sweatshirt.

The next morning, District Judge Frank Line arraigned King on a charge of open murder and use of a firearm in commission of a felony. He denied bond, saying King no longer had any ties to the community.

A thick stubble was emerging behind Brad King's temples. He shuffled out of the courtroom in wrist and leg irons. He no longer wore the sweatshirt, but an orange jumpsuit. It was the official prisoner uniform of the Calhoun County Jail, the place that would serve as Bradford J. King's home for the next eleven months.

3

Two camps of lawyers were still compiling their cases when a preliminary examination was held on March 12 in a Marshall district court to determine whether probable cause existed to bind Bradford J. King over for trial.

The prosecution team worked in a windowless room behind the elevator shafts in the basement of the county building. They called it the King Room. Gerry Woods was comparing reports and telephone numbers, associating calls with people, times and dates. Gary Hough still was searching for a motive. Legal research was being handled by a thirty-three-year-old assistant prosecuting attorney named Nancy Mullett. Mullett was an irreverent, but studious, attorney. She'd spent two years researching opinions as a Michigan Court of Appeals staffer, but had tried her first felony only a few weeks before the King exam.

They talked about the case all day in the King Room, then talked some more at the Winner's Circle after work. Woods's family saw so little of him, his daughter presented him with a sign for the King Room door, a circle with a line through it.

"The Brad Busters," it read.

James Brady's team included a legal assistant named Trish Hubbard and a young attorney named Matt Vicari, who researched and wrote the case's briefs. By exam time, some unexpected help also showed up. Her name was Virginia C. Cairns. The Battle Creek attorney had called Brady weeks earlier, asking him to allow her to assist in the case. Brady knew he needed someone to provide personal attention to Brad King at the jail. His office was more than an hour away.

"She seemed to have Brad's interest at heart," Brady later recalled. "She wasn't a dynamo, and I didn't need her to be. I didn't need her to give me one bit of legal advice. I would take it if she told me; but knowing the judges, giving me the lowdown on the judges, boy, she was good at that. She knew all of them. And help me with the cops, because I needed access to Brad. I needed somebody who knew the ropes in Calhoun County."

At first, the Brady team was swamped with reams of investigative material sent over by the prosecutor's office. The documents came dumped in no particular order in a large box, part of the process that allows the defense to discover the prosecutor's evidence before hearings begin. Trish Hubbard had been scrambling to organize the file since the arrest. A private investigator was researching a half-dozen potential witnesses. Much more work lay ahead.

James Brady wanted to stop the prosecution at the exam level. First, he tried to have the entire Tenth District Court bench disqualified, arguing the "appearance of impropriety" because King had been fired from the very same court. However, Marvin Ratner, the judge hearing the preliminary examination, said he did not know King. On the job only two months, Ratner said he'd made a point of not being "party of any conversation" about King among court staff.

As for the evidence, James Brady found the entire scenario befuddling, almost ridiculous.

"Why would Brad King be so stupid as to leave a gun and casings in a tidy package?" he would say. "Why would he be so stupid as to leave the gun on the property alone? Here we have a trained police officer, an intelligent man. A criminal justice instructor, no less. The whole case is ludicrous. It's ludicrous that he would even do it. He was *there*. He wasn't playing cards. He wasn't at a bar. He was at the scene."

As for the proofs, Brady said, "I really believed the evidence was not circumstantial. I'll go stronger than that. I believed it was weak. Then, the single most important piece of evidence that night, the boots, they give them back. Going back a year, I felt there wasn't anything essentially different between March and April of 1991 in the year since. Our strategy was one of attack."

Twenty-six witnesses were called in four days of testimony. EMTs and deputies testified to King's standoffish behavior at the crime scene. Pathologist Dr. Stephen Cohle detailed the autopsy and the killer's apparent marksmanship.

Freida Newton took the stand, took one look at Brad King, then shunned him. She was as stoic as granite, her features filled with a kind of expressionless anger.

Through Freida's testimony, Sahli established Diane King's weekend plans and the time she left for Marshall the day of her death. It was time for Sahli to choose a theory from all the previous speculation that had gone on in the task force.

Sahli asked about Diane's departure that Saturday.

"Did she take the children home with her?"

"Yes, she did."

"Did she make any comment about the fact the children were going home?"

"She did say, 'Boy, will your father be surprised when he sees you kids.' "

She talked about calling Brad King around 4:30 P.M.

"Do you recall what you said to Mr. King?"

"The only thing I said was, 'Diane was on her way home now.' "

"Did you mention the children?"

"No, I did not."

Brad King, Sahli would argue, had expected Diane King to be alone when she pulled up the driveway at twilight.

Jon Sahli called Gary Lisle to establish the dog track and the footprints he saw near the bridge and in the swamp near where the gun was found. Jim Stadfeld testified about the casing found in the loft and the .22 ammunition and cleaning rod seized from the attic.

Robert Cilwa, the ballistics expert from the Michigan State Police Crime Lab, said firing pin and ejection marks showed "conclusively" that the shell casing in the loft and the seven in the creek were fired by the Remington Model 511 Scoremaster.

Cilwa said some comparison was made between bullets found in Diane King's body and those test fired from the Scoremaster. The gun's barrel had rifling that imparted a spin on the bullet, making it fly true. The Scoremaster's rifling featured six lands and grooves in a right-hand twist.

"Did you form an opinion or a conclusion as a result of that microscopic comparison?" Sahli asked.

"Yes, I did. That conclusion was that the two bullets exhibit the same class rifling characteristics that the rifle left on the test bullets. In other words, it had six lands and grooves with a right twist being of the same dimension."

James Brady went after the comparison on cross-examination. "Now isn't it correct that there are twenty-two other manufacturers of (firearms) that exhibit the same characteristics, that is, or specifications of six lands and grooves?"

Cilwa wouldn't agree to a number.

Brady went through a list, asking the expert about Remington, Ruger, Beretta, and others.

When Brady was done, Cilwa had agreed there were at least nineteen.

Jon Sahli called neighbors to establish the time frame and the lack of suspicious people on Division Drive the night of the shooting. Joanne Karaba testified how Diane King wouldn't get out of the car without seeing her husband first.

Brady's cross-examinations, however, cast a different light on their stories. The attorney made Barbara Elgutaa look uncertain and confused about the Remington Model 511 Scoremaster. He poked holes in Tom Darling's memory about the gun in the house. He demonstrated the popularity of King's boots by pointing out Mark Karaba had worn the same kind to court.

He got Karaba to admit that his son's friends would also have had access to the bullets on his porch.

When Jack Schoder took the stand, James Brady took the detective to the woodshed.

No, the detective admitted at one point, there were no fingerprints on the box of CCI Stingers taken from the Karabas' porch cabinet.

"Was the cabinet dusted?" Brady asked.

"No," Schoder admitted. "It was not."

Later, Brady asked, "Did you take possession of the boots from the defendant?"

"Yes."

"How did that happen?"

"We were in the squad room and I was asking him about going out to his house, and quite frankly, Mr. Brady, he offered them to me to assist us. Very cooperative."

"He gave you the boots?"

"Very cooperative. Yes."

Schoder couldn't pin down when he was told about the path of the dog track. He wasn't sure when he first went in the barn loft. He could exactly remember personnel at the scene. He admitted the boot print in the swamp had melted by the time he got to the creek on February 11.

"Why did you seize (the boots) in Colorado then?" Brady asked.

"I was in Michigan."

"But you know there was a search warrant issued for those boots in Colorado?"

"I wasn't aware of that. I have subsequently found that out, yes."

"Aren't you the investigator on this case?"

"Yes, I am."

The tone of Brady's final question left serious doubts about that.

On the exam's third day, Nita Davis waited in a small room on the second floor of the courthouse, smoking cigarettes and imagining that a scarlet letter would soon be pinned across her chest.

She'd graduated from Western Michigan University, then promptly moved. She was afraid Brad King would find out that she had talked to the police. She'd lost weight, slept little, but mostly tried to forget, until she saw the arrest in the papers and answered the prosecutor's subpoena. A defense investigator would eventually show up at her door, asking her questions.

He would ask her for her opinion of Brad King.

"He's a liar," she would tell him. "You can not trust what he says. You can't form an opinion of someone who lies."

James Brady was leafing through his preparatory material as Nita Davis entered the courtroom. Brady looked up after she was sworn. Her hands were at her thighs, pulling her short black skirt over her black nylons toward her knees.

Brady turned quickly to Trish Hubbard and Virginia Cairns. Jon Sahli and Nancy Mullett could hear him all the way over at the prosecutor's table. So could Gerry Woods and others in the audience.

"Who the *hell* is she?" Brady asked, exasperated.

"The Brad Busters" knew immediately. Brad King had been less than entirely candid with his own attorney about his extramarital activities.

By now, Sahli was deep into his direct examination.

"Can you tell us what happened in the park?" he asked.

"The relationship progressed beyond just being friends. We talked and it became more of a physical relationship."

Brady was on his feet now, objecting, but he couldn't stop her. She detailed their sexual relationship, right down to their last evening together on the couch near the Christmas tree.

The headlines the next day were large ones.

Some relatives later complained to Nita Davis. They wanted to know if she still had the legal right to use her maiden name.

Smoking cigarettes outside on breaks, the Brad Busters tried to find highlights. They thought Brad King's courtroom demeanor might one day help their cause. King was somewhere between sullen and vacant at the defense table. At times he was outright menacing. "We've got to warm him up," his own attorney would later say.

The other highlight came to court with his hair neatly trimmed, his shirt smartly pressed. He was nervous at first. Then his stepfather told him: "Chris, you don't have to worry about acquitting or convicting Brad. That's not your job. All you have to do is go in there and tell the truth."

"Mr. Sly, how old are you?" Jon Sahli asked.

"Fourteen," Christopher Sly said.

The teenager told his story about seeing the gun when he was paid to mow the lawn in the summer of 1990.

"You believe that is the gun that you saw there at the Kings'?" Sahli asked, showing him the Remington Model 511 Scoremaster.

"Yes, I do."

James Brady tried to break him down.

"Now, Mr. Sahli showed you this rifle," Brady said. "Had you been shown this rifle before?"

"He had never shown it to me. No."

"Okay. Had an investigator shown it to you?"

"At my home, he showed me some pictures."

"Who is *he?*"

"Mr. Stadfeld."

"Now you said this was the rifle. This looks like the rifle, isn't that right?"

"Correct."

"You had no idea to know whether or not this was the rifle, isn't that right?"

"I knew that was the rifle . . . I had seen it at their home."

"Okay." Brady paused. "You've seen this?"

"Right."

Brady dug a deeper hole for himself. "How do you know this was the rifle you saw at the home?"

"Because I recognize especially the pull back chamber and the wood handle. I had seen it."

James Brady wasn't the only trial attorney in the room surprised by the boy's performance that day.

* * *

In his closing, Jon Sahli linked times, dates, and facts. He didn't need to present a motive. Motive wasn't required for a conviction in Michigan, let alone to bind a suspect over for trial.

James Brady began his closing on a somewhat astute note. "The prosecutor's own admission is that this is, I assume that this is a 'circumstantial evidence' case. We all know that circumstantial evidence is sufficient to bind the defendant over or to find the defendant guilty. It doesn't have to be direct evidence. It can certainly be by circumstantial evidence.

"But what's interesting there is that circumstantial evidence should lead the finder of fact to a point at which he or she can infer a fact or factual setting from that circumstance, not force the finder to make an inference upon an inference upon an inference. And *that* is what the prosecutor's whole case is here. . . . Mr. Sahli is asking this court to bind someone over on mere and pure speculation."

Judge Marvin Ratner deliberated less than two hours.

"There are circumstances upon circumstances that confirm each other," he said. "When taken all together, these circumstances are compelling and convincing to pass the threshold of probable cause."

Ratner bound King over for trial and sent him back to the Calhoun County Jail without bond.

Still, the botched boot prints and Jack Schoder's uncertain testimony made the investigation look comically flawed in contrast with James Brady's methodic cross-examinations. The jury box was filled with reporters covering the case. They talked among themselves when it was over.

"They're going to need a lot more than that to convict him," said one. "All this time and manpower, and that's all they've got to show for themselves?"

In the weeks after the exam, Gerry Woods holed up in the King Room, chain smoking as he continued the monotonous task of penciling in a time line of dates, phone calls, and events in the lives of Bradford and Diane King as contained in the 1,600 pages of reports. He strung the results on a roll of paper, taping it to the wall. Gary Hough had lined up a state police specialist who planned to put it in graphic form for court.

Woods was logging dates on telephone records when he came across a Brad King credit card call made on December 11, 1990, from student Kelly Clark's house to Denise Verrier's in Mt. Clemens. Suddenly, a pattern appeared. King appeared to have used the events of that week—the reported break-in at the house, the Wickware letter he gave to Lehmkul, his urging of Diane to stay in Detroit—entirely to his own ends.

Woods called Gary Hough over to the wall of paper.

"Gary, will you look at this," he said.

It was the first time they had linked the obsessed fan directly to Brad King's manipulations of people, places, and events.

"This, is exactly what we've been looking for," Hough said.

Days later, Woods began having chest pains. On a Sunday night in April, he went into the hospital.

It was his second heart attack in eleven months.

After the exam, Brad King wrote a letter to Susan and John Van Vleet back in Denver. It read:

> Well, the first hearings are over—we are bound over for trial. The real work begins now. We felt that there was a chance of charges being dismissed at the end of the hearing. But, as I know from experience, almost all preliminary hearings are resulted in a trial being set. We gave it one hell of a shot—you would like my attorneys. Jim would provide humor when he would see that I'm getting down. The cameras caught us laughing. . . . When we were in conference on several occasions he would say, "I wish you had a better mother-in-law. It would make my job easier". . . . When the judge gave his decision to bind me over to trial my thoughts were: The fresh air must have confused his mind, or having his head up his ass for four days just clouded his judgment too much.
>
> I know that I have a prejudice in this matter but—low is low. The prosecutor by the strictest (maybe not the strictest) guidelines has to show probable cause: One, that a crime had been committed (no doubt about that) and, two, that I might have committed that crime. Just to let you know they have circum-

stantial evidence, which can in conjunction with other real
evidence, leaves no doubt that I'm involved, then you can
convict on that kind of evidence. The real evidence is not even
conclusive as to its relationship to the crime. Well in the county,
cops and district judges are thick as thieves. We will win this. We
know where the prosecution is coming from—they don't know
what we are up to. I will be taking the case files and be preparing
this case as though I were the officer in charge of the investigation. There are some 1,500 pages of reports/interviews. This is
how I can assist my attorneys. We have four people preparing
the case for trial. I think the prosecutor is outgunned. . . .

4

Susan and John Van Vleet were surprised by Brad King's
focus in his letters. He was facing the possibility of spending
the rest of his natural life in prison, but was complaining about
his mother.

He wrote in one correspondence:

> You probably know that some neighbors of ours testified at
> the hearing and, well, they lied. My mother tells me you can
> only be sure that your family cares about you. Then goes on to
> say that I've had a hard time realizing this and doubts I ever
> will. Then she goes on to say that she wished she had raised me
> to make better decisions over the past twelve years, but will have
> to support me through it. The only real support in the letter was
> "I love you." Shit, I know she loves me, but where is the rest of
> her for me?

He wrote about leaving Gail and joining est.

> I was thinking, twelve years ago I got divorced and did the
> training. Two things my parents violently spoke out against. I
> made bad decisions. As I look back this was all really my mom,

with my Dad just going along with her. I remember a talk I had with my Dad about both decisions and he said he understood. . . . The conversation with my mother was very much opposite. How I was ruining my life and leaving God. Life went on from there and you know pretty much all of it. The overriding message from my mother has always been, you can't make good decisions. Now, I don't have my Dad to go to, to buffer that in my family. At least I have people like you in my life or I would begin to wonder about myself.

He wrote about other nebulous issues. He said the children were not being brought to him for visitation by the Newtons or a social service agency, though later it became clear he'd never asked. He lamented the fact that he was not attending powwows. He mused that jail brought home the fact that American society was racist and that anyone different from "the dominant white culture is victimized and abused by the government and its processes."

"I feel ashamed I'm even white," he wrote.

He's way off the mark, the Van Vleets decided. There was nothing in his correspondence about Marler's story or going out and trying to find the .22 rifle he told everyone he sold in Denver. There was no legal brainstorming, no suggestions on how they might find some exonerating evidence in his case.

"Susan had given him several grow up speeches," Jon Van Vleet later recalled. "And I said, this is all very sad that you're in jail. But gee, wake the fuck up and get it handled rather than sit here and cry in your beer about how your mother treats you. I don't think you have time to be upset about handling your mother."

Brad told them about his affairs. They found them more revealing than troubling. They still believed in his innocence.

"The fact that he had a series of affairs with students as opposed to women my age or women Diane's age, or women capable of taking care of him, showed me he was still committed to marriage," Susan Van Vleet later said. "These kids he was sleeping with couldn't take care of themselves, let alone Brad."

That's what it boiled down to, they thought, dependency and responsibility. For years, Brad had let everyone else make his decisions for him, starting with his mother, then Gail, and Diane. The Van Vleets had found themselves in the same role with the children's custody battle.

John Van Vleet recalled, "He didn't say, 'Goddamn it, I want you to do something with my kids. It's the only thing I got.' Brad didn't push it. We were pushing harder than he was."

Now he was alone, away from them.

"I told him when he was first in jail," Susan Van Vleet recalled. "I wrote to him. I wrote, Brad this is a learning experience for you. There is something in this you have to deal with before you're going to get out of jail. If you don't take responsibility for your life and deal with this, you ain't getting out of jail and there's nothing the rest of us can do about it."

At least there weren't any strong women to make his decisions for him in the Calhoun County Jail, they decided. Maybe that alone might force Brad King to act.

James Brady also was finding out about the strained relationship between Bradford King and the woman who was paying his legal bills. He found himself in the middle.

"There was great anger," he recalled. "I was the bridge. I didn't understand it at first."

Brady, however, had far more pressing problems, mainly what promised to be a lengthy and complex murder trial. Brady found that King had a tendency to get sidetracked on the issues of the custody of his children and bail. Both, he thought, would divert legal resources from the most important task at hand, preparing a thorough and spirited defense.

"I perhaps could be criticized for not getting him out on bail," Brady later recalled. "My point was that it was a waste of time and energy. They're just not going to allow that to happen. It's a waste of time and money. That money could be going to defense. A guy charged with first degree murder is not going to be free on bond . . . I don't know of anybody in the area where I practice where that has happened. I would say

Brad, cool it. Let's conserve our energy. Let's get you out of this thing."

Brady had a number of approaches underway. A private investigator was looking into the backgrounds of Tom Darling, Chris Sly, Nita Davis, and other witnesses potentially harmful to his client. He'd contacted the therapist that had counseled Brad and Diane King, obtained his records and psychological tests, hoping to show with them the marriage was not in as serious trouble as maintained by the prosecution. Brady did not see much opportunity with Marler King's story. The boy was too young to take the stand and his stories about the murder would probably not be admitted in court under the hearsay rule.

Brady decided to make detailed comparisons between police and witness statements. The paperwork alone was going to be a massive undertaking, especially when on May 1, the prosecution filed a list of 146 potential witnesses with the court. There were thousands of pages of materials seized in the search warrants to examine.

Brady also wanted to be prepared to attack physical evidence and statements crucial to the prosecution's case. He would try to get Brad King's statements to Jack Schoder suppressed and the casing found in the loft thrown out on the grounds that the search was improper. He ordered research on canine tracking, hoping to suppress the dog track itself, or at least be able to destroy its credibility in court.

As for the setting, Brady was optimistic that Brad King could get a fair trial in Calhoun County. He was impressed with the local jury pool. He was impressed with the judge they'd drawn in the case.

Calhoun Circuit Judge Conrad Sindt had served as the Calhoun County Prosecutor for nearly eleven years. He'd been Jon Sahli's boss and hired investigator Gerry Woods, but Brady wasn't alarmed at the old relationships. Sindt wouldn't be the first prosecutor who'd become a judge in Michigan. It was a natural career progression. The Battle Creek *Enquirer* had endorsed him for the bench, writing he had "the energy, brains and temperament to give full attention to all sides of any issue."

In fact, Brady was impressed with the level of professionalism among all the parties.

"I was impressed with the trial judge," he later said. "His reputation was outstanding and my own observations confirmed that. I relish good relationships. I sometimes think you go farther. Jon Sahli, who is not a very outgoing guy, I thought handled himself very professionally."

Brady also liked the possibilities of a jury impaneled in Calhoun County. He liked to think of careful jury selection as his trademark. As he began filing evidentiary motions in the summer, Brady sat in on a couple of jury selections in the county. He was devising a questionnaire for prospective jurors, probing their views on adultery and other issues. How they would respond, would shape how he tried his case.

"I want to know these people," he would say. "I want them to know me, and I want them to like me."

In Calhoun County, Brady decided there would be a lot of diversity in the jury pool. "There were two blacks on one jury I saw," he later explained. "I told Brad, come to Kent County or Ottawa County. The demographics for Battle Creek were really pretty good. Nice racial mix. Diversity. Working-class. This may not be all that bad a place to try this case."

But Brad King was adamant. He wanted to file for a change of venue. If they were going to do that, Brady suggested a professional survey of potential jurors and their attitudes about the case, something that did not come cheaply. Brad King insisted they go ahead.

By then, Marge Lundeen had already paid $50,000 for her son's representation. The firm had just sent Brad King's mother another letter, asking for $50,000 more.

In mid-May, Brady's resources were sidetracked. He received a call from a twenty-eight-year-old inmate in the Southern Michigan Prison at Jackson, saying he was involved in the murder of Diane Newton King. Brady sent Trish Hubbard and investigator Lee Coltson to interview David Albright, a repeat felon who was doing eight to thirty for breaking and entering. He was a short man of less than five and a half feet and had scars of self-mutilation on his arms. Hubbard later wrote in a memo describing her encounter:

The first statement Albright made was "I did it." He maintained eye contact during this time. His tone and demeanor seemed appropriate; he was quiet and definite-sounding. Albright did not want Lee (Coltson) to sit with us, as without him, it was "your word against mine." During the next hour and a half, Albright disclosed the following:

- He was "out and about" at the time of the murder. ("Out" date was September 1990.)
- He was taking drugs (PCP) for about three months straight prior to the murder.
- He was with a friend (male).
- He did not set out for the King residence. He found himself in the Battle Creek area, then thought of King.
- He did not intend to kill Diane. He intended to kill Brad.
- He knew Diane was gone—he saw her leave. He was hiding on the property for several hours. He thought he was well hidden. He does not know where he was hiding. He recalls only that in jumping down from wherever it was, he hurt his ankle.
- He does not recall if he took a weapon there, or if he got one from the house. He recalls going into the house, and that it appeared that no one was home. He recalls hearing a noise outside the door.
- He recalls that the weapon was long, like a rifle—not a handgun. . . . He recalls that he saw Diane still moving as he ran away, "as if she didn't die right away." He also recalls hearing a sound like crying, though he did not know if it came from somewhere nearby, Diane, or where it was from.
- He said, in response to my question, that he does not recall what Diane was wearing.

Albright provided other facts he could have gleaned from the news coverage of the case. Still, the firm launched an extensive investigation into Albright's background, talking with friends and relatives and trying to determine where he was the weekend of the murder.

In a few weeks, James Brady had another problem with
David Albright. He wanted a thousand dollars up front for his
statement. Then came another letter.

"My price is $20,000 when you're cleared and $500 a month
for twenty years," he wrote. "Now you know my price."

James Brady had told the King family the defense of Brad
King, if it went to trial, would not be cheap. And it wasn't.

By May, relations were growing more tense between the
Lundeens and the large Grand Rapids law firm. Marge Lun-
deen had already given the firm $77,000. In May, Marge and
Cliff had sent a letter pointing out what they thought were
$3,111.15 in billing discrepancies. Later in the month she sent
Brady $27,000, and told him "Brad will have to be responsible
for the rest."

On June 16, Marge and Cliff Lundeen drove up to San
Antonio to meet James Brady in a suite at the Airport Hilton.
He'd flown down, saying he wanted to discuss the case and his
representation.

It had not been a pleasant trip up from Kerrville. The day
was sweltering. They couldn't find parking for the hotel and
had to find a distant spot in the airport parking structure. They
rang his room from the lobby, but it was incessantly busy. He
was on the phone to his office back in Michigan, double-check-
ing on their appointment because the Lundeens had shown up
late.

Finally, they sat down to talk. There were some new items.
Trial was set for September 1. An inmate in Jackson prison had
confessed to the crime, "but it's probably not legitimate," Brady
cautioned. And, Brady said, his firm needed more money. The
work was more extensive than anyone realized, including a list
of 146 potential witnesses the prosecution had filed with the
court. Brady said the firm would need an additional $75,000 to
take the case through trial.

That was out of the question, she said. "One hundred thousand is all I can give."

"It's a man's life at stake here," the attorney said. "We have
to go Cadillac on this thing."

Marge shook her head slowly. "Mr. Brady, don't you think it's time we go Chevrolet?"

Brady came up with a counter offer. If she would provide $23,000, bringing the total to $100,000, and pledge another $27,000 in the future, he would try to get an okay from his partners to continue. He also would talk to Randy Wright about raising another $25,000 from friends. He asked her to sign a guaranty agreement pledging the $50,000. The Lundeens wanted time to make some alterations in the guaranty agreement.

A month later, Brady began discussing with the judge and prosecutor the possibility of withdrawing because of nonpayment. He filed a formal motion to that effect.

In late July Marge Lundeen wrote James Brady:

Dear Mr. Brady,

Enclosed you will find two checks totalling $27,000. I shall try to liquidate some funds soon to come up with the remaining $23,000 per requested. . . .

It is frightening to be 69 years old and have your money disappearing with no way to replace it. Not only am I frightened for myself but for Brad also. But facts are facts and I have very little money left.

For some reason Brad has the impression my funds are unlimited. After his father's death I tried to explain how my income had reduced, but he hears only what he chooses to hear. He has been asking and receiving money yearly since his divorce from Gail. With what I have given Brad and Diane in the past and am remitting to you, my capital will be depleted to a point that makes me very uncomfortable. I've had to change my life style, reduce church contributions and would not have sufficient funds for an unseen emergency or higher inflation.

I hope you can find a way to represent Brad with what I will send, but if more money is needed you will have to make arrangements with Brad . . .

Brad does not communicate with me. I've had three letters, but not much in them . . . (I) also send the jail money and have to assume Brad is receiving it. He mentioned once about getting $10 and to send either cash or money order.

This letter makes me very sad. I have spent many hours in thought and prayer and see no other way.

Sincerely,
Margie King Lundeen

James Brady had been saving money in one area. Virtually all contacts with his client were through Battle Creek attorney Virginia Cairns. She visited Calhoun County Jail's most famous inmate frequently, sometimes once or twice a week. By mid summer, her visits had become the talk among jail staff. Stories reached task force members. She was showing up with fast food, books and magazines for King. Cairns would later call those accounts malicious and untrue.

Some people called Virginia Cairns an outspoken, sometimes abrasive lawyer.

"Oh yeah, she's strong," King himself would say of her. "She doesn't let people walk on her."

"She was the only contact outside that jail Brad had," Marge Lundeen later said. "I'm sure it helped him emotionally."

5

Much had changed when the case of the People versus Bradford J. King finally came up for trial in Calhoun County Circuit Court in early November. Surgeons had grafted three new arteries on Gerry Woods's heart. Voters elected a new sheriff of Calhoun County during jury selection. Jon Sahli won the prosecutor's post unopposed, but he'd face a new opponent in court.

Bradford King had fired James Brady a month before.

Brady was blindsided by the move. He thought he'd resolved the payment problem with the Lundeens. King had waived a legal requirement that he be brought to trial within 180 days of arrest so more defense money could be raised by Randy Wright. Brady had given his word to Judge Conrad Sindt that he would try the case come November 3, whether the money was raised or not.

What he didn't know was that local counsel Virginia Cairns had been lobbying Brad King and the Lundeens to fire him for weeks. She made repeated calls to Kerrville, telling Marge and Cliff that Brady's fees were excessive and that he should have tried to free King on bond. There were "plenty of lawyers" in Battle Creek who would handle the case for $25,000, she told the Lundeens. Brady wasn't prepared, she charged.

"Brad is certain to be convicted," she said in one phone call.

Cliff Lundeen told Virginia Cairns that in his conversations with Brady, the attorney had always complimented her work.

"That's because I told him everything to do," she said.

Virginia Cairns, King told Randy Wright, "opened my eyes" to James Brady. In a long jail house conversation with his old friend, Wright tried to convince King to stay with the former U.S. Attorney. His fees were not bargain rate, Wright argued, but his trial abilities were highly respected.

"I told him I thought he was making a big mistake," Wright later said.

Brady was miffed, and later denied he'd done anything wrong. He'd learned King was considering his dismissal from Nancy Mullett, who Cairns tipped off one day during a pretrial proceeding. Brady confronted the Battle Creek attorney.

"Virginia indicated that she was shocked, that she was angry, and that she would not continue on as cocounsel," he later recalled. "She didn't just tell me that. She told my office that. She was surprised and sympathetic."

In November, Virginia Cairns had found Brad a new lawyer. His name was John Sims, a scrappy forty-year-old attorney from eastern Calhoun County. Sims practiced with two partners out of a restored farmhouse in Albion. His retainer was $50,000; $25,000 under the total Brady said he was going to need to take the case to trial. With Sims in place, Virginia

Cairns asked Marge Lundeen for $10,000 for herself. King's mother refused. She continued on the case anyway.

"Aggressive," was the word that dominated the news release put out by King through his attorneys. "I have directed John M. Sims and Virginia C. Cairns to obtain a substitution of counsel immediately and to begin an aggressive defense."

Sims tried only three or four criminal cases a year, but his resume included several lengthy, complex federal drug cases. His murder trial experience was limited to a juvenile homicide and a highly publicized case he worked as a law clerk. But his firm, and the two-fisted town of Albion, had a reputation.

"When Marshall people want to buy a home or get a mortgage or sign a contract they hire Marshall attorneys," Sims was fond of saying. "When they really want to get in somebody's shit, they hire us. We used to be referred to as those bastards from Albion."

John Sims also had something else that endeared Brad King. He'd faced Jon Sahli four times in court. His win streak was 4-0.

With only a month to prepare, Sims tapped time and resources trying to get his client out of jail with a bond hearing. Judge Sindt agreed to release King on a $750,000 bond, but attached several conditions. Randy Wright raised $75,000 in loans from old fraternity brothers, but when he showed up in Battle Creek with the money, the bail was cancelled. The Battle Creek *Enquirer* had published the location of a small apartment for King approved by the court, drawing neighborhood protest.

Brad King told friends and family it was all part of a larger conspiracy, a continuation of what had happened to him after his firing from the Tenth District Court. Randy Wright had no reason to disbelieve him. He made four long trips to the small city with the grain silos in its downtown skyline, but further glitches held up the release.

"I figured this is a Chinese fire drill," Wright later recalled. "They have no intention of letting this guy out."

However, the location of King's apartment had not come from authorities. The reporter simply had heard Virginia Cairns say it while talking loudly within earshot of journalists.

*   *   *

The preliminary exam headlines had been especially stark: **EX-LOVER: KING WAS UNHAPPY AND WITNESSES REVEAL SEXUAL AFFAIR, MARRIAGE ROCKED BY STRIFE.** The comments from James Brady's community survey were sometimes strident: "I think he did it. He hated his wife. She wore the pants in the family and he killed her."

But Judge Sindt denied motions for change of venue, despite the survey showing ninety-four percent of the people in the county were aware of the case and one in three thought King was guilty.

"Conrad Sindt was not going to change venue without trying to get a jury and he was going to get a jury," John Sims later said. "Come hell or high water."

It took four days to impanel a jury of twelve with two alternates. There were two blacks; the gender breakdown was seven women and seven men, among them: Two cashiers and a salesclerk. A Kellogg's factory worker. A licensed practical nurse. A social worker. An insurance worker. A retired health care administrator. Eight were married, four single, and two were divorced. A half dozen had children. All had high-school educations. The social worker had a master's degree, the retired administrator a bachelor's.

Judge Conrad Sindt offered the panel an unusual privilege in American jurisprudence. Jurors would be able to ask written questions of witnesses, after they were reviewed by the judge and both attorneys in the case.

John Sims remained guardedly optimistic when they finished with the voir dire.

"This is not a loser," he told Brad King. "This is a winnable case, but you're going in with the cards stacked against you."

Even a full trial by jury offers only a limited view of the people, places, and events associated with a particular crime. But nowhere is the window on reality more rigidly controlled than for the jury itself, which, unlike the courtroom audience, is restricted to panes determined by the rules of evidence.

On November 9 and 10, a struggle to fashion that window ensued before Judge Conrad Sindt. Sims had filed a blizzard of nineteen motions. He wanted excluded from the trial: personal documents, telephone and financial records, tracking dog evidence, crime scene photos, the clothing Diane King was wearing the day of the murder, mention of the Kings' security system, comments Diane King made to friends and coworkers, statements Brad King made to anyone outside of court and, most importantly, the testimony of Nita Davis and Kelly Clark.

With the jury box empty, Sims argued each strenuously.

One standard applied to most of the evidence. Admitted material had to be more probative than prejudicial. A crime scene photograph, for example, couldn't be used just for its shock value. It had to fit into the prosecution's argument of the case.

Sahli sought to make good use of his slide projector. During the debate over the motions, he flashed before the judge crime scene photos of Diane King's body for consideration.

Brad King looked away from the screen. He placed his forehead on his fist.

"What does this show?" Sims demanded, wondering why the jury would need to see a picture of the victim sprawled on her back in her driveway.

"Hair," Sahli said.

"What is the significance of the hair?" Sims demanded.

"The defendant stated to Detective Schoder that upon finding his wife, he shook her. The photograph shows that is not the case."

King snorted, as though the idea was preposterous.

Jon Sahli stopped in his tracks. He stared down Brad King for several seconds. It was the only direct acknowledgement of each other they made during the entire trial.

Judge Sindt denied some of Sims's motions and deferred others until they came up during the trial itself. He also applied some restrictions. On the matter of the King security system, for example, Diane King's declarations would be limited to what Joanne Karaba, Stella Pamp, Denise Verrier, and Freida Newton observed, not what Diane King told them. The judge ruled that was hearsay.

The attorneys argued over the testimony of Kelly Clark and

Nita Davis. The rule of evidence was an old and universal one. It's called Rule 404 in Michigan and federal books. Rule 404 (a) stated character evidence was not permissible to prove a crime. Rule 404 (b) stated other wrong acts by a defendant could not be introduced to show his behavior conformed with the crime.

Sims summarized the spirit of the ruling in his argument. "Let's paint Brad King as a bad person. If he did this bad act, then he must have done the other. I can see no reason for the admission of this evidence other than to prejudice the jury."

"We're not offering it as character," Sahli argued.

The extramarital issue aside, Sahli said, the women would offer testimony linking Brad King to the crime, an exception under Rule 404.

"Specifically, you're offering it as proof of scheme, plan, and motive?" Sindt asked, citing the rule's exact language.

"Yes, Your Honor."

After some consideration, Judge Sindt made his ruling. The prosecutor could not mention extramarital affairs in his opening statement, the judge said. He would rule on the admissibility of individual testimony of each woman as they were called during the trial, he said.

John Sims's strategy was straightforward. "I figured if I could keep out all the hoopla about the girlfriends, what Diane said here and there, and what Diane was thinking here and there, if I kept out all the guff, the chaff of this case, I hopefully could get a jury to see that: Number one, this case was botched from the word go by the police. Number two, there isn't a whole lot of evidence here and it's all circumstantial. Can you convict a person for first degree murder on this kind of evidence? And number three, there is no motive. There was never any motive that I could find."

After the 404 ruling, the Brad Busters met in a stairwell at the back of the courthouse, smoking cigarettes and comparing notes. Sahli believed the most critical evidence was still intact, despite Sims's motions. The prosecution had lost the extramarital testimony from the coeds, but not the coeds themselves.

"Look, it will work in our favor," Gary Hough predicted. "When that jury sees these good-looking gals come in here one after another, they'll put two and two together. In fact, because they can't testify to it, they'll start thinking he was sleeping with some that he wasn't."

Rule 404 also was a two-edged sword. Sims's own defense would also be severely limited. True, Sahli could not make Brad King's character part of his prosecution, but then neither could Sims make it part of his defense without consequences. If Sims brought King's character into play, it would be open season for an attack on King's virtue, and they had plenty of ammunition in stock.

If the People's case was a small-town vendetta, as Bradford King kept telling friends and family, it was going to be one like Calhoun County had never seen. The prosecution had tapped every available resource. They'd built a model of the crime scene. The state police graphics expert had produced a time line that covered four easels of placards. Another staffer loaded the key preliminary exam and interviews into a notebook computer and would also summarize trial testimony. A program called Discovery-ZX would give Sahli instant electronic access to past statements. A staffer was assigned to manage seventy-three witnesses now listed in the prosecution's case.

Sahli had pared his own witness list down, but during jury selection, added one as well. The tip had come out of the jail. A forty-year-old former jail inmate named Ricky McClain had told detective Jim Stadfeld that he was playing a game of spades in jail in October when Brad King began puffing about how tough he was to cell mates.

"Yeah, I killed the bitch," he quoted King as saying. "And I'll kill any other bitch that crosses me, too."

Nobody was going to call little Marler King. John Sims subpoenaed the boy in October to one of the bond hearings, mainly to give his client an opportunity to see his son. Judge Sindt allowed a noncontact visit in the courthouse law library. When King reached out to touch the boy affectionately during the visit, it was over before it really began.

"You're assholes," King exploded. "You're all fucking ass-holes."

John Sims considered putting Marler King on the stand counterproductive. "Mainly, I think it would reflect badly on Brad," he later said. "I didn't want to take the chance that my client could be blamed for putting a child that young through that."

Unknown to the defense, the prosecution in April had sent Marler King to be evaluated by a child psychiatrist at the University of Michigan. The boy avoided the subject of the shooting during three sessions.

"If he had to testify, he couldn't tell the difference between reality and fantasy," the psychiatrist told Gerry Woods.

Woods was hoping John Sims would call David Albright, the inmate at Jackson prison who had contacted James Brady. The attorney had sent over a memo to the prosecutor, saying the inmate was confessing to the crime. On February 8, 1991, Woods discovered, Albright was arrested for breaking into a Lansing business. Police found him because he'd left his wallet and ID at the scene. On February 9, the day Diane Newton King was killed, David Albright was in the Ingham County Jail.

"That's one good break," Gary Hough said. "There may be more. We're gonna get a lot of attention with this trial. Some-where along the line, you gotta expect to get a break when this thing goes live."

On the morning of November 12, a line formed outside the largest courtroom in the county courthouse in downtown Battle Creek. Authorities would need every bit of space and more. The prosecutor's staff filled the first row. Diane King's extended family and friends filled the second and the third. The prosecutor's office offered Freida Newton, and other sequestered family witnesses, a small room just outside the courtroom doors. Rela-tives, friends, and well-wishers filled it, keeping the victim's mother company until her day in court.

There didn't appear to be a soul in the courtroom in Brad King's camp. His family was absent. Brad King himself walked in wearing an impeccable dark blue, double-breasted suit with

a starched white shirt and red-and-white striped tie. He walked
erect, eyeing the courtroom, his chest out.

It was all being captured by a camera and microphones and
fed to a video control center set up in a small room off the
outside hallway. The national cable network Court TV had
wired Judge Sindt's courtroom for picture and sound. Outside,
electronic reporters with their own monitors tapped into the
Court TV feed to get their sound bites for local news.

Nationally, the trial would be broadcast live, interrupted
through the hour by mandatory commercial breaks and analysis by guest commentators and a New York anchor when the
action slowed. A Court TV reporter would also do cut-ins from
Battle Creek.

The coverage reached beyond cable customers. For the next
month, it would be hard to find a bar or restaurant TV in
Calhoun County that wasn't tuned in.

6

Jon Sahli's opening argument was about dates, of one sort or
another.

"This case begins in the summer of 1990, when the deceased
received calls for lunch from a male caller," he began.

Seconds later, Sahli approached the jury and one of the stark,
black-and-white placards he'd set up across from them. He
pointed to October 30, 1990, on the time line. It was the day
Diane King received the stalker letter.

"That note stated: You Should Have Gone to Lunch with
Me," Sahli said. "When she received this note, she became very
concerned. She became frightened."

Every date had a story: October 30 at Cindy Acosta's house.
November 20 at the hospital. Diane King alone after Kateri's
birth. December 11 and 12 at Denise Verrier's with Diane and

the children. Brad King seeing *Dances With Wolves* with Kelly
Clark, then reporting the break-in.

On December 12, Sahli said, Brad King would "visit" Kelly
Clark. On December 19, Nita Davis would "visit" Brad King
at his house. On February 7, Brad King would make another
"visit" to Kelly Clark's.

Every significant date was on the time line. But the jury was
sent out for its mid-morning break before Sahli ever got to the
afternoon of the murder.

That's when John Sims rose to make a motion.

"Your Honor," he said. "I want a mistrial."

He wanted a mistrial, for among other things, Sahli's introduction of the extramarital affairs in his argument and on the
placards. He charged Sahli had flagrantly disregarded Sindt's
ruling on the Rule 404 (b) character issue. Soon the defense
attorney was livid, nearly shouting.

"I want a mistrial," Sims said, pacing near the defense table.
"I want a mistrial, and I can go home and take a nap and forget
this mess."

Sahli shrugged, looking at the judge like Sims was hallucinat-
ing.

"I only referred to them as friends, Your Honor," Sahli said
of the coeds. "I didn't introduce any sexual references whatsoever."

Sims pointed out the wording on the time line: "Date with
Brad King." "Lunch date with Brad King." "Movie date."

Sims laughed sarcastically, eyeing the packed courtroom.
"Let's take a poll, Your Honor. I think everyone in here knows
what's going on."

Sahli offered to take the word "date" off the placards.

Judge Sindt pondered more verbiage. When the attorneys
ran out of words, he decided. Sahli's terminology was ill-ad-
vised, he said, cautioning the prosecutor to go more carefully in
future references. But a mistrial required flagrant prejudicial
conduct, he said.

"I don't find those references so blatant that they are grounds
for a mistrial," Sindt concluded.

It would take the rest of the morning for Jon Sahli to outline his case. It appeared to be a four-prong attack: The crime scene pointed to no one but Brad King as the killer. Brad King had been seen with a rifle similar to the murder weapon. The King marriage was in trouble. Brad King's demeanor in the hours, days, and months after the killing was atypical of a man who quite suddenly and tragically lost his wife.

When he was finished, John Sims made another motion for a mistrial, contending the prosecutor was introducing exhibits before they were admitted. Judge Sindt denied the motion.

The judge would deny nearly two dozen such motions for a mistrial from John Sims in the days ahead.

"Here are the facts of this case," John Sims told the jury. "Fact one: On February 9, Diane King was shot and killed. She was found lying in the driveway. Fact two: A shell casing, not a bullet, a shell casing, was found in the barn. Fact three: Two days later, not that night, they found *that* gun. And right next to that gun, seven casings."

Sims paused. *"Those* are the facts. That's it.

"Oh, I forgot," Sims said, gesturing. "I forgot. One year later. January 31, 1992. They arrest Bradford King. Not February 9. Or February 11, or 12. Or March, or April, or May, or June, or July, or August, or September, or November, or December. . . .

"Why are we here? I'll tell you why. You know I will . . . this is the power of the state arranged against Bradford King. That's what you're going to see. You're going to see that if you want somebody bad enough, you can get them. That's what you're going to see."

The prosecutor had the burden of proof to show Brad King's guilt, he argued, and the prosecutor's case was built on "innuendo," police errors, and "an assassination of Brad King's character." Sims told the jury they would see outright deceit. He charged the prosecution would introduce statements they knew were blatantly false.

"Now, *I know,* you're going to hear out-and-out lies. Fabricated lies."

But when it was over, the attorney predicted, the result would be anticlimactic.

"It's all, as someone once said, all sound and fury signifying nothing," he said. "When it's over, that's what you're going to hear—a big, resounding silence."

Jon Sahli's first battery of witnesses were the first people responding to the call on February 9, 1991, from Marshall dispatcher Joe Delapas to Guy Picketts to the EMTs first arriving on the scene.

As Sahli questioned EMT Jeffery Caison, he flashed slides of a prostrate Diane King, the hum of the projector fan accented by Diane King's sister Darlene crying in the second row. Something was wrong with the picture at 16240 Division Drive during the fourteen minutes the ambulance was on the scene, Jeffery Caison testified. He said Brad King never approached his wife's body. He never inquired about his wife's condition.

"Out of eight hundred runs (you've done), how often do you have family members not approach you?" Sahli asked.

"Very few, at best."

"How often do you have family members not approach the victim?"

"Very few."

"How often do you have family members not inquire about condition?"

"Again, very few."

Under cross-examination, Sims asked if family members ever got in the way of his work.

"Yes."

"Police try to keep people away, isn't that correct?"

"Yes, at my request."

Questioned by Sahli, Caison said he never requested King be kept away.

"Because nobody got in the way, is that correct?" Sims asked.

"Yes."

After lunch, the People called Guy Picketts. For an hour,

Picketts detailed what he found at the scene, Sahli lighting up his silver screen again with slides.

The Jeep. The body. The children inside. The husband on the porch. The camouflage outfit he was wearing.

As he approached the EMTs, Picketts testified, one of them called out the victim had been shot. He told the jury how he then approached Brad King.

"You said you asked Mr. King if he had any weapons," Sahli asked. "And his response was what, sir?"

"All he said was, 'Only a shotgun.' "

"Did you then at that time stay with Mr. King?"

"No, sir. I advised him to stay right in that little porch area. . . ."

Picketts continued. There were more pictures: The open loft door. The chained Doberman. The casing in the straw. The key case and barrette in the driveway.

His testimony took everyone from the barnyard to the foggy footbridge at Talmadge Creek. The boot print found there.

They moved to the search on February 11.

"I show you now what has been marked as People's proposed Exhibit Number Five," Sahli said, lifting up the Remington Model 511 Scoremaster from behind the defense table and approaching the witness-box. "Do you recognize that, Deputy Picketts?"

"Yes, sir."

"How do you recognize that?"

"It is the gun I located in the creek."

The seven casings were introduced. Picketts testified about his field tests, how he ran the dog track and heard gunshots from the far set of bales.

When John Sims had trouble opening an evidence envelope the prosecutor handed him for inspection, he and Brad King chuckled. The defense attorney was trying to break the tension.

No one on the jury laughed. No one even smiled.

Guy Picketts said it in direct testimony. Under cross-examination, John Sims had him say it again.

Yes, he'd ordered Brad King to stay by the porch.

Sims's message: As a former cop, King knew to give emergency personnel room.

"Isn't it true that family members that generally jump into an emergency scene present a problem?" he asked later.

"Yes."

"And as a police officer you know that they generally get in the way?"

"Yes."

Then Sims used the former resident of the old Zinn farm to expand the potential crime scene, making it a much larger and louder place. Yes, Picketts agreed, there was a pipeline to the east and another lane coming into the back property from the west, hinting there was other easy access.

"I-69 is nearby, isn't it? You can hear traffic night and day, isn't that right?"

"Yes."

"Mr. Zinn has acreage there, maybe five hundred acres?"

"Yes."

"No hunting there, though."

"No hunting."

"But lots of deer."

"Lots of deer."

"So many deer that their tracks obliterated the track you found out there, didn't they . . . or, do you know about that?"

No, Picketts didn't know about that.

When both attorneys were finished with the deputy, there was a question from a juror. It was passed on paper to the bailiff. The juror wasn't thinking about demeanor, he was thinking about a weapon. He wanted to know about the test firing. What caliber was it? How far away was Picketts?

Picketts couldn't provide the distance.

"And I believe it was the same weapon that was recovered on February 11."

Another question on paper from a juror. Did Picketts hear a dog barking?

"No."

Sims followed up. "In fact, you didn't even notice the dog until you entered the barn, did you?"

"We checked during the building search."

"If you hadn't, you would have never noticed him, would you?"

"That's correct."

The two attorneys seemed to fight the demeanor question to a draw. Typical of the gains and losses was the testimony of Sergeant Harold Badger, the first supervisor on the crime scene. His three sergeant's stripes hardly covered his large biceps, but his voice was nearly inaudible.

Badger recalled his initial exchange of words with King as to what had happened, how the defendant said he'd been out walking. The sergeant testified he could not recall King ever inquiring about Diane King's condition, nor did he ever ask to approach her or the children.

"What was Mr. King's demeanor when you were speaking with him?"

"Throughout the time I had contact with him, he didn't appear to be upset. He didn't seem to be too concerned. He was kind of distanced from what was going on."

Sahli wanted to know King's reaction when he was informed his wife was dead.

"At that time he began to cry."

On cross, Sims brought out a statement Badger had given sixteen months earlier to Jack Schoder. In it, the sergeant said King had asked one time about his wife's well-being, talked of going to the hospital, and asked to get the children out of the car after the ambulance left.

Sims refreshed his memory in front of the jurors.

Badger also admitted he had no knowledge that Deputy Picketts had told King to stay put near the porch.

"You also were not privy to the conversations that Mr. King had with Deputy Picketts?"

"No, sir."

"So you don't know that maybe for as many as fifteen minutes to a half hour, this man had been yelling and screaming and crying before you showed up there."

"Prior to my arrival, I have no knowledge."

Sims used Badger to remind the jury King *was* capable of emotion. "When someone told him his wife had died, he broke down and cried. Those were your terms, right?"

"Yes, sir, he did."

While Sahli was introducing the demeanor matter, a note came up to the prosecution table. The Battle Creek Police Department had a message on the department's Silent Observer tip line. An anonymous caller said he'd overheard two women talking about the King case that everyone was watching on Court TV. They knew something about the rifle everyone was talking about, the tipster said. He left their names.

Sahli and Woods asked Jack Schoder to investigate.

After the first day of testimony was over, the Brad Busters sped over to the basement of the county human services building to meet the detective. He was pacing the halls with anticipation, simultaneously smoking a cigarette while chewing a stick of gum. Nancy Mullett's office filled with smoke as everyone listened to the detective. He'd found the two women.

"This is great, man," Schoder said. "This is *really* good."

The two women worked in a cleaning service. They used to clean the Kings' apartment back when they lived in Battle Creek. They cleaned it every Friday for more than six months. One cleaning woman saw two long guns in the house. She didn't know much about weapons. The other woman saw one gun, sitting on a bar near the basement stairs.

"She's pretty familiar with guns," Schoder said.

Schoder not only had already taped an interview with the two women, he had them waiting in Gerry Woods's office across the hall. The detective had shown the woman familiar with guns a picture of the Remington Model 511 Scoremaster.

"Well, what did she say?" Nancy Mullett demanded.

"She said it looks like the gun," Schoder said. He stopped puffing and chewing and smiled.

"Damn, this is going to be great," Schoder continued.

"Why's that, Jack?" Sahli said dryly.

"If Sims says to her why didn't you come in earlier with this information, she says she's afraid of Brad. She says, 'I'm scared to death of that guy.' "

Woods was cautious. He wanted to know exactly what the woman remembered. "Did she remember the leather strap, the bootlace?"

Woods decided to go ask her himself.

He came back smiling. "She doesn't remember the strap at all. She just remembers it being long and dark. My suggestion is we take them over to the apartment. Get permission to go in."

Sahli lit another cigarette and exhaled. "Well," he said. "I guess this makes it awful difficult for them to put the gun out in Colorado in the hands of some unknown stranger."

"It sure do," Schoder said, smiling. "Big time."

An hour later, Gerry Woods slid in half soaked into his idling car, a driving fall rain hammering a beat not too far out of sync with a *Best of Conway Twitty* tape playing on his deck. He was waiting in the dark parking lot of the Oakwood Apartments, hoping the tenant of the Kings' old apartment unit would come home soon. Schoder had driven off to baby-sit the two new witnesses.

"Well, we just got a good one," he said. "This is the stuff you hope for. Just like Gary said."

It almost seemed to be a pattern now. Every time there was a big development, something came along to add some agony to the ecstasy for Gerry Woods. But he wasn't flinching, just waiting.

He had no way of knowing Gary Hough would soon be taking his place at the prosecution table or that he would be heading for Brighton, Illinois, for a funeral. His sister would call him with the news of his mother's death.

7

J on Sahli told the court during the next morning break about the two new witnesses, just about the time his effort to portray Brad King as the crime scene's disinterested bystander was starting to look like a real stretch.

Sims objected, then did just what Jack Schoder predicted.

"My concern is these are people who have been aware of coverage, and they come forward saying, 'Gee, I saw something like this gun,'" Sims said, indignantly. "This was in 1989. It's too remote, Your Honor. And it's improper."

"Your Honor, these witnesses were reluctant witnesses," Sahli argued, adding the prosecution had no chance to discover them before the trial.

Judge Sindt offered John Sims the opportunity to interview the women, then took the matter under advisement.

When the jury came back from break, Sahli put a deputy who'd gone to the hospital with Diane King's body on the stand to help introduce exhibits. He started with Diane King's gray Operation Desert Shield sweatshirt, with its bloodstained American flag.

"Your Honor, I'm willing to stipulate these are the clothes worn by the victim," Sims said.

"Your Honor," Sahli said. "I want the deputy to identify them."

And identify them he did. Diane King's pants. Her red underwear. Her white bra. The dark scarf she was wearing around her shoulders.

Sims watched, slouching in his chair, Brad King at his side, his shoulders hunched. The attorney was coming down with a bad case of bronchitis that would last through the entire month-long trial.

He looked more exasperated than sick.

* * *

On November 17, Trooper Gary Lisle was called, looking as much like a soldier as a cop in his snappy, dark Michigan State Police blues. He was girded in black leather at the waist as well as crosswise at the chest.

As the jury waited in the jury room, Sims argued against the admission of the dog track evidence. It was the last in a series of efforts by Sims to keep the dog track evidence out of the trial. Sims argued the prosecutor hadn't met the conditions of allowing such evidence. The prosecutor had to show the dog was qualified and the trail wasn't contaminated.

"I take it Travis can smell police officers?" Sims asked the trooper during voir dire.

"If they're human, yes," he said.

Everyone was laughing, but Jon Sahli knew if he didn't get the dog track in, his case might entirely fall apart. Sahli laid more foundation for the trooper to be qualified as an expert. Lisle had testified more than a hundred times in previous cases.

"What is a contaminated scent, Trooper Lisle?" Sahli asked.

"A contaminated scent is where you have a number of things that have masked the scent. A large crowd of people have walked over the scent . . . which makes it impossible for the dog to get a good start."

Lisle said he "knew" his dog. Travis's behavior let him know when a scent was contaminated or old. Travis had tracked scents as old as thirteen hours, he said. He and the dog knew how to discern the proper trail.

Judge Sindt decided to allow his testimony, but not without cautioning the jury of a reservation cited by previous courts. "Tracking dog evidence is not to be considered proof in and of itself," he later told the jurors. "There must be other proof to convict the defendant of the crime."

Jon Sahli asked the trooper to explain how the tracking process worked. Lisle explained how the dog was trained, how the dog was ready to go to work when he was taken from his kennel into the station wagon and arrived on a scene.

Lisle explained to the jury how Travis found the scent, then using a pointer traced their track the night of February 9 on a large diagram. Lisle testified how the dog lingered at the water where the gun was eventually found. He discussed their failure to pick up other scents in adjoining areas that night.

They moved to February 11. The dog handler testified about speaking with Bradford King at the sheriff's department earlier that day.

"What did you speak to Mr. King about?"

"I wanted to find out exactly where he had walked."

Sahli introduced the cryptic diagram King drew, and Lisle detailed King's supposed route on the large one for the jury. The dog handler detailed finding the stuck Jeep Wagoneer back near the hay bales on February 11. He told of seeing the pair of tennis shoe footprints in one snow patch, but noted there were no boot impressions in the same area.

On his cross, John Sims went after Travis and scored no points with dog owners.

"When Travis did this track, he was ten years old at the time?"

"Yes."

"Is Travis still alive?"

Lisle chuckled. "He's still running tracks."

Sims wanted to know what Travis did when he finds the person he was tracking.

"He wags his tail and comes up to the person because he expects to be petted."

"Did he wag his tail or come up to Mr. King that night?"

"No, he did not."

"In fact, Travis failed in his assignment that night because he lost the track, didn't he?"

"He took it as far as he could."

"He lost the track, didn't he?"

"Yes."

"So you don't know where that track went after he lost it?"

"No."

"You don't know that Travis actually played a trick on you that whole night, that he was just leading you down the merry road. You don't know that, do you?"

Lisle looked Sims right in the eyes. "Yes, I do."

"You can read your dog's mind, right?" Sims said, condescending.

"No, I can read my dog."

"So you know when your dog is fooling."

"Yes, I do."

Sahli interrupted. "Your Honor, this is argumentative."

"Overruled."

"Do you talk with Travis?"

"No, sir."

"Do you speak dog language and he tells you what he's thinking?"

"No, sir."

Later, Sims asked him about ground conditions.

"You indicated this one (boot print) was in slush and mud."

"Yes, sir."

"That was a very muddy area."

"Yes, sir."

"When you completed this track walking through there, did you have mud on your boots?"

"No, sir."

"Did you have mud on your pants?"

"I might have."

On his redirect, Jon Sahli let the jury see why Travis never reacted to Bradford King.

"Did you observe the defendant on February 9 at 16240 Division Drive, the Saturday you were there?"

"No, I never saw the man," Lisle said.

Perhaps unfairly, Jack Schoder was being made the fall guy for every mistake made early on in the King investigation. But after Schoder's testimony in the preliminary exam, Sahli knew one thing about the detective. When he took the stand, it was difficult to predict the results.

Sahli wanted to get Schoder on, let him summarize his involvement in the case and King's behavior in the hours and days after the murder and then get him off. He needed Schoder to introduce the striker plate from the porch door and two

Microcassette tapes of the interviews with Brad King on February 9 and February 11.

Schoder set up speakers for the jury, stringing long, thick speaker cables to a small Microcassette recorder, the ends rigged with electrical tape. The sound system was exceptionally inferior, especially considering the cost of the entire case. Some of the speakers cut out on playback. Jack Schoder left the witness stand to jiggle the wires. The second tape changed speeds abruptly during the interview, momentarily turning their voices into cartoon quality.

On the detective's second day on the stand, John Sims stood at the podium with a pile of notes and documents, hurling inconsistency and error at the detective.

Sims questioned him about Brad King's boots and the footprints.

"And you did not take his boots from him, he volunteered them to you, isn't that correct?"

"Yes, sir."

Sims set up the detective for his use of the term "soft denials" in describing King's responses in their second interview. Schoder had introduced the term without ever explaining it was a technical reference in the Reid interrogation method.

"Would you agree there are twenty-seven denials by Mr. King in nine pages of transcript?" Sims demanded.

"I haven't counted them, but I wouldn't disagree."

"Are those soft denials?"

Schoder looked bemused.

"If twenty-seven is a soft denial, is ten a confession?" Sims continued. "I'm trying to get your scale here. Does it get to be a moderate denial if he does fifty? I suppose you would have preferred he got up and pounded you in the teeth, that would be a strong denial. Then you could put him in jail and sweat him some more."

Sims questioned Schoder's time and distance measurements. He pointed out he'd failed to search the Jeep Wagoneer the night of the murder and failed to administer a nitrate test that might have shown King had shot a weapon. Sometimes,

Schoder gave concrete answers to questions only seconds earlier he said he didn't know.

Sims attacked the detective with his own words on the handling of the crime scene. Under questioning, Schoder admitted the farmhouse and property were left unguarded when they cleared the scene in the early morning hours.

"When you left did you bother to lock the door?" Sims demanded.

"I don't believe I was the one who secured the house," Schoder said after a long pause.

"So, to your knowledge, nobody even bothered to shut the door."

"The doors were shut."

"To your knowledge? Or are you offering something you don't really know again?"

"The doors were shut. I was there when we left."

"I thought you just said they weren't," Sims scowled.

Schoder tried to fend off the attack with obsequiously polite responses, only sounding more uncertain.

Sims pointed out he was relieved in June as head of the investigation.

"You were fired, weren't you?" Sims boomed.

"No, sir."

Sims continued the punishment for more than an hour, charging Schoder had fallen down on the job in his initial investigation of the stalker letter, failing to eliminate fingerprints on the paper right away. Surprisingly, he didn't go after the detective on the matter of James Wickware, Jr., the young letter writer.

"You did most of those things after Diane was dead."

"Yes."

"Is your conscience bothering you?"

"No, sir."

Schoder didn't answer Sims's last question.

"You just didn't do your job, did you?"

When Sims was done he plopped down into his chair at the defense table and turned to Brad King.

"How did I do?" he asked his client quietly.

"Excellent," King said, smiling slightly.

Afterwards Jon Sahli asked a writer, "How do you think that went?"

The prosecutor answered his own question. "I think it went for shit."

Soon, John Sims was motioning for a mistrial again. Jack Schoder had asked King if he would take a polygraph examination on the tape played for the jury. So-called lie detector tests were not admissible. But King never answered the question one way or the other in the interview. Judge Sindt ordered it removed from the tape for future listening and the trial continued.

His most treacherous waters behind him, Jon Sahli returned to safer evidentiary seas. The neighborhood witnesses were largely unimpeachable. One by one, they detailed seemingly uneventful activities in their lives on February 9, 1991, activities that became meaningful only when put into the context of Jon Sahli's grand circumstantial scheme.

The jury heard from a Gerry Stepp. He was cutting wood on his father's property across from the Kings' from 11:30 A.M. until 2:30 P.M. on the day of the murder. He saw Brad King working on his porch. He heard no gunshots that day. It wasn't often anyone heard shots in February, he said. Deer hunting season was in November in Michigan.

Under cross-examination, he acknowledged he couldn't hear everything. He was running a chain saw.

They heard from his wife, Cheryl, who rented Brad King the Patrick Swayze video, *Next of Kin*. The customer came in the store around four o'clock, she said. She knew it was around four because it was close to quitting time. The receipt put it exactly at 3:52 P.M. Records showed it was returned the next morning sometime before noon.

Young Tonya Scott testified to hearing two shots from the direction of Thunderspirit as she carried moving boxes out to the truck at around 6:25 to 6:30 P.M. She knew that was the time because her mother got to the new house at 6:45 P.M., about five minutes away, and the shots were fifteen minutes before she left.

"Is it possible that it was as early as 6:20 P.M.?" John Sims asked.

"I doubt it," she said.

Elsie Scott reinforced her daughter-in-law's testimony, but also noted there was no suspicious activity along Division Drive. She knew it was 6:45 P.M. when she arrived at the new house because she looked at her watch. She looked at her watch, like any parent would. Her daughter was baby-sitting and complaining she was supposed to leave at 7 P.M.

"I looked at my watch and told her it was 6:45 P.M.," she said in a slight, but certain, Southern twang.

The same strong accounts came from Doug Nielsen, his wife, and friends who were their dinner companions that night. The jury heard about their pizza run and the trips past the residence before and after the shooting. Again, no strangers on the road. No unknown cars.

Save the possibility of one.

From the police statements of Joanne Karaba and two other witnesses, John Sims knew there was a certain cream-colored Oldsmobile parked in front of a gate of the pumping station where Division Drive turned north at the I-96 freeway. It was a quarter mile west of Thunderspirit. It was the one blatant variable left in the prosecution's crime scene. The task force had never been able to pin down who owned it or what it was doing there.

John Sims was hoping it stayed that way. He planned to use the other avenues into Thunderspirit and the tan Oldsmobile vehicle to carry an argument of reasonable doubt.

James Stadfeld was wearing his FBI academy medallion on his left lapel when he took the stand. But with Jon Olson defeated in the election, prospects for his advancement to undersheriff had in one day become slim to none. Stadfeld's role in the trial was largely perfunctory, introducing the small-caliber cleaning rod and the seven shell casings found in the creek.

John Sims couldn't resist taking a few swipes at the other original detective on the King case. Stadfeld answered his question without a hint of passion.

"You know Jack Schoder?" Sims asked him at one point.

He said it as though the mere association should be enough to discredit what he said.

But most of the basic evidence held up to scrutiny. John Sims made no gains with Robert Cilwa, the polished ballistics expert from the Michigan State Police Crime Lab who had testified hundreds of times all over the state. Sims couldn't challenge the basic facts. Firing pin and ejection markings showed the casing in the loft and the seven in the creek came without doubt from the Remington Model 511 Scoremaster. The bullets in Diane King's body could have come from another weapon, but they were also consistent with those shot by the Remington.

On November 19, Sahli finished up with most of the hard proofs. A Bell official verified the telephone records associated with the case. A climatologist with the state agriculture provided the weather the day of the murder and thereafter, also setting sunset on February 9 at 6:04 P.M., with twenty-nine minutes of "civil twilight" thereafter.

It meant the person in the loft had good shooting light. What remained unclear was would an escaping killer have some cover of darkness and thus avoid Brad King if he were walking back from the hay bales?

John Sims never explored the question.

The following evening, the end of the second full week of testimony, the Brad Busters met at the corner table at the Winner's Circle across from the cereal plant. Gerry Woods had just returned from his mother's funeral. They explained the trial's progress to the investigator, as reruns of Court TV testimony played on a television over their heads.

There was a consensus. John Sims was a feisty competitor, who seemed to start strong in his cross-examinations, but also let others off the hook. Ostensibly, he seemed to be fighting them alone. His cocounsel Virginia Cairns was in and out of the courtroom, granting TV interviews in the halls or attending to business in her own practice. Unlike Sahli, who had Nancy Mullett at his side, Sims was largely depending on Brad King as his second set of eyes and ears.

"I'm almost ready to rest a little bit," Sahli said, nodding as he lifted a glass of beer to his lips. "With the crime scene in, I'm also tempted to say I can rest now and get a conviction."

Tempted, but not quite yet.

8

There were a dozen days of testimony spaced across November. During the entire month, the sun virtually didn't shine, and Battle Creek seemed like the grayest place on earth.

On the morning of the third day, Brad King seemed to light up the courtroom for the first and only time when his mother took a seat with her husband Cliff and a local Presbyterian minister in the second row near the wall. King beamed as the deputies allowed him to chat with her awhile at the rail before the break. It was more emotion than he'd shown in days.

On the afternoon of the sixth day, the defendant was not so animated as he watched his mother take the stand as a witness for the prosecution. She was talking about the .22 her first husband Willis had bought to teach gun safety to her eldest son.

Sahli held up Exhibit Number Five, the Remington Model 511 Scoremaster. Her answers were curt.

"Does that look familiar to you?"

"No."

"Can you say it is or is not the rifle?"

"No."

"Does the cleaning rod look familiar to you? Are you at all familiar with guns?"

"No."

"Do you know who last had the .22 rifle?"

She paused. "Under oath I really can't say, because I always assumed Brad had it."

John Sims interjected. "Your Honor, I guess I'll have to object to my client's mother's assumptions."

She was one of a half-dozen witnesses that would testify that Brad King, at one time or another, possessed more than one gun or had a .22 not dissimilar from Exhibit Number Five. Every other day, a new one would take the stand, allowing Jon Sahli to brandish its black walnut stock and gun-blue barrel one more time.

The gun witnesses cast a shadow over the proceedings, but on any given day failed to strike lightning. Gail Hietzker testified she knew that her ex-husband had two or three rifles. Barbara Elgutaa offered her poorly defined sighting of the gun.

Tom Darling, after indicating he was at a church camp the day of the murder, told his story about offering his rifle to kill the troublesome woodchuck. He testified Brad told him, "If it comes to that, I'll use my .22." He testified he might have seen the Scoremaster in the King home.

"I can't be sure, because I've been throughout the house, but I believe I saw a .22 in the house there."

"Do you recall anything about it?"

"That it was an old bolt-action gun."

Sahli showed him Exhibit Number Five.

"It looks similar to the gun I saw."

Sims aggressively cross-examined the hardware owner, who sat with his hands folded in a green plaid shirt, confronting him with his statements to police, trying to imply his memory improved with time. But when he went to bring up Marshall rumors about his involvement in the crime, Jon Sahli rose to object and the jury was sent out. Sims argued he was entitled to show that the rumors may have influenced Tom Darling's memory. But Sahli made a spirited argument, contending that Darling's statements were in fact consistent and didn't change.

Judge Sindt questioned Darling directly.

"When I called Detective Stadfeld I said there was something about that gun that I saw it before," Darling told the judge. He also contended he didn't hear rumors until late summer, after he'd recalled seeing the gun.

Judge Sindt sustained the prosecutor's objection. It spared

Darling the cross on the extramarital affair rumors, but not the Court TV camera, which detailed the entire sordid story as attorneys argued it with the jury excluded from the courtroom.

"I'm sorry," Nancy Mullett apologized to the hardware owner after his testimony. "That was a dirty trick."

Darling's stepson, Christopher Sly, was as certain as he was in the preliminary examination that he'd indeed seen Exhibit Number Five on the chest freezer on King's porch.

"Do you recognize this?" Sahli asked, showing him the weapon.

"Yes," Sly said. He came to court dressed in a white shirt and tie.

"How is it you recognize that?"

"The bolt action and the main part of the gun."

"Is that similar to the gun you observed or is that the gun you observed?"

"That *is* the gun I observed."

Sly acknowledged he was generally unfamiliar with guns, but he'd seen other bolt-action .22s in other places, he added.

"You're not confusing that rifle with any other rifle you've seen," Sahli asked a little later.

"No."

He remained unshakable on a short cross-examination.

Scott King took the stand as a witness for the prosecution. He recalled the family .22 that he hadn't seen in twenty years, the one as far as he knew had gone with his brother when he graduated from college.

"Can you describe the .22 for us, please?" Sahli asked.

"About all I can recall is it was a bolt action."

"Do you recall the brand name?"

"No, sir."

Sahli showed him Exhibit Number Five.

"In looking at that gun, is that similar to the gun you had as a youngster?"

"Yes."

"Is there anything different with that gun and the one you had as a youth?"

"I can't recall it that well."

On cross, Sims asked, "The .22 you saw, was it a single shot?"

"Yes," he said after a long pause.

"Did it have a clip?"

"I don't remember."

Afterwards, Scott King was allowed to visit his brother briefly in the courthouse lockup during the break. He embraced Brad King and wept.

Employing nearly another dozen witnesses, the prosecution detailed the threat of the mysterious phone calls, the stalker letter, and the security practices used by the Kings up until the week of her death. Cindy Acosta flew up from Caracas to detail the night Diane King received the letter. Joanne Karaba, Stella Pamp, and her baby-sitter Kameron Knowlton detailed the measures Diane took until she knew her husband was at Thunderspirit.

Jon Sahli appeared to be building an indestructible mosaic that the security practices were in place right up to her death. Debbie Rich, a TV newswoman from Grand Junction who kept in frequent touch with the Kings, put in the last piece. Gary Hough and Gerry Woods had found the woman in their first trip to Colorado. Rich's source about the security system was none other than Brad King himself when he returned her phone call right after Diane's funeral.

"He said that . . . she would pull up into the driveway and honk the horn if he were there, and if not then drive around the house to make sure all the windows were secured and . . . then she would go in."

"And that was in effect on the date of her death, according to the defendant?" Sahli asked.

"Yes."

While Joanne Karaba also testified how Diane King refused to get out of the car at twilight, she created other problems for the defense. All hearsay was not prohibited under Rule 803 of the Michigan Rules of Evidence. There were a number of exceptions. Judge Sindt had made specific rulings on hearsay statements from Diane King. Allowed were comments she made under the stress of excitement or while she was perceiving an event or condition. Under another exception, Judge Sindt had ruled that the jury could hear some of Diane King's statements about the stalker and getting out of her car. Not allowed, however, were statements she made that would cast a prejudicial view of the state of mind of Brad King.

"Earlier Mrs. King had mentioned telephone calls," Jon Sahli said to Karaba when she took the stand on November 20. "Did she describe the voice in those calls?"

"Yes, she did."

"How did she describe the voice of those calls?"

"She said it was really slow. Every word was precise. . . ."

"Did she say anything else about the telephone calls?"

Sims objected, saying the question was too broad in light of the judge's hearsay rulings.

Sustained.

Sahli was more direct. "Did Mrs. King have any idea as to the identity to the caller?"

Sims objected again. "Clearly hearsay."

Sustained.

"She was concerned, correct?" Sahli continued.

"Yes."

"Did she mention the letter she had received to you?"

"Oh yeah . . . that's why . . . she wouldn't let the kids play in the yard. This letter frightened her. At one point she even said—"

Sims jumped up. He wanted a brief sidebar.

"What did Mrs. King say about her concern?" Sahli said when he resumed.

"She was just really scared. . . . She said at one point, I thought it was Brad playing a sick joke, and we laughed about that, but then it became real serious. . . ."

At the break, with the jury out, Sims grabbed the court rail behind him with both hands and began yelling.

"The jury caught it. She planned. I tried to warn ya. That's why we went to sidebar. She's about to do it. She's opening her mouth. Keep an eye on her. And he went right on in there and got it out. It is a clear violation of this court's ruling, and I want a mistrial on his misconduct." He pointed at Jon Sahli.

"What's your response, Mr. Sahli?"

"My response is take a look at my question. My question was not meant to elicit that response."

Sindt denied the motion, but agreed to Sims's request to instruct the jury to disregard the "sick joke" statement and give it no weight.

If there was a grand courthouse conspiracy, as the King camp was known to murmur, it sometimes seemed to be failing miserably. During the second week of testimony, the prosecution began taking direct hits as Jon Sahli moved to more subtle aspects of the case having to do with marital trouble, Brad King's gamesmanship, and possible motives. They came in the form of evidentiary rulings from his old boss, Conrad Sindt.

The first loss was when Judge Sindt severely restricted the details of the purported break-in at the King residence when Diane King was at her sister's and Brad King was with Kelly Clark. Sahli wanted to show circumstantially that Brad King made the pry marks in the doorjamb and filed a false police report. Sindt cited Rule 404 (b), "evidence of other crimes, wrongs, or acts, is not admissible to prove the character of a person in order to show that he acted in conformity therewith."

Sahli had argued unsuccessfully the apparent phony break-in went to motive, thus making it admissible. Other crimes or wrongs by the defendant were allowed under Rule 404 (b) if they were "proof of motive, opportunity, intent, preparation, scheme or plan." Brad King's overall scheme to use the stalker to his advantage *was* intertwined with the motive to destroy his wife and avoid divorce in a troubled marriage, Sahli was trying to argue.

Sindt ruled against him, saying it not only fell under Rule 404, but Rule 401, which outlines relevancy, as well. This prevented Sahli from linking the break-in directly to King with the skeptical remarks by the deputy who investigated the break-in. It threatened to make the B&E not only a nonevent, but an argument for the defense that someone was indeed prowling 16240 Division Drive.

A small rip was opening in the fabric of Sahli's case, and John Sims began tugging on it wherever he could. He levied objection after objection. More than two dozen times the jury was sent from the courtroom while the judge "took proofs," listening to testimony before deciding whether it was appropriate for the jurors' ears. Sahli was ordered to caution witnesses about what they could say and couldn't say.

Another Rule 404 argument ensued when the prosecutor tried to introduce testimony that the CCI Stingers showed up missing on Joanne Karaba's porch after King had taken an unusually long time getting a diaper out of the car. Sims argued it was another "bad act" meant to slam his client's character.

"It seems to me that everything that points to Mr. King's guilt is a bad act and should be excluded from this trial," Sahli argued, sarcastically.

Again, Sindt went with the defense. The jury would not hear about the missing Stingers.

Then, the prosecution faced a major setback, this time on a hearsay ruling. On one hand, Sindt ruled Diane King's talk of quitting her job was admissible. On the other, he ruled that virtually everything Diane Newton King had said to more than a half-dozen important witnesses about her marriage being in trouble was not.

With Nancy Mullett feeding him higher court citations, Sahli argued it was admissible under Rule 803.3, in that it went to her "existing mental and emotional" condition and was relevant to Brad King's scheme to harass, then kill her.

Judge Sindt went with the defense, ruling most of it was more prejudicial than probative. Out were Diane King's comments on how she wanted "out of this marriage," her concerns to Barbara Elgutaa on the night of Kateri's birth, her confessions to her hairstylist and her surrogate mother, Nancy Gwynn. Out were a litany of other complaints she'd made about Brad King.

As Thanksgiving approached, the rip grew into a gaping tear.

* * *

The same day Sahli was losing the evidentiary battles, the Newton family showed up wearing large buttons on their lapels. They bore a picture of Diane Newton King. Sims didn't notice them until well into testimony, then demanded a mistrial, saying it was "a blatant attempt to influence the jury."

Sims didn't get the mistrial and Sindt took the issue under advisement. Outside the courtroom, the Brad Busters had another battle on their hands. Royal Newton was prowling the halls, vowing to reporters that the buttons would stay, citing something a judge said at a Parents of Murdered Children (POMC) meeting.

"He said you can display anything you want in the courtroom," he groused. "You can put up a full-sized poster of your loved one if you want."

There was more tension and trouble building in and outside the courtroom. Sims threatened another mistrial when jurors arrived one morning to find the courthouse besieged by picketers demanding justice for children. It turned out to have nothing to do with the King case, but was staged by a client of Virginia Cairns. In another incident, Cairns pushed a writer and accused him of trying to wiretap the defense table. Diane King's sister Darlene outright hissed at John Sims during his arguments from the second row, just out of earshot of the judge. Gerry Woods almost decked Royal Newton one night when Newton told him he only worked hard on the case because, "I pay your salary, buddy, and don't ever forget it." A schizophrenic stood up in the middle of the trial and was forcibly removed, claiming murders were being committed based on a system of numbers on freeway exit ramps. Two dress coats were stolen off a rack of a dozen just outside the judge's chambers. They belonged to Jon Sahli and Nancy Mullett.

Word reached the judge that "some kind of Indian observance" was being conducted in the witness room. Stella Pamp had brought medicine bags and "some kind of altar was being built to Diane King" on the table, somebody told the attorneys.

Judge Sindt ordered Gerry Woods to look into it.

The "altar" was Diane's picture. Pamp later explained that the medicine bag had sage, sweet grass, tobacco, and cedar in them, the four sacred substances meant to bring good will. She'd also added some corn, a symbol to signify its bearers should not go hungry.

The other concern had a different kind of spiritual connection. Allen Marler began showing up every day for testimony. A sequestered witness, he spent his time either with his mother and friends in the witness room or making friends in the courthouse. He passed out a few copies of the Rush Limbaugh newsletter to interested conservatives and walking across the street from the courthouse to fetch fresh coffee for attorneys and cops.

He wasn't so gracious to the defense. Every time there was a break and Brad King was taken down a long hallway to the lockup, Allen Marler made sure to position himself on a corner as his former brother-in-law walked by. He stood glaring at him, arms folded. Some days he wore an Indian choker of turtle and buffalo bone, looking like a warrior suited for battle.

"I want him to know I'm standing there," he told a friend. "Every chance I get, I want him to know I'm looking at his ugly face."

On his belt he had a six-inch buck knife. He showed up one day with the knife and a black POMC sweatshirt with a massive red broken heart on it. When someone told Judge Sindt about the knife, he ordered it taken.

Sindt put his concerns on the record by the end of the second week.

As the defense attorney walked to the parking lot each day, a Battle Creek detective that Sims had successfully defended in a police assault trial returned a favor.

"John, let me watch your back," he said.

"We may have some kind of trouble with him later on," Gary Hough was telling everybody at the Winner's Circle. "If old Bradley is acquitted, Allen Marler may not take that in stride."

Acquitted. Several of the Brad Busters at the table were thinking it, but nobody wanted to hear the word. On the overhead television, Court TV commentators were talking about that afternoon, how they'd been taking proofs from Kelly Clark. It looked like Judge Sindt was about to restrict King's "visit" to her apartment and its relationship to the B&E.

Most of them had colds. Most had to deal with Thanksgiving company. It had been another sunless day.

"Well, tomorrow's Turkey Day," a writer who had joined them said.

"Ole Conrad, he don't give a shit about no turkey day," Woods said, his drawl deeper than ever. "Hell, I seen the man cancel a European vacation because of a case."

Jon Sahli didn't want to hear the name of his old boss. Only five days had passed since the prosecutor had confidently said they'd all but won the case with the crime scene in evidence. Now Sahli was transfixed on his ashtray as he rolled his lit cigarette into a sharp red point.

The prosecutor of Calhoun County looked at everyone at the table. The bright testimony of Chris Sly and dog handler Gary Lisle were less than echoes now.

"You know, we're not going to win this case," Sahli said, just loud enough so only his table could hear it. "We can't win it if we can't show any marital discord."

9

Cindy Acosta brought in the small leather pouch on one overcast morning. Inside, was a small wooden circle with sinew stretched into a five-pointed star. Diane Newton King had given it to Cindy Acosta when a friend's boy came down with cancer.

Indians called it a "Dream Catcher."

"Put this above his bed," Diane told Cindy. "It catches bad dreams. Then you put it in the sun and it burns them all up."

The cancer had gone into remission.

Cindy Acosta saw no signs of the troubled family Diane

talked about from her youth. In fact, she was impressed how close everyone appeared. The Dream Catcher belonged with Diane's family, she decided. It belonged with Stella Pamp's medicine bags and Denise Verrier's born-again prayer circles, usually held in the hall as defense attorney John Sims was leaving the courtroom at the end of the day.

"It's bad enough I've got to try this case with a community against this guy," the defense attorney once complained. "Now they're out there praying against me, too."

Freida Newton was clutching the pouch with the Dream Catcher when she took the stand.

"Are you familiar with Bradford King?" Jon Sahli asked.

"Yes, I am."

"Is he present in the courtroom?"

"Yes, he is."

Freida Newton stared down Brad King for a full five seconds.

John Sims asked for a sidebar. Once more the jury was sent out for proofs. Increasingly, jurors were showing exasperation with the daily ritual of being shuffled in and out.

Judge Sindt made another string of damaging rulings to the prosecution, deciding Freida Newton couldn't testify Diane King's hearsay statement on February 9 when she said, "I guess your daddy is going to be surprised to see you" as her daughter left with the children for Marshall.

When the jurors returned, Jon Sahli led Freida Newton through other events the weekend of the murder, including her 4:25 P.M. phone call to inform King that "Diane is on her way home."

By then, Freida Newton's shoulders were slumping, her voice softening. The transformation continued as Sahli asked her about finding out about the tragedy.

"When did you learn of your daughter's death, ma'am?"

She sighed. "Probably around eleven o'clock Saturday night."

"And how did you learn of your daughter's death?"

"We had to call the sheriff's department."

She'd talked to Brad King earlier, she explained, at eight o'clock when she called to see if Diane got home okay.

"Brad answered the phone," she said, her voice breaking now. "I said did Diane make it home. And he said, 'There's been an accident,' which I'm assuming was on the express-way—"

"Your Honor," Sims said, ready to launch an objection. The judge and witness ignored him. Freida Newton was breaking down.

"—and I said how are the kids. And he said, 'They're fine.' And I said, 'Where's Diane?' And he said, 'At the hospital.' At this point I was very upset, and I said, 'Why are you not with her?' And he said, 'They won't let me.'"

"What was the tone of Mr. King's voice?"

"He didn't sound any different than he usually does." For a moment she was cold, inward.

She said she woke Royal, who convinced her to wait for news before going to Marshall.

"He got one of the detectives on the phone, and apparently they handed the phone to Brad, and his statement to my husband was Diane is dead. And that's all he said. And never got back on the phone again."

"Did you then leave to go to Marshall, Michigan, ma'am?" Sahli asked.

She looked downward, at the Dream Catcher, and sobbed.

"No," she said when she looked up. "There was no use to go. My daughter was dead."

"Ma'am, I think you've made the statement before that you and Mr. King, here, just didn't get along, is that true?" John Sims asked on cross-examination.

"Made no statement like that."

"Would it be fair to say you didn't care for Mr. King?"

"That's not a fair statement, no."

John Sims tried to show that many family and friends observed Bradford King with a jaded eye. Nearly half of the prosecution's six dozen witnesses had something to say about Brad King's demeanor as a widower, but not all were as potentially biased as Freida Newton. Cindy Acosta detailed his cavalier tone in their phone conversation. Nancy Rapo spoke about his smugness over the investigation. Kristina Mony told of his vows not to let anyone cross him. Reporter Debbie Rich from Grand Junction said weeks after the murder she'd posed questions few had the nerve to ask.

"I asked Brad since this was his background why he wouldn't investigate the case and go after the person that supposedly did this to Diane," she testified. "He said that it just wouldn't be proper to do that, that they had destroyed a lot of the evidence that was on the property as far as the investigation went."

"Did he mention anything specifically?" Sahli had asked.

"Footprints and driving the car around on the footprints. Driving the cars around the property. Destroying evidence." The jury already knew that the only vehicle driven near footprints carried Brad King and Randy Wright.

Day after day, jurors saw the same kind of behavior in the courtroom that others described in the witness-box. King was either cold or crying, and even then he covered his eyes with the tissues handed by Virginia Cairns.

"I had many people tell me: 'Couldn't you try the case with a bag over his head?' " Sims later said.

Then came Virginia Colvin, the wife of Channel 41's general manager and herself the general manager of a large mall in Kalamazoo where Diane King hosted events. She testified she was aware of some "tension" between the Kings at the company Christmas Party in 1990. She also testified, as did station staffers, that she expected Diane and Brad at a party at her home on February 9.

Sahli asked her about the funeral. "Would you describe his demeanor, as you observed it?"

Sims objected, but Sindt let her go on.

"How I would describe it?" she continued. "I thought that he was crying. And my thought was that, I related it to my children, when I was raising my children. My children when they wanted something, cried one way. And when they were really injured or hurt they cried another way. And, I felt that it was forced like my children when they wanted their way. . . ."

Other people, places, and things began to swing momentum.

Every day, Sims carried his own case file into the courtroom in a large cardboard box. It was part of a planned strategy of appearances. Back at the law firm in Albion, a team of lawyers helped him every night. He was putting in twelve- to eighteen-hour days. However, Sims wanted jurors to think King was a David facing a state Goliath.

But the strategy also took a toll. Jon Sahli and his team seemed refreshed after Thanksgiving. Sims appeared to be showing the strain.

On December 1, Stella Pamp was allowed to detail what Diane King had told her about receiving mysterious phone calls at work, but restricted from saying Diane's comment that she thought it was her own husband on the line. Nevertheless, when she finished, jurors sent up two questions. They had not forgotten Joanne Karaba's testimony days earlier, despite the judge's order to ignore it.

"Did Diane King say whether she knew who was writing letters or making phone calls?" the first question went.

"Yes," Stella Pamp said.

"Did she think the same person was doing both?"

"Yes."

"May I ask who, Your Honor?" Sahli asked.

Sims objected. Sustained. But it was too late.

At that point, Jon Sahli didn't need to ask.

There was a new surprise witness.

The day after his testimony, Doug Nielsen told a coworker named Terry Saylor about his court appearance. Saylor told Nielsen he recalled the day of the murder. He was ice fishing in the neighborhood, on a lake behind the pumping station near I-69. He'd parked his 1985 cream-colored Oldsmobile near the gate. They left sometime after five.

"You mind if I tell the prosecutor about that?" Nielsen asked.

Terry Saylor took the stand and John Sims's opportunity to argue the Olds could have been the killer's was gone.

Sahli eliminated another defense possibility. Diane King apparently had been exaggerating to intern Kristina Mony when she said she was worried for her safety in Colorado. TV management and staff from the Grand Junction TV station testified that her "investigation" into suspected drug activity had amounted to nothing more than a call to a DEA agent.

On December 1, the cleaning women, discovered on the trial's first day, were called.

The first, Lori Olsen, produced records documenting that she and a partner had cleaned the home weekly from November of 1989 until April of 1990. Olsen testified that she at least once saw two long guns on the bar counter while vacuuming the basement step, but backtracked some on cross-examination.

The second, Carol Mendez, who ran the cleaning service, was far more certain of what she saw on the basement countertop.

"Are you familiar with firearms at all, ma'am?" Sahli asked.

"Some, yes . . . my husband's a hunter and he has a few firearms of his own."

"Did you have occasion to observe firearms at the King residence?"

"Yes."

"How many times?"

"I can recall seeing it every time I was there."

She said she saw the firearm, lying so the barrel was pointing at the stairway.

"Can you describe the firearm?"

"It was a .22 rifle."

"You're familiar enough with weapons to know that it was a .22 caliber."

"Hm-hm," she nodded.

Like Chris Sly, she recalled the wood. "The stock of it was really dark, the wood," she said.

Sahli approached her with Exhibit Number Five, the Remington Model 511 Scoremaster.

"Does that look at all familiar to you, ma'am?"

"Yes."

"And how is it that it looks familiar?"

"By the stock and the barrel, especially the barrel, because it was pointed toward me at the bottom of the stairs." She'd looked right down its small bore.

On his cross-examination, John Sims eventually asked, "Ma'am, counsel has shown you this particular gun here. Did they show you any other rifles?"

"No."

"Did they show you any other shotguns?"

"No."

No, Mendez acknowledged, she couldn't be "absolutely certain" Exhibit Number Five was the gun on the counter. Then, Sims tried to get her to admit she'd just glanced at it.

She shook her head. "What brought my attention to the gun was it was pointed toward me."

Sims hurt his own cause with the follow-up. "Did that make you a little nervous?"

"Yeah, you don't know whether it's loaded," she said, shrugging.

It was hard to escape the irony. Judge Sindt would allow neither the testimony of crime scene specialist David Minzy nor most of the other prosecution's vehicles to show acrimony in the King marriage and at least hint at some kind of motive. But, unexpectedly, as the prosecution moved toward its conclusion, a door opened in the form of the most restricted of all witnesses.

Brad King's comments to the women he was trying to impress or coerce at Western Michigan were admissible. Unlike other hearsay, he had the opportunity to testify and refute this if he wished. Jon Sahli had found a way to introduce marital discord. He would do it through none other than Bradford J. King.

Heather Taylor began it. There wasn't a shred of evidence that Taylor had been anything more than the unwilling end of an obsessive courtship by Brad King. But every time an attractive young coed took the stand, the jury found itself sent out for proofs.

When they returned, the Chi Omega detailed King's frequent visits to the yogurt shop. Sahli asked her about a dinner just before the murder.

"Did Mr. King say anything about his marriage?"

"He said they were having a few problems," she said.

She told the jury how King called Freida Newton "a bitch." She said he told her he preferred Colorado, but had to follow his wife's career.

"He said the job was conflicting in their relationship," she said, adding she didn't know why.

Sahli asked Taylor to describe their conversation on campus about the investigation three weeks after the murder.

"What did the defendant say?"

"It doesn't matter, because they can't prove a fucking thing. . . ."

"Did the defendant ever call you?" Sahli continued.

"Before his wife's death he did."

"How frequently would he call you?"

"Maybe twice a week. Leaving messages."

"Did you ever return those calls?"

"No. . . ."

After complaining the jury might draw some kind of inference, John Sims had received permission from Judge Sindt to inquire of Heather Taylor in front of the jury if indeed she was involved with King. Sindt ruled he could do this without fear he was opening the door to the prosecution to introduce the issue of extramarital sex.

But when it came to his cross, Sims never asked.

Kelly Clark took the stand, her long, wavy walnut hair cascading past her shoulders. She was restricted to saying that her former instructor had only visited and called her house during December.

"Going back to the twelfth of December, did you ask Mr. King whether he was married?" Sahli asked.

"Yes, I did."

"And what was his response to that?"

"He said technically, yes, but his wife had left him in mid-November."

"Had he ever mentioned his wife prior to December 12?"

"No."

John Sims didn't have any questions. He just wanted her out of the courtroom.

It took Jon Sahli two hours and twenty minutes to go over Nita Davis's testimony outside the presence of the jury. The judge also granted her request that her face not be shown on camera.

When they were done, Judge Sindt would allow Nita Davis to recall much for the jury, simply because so much of it had come directly from Brad King. With Nita Davis, Jon Sahli would paint a portrait of a man who was either a compulsive liar or a severely troubled husband, often a good deal of both.

Nita Davis told the jury about their many long talks in campus bars, the dates corresponding to those on the prosecution's time line placards.

"Did you know Mr. King was married?"

"I knew he was married, but he told me he was separated."

"When was it that Mr. King first told you he was separated from his wife?"

"It was in September. He said he was a single parent."

"Did he say how the separation came about?"

"No, at that point in time he just said he was separated, and he had custody of the son."

"Did he ever later tell you how the separation came about?"

"He said she had initiated it."

She testified about him breaking class early on October 30 and having a two-hour conversation with him the night Diane King received the stalker letter.

Sahli asked about seeing him two days later. "With reference to November 1, did Mr. King make reference to October 30?"

"Yes, he did. He said that Diane was very upset because he had been late coming to pick up his son."

She testified about finding out that Kateri was born, seeing Diane and the baby in the hallway, and King's apparent lies.

"What did Mr. King say?"

". . . he said this was the first time he'd seen the baby since the day she was born."

Nita Davis talked about visiting the home in Marshall on

December 19 at King's invitation. She testified about seeing the Doberman chained to a tree in the yard and meeting King on the porch.

"Did he make any comment with reference to the Doberman?"

"He said she was a guard dog and she had been trained . . . to protect the family. He said the dog looked chained, but was not actually chained very securely so that if anybody in the family were attacked the dog would immediately attack."

"Did he say what you should do?"

"Not do anything threatening . . . to the children or himself."

She testified the children weren't there that night, that she'd been told they were at their grandmother's with Diane King. She talked about seeing the makeup brushes and hair dryer.

"Did you form an opinion or conclusion?"

"I assumed they were for a woman."

"From the time in September to December 19 of 1990, on how many different occasions did Mr. King make reference that he was a single parent, separating and divorcing his wife?"

"He said it on many occasions. I couldn't count how many. He said it that many times."

Sahli moved closer to the killing. He asked her about her January 7 conversation with King in his office. He wanted to know how he was acting.

"He was upset."

"What specifically did he do that led you to the conclusion he was upset?"

"He was upset about his bank account. That his wife had frozen the account and he could no longer pay for his classes he'd signed up for that semester. . . . He told me he'd spoken with an attorney who said he couldn't do anything about it."

"How did he appear at this time?"

"He was both upset and angry. He said . . . that meant an interruption in his education and he couldn't pay for anything for a while."

That included his older daughter's college tuition.

"Did he say why he wanted to pay for his daughter's education?"

"To show other people that they were wrong about him."

She testified about Brad King's call to her answering machine the night before the murder. Jon Sahli played the tape, King's voice saying he'd be away for the weekend. She told the jury how she'd returned the call the morning of the killing and King's excuse that he was heading out the door.

Nita Davis testified how King had bragged of being an "excellent shot" with a rifle and of his hunting prowess.

"He said he could kill instantaneously with a rifle," she said.

Nita Davis also testified about another aspect of King's outdoorsmanship, a revelation that appeared on none of the earlier police statements. She said during her December visit he'd talked about an outing he'd just made on his property.

Sahli asked if they had any conversation that day about the creek on the farm where the gun was later found.

"He said he had been tracking a deer and tried to leap the creek, but fell into the water."

"Did he say anything with reference to the mud in the creek?"

"He said that he was laughing about the fact that he almost broke his legs at the knees because it went beyond his knees when he fell into it."

"Into the mud?"

"Into the mud."

"Did he indicate surprise that the creek was so muddy?"

"Yes. It was in the middle of winter, it should have been frozen. He was surprised he had gone into the mud."

On cross-examination, John Sims ignored the creek and tried to undo other damage by impeaching the witness.

"Did you ever see a complaint for divorce involving Mr. King and Mrs. King?"

"No, I didn't."

"Did you ever see a custody order?"

"No, I didn't."

"You would not be surprised to find out there wasn't any such divorce, would you?"

"No."

"The fact of the matter is, with all the statements Mr. King made to you, they were in fact all lies?"

"Given the fact he wasn't getting a divorce, yes."

"And given the fact you saw makeup and hair dryers, you knew a woman was living there, didn't you?"

"I assumed that if not full-time, somebody was living there."

"Thank you, ma'am," Sims said angrily. "I have nothing further."

Later, the prosecution team couldn't understand it. Sims must have been getting tired. Jon Sahli had never seen a defense attorney so perfectly portray his own client as a liar.

On December 3, extra security was added at the courthouse. A rumor was spreading that the next witness might be accompanied by her husband. Somebody also had to guard her full-length fur coat.

The attractive blonde confidently walked up the aisle and took the stand. Shemane Nugent, aerobics instructor and wife of rock star Ted Nugent, looked as though she'd dressed for an episode of "Perry Mason." She was wearing red heels, a red skirt, red jacket, and a red V-neck ruffled red blouse.

"Mrs. Nugent, did you ever meet Diane King?" Sahli asked.

"Yes."

"On how many occasions?"

"Two."

They'd met during an interview of her husband at a concert and open house of Ted Nugent's Bow Hunter's World in January of 1991.

"Was she invited to that as a member of the media?"

"Yes."

Nugent said she gave Diane her home phone number because Diane thought she might be able to help her find some production assistants for her husband's videos.

"Did you have any conversation with Mr. King?"

"No, other than being introduced to him."

That's all she knew of the man—until she received an odd phone call on February 11, two days after the murder of his wife.

"What did he call to tell you?"

"He called to tell my husband and I that Diane was dead."

"Were you surprised to get this telephone call?"

"Very."

Sahli wanted to know why.

"I was surprised that he was concerned enough to call us. Because we weren't the immediate family and our relationship with Diane was being interviewed with the media. We didn't know her very well."

"Did he say anything about the circumstances of his wife's death?"

"He said she was being stalked and had received letters at work from an obsessed fan who had threatened her. And he supposed that she was killed by him, this obsessed fan, who had spent the afternoon in his barn waiting for her to come home."

Sims asked one question.

"Did Ted get his deer?"

"Yes," she smiled. "So did I. A ten-point buck."

Considering all the prayer out in the hallway, it seemed fitting that the prosecution's last witness was a Catholic nun.

Sister Anne Jeffery, who had counseled Brad King during the funeral, requested her face not be shown on camera. But the jury saw her. They saw her habit. They saw the simple wood crucifix hanging from her neck.

Adding to Sahli's ever-present demeanor theme, Sister Jeffery said King's funeral demeanor was not typical of grieving families she'd counseled. She described his dancing at pow-wows.

She also talked about sitting down with Brad King at the farmhouse the Monday after the funeral and having a long chat about mostly "trivial things." Sister Jeffery said she brought up a hobby she'd had for years. She'd started years ago on a farm and kept practicing for relaxation.

Jon Sahli asked her to explain.

She smiled and said calmly, "I made a remark that I had a .22 and I liked to target practice. Brad said, 'So do I, and I'm an expert shot.'"

On cross, Sims didn't point out the ambiguity of King's response. Was King talking about having a gun or target practicing?

He left the comment alone. He said later he didn't want to risk challenging the Lord God.

10

Brad King passed recesses in the courthouse lockup, staying alone in a small cement block cell with two poignant pieces of graffiti: "Jesus Saves" and "Fuck You." He napped on some breaks and read on others. The novel was Lawrence Sanders's *The Third Deadly Sin*—the sin of lust.

Already, King was facing severe condemnation, before he even presented his formal defense. The jury hadn't heard any testimony about his campus philandering, but his mother had. She paid him a visit in the Calhoun County Jail one night.

"If you were living the kind of life you were raised to live, you wouldn't be in the trouble you're in now," Marge Lundeen scolded. "Brad, you were not brought up in that kind of home."

The lecture turned into a litany about the years of mistakes he'd made, how he'd never shown good judgement, how he'd failed her as a son.

Brad King sat silently, his shoulders hunching in his prison suit.

"Marge leaned on him pretty hard," Cliff Lundeen later said. "She worked Brad over pretty well."

The decision to put the accused on the stand in a murder trial is often the most difficult faced by a defense attorney and his client. But John Sims had to consider more than what Brad King could offer in the way of rebuttal. Sims had a criminal justice expert for a client, an expert who seemed to have no answers.

What he suspected, but didn't know, was that Jon Sahli had four pages of questions waiting for Brad King, and another page of bets logging better odds if the former cop took the stand.

"I was concerned that Jon Sahli would have four or five hours of cross with him," Sims later said. "And Brad would break down to the point he did with Schoder. If he gets into that argument he got into with Schoder, which is, 'Look, I don't know what happened.' That doesn't play well. I didn't like the way it played on tape. I wouldn't like to see it played live before a jury as well."

Sims didn't want to risk negating the gains he made during the long prosecution case. He'd cast doubt on demeanor. He'd painted the early part of the investigation as buffoonery. He made suspect the observations of Diane Newton King's family. In the cross-examination of Allen Marler, he appeared to link police and family hand in hand. Sims all but accused the anchorwoman's younger brother of driving in a drunken blackout to Marshall the night of the murder. Marler's answers sounded confused. Sims's last question punctuated the connection.

"You wouldn't happen to be a good friend of Detective Schoder, would you?" Sims asked, mocking.

On the other side of the aisle, the prosecution team waited with anticipation as to what John Sims would present. Gary Hough still worried another King gun would surface. Jon Sahli had psychiatrist and stalker expert Park Dietz on standby for rebuttal, should Sims begin to explore the possibility of an obsessed fan.

What only John Sims knew was that his defense had already been dealt a damaging blow. The last prosecution witness was supposed to be the former Calhoun County Jail inmate who supposedly had heard Brad King say, "I killed the bitch." Sims had fought Sahli on the admission of the witness, calculating that would only make the prosecutor try all the harder to call him to the stand. Sims had planned to climax his closing with the argument that the state would sink to dealing with a prisoner to convict his client.

"I hoped and prayed he'd bring in the jailbird," he later explained. "I was waiting. I had seven witnesses lined up. I was going to tear him apart."

But the bird took flight. The last day of the People's case, Ricky McClain disappeared. He was dismissed as a witness by Judge Sindt. Sims later credited Jack Schoder and Jim Stadfeld with unknowingly making their final contribution to the case.

"I hoped against hope that they had tied him down and would present him," Sims said. "I should have known that with who was in charge of keeping him, Schoder and Stadfeld, that he would be gone."

With seven witnesses no longer needed to rebut McClain's testimony, another seven logged not even two hours of court time as a thick, wet snow began to fall outside on the morning of December 4.

Sims called Channel 41 receptionist Rita Gillson who said she knew Brad King's voice and the mystery caller did not sound like him.

"It did not sound disguised to me, not mechanical or cloth over the phone," she added. "It sounded like a normal, talking voice."

Sims produced another stalking report filed by Diane King, one that the prosecution team became aware of only when Sims began checking records in Battle Creek PD. Diane King had filed a police report after she thought she was followed by two teenagers when she drove her Jeep Wagoneer to Marler's preschool on November 9, 1990, ten days after the stalker letter.

Sims called two Tekes who helped clean up Thunderspirit. They testified they never saw a rifle on the property. Another neighbor testified she saw Diane King's Jeep parked on the property around 6:15 to 6:20 P.M. on February 9, 1991.

Most spent no more than ten minutes on direct testimony, many less than five. Jon Sahli asked no questions of some. The defense moved so fast the judge had to take breaks to allow witnesses time to get to the courthouse.

Sims called a neighbor who had just moved into a second Zinn farmhouse near Thunderspirit. Of all things, he'd found a Remington Model 511 Scoremaster in an upstairs storage room. The Zinn family stored it there. The man called the prosecutor's office about the weapon the weekend before Thanksgiving after hearing about the .22 associated with the King case. The sheriff's department had taken the gun.

The final witness was Timothy Knowlton, who used to live in the Zinn farmhouse where the second Scoremaster was found. He'd seen weapons in the storage room, he said.

Sims wondered who else had access to his house.

He said he'd used a house sitter when he and his family went in and out of town.

His name was Christopher Sly.

Minutes later, New York anchor Fred Graham was reporting on Court TV that Christopher Sly used to "live" in the house where the second Remington Model 511 Scoremaster was found. "Another odd twist in this case," he called it.

Kristin Jeanette-Meyers, the reporter Court TV had working at the courthouse, corrected the anchor. "Actually, I have to slightly correct you, it's that Chris Sly *house-sat* at the house where the gun was found. *That's* been the testimony."

Meyers began speculating. "This has been very confusing," she said, excitedly. "But it *appears* that the defense is trying to put forth the possibility of another person who could have fired the shots at Diane Newton King, and it appears they might be pointing the finger at young Christopher Sly."

"But Kristin, what could be a possible motive for a thirteen-year-old lad to conduct an assassination?" her anchor asked.

"Well, Fred, as I said, it's unclear that's exactly what the defense is saying, but no one can think of any other possibility."

Soon she was talking about the "unsubstantiated rumors" of the affair between Tom Darling and Diane King.

The news was spreading through downtown Marshall just after Tom and Sue Darling received a call from a prosecutor's office that Chris Sly was being called back to Battle Creek. The prosecutor had faxed a subpoena to the high school. A cab would be sent to get him if necessary.

One of the workers at Darling and Daughter Variety had just returned from the bakery.

"My God," she told everyone. "Chris is being called back. The defense is going to try to make him a suspect."

The Darlings sped to Marshall High School, picking up their son. The couple later said they didn't tell him what everyone in town was saying or what had been reported on Court TV.

"You know Sims, Chris," Tom said. "I think it's his turn to question people."

"Oh, yeah," the boy said, unalarmed.

Tom Darling was upset, but grateful. He was grateful he'd volunteered to chaperon that church outing the weekend of Diane King's murder.

"You know, I think God was watching over this whole family," he later said. "He couldn't have had us in a better place."

There were no more defense witnesses—nobody to point a finger at Chris Sly or anybody else. Following the prosecutorial marathon, the defense case seemed to be "the big, resounding silence" Sims had promised in his opening.

It took Jon Sahli only one hour to rebut. He called the patrol officer who took Diane King's report in Battle Creek. The car that had followed Diane King had apparently turned into its own driveway. A teenager had taken his mom's car out for a joyride.

State Police Crime Lab expert Robert Cilwa testified that ballistics revealed that the Scoremaster found in the attic couldn't have fired the bullets that killed King. It had five lands and grooves with a *right-hand* twist.

The second Scoremaster was now in evidence. Its stock was much lighter than Exhibit Number Five, its condition pristine.

When Chris Sly took the stand, Sahli asked him, "Did you ever house-sit for the Knowltons when they went away?"

"Yes."

"Did you ever see any guns or firearms there?"

"No."

"Were there areas of the house you didn't go into?"

"Yes." That included upstairs.

He laid the second Scoremaster in front of the teenager. He wanted to know the differences between that gun and Exhibit Number Five.

"On the bolt action, the ridges are very evident," Sly said, confidently. "There's a red stripe on the bolt."

"Is this the gun you saw at the King residence?"

"No."

"You're certain about that?"

"Yes, I am."

There was one more matter before final arguments. Jon Sahli requested the jury be allowed to visit the crime scene. John Sims vigorously argued against the outing, calling it "a trip fraught with peril."

Judge Sindt allowed it, but restricted the jury to four areas: The barn. The creek. The swamp where the gun was found. And the hay bales where Brad King said he'd been watching deer.

An inch of snow covered the ground on the morning of December 8 as the jury filed from the courthouse into a gray county school bus. Some jurors covered their faces with notebooks. They'd come prepared with outdoor clothing, as had the attorneys, the judge, and his staff.

Brad King would not accompany them. John Sims had waived his client's appearance. The last thing he wanted the jury to see was Brad King being escorted around the crime scene in belly chains and leg irons.

In Marshall, Michigan Avenue was decorated for the holidays. Holly hung from the street lamps, antique shop windows glistened with antique American Flyers and nineteenth century ornaments. "The Little Drummer Boy" played from loudspeakers on Main Street, piped in by a single sound system downtown merchants had purchased a few years back.

At the corner of Division Drive and Old 27, a horde of media vehicles were kept at bay by a state police cruiser. The judge had allowed only a pool of three reporters on the outing. He'd ordered the air above a no-fly zone.

At Thunderspirit, it was white and cold and still. Mostly it was silent, save a nervous laugh or comment here and there about the rigors of the trip. When they went on the record, the court reporter set up her machine and sat in a plastic chair, the judge's secretary feeding paper to the three-legged machine. There were few questions. Neither attorney could provide directions or details. Gerry Woods and Gary Hough were restricted to the barnyard.

The judge gave the jurors the option to go to the stipulated locations. All but one climbed the narrow, steep stairs into the loft. There were echoes of February 9, 1991. The new tenant, who happened to be a staffer at the prosecutor's office, kept her large mixed breed chained at the barn entrance just like the King's Doberman. There were remnants of straw on the barn's wooden floor in the loft, a small accumulation left near the spot that once made a bed for the CCI Stinger casing.

From below, Gerry Woods watched as a juror began examining the wrong loft door.

"Great," he complained to Hough under his breath. "All these pictures and diagrams and models, we really got our goddamn point across, didn't we?"

"Settle down, Gerry," Hough said.

Seconds later, someone was opening the correct door, peering out the crack as the killer apparently had. One juror wanted to know where the dog was kept. Downstairs, the attorneys showed the group the tack room.

At the Talmadge Creek makeshift footbridge, three people turned back. Seven jurors pushed on to the area where the gun was found. They had to find their own way, the group picking their way along the same route as the dog track. They ducked into deer tunnels cut into the deep brush and pushed aside branches. One soaked her boot in mud, but most remained surprisingly spotless.

Eight went back to the hay bales. A juror wondered if somebody could sound a car horn back up at the barn while they listened. The judge denied the request.

"I think the distances were the most surprising," said one pool reporter later. "It took twelve minutes to get back to the barn from the hay bales."

Another reporter was struck by the difficult route back to the gun area, adding afterwards, "It was apparent to me that you had to know where you were going to get back there."

Said Gerry Woods: "That was the objective for the whole trip."

11

If he was defending Bradford J. King, Jon Sahli later said, he would have let in all the sordid details. The affairs. The lies. The sessions with the marriage counselor. Then, it would have been very difficult to do what he did in closing argument in front of a packed courtroom audience.

The prosecutor started again with dates.

October 30, 1990, the day Diane Newton King received the note: "When we read the note, 'You should have gone to lunch with me,' that obviously tells us one thing. The person who prepared this note. The person who pasted this note together. The person who placed it in the mailbox. *That* person knew about the telephone calls. . . . This note was designed to cause terror. We know the person knew about the phone calls simply by the wording of the note."

The person who left it in her mailbox knew more.

"Not only would a person have followed Mrs. King home and found out where she lived, that person would have had to know the schedule of Diane King. When she left for work. When she came home from work. That person would have had to know the schedule of Brad King: When he left for work. When he returned. That person in order to avoid detection, if he was indeed an obsessed fan or a stranger, would have had to have known the schedule of both these people."

Sticking with Devil's Night, Sahli led the jury down a path created by the defense's effort to keep Brad King's sex life secret, a strategy that seemed to only make Brad King's agenda more dark, more deceptive, and more obscure.

"Now, where was the defendant?" Sahli asked. "We know he was teaching a class at Western Michigan University. We know he got the message, because he went to the Acosta residence. We know he arrived some three and a half to four hours later. And we know where he was from the time he let the class out early to the time he went to his wife, who was crying hysterically. He was with Nita Davis, telling her . . . my wife left me. We're getting a divorce. I'm a single parent. I've got custody of my son, Marler."

Two days later, November 1: "What was the defendant doing? Again, with Nita Davis. Again, I'm separated. I'm getting a divorce. I'm a single parent. Boy, was my wife upset the other night. Tuesday night. *Not* because she received a letter. She was upset because I was late. Nothing about concern for his wife's safety. Nothing about concern for his wife's reaction to the note."

November 20, the birth of Kateri: " 'Our single parent' was not with Diane King at the hospital. And where is the defendant? Same place. Nita Davis. And what is the defendant telling her once again. My wife left me. We're separated. We're getting a divorce. By the way, I had a daughter born today."

December 11, 12, and 13, the "visits" with Kelly Clark: "What did the defendant do on December 12, after Diane King changed her plans, stayed at her sister's an extra day, what did the defendant do? Same old story. My wife left me. We're separated. We're getting a divorce. I'm a single parent.

"Ladies and gentlemen, I submit to you that this is part of the defendant's plan for what happened. The defendant was not concerned about the fan letter, but it fit his plan. So he mentioned it on the twelfth of December. I submit to you on October 30, the defendant used his wife's concern for his own advantage, rather than going straight from the class he dismissed early to be with his wife, he was talking with Nita Davis. Rather than on the twelfth using his wife's concern, he was visiting Kelly Clark. . . . This single parent again used his wife's concern to visit someone else."

John Sims said it without alarm. "Your Honor, may we approach the bench?"

The jury was sent out.

John Sims demanded a mistrial. He claimed the prosecutor had gone over the line.

Judge Sindt only cautioned Jon Sahli. "The statements made by Mr. Sahli are within the evidence presented," he said.

The jury back, Sahli worked his way to the day of the murder, using his time line cards, approaching the jury as he appealed to them, returning to the podium to start off every new point.

He returned to Nita Davis, the message he'd left on her machine about being gone for the weekend. "Was that a true statement, ladies and gentlemen? I submit to you, no, it was not. Again, I submit to you, it's evidence of the defendant laying groundwork."

He argued that the testimony of four witnesses indicated King wasn't expecting the children home that day. He argued that Diane King was still too frightened to get out of her car at dusk alone. The prosecutor employed the defense's own evidence of the Battle Creek police report to make his point.

"I submit to you what you've heard described in this trial are the actions of a terrified person. A person who was in fact placed in terror by the person who authored that note. So frightened, that on November 9 she called the Battle Creek City PD about a car she thought was following her, a car that pulled in to its own driveway. November 9 she was frightened. January 10 she was frightened. February 3 she was frightened. On February 9 she was frightened."

Sahli eyed the jury, his voice booming now. "I submit to you that Diane King saw the defendant, her husband, on February 9, 1991, and after seeing him she then got out of her Jeep Wagoneer. And that's when she was shot two times. Once in the chest. From right to left at a downward angle, consistent with seven degrees, the fatal shot, a shot that went through her heart. And a second time. Shot in the vaginal area."

Sahli turned on his slide machine. It was a picture of Diane King's swollen belly and the bullet hole. A haunting chorus broke the silence. Denise Verrier was crying on one end of the second row; Freida Newton on the other; their stuttered wailing joining in a perfect harmony.

"A shot, which according to Dr. Cohle, traveled straight up her body. Two inches under the skin. Straight up her body. Ladies, I submit to you *that* is not the shot of a stranger."

He was pointing at the screen when Sims jumped up, his hands up like a traffic cop. "Your Honor, wait a minute. Wait a minute."

"Send the jury out," Sindt said. He sounded irritated at another interruption.

Sims was shouting. "Your Honor, there's no foundation of that in this case whatsoever. Nobody has testified in this trial that that shot indicates that it couldn't be made by a stranger. To make that argument is impermissible under the circumstances here. It's exceedingly prejudicial in light of the prosecution theory. Once again, I move for mistrial."

He stomped around the podium, adding, "This last one is ridiculous."

"Mr. Sahli?" Sindt asked, calmly now.

The prosecution, particularly Nancy Mullet, had fully expected a legal tantrum from Sims on the comment. The prosecution was prepared.

Sahli read off a list of cases to support his position that the prosecutor has the right to draw inferences from the facts appearing in the record. A prosecutor can draw inferences and comment on the testimony.

Sahli looked directly at the judge. "I submit that the jury can draw the inference that that is not the shot of a stranger."

"Absolutely ridiculous," Sims retorted. "You know, he tried with Trooper Minzy, but that wasn't relevant or admissible, and now this is completely out of right field. This isn't proper."

Sims was pointing at Sahli as he shouted.

The prosecutor was leaning on the podium with his elbow,

as relaxed as a gentleman resting on the mantel over a roaring winter fire.

"No, I'm going to overrule the objection," Sindt said. "You can obviously address it in your closing argument. Bring the jury back in."

Given the green light, Sahli returned to the argument like a record stylus dropped back down in a groove during mid-play.

"Ladies and gentlemen, I submit to you this is not the shot of a stranger. Not the shot of an obsessed fan. But the shot of someone who was close to Diane King. The shot of someone who was *enraged* with Diane King."

Indeed, Sahli was employing profiler David Minzy's logic. "The defense may try to argue to you that there is no sign of anything but a stranger or an obsessed fan. But there has been no testimony of any signs of a struggle taking place. There has been no testimony of any sign of self-defense. There has been no testimony of any sign of a robbery. There has been no testimony of any signs of a sexual assault. No indication that these shots were accidental. No indication that these shots were self-inflicted."

Sahli worked the inconsistency of King's statement with what others in the neighborhood heard. King heard shots throughout the day. No one else did. King heard one shot. Tonya Scott heard two.

Another slide: Diane King on her back in the driveway. "You can see Mrs. King's hair is still out. Does that photograph appear to you that Brad King picked up his wife to see what was wrong? Laid her back down. Or does it appear that she's laying exactly as she laid when she was felled by a gunshot from a .22 caliber?"

More family wept.

"The children are in the car. He goes in and calls for help. He *leaves* the children in the car. His wife is laying in the driveway and he doesn't take the children from the car. He's been a police officer for thirteen years for Pontiac City Police Department. He's trained in emergencies. According to Nancy Rapo and Allen Marler, he'd told them he'd investigated seven homicides. According to the defendant, it was someone other than him who shot Diane King—and he *leaves* the children in the car?

"Even if you took his word that he didn't know what was wrong, why would he leave the children in the car? Why would he not take them in the house? If he went in to call for help, why wouldn't he immediately get his children after calling for help? Does it make sense to leave the children in the car? I submit to you it makes no sense. If there's a stalker on the property as he told Shemane Nugent two days later, would he leave the children in the car?

"Then if you recall the first witness in this case, Dispatcher Joe Delapas, after saying something is wrong with my wife, I don't know what's wrong with her, he then starts saying, 'Why did this have to happen? All I want to do is be with her.' *This*. Why did *this* have to happen? Did he go with her? Why did she have to have a heart attack? No, why did *this* have to happen? He didn't go to her side. He doesn't go to the children."

At the defense table, Bradford King appeared visibly tense for the first time in the trial. He kept pushing the hair on his temples back.

Sahli pulled out Exhibit Number Five, the Remington Model 511 Scoremaster, wielding it as he paced back and forth from the podium to the jury rail. He reminded the jury that six witnesses said they had seen a gun like it connected with Bradford King. Chris Sly said it was the gun. King had to dump the gun in the creek quickly when he realized the children were in the car, Sahli argued.

He reminded the jury what King said in his statement. "Detective Schoder asks the defendant about a Remington Model 511 Scoremaster rifle, and what was the defendant's response? 'I don't know what you're talking about, Jack.'"

For two hours Sahli probed every detail. Finally, he began working toward his conclusion. "The defendant wants us to believe that a stranger killed Diane King. He wants us to believe a stalker killed Diane King. He wants us to believe someone other than himself killed Diane King. I ask you, ladies and gentlemen, is there evidence to support that theory? There isn't any. There's not one iota—"

John Sims jumped up again, objecting, saying Sahli was shifting the burden of proof.

"Overruled," Judge Sindt snapped.

"There isn't one iota of evidence in this case that a stranger or an obsessed fan killed Diane King," Sahli continued. "For a stranger or an obsessed fan . . . if they were watching, they would know that Diane King drove the Jeep Wagoneer. They would have known that the Jeep Wagoneer hadn't been on the property since February 7. If they were watching, they would have known that the defendant's car had been present on that property in that time period."

Sahli approached the jury, his right hand in his suit pocket. "If they were watching, they wouldn't have known when she was coming home. The defendant was the only one who knew she was coming home. . . . Could it have been someone who followed her into the driveway with her habit of not getting out of the car, with her habit of watching who was around her?

"The defendant was there most of Saturday, February 9. Yet he wants us to believe somebody entered the property and hid in the barn and killed his wife. Someone killed his wife while he took his walk. Well, if we accept that theory, that this person in the barn, waiting for Diane King to come home . . . this person hiding in the barn who shot Diane King would then have left the barn, headed south, in the area he had just seen the defendant walk."

Sahli pointed out the route on the diagram of the property. "That person would have walked in the same direction he saw the defendant go. If you accept the theory that it's a stranger, who made his way through this passage, which seven of you saw, if you accept the fact that the defendant is here at the bale of hay and started walking back, wouldn't they have run into each other? Wouldn't he have seen him? Wouldn't he have heard him going through that marsh?"

He moved to the dog Travis. "Now, perhaps the defense counsel will attack Travis. 'The deer confused Travis.' Now we saw deer prints out there. Well, then you'll have to forget Travis's training, have to forget Travis showed interest where the gun is found. And if he's following a deer, did the deer put the gun in the creek? Travis started at the shell casing. Did the deer fire that shot with the shell casing?"

Sahli carried the Remington Model 511 Scoremaster around the courtroom with him for the entire last half hour of his closing. He leaned on the rifle like a cane as he returned to Brad King's track record when it came to relaying facts. He reminded the jury of Virginia Colvin's comment that King's tears were like those of a manipulative child.

"Defense counsel asks Nita Davis, 'Well did you ever *ask* to see a judgement of divorce?' No. 'Did you ever *ask* to see a judgement of custody to the defendant?' No. 'You knew it was a lie. You *knew* these were all lies.' "

One of the jurors was nodding in agreement.

"Yet, the defense would ask you to believe that the defendant can tell these lies and there's nothing wrong with it, but *please* if he's accused of murdering his wife, *please* believe that on occasion, the defendant told the truth." He said "please" like a plaintive child.

"The defendant can tell lies to benefit himself in the past, but these certainly aren't lies. When accused of killing his wife there's no basis for you to conclude *that* was a lie. It's okay for the defendant to tell Nita Davis that he's alone the weekend of December 19 because his wife took the children to visit her mother. It's okay for the defendant to tell Nita Davis all these other lies, but *please* believe the other. Don't think the defendant is a liar just because he told Nita Davis and Kelly Clark all these other lies. Don't believe he's lying when he said that he sold his .22 rifle in 1984 in Colorado. *Please* don't believe he's lying when he's questioned by Detective Schoder about Remington Model 511 Scoremaster and he responded, 'Jack, I don't know what you're talking about.' *Please* don't believe that's a lie. *Please* don't believe it's a lie when he said he walked at six o'clock, even when there's no evidence to prove it. *Please* believe Diane King varied her routine and got out of the car when the defendant wasn't around. *Please* believe that the defendant is such a concerned husband he left his children in the car while his wife lay motionless besides the Jeep."

Sahli was next to the podium now, his fingers wrapped about the barrel of the gun.

"Circumstantial case? Yes, there is circumstantial evidence. And I submit to you it is *strong* circumstantial evidence, and that the direct evidence, which the People have produced, link those circumstances up. They make this case a *strong* case."

Then Jon Sahli asked for a guilty verdict for murder in the first degree.

12

John Sims asked, "Your Honor, can I make some room here?" People cleared away the projector and the placards and the other prosecution props.

It was late afternoon when he started. His mystery Oldsmobile gone, his own evidence used against him, John Sims tried to fashion a symbol of reasonable doubt. As he walked toward them, he seemed to be yelling at the jury.

"What are the facts? Fact number one they found a shell casing. No, fact number one. Diane King died. And I'm sorry about that. And I feel sorry for her family. And I feel sorry for her husband. And I feel sorry for all us we have to put up with all of this and why we're here.

"What *don't* the facts show. Nobody testified that Bradford King shot his wife. There's no evidence that Bradford King held a gun, fired a gun, or even had a gun in his possession of February 9, 1991. Where's the evidence to that? There's not evidence of that. There's nobody standing there. We don't have a witness. If we had a witness, we'd know who did it, but we don't.

"There is a failure of evidence here. And the charge they want you to convict on is murder. Because they want you to make that leap of faith, that little step, to make an interpretation of one of the eighty-five or so theories they've offered you as to why he did it. And do you know what is at the bottom of each and every one of those theories? No evidence. Think about it."

Sims paused, then continued. "Bradford King was on the property and they don't have a butler. Otherwise, the butler did it. We all know that. This whole case is built on, just as I told you before a long time ago, insinuation, innuendo, opinions, thesis, theories—"

Sims slammed his notebook down on the podium.

"Suspicion, belief, thoughts, guesswork, hunches, think-sos, maybes, I-don't-knows, unanswered questions and unanswerable questions. That's what this case is all about. And they want you, on a charge of murder, to make a giant leap of faith and say, well you know maybe he didn't behave the way I would want him to at his wife's funeral so we have to accept their theory."

Sims pointed at the jurors, approaching them. "You can't do that. You can't do that."

Sims said he wanted to go home, but first he had some things to cover.

"What is this prosecution?"

Sims pointed directly into the lens of the Court TV camera.

"There's what it's all about. It's The Big Production. The Calhoun County Prosecutor's Office, in conjunction with the Calhoun County Sheriff's Department, the Michigan State Police, the Michigan State Police Crime Lab, the FBI, and every other police agency in the whole county, have put together The Big Production. We don't have the proof. Gosh, we waited from February, 1991 to Jan, 1992—if that's not a reasonable doubt, I don't know what is—so let's put together The Big Production. See the script? I've seen it. We've got screenwriters. We've got lighting. We've got a big budget. We've got locations all over the world. We've got lasers, tasers, microwaves, you name it!

"The big trial. And this dog and pony show, this circus act, complete with its own magic, that's what we're all about here. Sound and fury signifying nothing. 'Cause when you haven't got anything and you got the power of the state and you got The Big Production you can get anybody you want. That's what it's about. We didn't have any proof. We couldn't arrest this guy. We didn't have any grounds to arrest him. We didn't have grounds to charge him. We waited a whole year. So let's come up with the theory of The Big Production, and we'll try him. Makes for interesting viewing. Good press. Lots of grist for the author mill. We're going to write books, oh yeah. We have commercials sold. TV audiences increase."

Jon Sahli stood up. "Your Honor, there's no evidence of any of this. I object to it."

He was overruled.

"But how do you critique any of this?" Sims continued. "If you were Siskel and Ebert? . . . Big Production. Lots of money. Lots of witnesses. Lots of time. Fairly interesting topic. The story line is decent. You got a celebrity here. But there's a problem. There's a real problem here. The whole thing falls apart. The plot just doesn't make it. It falls apart at the most interesting point. Thumbs-down. Because it all is fantasy, conjecture.

"Think about it. This whole case is based upon the fact that nobody saw anything, so it happened this way. They didn't see anybody on the road. What did they expect? Some guy wearing a big sign saying, 'I killed Diane King.' No, that's not going to happen. Whoever did it wasn't going to be seen, because they didn't want to be seen. The other fact is, you know what the trouble with all this is, nobody saw Diane King, either. Not one of them saw Diane King coming home either. Diane King got in and out of there without anyone seeing her.

". . . I'll tell you, folks, behind all the smoke and mirrors, behind all the illusions and twists, behind all of that, you know, there's a lot of movie magic. But when you know how it works, it gets a little weird. It's like those old sci-fi movies where you see the toy rocket ship with the wire attached to it. Once you've seen that, it goes bust."

Sims summed up his witnesses, saying they showed that the prosecutor neglected facts. The defense had to bring Rita Gillson to the stand to show the caller's voice didn't sound like Brad King's. The defense had to bring in a neighbor to show that the time of Diane King's arrival at the farm could be off. The defense had to show the jury the second Scoremaster and Diane King's complaint to the Battle Creek police.

"Why?" he said, pointing at the prosecution table. "Because it doesn't fit the script. It doesn't fall into The Big Production."

Sims waged a war of perception.

The children: Sims pointed out Denise Verrier heard Diane say she wasn't going to leave them on February 7. "How many phone calls, conversations, does the prosecutor show himself between Mr. King and Mrs. King after that decision was made?"

Brad King's demeanor at the scene: "I don't like the connotation. He *left* his kids in there. Ladies and gentlemen, how many police officers were there? Did one of them grab those kids out of that Jeep? One of them? The father was being told to stay up there. Did anybody stop to think about those kids? No. Not until, remember I had to remind him, Sergeant Badger, not until Brad says, 'Can I go get my kids now?' And they're hoping to use *that* against him. Because he did what he was told."

The stalker theory: "I'm not here to tell you there was a stalker. I'm here to tell you *they* haven't proven their case." And, "(Police decided) it can't be a stalker. It couldn't be someone who was pursuing her because then we blew it. We blew it big time. It's gotta be the husband. It's gotta be."

The investigation: "I swear to you folks, I think if Jack Schoder had seen some guy standing out in the middle of the street with a sign saying, 'I killed Diane King' and blood on his hand and a gun in his other hand, I think he would have run him over trying to get Brad King down there to sweat him a little bit, because he already made up his mind."

The gun: People could have seen a neighbor's gun, Sims said. "The major failing in this case is quite simply Exhibit Number Five, the .22 they found in the creek. Their own expert says I cannot say that this is the weapon that fired those bullets. They want to say that it's *consistent* with being the gun that fired those shots. . . ."

Sims focused on Chris Sly. He said he'd only introduced the second Remington Scoremaster to show that both Sly and his stepfather Tom Darling could have seen a similar gun somewhere else.

"Now you will observe that I'm a nasty individual sometimes and I may get after someone. But I didn't go charging after Mr. Sly. He's a young one. And only the young can be that certain, folks. When I was thirteen, my old man didn't know anything. By the time I got to be twenty, it was amazing how much he had learned. . . . So, so certain."

The dog: "Travis is a good tracking dog. And I'm sure Trooper Lisle loves him greatly, and I believe in that. But ladies and gentlemen, you're going to hear the judge say, that type of evidence is very suspect. You have to treat it very lightly. Why, because it's an animal. And as my daddy always said, you never bet on anything that eats. And Travis eats . . . Travis didn't do his job. Travis's whole purpose is to track down a person, and he didn't do that."

The crime scene didn't make sense, Sims argued. Anybody could have found out Diane King was coming home on Saturday. The Colvin party was noted in her appointment book at the TV station. He suggested the gun was planted by someone trying to frame his client.

"Anybody could have gone on that scene at any time. If Bradford King is such a wonderful whirlwind of a planner, he knew he could have gone out there on the tenth, why not in the heck go get it and get rid of it before anybody gets it because the cops haven't been there? Great plan. The plan is you're going to tell these gals 'I'm a single parent.' You're getting ready to off your wife. How much more trouble can he put himself in? Huh? Great plan."

Sims walked away from the jurors, shaking his head. Then he lay some of the blame for Diane King's death on a family feud.

"This is the tragedy of this whole case. He got a phone call at 4:25 P.M. from his mother-in-law. And that phone call was: 'Diane's on the way home.' Click. Those people didn't like each other. If she had stopped and said, 'Diane left fifteen minutes to a half hour ago,' if Bradford King would have known that, maybe he would have tried to make the point of getting home from the hay bales a little quicker. . . . His time was off by a half hour."

Sims stood halfway between the podium and the jury, and concluded, "Over a month ago, in this dog and pony show, I told you I would demand you find this man not guilty. I'm demanding when you go back there you do what the law and what this evidence is going to require of you. You send this man back to what's left of his family. You find him not guilty. 'Cause they just didn't prove it, folks. They just didn't prove it. Despite all the media. All the hoopla. It comes down to the fact that there isn't enough facts to commit this man. Not of this charge. Not at this time. Not at this place."

Michigan law allowed the prosecutor the final word. Sahli kept his rebuttal to fifteen minutes, covering the points quickly. Outside, it was civil twilight.

"If there's a neighbor out there that left a .22 rifle at the defendant's home," the prosecutor boomed, "bring that neighbor in."

Later: "He said people got in and out of there. Diane King got in and out of there. Diane King got in, but she didn't get out."

The prosecutor made a passing reference to a motive. "Why would he want to kill the breadwinner? The breadwinner wanted to quit her job. Mr. King was upset. They moved here because of her job. And he was only working part-time. And he was upset. That's why he would want to kill the breadwinner."

Jon Sahli rejected the foundation of John Sims's argument, The Big Production.

"He said that the People have given you eighty-five or eighty-nine different theories," Sahli said, pausing. "Ladies and gentlemen, the people have given you *one* theory: That the defendant shot and killed his wife."

The next morning, a Thursday, the jurors negotiated a six-inch snowstorm. The first vote was 6-6.

On Friday, the panel asked for all the exhibits. One juror brought in a portable stereo to play King's recorded statements.

One, Diane King's calendar marking the Colvin party, also had a reference to the Oakridge Counseling Center. Some jurors knew it as a marriage counseling facility. A court reporter read Guy Picketts's direct testimony at their request. Before they broke for the weekend, the vote was 9-3.

One of the majority jurors was a retired U.S. Air Force master sergeant. He'd not taken a note during the entire trial, saying later he wanted to watch rather than write. On Monday, he showed up with his first writings, a twenty-two point list why he was changing his vote. The jury received a transcript of Jack Schoder's testimony, as requested. Another juror changed with the master sergeant. The vote was 11-1.

At 11 A.M., the jury passed a note up to Judge Sindt. "At this point, we are a hung jury and need further instruction."

Judge Sindt brought them in the courtroom and read a charge reserved for deadlocked juries. "I am going to ask you to return to the jury room and resume your deliberations in the hope that after further discussion you will be able to reach a verdict," he said.

It was December 14, ten days before Christmas Eve. Brad King smiled at the defense table. "It's almost time for lunch anyway," he told John Sims.

The jury broke for lunch at noon. They returned to deliberate at 1:20 P.M. At 1:55 P.M. another note was passed up to the judge.

Word spread through the courthouse. They had a verdict.

Everyone converged on the courtroom. Deputies found Brad King sound asleep on a bench in his holding cell. Freida Newton clutched a rosary in the second row, speeding through Hail Marys under her breath. Allen Marler sat in the first row behind the prosecutor, next to Jack Schoder. Denise and Don Verrier were speeding to the courthouse from points east after hearing that the jury was hung.

Marge Lundeen was at the home of friends in Albion, on the other side of Calhoun County. The verdict might be too traumatic, she'd decided.

When the jury foreman stood, Brad King leaned forward, his

palms down on the table as he waited. Five Calhoun County sheriff's deputies flanked him. One was Guy Picketts, the cop who'd led the charge to 16240 Division Drive.

"We the jury find Bradford King, as to count one, guilty of first degree premeditated murder, and as to count two, guilty of carrying a firearm in the commission of a felony."

King lowered his head at "guilty," then he sat back in his chair.

One female juror was crying. The man next to her gently rubbed her shoulder.

Sims asked that the jury be polled.

"Is your verdict as stated by the foreperson?" they were asked one at a time.

Three said "yes." Nine said "guilty."

Denise Verrier heard the word just as she raced through the courtroom door.

Not an hour later, Jon Sahli, Gerry Woods, Gary Hough, and Nancy Mullett were sitting in Bobby's, a small jazz bar behind the county building. The Brad Busters ordered a round of whiskey to toast the victory. The club was empty. Bing Crosby's "White Christmas" played on the jukebox.

Everyone was at a loss for words. Everyone drank silently.

"I guess we did it," Jon Sahli finally said.

The scene changed to a raucous one an hour later. Royal Newton threw a full-scale party at the Moose Lodge in Marshall, buying drinks for dozens connected with the case. Jack Schoder. Jim Stadfeld. The Brad Busters. The Newton clan.

Somebody put on Bob Seger's "Old Time Rock and Roll" on the jukebox and the floor cleared for dancing. The prosecutor of Calhoun County was doing the twist with one of Diane King's aunts. Not a half hour later he decided to leave. Nancy Mullett offered to drive him home. Royal Newton led a chorus of "For He's a Jolly Good Fellow" as Jon Sahli was led away by his driver, a new cashmere coat draped over his shoulders like a tired fighter.

Royal Newton turned to Gary Hough and Gerry Woods. "I should have sung that for you, too," he said.

A local reporter, meanwhile, reached Marge Lundeen at a Battle Creek motel room as they were packing. "I just want to get out of this town," she said. "I feel sorry for the people who live here."

When they left, the Lundeens didn't stop to rest until they reached the Missouri border.

The last anyone at the party saw of Bradford J. King that day he was in the sheriff's prisoner transport van. On a street corner near the courthouse, a lone figure dressed in a dark topcoat waited for the van to pull out and head for the county jail back in "the town of hospitality."

Allen Marler smiled and waved as it passed.

From the View of

BRADFORD KING

I knew that going into any trial that our system says you're presumed innocent. However, human beings don't view it that way. The community, the jury, the prosecutor, everybody views you as guilty if you've been arrested. The truth is you have to prove you're not. That's the reality of a trial.

The way the trial is held is that the prosecutor has the burden of proof. You don't have to prove anything. But the problem is that that goes on in front of a group of fourteen people who don't think that way. I knew that going in and so did John Sims. We weren't kidding ourselves.

In other words, they were waiting for me to prove that somebody else did it, or that I didn't do it. The analogy John made in his opening arguments was that you're not going to see what you see in "Perry Mason." And I think

people expect that. They expect the guilty party to be unveiled. And if the guilty party is not unveiled, then whoever
has been arrested is guilty as far as they're concerned.

In real life it's not that way. It's never that way.

We knew going in we were on Jon Sahli and Conrad
Sindt's road. They're the ones with the roadblocks and the
keys to the roadblocks. Either we break through those on
our own or they let us through. We broke through none of
their hurdles. You look at the twenty-two motions John
filed. One was granted in court and part of a search warrant was quashed. We had to do this trial their way. They
weren't concerned about the rules of justice.

It's always a game, but so much more so in that courtroom because it was a small county. We were dealing with
Conrad Sindt who was Jon Sahli's boss at one time. We
were dealing with dynamics that in a large county we
wouldn't have encountered.

Jim Brady was ignorant of the politics of that community. They're as thick as thieves, to use the cliche. It was
part of the reason I dismissed Brady. He needed to kick
some butt, and he refused to do it. He wasn't ready for
court. He had six months to be ready, and he wasn't ready
and he led me to believe he was ready all along, or getting
there.

When we were doing voir dire of the jury, it became very
clear to me we were doing it Conrad Sindt's way, no matter what the rules were. It was his courtroom, and that's
just how it was going to be. In the voir dire, if potential
panelists were aware through the media of the case, they
were taken into the back room. We all went back there,
and they were questioned. Conrad, in my opinion, if he's
going to be fair and do it right, should have had a set of
questions that he was going to ask and asked every juror
those same questions. He didn't do that. He arbitrarily determined whether people could be unbiased.

John asked for additional preemptory challenges, which
by court rules can be granted. They were turned down.
That shows you clearly Sindt was going to make sure he

had his jury. We don't get a shot at having our jury. And it's really for us to get a jury, not him.

For some reason Conrad Sindt had a lot at stake in this trial, personally. And that's not a position for any judge to be in. It was his former staff that prosecuted this case. He wanted to make a name for himself. He would be in the world's eye, so to speak. That's abuse of judicial discretion, clearly. My impressions of him as a judge: I wouldn't piss on him if he was on fire. I'd let him burn. . . .

I knew the children were coming home with Diane. I had just gotten back with my lunch that day, and we talked. She said get us a video. She said she was bringing the kids because Marler was being a pain, and her mother wouldn't take him when he was like that. Actually, she told me that on Friday, too.

They twisted about leaving the kids in the car. What happened in the space of ten minutes, they made it look like a half hour. I had to make a choice. She was the one on the ground. I had to get her help. The children were shut in the car. They were safe.

I questioned the dog track. It didn't track me. And if it *was* me, I would have been a sweaty mess when that deputy met me. To do all that, I would have been dripping wet. I would have stunk. He would have noticed that. My pants and boots would have had to have been wet and muddy. My boots were dry and without mud on them when I gave them up. There was no mud in the house.

I don't know what the dog tracked. It may have tracked nothing. Or, it may have tracked something. But it did go by where the gun was found, so it probably tracked the person who did it.

As for my gun, my dad bought one to teach my brother and me how to target shoot. I don't know how old we were. Around fifth grade. We were in Tustin, Michigan. Might have been before that, but that's when I remember it coming out for us to use. He taught me gun safety. It was a single-shot .22, as I recall. I don't know what the make of it was. I don't remember. It could have been a Remington. It was a bolt action. I recall the one in the trial there was a spot for the clip, but no clip. My father's was a single shot. You put one bullet in, shot it, pulled it out, and put another one in. I asked him, how come there's no clip? Because as a kid you see the Army pictures. Everybody's got clips. And he says because for safety reasons, you're learning how to shoot. You only need one bullet at a time.

I got rid of that gun. I just kept dragging it around and never used it. So I got rid of it. Gail doesn't even remember it. I never had it out. I'd taken the .22 and the shotgun to Colorado. Diane wanted me to get rid of both the guns. She was nervous about having guns. I said I can't get rid of the shotgun because it was my grandfather's. It has sentimental value. It's old. But I will get rid of the .22. There's no sentimental value. It's just a .22. So I just sold it at a garage sale right after we moved to York Street. It was the first thing that went, by the way. I sold it for $35. The guy who bought it wasn't a neighbor. If it was a neighbor, I could have told them who to talk to.

Barbara Elgutaa saw the shotgun. I remember the day she was referring to. I came back from deer hunting. I would have not had a .22 rifle with me. You can't hunt with a .22 anywhere for deer in Michigan. It's against the law. Now, if you look closely how she was interviewed, and how Tom Darling and his stepson were interviewed, you'll see it was like: We have this gun. Isn't that it? Guiding them. They only showed them two guns. The shotgun and the rifle.

Barbara Elgutaa's identification didn't hold up well in court and neither did Tom Darling's. Now Chris's did, but he's a fifteen-year-old kid. I have no idea what he saw. He was there so much. But look, I've got a little child, am I going to leave a gun laying out on the porch? I think he wanted to see it because of what he heard his dad talk about and he wants to help his dad look good.

The hardware story. I remember when he offered me a .22. I told him, "No, I'll use my gun," meaning my shotgun. Tom Darling is not sure exactly what I said.

The cleaning lady. I'm convinced she's confused between our apartment and a neighbor's apartment. Because our neighbor had all kinds of rifles. They cleaned their house, too. The apartments were identical. The floor plans are identical.

The .22 cleaning rod. I don't know where that came from. That's not mine. I don't know where they got it. I can't prove anything about it, so we just left it alone in the trial.

The prosecutor's time line I thought was a good trick. It really didn't show anything of evidentiary value. It was just a trick to implant things in the jury's mind, like the infidelity. The jury wasn't stupid. But take the Christmas party, there wasn't an argument. I was late getting there. And I called her. She had problems. Marler was throwing a fit, as she described it.

The night at the hospital. They tried to make it look like she just had a baby and I wasn't there. But she hadn't just had a kid. She had that kid at eight o'clock in the morning. I spent the whole day with her. They made it look different than it was.

What they did was illegal. It was against the court rules. They cannot introduce my character, unless I do. They claimed it went to motive. Motive, scheme, and plan, which is an exception. But where does that go to motive, scheme, and plan to kill. That's a stretch of the imagination. And I think the Michigan Court of Appeals is going to agree that's an awful big stretch.

Looking back, I would have gone on the witness stand. I don't make a bad witness. First of all, I know how to testify in court. I know how to talk to the jury, and how to irritate the prosecutor, and not look as though I'm irritating the prosecutor. I did it with defense attorneys all the time. I could have just sat there and admitted to the jury, yes, I did have an affair, clearly being honest to them, showing the emotion that goes with that. I'd let myself admit my faults, my shortcomings, so they could see I'm a human being.

I think I could have handled Jon Sahli's cross-examination. Under the rules, he can't probe into anything outside of what John Sims would have asked me on direct testimony. My arrogant side would come out. But I have testified in front of some tougher attorneys than Jon Sahli will ever think of being and held my own.

If I would have been on the stand, they would have seen some other sides of me. At the table, it was hard to be anything but intense. The way I react to serious things is I get intense about them. Other people laugh and tell jokes. I can't. I have to be glued to the issues.

What the jury got was me. I didn't like when they put up pictures of Diane. I didn't look at them because I didn't want to cry. I did anyway. I had either sadness or seriousness. I had no other emotion between that. I know I'm speaking from a prejudiced point of view, if I was sitting in a jury, looking back at me, and seeing he's either removed or sad, I'd say, well at least he's true to his emotions. The time of Diane's death was serious and sad. And I was reliving the same emotions I had that night. It was me being me, there wasn't anything different than what the witnesses said. Shouldn't that have shown a rational human being; that's how he deals with it?

I think all that was in their minds was: When are they going to tell us who really did it? Ultimately that's what happened. Somewhere the burden of proof shifted. Somewhere, the burden of proof shifted to us, and that's where the case was lost. That jury all of a sudden said, *wait, he's got to prove he didn't do it or show us who did it.* Give us somebody. I'm not sure when it happened, but it happened.

When the jury went out I thought it was a flip of the coin. The longer they were out, the more I thought they were hung. But then going back to what I said about Conrad Sindt, he made sure it wasn't. He threatened them with spending Christmas on this case by telling them to go back in and deliberate.

That's why they found me guilty, so they could spend Christmas with their families. They wanted to get the hell out of there, and the judge gave them permission to not do their job.

Conclusion

Brad. . . . Lot's of luck in the future with all the women. Be good so your mother won't find the truth out.

—senior picture inscription from a
high-school classmate

1

I suppose seeing a convicted Bradford J. King appear in shackles for sentencing on January 6, 1993, made it easier for some to be absolutely sure he had killed his wife in cold blood. In the eighteen months I'd spent on the case, I'd often find such days of certainty elusive.

A probation agent with the Michigan Department of Corrections named Timothy G. McCaleb also wanted more answers when he compiled a confidential presentence report on King for Judge Conrad Sindt. The report would not influence penalty. The mandatory sentence for first degree murder in Michigan was life imprisonment, or "natural life," as inmates called it. There was no chance of parole.

McCaleb's report was meant to probe family background and King's state of mind, factors sometimes helpful in prison assignment. For the officers of the court, it provided more glimpses into the quiet man who had sparked what amounted to a media siege a month before at the courthouse in Battle Creek.

King's session with McCaleb was exceptionally long, nearly six hours. "Mr. King was cordial, articulate, though occasionally guarded," the agent wrote. "Regarding the commission of the offense, he simply stated, 'I didn't do it.' "

McCaleb wrote a four-page personal history. King talked at length about his father, who he described as "loving, but strict" and "not as accessible as he ought to have been." There were

several references to his brother Scott, but only one paragraph
dealing with his mother.

"Mr. King states that he was closer to his dad and always
took his problems to him. He recognized that his brother was
the spontaneous one, while he was reticent. In that respect, he
is more like his mother, whom he describes as guarded, careful,
status conscious. As he put it, 'My screw-ups sometimes offended her social shame and she'd run a guilt trip on me. My
dad would just ask me what I'd learned.' "

King offered McCaleb a personal inventory, stating he had
"empathy," "compassion," and a "high energy level," traits
very few had ever affixed to him. "In expanding on these
introspections, Mr. King noted that he is very careful who sees
his emotions. He feels that the male onus against crying or other
display of emotions is very detrimental and at one point he
stated, 'We should be able to cry and still do our job.' "

King rationalized his lack of emotion about his wife's death.
"Mr. King states that it is something that you cannot prepare
for and that in his case has been made especially problematic
by the court process. 'The court matter blocked the grief process. I was thrown into a survival situation and had to put
grieving aside.' "

King confessed to affairs with two women, calling the behavior "selfish," but said he was trying to work it out in counseling
sessions at the Oakridge Counseling Center before his wife's
death. There was more about Diane.

" '. . . I was committed to teaching. She *was* considering
leaving the job, but it was by no means cut and dry. We were
just beginning to discuss it. I wasn't too happy about it, but if
we could do it and make it work I would have been for it. The
unhappy part of it would be I would have to abandon my plans
for a while. She was not only thinking about the kids, but she
was disillusioned with the media. . . . Our marriage problems
were based on several things: bad communication, my liaisons,
she was getting increasingly moody, and budget problems. I
wasn't dealing with her moodiness well.' "

King volunteered more. "He noted that his wife was Catholic
and dead set against divorce. Marriage was a 'forever thing'

with her. He stated that most people did not know her well, even her family. She was very spontaneous and would say things because of strong feelings that were quite beyond what she would eventually do. In other words, she would speak rashly in the heat of the moment."

As for his pending prison sentence, King told McCaleb Michigan prisons worried him because of his police work. He wanted to be sent to a federal prison. He wanted to pursue "college courses on the graduate level." He said he wanted to study computers. "One can't live without them anymore," King said.

The report noted that Brad King had already accumulated 342 days of jail credit. Presumably, that meant he had nearly a year's head start on the rest of his life.

A gaggle of reporters, Diane King's family, and three jurors who convicted Brad King attended the sentencing. Court TV had arranged for a camera and sound for its updates.

Denise Verrier had been anticipating the sentencing for days. She'd written out a victim's impact statement. Tears stained the pages as she read it at the podium.

"Diane was devastated by the death of her father," she said at one point. "And now, ironically, her children have to suffer the very loss she hated so much. But her children have lost two parents."

She began weeping, but kept reading. "Our lives have been affected in so many ways. I have nightmares of her struggling, trying to turn over to get to the car to protect her children. Only last night I dreamed Diane did not die and she put my hand on her wounds. It was so real. If only it were real. She would be here for the children today. I'm sure for the rest of my life I will look out the window every year on February 9 at six-fifteen or six-thirty and remember her and how alone she was out there on the cold gravel drive—all alone, with only her crying children to be heard.

"In the light of events that have taken place in the last two years, I have asked why. When there was no arrest, why do the wicked go unpunished? Why do the innocent suffer so many times? One thing I came to realize was through all this there comes a time to stop asking and start trusting. And that's what we did. I know this may sound simplistic, but I do feel this is really what God wants. We are people called to live by faith. There is nothing wrong with inquiry, but the enemy loves to have us linger and doubt our God who says, 'Though they join forces, the wicked will not go unpunished.' "

She continued quoting scripture. "Seven things the Lord hates: A proud look, a lying tongue, hands that shed innocent blood, a heart that devises wicked plans, feet that are swift in running to evil, a false witness who speaks lies and one who sows discord among brethren.' Part of me desires vengeance on the perpetrator, the other part fears greatly the judgement of God on this type of crime. . . . Only one thing is for sure, and the very heavens and earth would have to pass away before His Word fails when it says, 'Take note; you have sinned against the Lord; and your sins will find you out.'—Numbers 32:23."

When he was asked if he had anything to say before sentencing, Brad King stood and took the podium. His shoulders back, he faced the judge and read from two hand printed sheets. He would employ the term "law suit" to his case, a term usually reserved for civil proceedings, but accurate under the strictest legal definition of the term.

"Presumed innocent," he began. "The basic tenet of the justice system. Presumed innocent did not exist in this case. The press, in their zealousness of the public's right to know, is to be condemned for obliterating the foundation of justice. The actions of the justice system professionals in this law suit have set the concept of professionalism back to the 1950s. The answer to the question—what price justice?—is, in the law suit, easily and obviously answered. Throw out the foundation of presumed innocent and ignore the search for truth. Throw out professionalism. What occurred throughout the investigation and the trial is a conspiracy to convict at any cost—vigilantism.

"The obvious victims of this farce are my wife, myself, our children, and our families and friends. The not so obvious victims are the citizens of this county and the justice system. My heart is saddened and angered for the loss of my wife, my freedom, and the effects this has had on our children, families, and friends. For those who have to live with a corrupt justice system I should have pity. I don't. You have the ability to change your justice system. You deserve what you have until you change it. If you think this statement is harsh, I will explain my position."

King addressed the judge. "First, you forced a trial in this county on me. You forced a jury on me, a jury with considerable prior knowledge of this case and obvious opinions. Second, you allowed the prosecutor, your friend, to continue to attempt to enter inadmissible testimony into this trial. Third, you remained the trial judge when you knew that you were biased for the prosecution. Fourth, you knew that to ensure a conviction would be the only way to cover the incompetence of the investigation into the death of my wife. First, this case carried a lot of media coverage and political impact. To control the trial process was necessary in order to ensure a conviction. Why were these points carried out in this trial? To cover your guilt in the conspiracy to convict me. To cover your guilt about the travesty of justice you knew this would be."

Judge Sindt looked up from papers he was signing. He glared momentarily, then resumed writing.

"To the jury, I charge you with failure to follow the court rules. I charge you with lying during the selection process. I charge you with willful misconduct. You also threw out the basic tenet, presumed innocent. I say you chose to act in the manner you did for your own comfort, not in the interest of justice. I have nothing but contempt for you."

King paused briefly, pushing his shoulders back farther. "Finally, I stand here a proud man! I *did not* kill my wife. I am not guilty. I am taught that all things are related. Everything is a part of the greater whole. I have asked the Great Spirit to guide me on my path and help me to restore balance and peace to my life. I am taught that your actions are not actions of true humans and you have forgotten about being human so you have acted as you did toward me. I forgive your actions. But this does not erase your responsibility in perpetrating this travesty."

* * *

With that, and without a hint of acrimony in his voice, Conrad Sindt sentenced Brad King to life imprisonment, adding another two mandatory years to run consecutively for using a firearm in the commission of a felony.

A Mohawk quoting scripture. A man without a drop of native blood evoking the Great Spirit. The irony did not go unnoticed as he was led away.

A few minutes later, I was sitting with Bradford King in his courthouse holding cell, there to arrange details of a series of upcoming interviews. There was no sign of the angry figure at the podium. Attorney Virginia Cairns joined us. She was saying goodbye, and King was crying. She gave him a tissue.

"I won't be here anymore to hand them to you," she said, sentimentally.

"I'll be damned if I'll let those bastards out there see me cry," he said.

"You take care of yourself," she said. Then she gave him a farewell peck on the lips.

I told him I'd see him in Jackson, Michigan, in a few weeks. It was the home of the largest walled prison in the world.

2

He inspired intense loyalty among friends. This became even more clear when Randy Wright and I met one month later at Southern Michigan Prison in Jackson. Wright would accompany me on one visit, then, I'd have King to myself for months.

Randy Wright was anxious for him. Soon, King would be transferred to a much smaller facility, his request for federal housing denied by the department of corrections. The attorney recently had thrown a Super Bowl party for some of the old

Tekes who had helped raise the $75,000 in his ill-fated attempt to free King on bond.

"Some of the guys were sneaking the money," Wright told me as we waited to go in. "They had to sneak it because their wives thought he did it. They thought he'd killed her."

Of course, the wives knew as little about the evidence as the husbands, or Randy Wright, or the Van Vleets, or any number of his supporters who had not been at the trial. Some had watched the Court TV coverage, but even then significant testimony was lost to commercial breaks.

In the visiting room, they hit it off like a couple of old frats at a founder's day function, talking about past friends, old places, past lives. King, dressed in state-issued blues, made snide cracks about the prison staff and clever observations about his trial. There was little resemblance to the menacing figure I'd watched for five weeks in Battle Creek.

Except for the eyes. Eye contact was like a psychological game of chicken, a contest to see who would look away first. When I did not, he stopped trying. Besides, soon I found him easy to talk with. Soon, I found him easy to like.

King brought up a letter he got from his mother, rolling his eyes. "She's a fatalist. She's worried I'll spend the rest of my life in prison. Her health is bad. Of course, that's entirely my fault."

Later, in the parking lot, Randy Wright sighed with relief as we walked to his new Cadillac. "Well, I was worried about him, how he'd be handling this. But he sounds great, doesn't he? I don't think I'd be in such good spirits if I were in his shoes, but I think he's going to be just fine."

Our visit had lasted no more than an hour. I told King what I needed: unrestricted access to him, his family, his friends. Not expecting to get it, I asked for all of his defense files. He formally waived attorney-client confidentiality and gave me everything.

A couple weeks later I picked up two large file boxes of discovery, private investigation, and personnel notes from attorney John Sims. It was an impressive gesture. Such materials usually are not offered by guilty men.

Later, John Sims said something compelling. "When you get done with this do me a favor, will ya? When you figure out whether he's innocent or guilty, let me know. I've never been able to determine that."

The case was not an easy call. Jurors struggled with the evidence and the pressure. Christmas was one of the furthest things from their minds, they said. Several had nightmares. Another kept a journal. Of the twenty-two reasons brought in by one of the holdout jurors on the day of the conviction, most had to do with King's association with a .22 caliber rifle, his movement on the crime scene, and his apparent lack of commitment to find his wife's killer.

Brad King was right about one thing. The jury had convicted him because there had been the absence of another suspect.

"The last thing we marked off was the stalker theory," one juror said. "We didn't know how it could be someone else. There were a lot of things that just didn't make sense for someone else to have done it. It just didn't add up."

However, the crime had not occurred in a courtroom. It had occurred in an environment neither controlled by evidentiary guidelines nor hearsay rules. It had taken place on a vast, rural crime scene one winter evening in unstable weather conditions. The investigation involved people the jury would never know.

On the land at 16240 Division Drive, I found some of the evidence suspect. Using the prosecutor's own times, I decided Brad King could have missed someone moving through the swamp as he came back from the hay bales. By 6:40 P.M. it was nearly dark. On the other hand, that same darkness also gave someone in camouflage much cover.

I had someone fire three rounds of CCI ammunition with a bolt-action .22 from the loft, the barn door, and the driveway in conditions similar to those of February 9, 1991. I sat back at the hay bales. All I heard was an airplane landing at Brooks Field airport. We repeated the test. The wind kicked up to fifteen miles an hour. I barely heard only one of the three shots fired. It was not the sharp crack I expected. It sounded like a screen door slamming on a very distant farm.

Tonya Scott's testimony about the shots being a "few seconds" apart was troubling. It took at least ten seconds to scramble from the loft door down the treacherous, narrow stairs in the dark.

Then, there was the matter of James Wickware, Jr., the young man who'd been interviewed by Jack Schoder and eliminated as a suspect. Indeed, the younger Wickware was a timid, shy man. He allowed me to log 225 correspondences he'd accumulated by the summer of 1993, mostly with TV newswomen. The first person he began writing was a reporter named Cynthia Canty, who worked for WKBD-Channel 50 in Detroit. He described himself in his letters as an elderly person, she told me. She thought he was a shut-in and sent him a promotional photo.

"The amazing thing was how much he knew, about my career, where I had worked, what shows I'd done, going back years," she said. "That's what was unsettling. That's what really gave me the creeps."

Young Wickware had his own car, but his father said he was in by 7:30 P.M. the night of the murder. "Hell, he can't even shoot a gun," James Wickware, Sr., said. "He's more afraid of me than anything else."

I did not find the proper, mild-mannered father Schoder described in his report. James Wickware, Sr., was an angry man. There was much talk of people and institutions in our two visits, talk of violence, the need to kill, to decapitate even, the people who had wronged him.

It was unsettling.

But no more so than Brad King's reaction to these discoveries when I detailed them to him during our interviews. King was transferred to the Gus Harrison Regional Facility, a new prison in Adrian, Michigan. In a small interview room, new leads and inconsistencies were met with a silence or flat responses that could be interpreted as anything from indifference to caution.

There simply was, as psychologists say, a lack of affect. King asked no questions about my findings. Most days, he seemed content to listen and watch and answer questions—or cry. In the first half-dozen visits, he cried passionately, calling it his "therapy." That was unsettling, too. It was the only emotion he seemed capable of displaying at will.

The first crying spell came forty-five minutes into our first interview. He told a story about homecoming time at Cross-Lex High School. He tossed an apple out of his car and shattered the windshield of a vehicle trailing him on a country road. The next day the school made an announcement, trying to find the culprit. It turned out the girl driving the car was the daughter of Willis King's second in command at the bank. The girl was waiting in the principal's office.

"I went to the office, skipped football practice and everything," King said. "The girl was shocked. She said, it couldn't have been you. And I said, 'Well, it was me.' I threw out the apple because I'd taken a bite out of it and it was rotten. I didn't mean to do it. It was just one of those things.

"So, nothing happened to me at the school, but I wanted to tell my dad before anybody else did. So I got permission to leave the school. I drove right down to the bank. He got his second in command in there and I told her, too. That was probably the hardest part. But I didn't even get disciplined.

"My dad said, 'You told the truth. You handled it like a man so we're going to leave it at that.' "

King cried. With no tissues from Virginia Cairns, the waterworks were plain to see.

"I guess that was the first time he acknowledged that I was a man," King continued, his eyes red, his lip shaking slightly. "And I wasn't a man, but he treated me as though I was a man, because I handled the situation."

The story was perfectly crafted and quite moving. On the drive home that day from the prison, I thought about the message. It was in anecdotal form, but clear enough: *When I do something wrong, I'm man enough to admit it.*

I couldn't shake the feeling he was trying to manipulate me.

We talked in great depth over the next ten months. In time, King stopped wearing prison blues, showing up in a purple jogging suit and new running shoes his mother had sent him.

"Gee, do you think he's trying to draw attention to himself?" one administrator quipped later in the prison lobby.

King grew his hair out. By late summer, his increasingly silver hair was in a ponytail, his face and dome deeply tanned. He wore shorts or khakis with shirts in attractive Southwestern patterns. Some days he looked like he'd just broke eighty on a brisk eighteen. Other days he looked like a slim Marlon Brando during his Native American phase.

For help, I drew upon an FBI Behavioral Science Section and an article agents wrote called "Interviewing Techniques for Homicide Investigators." The paper was compiled for the FBI *Law Enforcement Bulletin* in 1985 after agents conducted detailed interviews and research with some of the country's most savvy convicted serial killers. The section made a study of interview patterns among killers, just as David Minzy had with crime scenes.

One interview pattern was: "What the subject avoids or refuses to talk about provides information on areas where strong emotions may exist."

There was nothing Brad King refused to talk about, but there were important areas where avoidance appeared to take the form of missing or inconsistent details.

I brought up several times over the months the .22 caliber rifle he said he'd sold in Denver. For boys who grow up in rural Michigan, boys such as myself, a first rifle is usually a childhood milestone. I not only remember every detail about the first gun my father brought home and let me shoot, I remember a good deal about the guns of his friends I was also allowed to shoot. My younger brother does as well, though he hasn't held the family .22 in his hands in a dozen years.

King distanced himself from his first firearm, as did his brother, Scott, the only family member who never returned my calls. Brad King struggled and hesitated when I asked him about the weapon in our first full interview. His ignorance was curious, especially for a boy who would grow up to brag to so many about his marksmanship.

A few months later, I asked him to give me an inventory of

all the guns he'd owned over the years. He listed more than a half dozen, providing great detail:

"I bought a revolver, a Smith & Wesson. It's a five-shot Chiefs Special. Revolver. It's a five shot as opposed to a six shot. Small, lightweight."

Or, "I carried a six-shot snubnose with a four-inch barrel, which was our uniform issue. A Smith & Wesson."

Or, "I purchased a 7 mm Magnum. It's a bolt action. It was a BSA. Bought it at Williams Gunsight. . . . The bullet is small, shoots very flat, so it's good for hunting out West. Doesn't have a lot of knockdown power. Thousand yards you're taking chances."

He fondly remembered golfing with his father and their man-to-man talks. He recalled them target practicing outside of Tustin. He remembered being taught gun safety.

"What was the make of the .22?" I asked.

"I don't know what the make of it was. It could have been a Remington." And, later, "No sentimental value."

The second troubling hole was Brad King's lack of clarity on exactly when, where, and how he found out his wife was a murder victim and not struck down by a seizure or heart attack. In an early interview, King said he couldn't recall an EMT telling Deputy Guy Picketts "she's been shot."

"When were you told that she'd been shot?" I asked.

"Quite a long time. I don't think anybody told me she'd been shot. They just told me she was dead."

"When did you first realize she'd been shot?"

"When I was being interviewed. Or, maybe . . . maybe, no, I think it was when I was being interviewed. I was trying to think maybe, you know, it was in the process of leaving the house."

A month later, King came up with more detail about what he knew about his wife's condition.

"You didn't hear the emergency people say anything to Picketts?" I asked.

"I think they called him, but I didn't know. I mean, when I look back at it and I can look at myself, I think I knew it. You know, I could say it, but I wasn't allowing it. I didn't want to admit that to myself that she was dead."

"You think you knew she was dead, or shot?"

"Both. One or the other, both. You know, I've come across. . . . I've been involved in hundreds of shootings. You just get so you know. But when it's someone close, you don't want that to be the truth."

I left the subject alone for three months, then asked again, "When did somebody tell you she'd been shot?"

"It was in the house. . . . It was when they told me she was dead. See . . . I mean, I knew she'd been shot 'cause I heard the paramedics say, 'She's been shot.' "

"Oh, you heard that?"

"Yeah."

There were more holes. King told Jack Schoder he did—then did not—watch the video *Next of Kin* in the hours before his wife's murder. I asked him about it.

"Well, I've seen it since, but I don't know if I watched it that day. I might have."

The time he *might* have been watching the movie would have also been when he was setting up his wife's ambush, detectives believed. King was also sketchy on details as to what he did on Friday the day before, a time detectives believed he was zeroing in his gun.

There were more inconsistencies.

King seemed oblivious to the fact he'd slept with Kelly Clark, then tried to bed two other women the Thursday before Diane's death, a time he said he'd stopped fooling around. He told Jack Schoder he'd not walked in the marsh near the creek for weeks, but told me he'd walked on both sides twice in the days before the murder. Of finding Diane in the driveway he said, "There was nothing I could do for her, I'm not medically trained." Seconds later he noted he was "CPR certified."

King never once expressed remorse that he'd not returned from his walk earlier, until I finally brought it up. Then, he said he thought about it "all the time."

"Maybe it would have been worse if I had," he said. "Maybe I'd be lying there next to her, too."

3

The article in the FBI *Law Enforcement Bulletin* also described a specific technique agents employed on convicted killers who refused to acknowledge their guilt.

> There are reasons why a suspect might deny a crime. The denial might serve to protect the subject from legal action as well as from the psychological impact of admitting such a crime. . . . We found that when someone outright denied they had murdered or had anything to do with the crime, the use of an imaginary third person was helpful. The agents would go through the details of the crime and ask the subject why he thought this third person would commit such an act. This technique projected responsibility or guilt away from the subject and onto somebody else.

It had worked on no less formidable a subject than Ted Bundy, who only directly admitted responsibility hours before the electric chair.

When we began talking about the details of the crime scene at 16240 Division Drive, I decided to employ a third person role for Brad King, one that he'd already created for himself.

"You're the former cop here," I said. "You know how these crimes work, and I respect your opinion. I want you to help me as an investigator. Remove yourself personally, and try to give me some reasons why you think things happened the way they did."

The results were more than intriguing.

We began with King's analysis that the husband would be the most likely suspect on such a case, an angle that—despite John Sims's argument otherwise in court—Jack Schoder ignored because he was so worried about the stalker case back on his desk. Then, King moved on to other theories. He usually preferred to discuss the murder in context of two mystery assassins killing his wife.

I took the discussion to a more detailed level, ignoring who and how many, concentrating on why instead. We talked about the kill shot.

"What do you make of that?" I asked. "He couldn't have picked a more deadly shot."

"That's right," King said. "It's somebody who knows how to shoot."

"But also somebody who knows a little about anatomy."

"Yeah. . . . She didn't suffer."

"That's right. She was gone very quickly."

"I'm glad of that," he said. "In a way."

I was curious about the wound to Diane King's pelvis. If the shot was fired just outside the barn door after she fell, the angle of entry indicated the barrel was not more than a foot off the ground. The prosecutor argued King had just lowered the gun and fired in anger. I asked King "as an investigator" what he thought the significance of the second shot was.

"I think it was just a precautionary shot. I think it was just done just to be sure."

I asked, why would an "insurance shot" be fired to such a non-vital area?

"Instead of walk up and put one in the head?" he asked back.

I nodded.

King switched to the present tense. He often did that, and used the term "they," when he speculated. "Um, discovering that there's somebody in the car so not wanting to be seen. Wanting to get away. Not knowing if they were seen. Well, I'm not gonna go up right now, there's somebody in the car . . . you know, so I'll have to take my shot from here."

"I never thought of that," I said.

Neither had the detectives. The shooter stayed low with the gun to avoid being seen by Marler King. The bullet was headed for the vital center organs, but had to be delivered low and flat. Once the second shot was fired, the shooter could quickly run south and find cover from utility buildings south of the barn.

I wanted to know about the cartridge in the loft. Why would someone leave such evidence?

"Couldn't find it? Getting dark? It'd be dark in the barn. It's brass colored so you got straw all over the floor, which is kind of brass colored. You're not going to be able to see it without a flashlight."

I asked why a killer would dump seven casings with the gun. (There had been no trial testimony that the casings in the creek might have been used to zero in the rifle's sights.)

"They don't want to get caught with them. Maybe those are the ones he used zeroing in his, you know, his .22. And, uh, had 'em in his pocket so he dumped 'em. Makes sense to me."

Weeks later, I brought up the gun and shells in Talmadge Creek again.

"Do you think that's the murder weapon?"

"I don't know."

"As an investigator?"

"If I were the investigator, I would say that's probably my murder weapon. . . ."

"Why are the seven shells with the murder weapon?"

"Uh, distraction? To show the weapon's been fired. See, that explains, why I heard rifle shots out there that week. That was one way of explaining it. I forget how many shell cases they have, but that's one way of explaining it."

"Seven, isn't it?"

"So that's one way of explaining why I heard shots out there, out towards the woods."

"Didn't you say the shells were from zeroing in the gun?"

"Possibly, yes."

It was an astounding connection. He seemed to be saying the gun that "probably" killed his wife was zeroed in near his property. I thought, would an unknown killer take such a risk?

"Why would someone not put the gun clip in the creek?"

"Maybe the clip is still in the creek bed."

"I wonder how well they searched the creek bed?" I thought out loud.

"Well, once they found that gun they quit searching for anything I'll bet you."

What King didn't seem to know was that the sheriff's department made several digs in the creek bed. They kept picking up a faint signal on a metal detector, but never found the clip.

King frequently criticized the sheriff's department, calling Jack Schoder and Jim Stadfeld "stupid," "dumb," and "incompetent." This set up more opportunities. I pushed his hypothetical role further, asking him now not only to investigate the death of his wife, but tell me what his thinking would be using his own reasoning. Brad King as the investigator, I pointed out—unlike "incompetent" Jack Schoder—would consider the husband the prime suspect in the early days.

"Okay, if you're investigating and you think it could very well be the husband, why would you think that he would leave the gun there? I mean, that would be stupid," I began.

"Yes, that would be a big hole for me to fill. Okay. The husband did it. Why is the gun where it is?"

"Right. Wouldn't that be kind of stupid?"

"Yes, very stupid."

"So why would he have done it?"

"Maybe he thinks I'm stupid," King the investigator said. "Maybe he was trying to throw me off. Maybe he didn't put it there."

"How would he be trying to throw you off?"

"Being stupid. It's so stupid, it *couldn't* be him. Or, maybe he didn't put it there. Maybe there's another person. The husband being somebody like me, I would throw out being stupid."

I asked King to be more analytical. "I'm asking you to remove yourself here," I urged.

"That's hard to do," he said.

"I know, but I respect your ability as a criminal justice instructor. I respect your abilities as an analyst."

King thought about it a second, then continued. He began speaking in the first person, as though he were the shooter. "Right. What's the difference in running back on the property and jumping in my car and running a quarter mile away or half a mile away and ditching the rifle and coming back? It'd take the same amount of time."

Then, not a minute or two later, he pointed out who he indeed thought was "stupid." He was talking now as the husband at 16240 Division Drive.

"Cops are stupid," he said. "They're stupid. They get

focused. They forget. They think because people are involved in criminal activity, they're not smart. Well, that's being stupid."

The connection became more striking a few weeks later as we talked about the Calhoun County Sheriff's Department investigation of the stalker letter.

"Did you have the feeling that this outfit wasn't up to snuff?" I asked.

"Yeah. Certainly did. I heard a lot of rumors in the community. Marshall and Battle Creek. The department was something less than it should be."

I was more specific. "Any specific cases people talked about? I know they had open homicides."

"Yes. They do. Exactly. This is probably the only un-open homicide they've had in recent years."

"So you heard they had a lot of open homicides?"

"Yeah, it was one of the big complaints in the community. They'd find bodies and couldn't do anything with them."

A minute later, he pinned down the time frame.

"I would hear those things. I heard 'em in Battle Creek even before we moved to Marshall. The sheriff's department was the brunt of jokes in the Battle Creek Police Department."

He'd also heard top Battle Creek cops, he said, talking about the sheriff's limited abilities at Salvation Army dinners he attended with Diane. Long before the week of February 9, 1991, Brad King had decided the police in the jurisdiction where his wife would be murdered were of limited ability.

Maybe he was counting on it.

We discussed the obsessed fan scenario. When I brought it up, I didn't tell him I'd recently received a copy of psychiatrist Park Dietz's six-year Justice Department study, published in a 1991 edition of the *Journal of Forensic Sciences*. It was no help to Brad King's case.

Dietz's study specifically looked for signs obsessed fans left in correspondences before trying to make face-to-face contact with public figures. The research team looked at content, appearance, volume, and other factors in letters. They chose from

1,500 letter writers in the files of Hollywood security specialist Gavin de Becker, Inc. Of that number, 170 had tried to approach the public figure. The rest had not. For their sample, the team stratified the work of 107 letter writers who had approached and 107 who had not.

The study looked at the percentages. Only 7.5 percent of letter writers who wrote once tried to visit a celebrity. Only five percent maintained complete anonymity in letters, as Diane King's would-be lunch date had. Both anonymous and identified writers were equally likely to approach. Only twenty percent had tried to deliver a letter to a celebrity's home, studio, or agent. Only twelve percent used no greeting.

The study also looked at the letter writers' perceived relationship with their public figures. Most thought they were friends, lovers, would-be spouses, or other delusional roles. None were would-be protégés or students, as Diane King's caller had been.

Other high-risk factors didn't fit the King scenario. Approach-oriented letter writers tended to write over a period of a year or longer. They announced specific times and places where something would happen to a celebrity.

The study looked at actual appearance of the letters. Only four percent had "undulated or wavy" writing as the King lunch letter had. And finally, in the most revealing statistic in the Dietz study, of 214 letter writers: "Contrary to popular stereotypes, only 1 (less than 1 percent) sent a letter which had been cut and pasted from printed matter."

Brad King seemed to know this intuitively: "I thought this is somebody who watches too many crime movies. Scriptwriters do it all the time."

As I talked with friends and King himself, it also struck me Diane King at one time had an obsessive admirer well before she moved to Marshall, Michigan. His name was Bradford J. King.

Other criminal studies show that eighty-five percent of all stalking cases do not involve celebrities and mysterious fans in mental institutions, but former boyfriends, husbands, and other people the victim knows. King's behavior toward his wife appeared at times marginally abnormal: His deep, early infatuation with her. His breakdown when she left for Grand Junction. His fixation with her TV appearances. His following her from room to room and to a lunch date with a friend. His appetite for the attention she brought him. The special treatment her celebrity brought. His phone call to Shemane Nugent.

"He liked being Mr. Diane King."

Such behavior seemed at odds with his self-perception as the stoic, ex-cop unfazed by fame.

King had talked so frequently about the two mystery killers in cowboy hats, I decided to throw the stalker into the mix, into his criminal justice expert speculations.

"How much stock do you put in the obsessed fan?"

He couldn't seem to answer.

I rephrased it. "Given a choice between the obsessed fan and the two guys in cowboy hats."

"Could be one in the same, for that matter," he said.

Yes, I thought, they both could be made up.

"Why would somebody bring someone else?" I persisted.

"Okay, that's a good question. I don't know. So throw that out." He agreed the obsessed fan was the most likely.

"Do you think it would have made a difference that she was alone or that the kids were in the car?" I asked. I was thinking of Jon Sahli's argument.

"No. I don't think the guy knew that. It would have been hard to see the kids in the car so, I don't think that was an issue. I think the issue was Diane. Because if they were the issue, they'd be dead. The fact that they were unharmed leads me more into the obsessed fan thing. . . . The children were not part of his fantasy. So I don't think it would have mattered if the kids were there or weren't there. I don't think that mattered. You look at the obsessed fan and what you've got is: The object is Diane, period."

She certainly was. In fact, the birth of the children ended the fantasy, meant the disappearance of the woman he once worshipped. Perhaps the stalker's note said as much about the sender as it did the recipient. After all, Diane King herself told Nancy Gwynn that she believed her husband had sent it to "get me back in line."

Maybe he did know the children were coming. Then everything about that night made sense. They were supposed to get a pizza. Blow off the Colvin party. Watch a movie. He'd just rented it, he could tell police who were supposed to be too stupid to find the gun.

There was no such thing as a perfect crime. You always overlooked something—like the Michigan State Police or a tracking dog.

In another interview, I pushed our speculation game to the limit.

"Motive," I said. "That's the big missing piece."

"And I've been trying to do that," King said. "And I got nothing. I mean, you know, that I can hang my hat on."

"You want to take this exercise even further, on a hypothetical basis? Let's say you killed her, okay? Let's make the assumption that you killed her."

"That's hard for me to do."

"Why did you kill her?"

"I don't have an answer."

"Nor did the prosecutor. . . . Okay, assuming you were investigating, what would you look at in the husband, being you?"

King didn't hesitate. "Well, overly jealous."

There was a long pause. Then he offered a couple more, pausing between each. "Uh, is the wife having an affair? Uh, history of violence between the two. Mental illness on the part of the husband. Substance abuse on the part of the husband. Uh, fanatical behavior. Obsession with weapons."

"Nobody says she was having an affair," I said.

"And then there's no input, I'm not the jealous husband," he added quickly. "We didn't live in an atmosphere of violence."

"Right."

"I'm not a gun fanatic. I'm not mentally ill."

But the homestead was becoming violent. Cindy Acosta and others did see his attachment to Diane as fanatical. King was drinking heavily with students, including the Thursday before her death. King may not have been obsessed with weapons, but he couldn't seem to stop bragging about his ability to kill.

I wanted a definition of his first utterance. "What do you mean by *'overly jealous'*?"

"Well," King said, "I've seen husbands who when their wife just is, like, at parties and spends too much time talking to a group of men or a single man, he's like, weird. He gets weird."

It was entirely too similar to the party scenes I'd already heard described by Cindy Acosta and Nancy Gwynn.

4

In their ambitious and encompassing book *Crime & Human Nature,* Harvard professors James Q. Wilson and Richard J. Herrnstein offer the belief that crime is a matter of choice.

> Our theory rests on the assumption that people, when faced with a choice, choose the preferred course of action. . . . When we say "choose," we do not necessarily mean that they consciously deliberate about what to do. All we mean is that their behavior is determined by its consequences. A person will do that thing the consequences of which are perceived by him or her to be preferable to the consequences of doing something else.
>
> The consequences of committing a crime consist of rewards and punishments. The consequences of not committing the crime also entail gains and losses. The larger the ratio of the net rewards of crime to the net rewards of non-crime, the greater the tendency to commit the crime. The net rewards of crime include, obviously, the likely material gains, but they also include intangible benefits, such as obtaining emotional or sexual gratification, receiving the approval of peers, satisfying an old score against an enemy, or enhancing one's sense of justice.

Among the material in the defense file were notes and test results of Bradford and Diane King's therapy sessions with marriage counselor Donald Eckerty at the Oakridge Counseling Center in Kalamazoo. Brad King also saw the psychologist for a half-dozen sessions of grief counseling.

The couple's first appointment with the marriage counselor was fifteen days before the murder. They contracted for a half-dozen marital sessions "to resolve the distancing that had occurred in their marriage," the counselor noted. He also indicated they wanted to deal with stresses from Diane's recent pregnancy, the uncertainty of her employment because of the station's pending sale, and Brad King's desire to obtain his PhD.

The Kings had two individual sessions each with Dr. Eckerty, including Brad's on February 7, two days before the murder.

In an initial interview with Jim Brady in April of 1991, the psychologist praised the couple. "Mr. Eckerty believed that they both loved each other very much and said in no uncertain terms that neither was contemplating divorce," Brady wrote in his own memo. "He said that he wished more couples who he counseled had the commitment and desire to make their marriage work that they had."

Brad King appeared to be the supportive husband in his sessions, wanting to learn how to deal with his wife's moods. In the February 7 session, King talked about his love for teaching. Also, Diane had come up with a new idea. She wanted them to go into Christian missionary work. King told the psychologist he didn't have an interest at all in that. He said nothing about his extramarital affairs.

Diane King was in a precarious mental condition, Dr. Eckerty told Brady. She needed immediate attention. She was clinically depressed. She had deep resentments against her mother. She had a big agenda for six sessions. She not only wanted to straighten out her marriage, she wanted to see if she was capable of staying home as a mother and wanted to "renew her Christian faith principles in the home." Overall, the psychologist noted, "Diane states she feels she has been depressed all her life."

Diane King took a test known as the Milton Clinical Multiaxia Inventory-II, or MCMI-II, a 175-question psychological evaluation used by many therapists to provide guidance on a patient's personality traits and pathology. (Brad King later told me that he took the same test as well.) Her MCMI-II profile was included in the file.

It was not a flattering portrait. Diane King was a woman with a "veneer of friendliness and sociability," but her "basic irritability, argumentativeness, and moodiness are seen frequently by family members and close associates," the test profile went. She used anger to "badger and control" others. She was insistent on getting her way and "typically acts on her impulses with insufficient deliberation and poor judgement." She readily projected blame on others and was capable of "explosive outbursts." The test noted she was suffering from generalized anxiety. She was histrionic—capable of self-dramatizing behavior—the clinical equivalent of Gina Zapinski's Big Event. Her histrionic tendency, in fact, threatened the validity of the test, as she was likely to exaggerate on questions.

She was a "basket case," Dr. Eckerty told Brady's legal assistant Trish Hubbard in July of 1992, when he was re-interviewed after King's arrest.

In that same interview, the psychologist expressed disappointment that Brad King had not told him about his extramarital affairs and acknowledged he might have been living some kind of double life. Dr. Eckerty told Hubbard each of the couple's faults played into the other's.

"(Dr. Eckerty) advised in a straightforward way that Diane was 'mean to him,'" Hubbard wrote. "And that Brad's sense of never reaching his goals was reinforced by this, and Diane's role as the 'boss.'"

The psychologist also noted Brad King underwent some psychological testing. Whether this was the MCMI-II or another kind of test was unclear in the documents. The results could be obtained from the company that scored it, Eckerty told Hubbard, adding he believed the results "would be favorable to Brad."

The law firm wanted the results. It was the only document I found missing from the entire defense file I received.

Brad King was evaluated by a Michigan Department of Corrections psychologist when he first was assigned to the prison in Jackson. King agreed to have a summary of those results released. King took the Minnesota Multiphasic Personality Inventory, or MMPI, a lengthy, standard test that looks for psychosis and personality disorders. He took two other more subjective tests.

Department of corrections psychologist James J. Glades wrote King showed no signs of psychosis, but did not rule out King might have a nonspecific personality disorder with "dependent, paranoid and passive-aggressive personality features." He wrote in his report:

> Mr. King is an emotionally dependent and somewhat emotionally immature individual. . . . He tends to minimize his own anger and rage, has remained somewhat defiant and rebellious of authority. This may be related to his own feelings of inadequacy and lack of accomplishment in a manner which he feels entitled to obtain. . . . It appears he duplicated his father's behavior in the sense that he married a second time (a woman) who was somewhat younger and was rather outgoing and entertaining. There is some question as to whether he has been able to accept the full responsibility of adulthood. . . .

Under the supervision of a forensic psychologist, I asked Brad King to retake the MMPI as well as the MCMI-II, the test he'd taken before with Diane at Oakridge. It was the only area of my research where he repeatedly asked me questions, wondering what his results were, wondering if they showed him to be normal.

"They show you're not psychotic," I told him. "And that you're an arrogant son of a bitch."

King's MMPI score exhibited a largely well-adjusted individual. The results noted: "This person is presenting himself as very masculine. Associated features include: adventurous, coarse, easygoing, aggressive, emphasizes physical strength, compulsive, preference of action to thought, and inflexibility about masculinity. Doubts about masculinity are possible."

The test did show some problems with validity, calling for a "guarded" prognosis. "These patients tend to be somewhat defensive and are reluctant to admit problems," it noted.

The MCMI-II, the test that was not included in the Brady materials, presented a disturbing personality profile, though, as the test itself cautioned, the results should not be considered definitive.

King's MCMI-II profile stated he had a "deeply ingrained and pervasive pattern of maladaptive functioning" in his personality. He had a "sadistic personality disorder" and a "dependent personality disorder with prominent obsessive-compulsive traits." His obsessive relationship with Diane aside, three features stood out in the testing. King was highly dependent, had severe aggressive/sadistic tendencies, and showed an abnormally low level of anxiety in his personality.

In his own book *Disorders of Personality,* Dr. Theodore Millon, the noted psychiatrist who designed the MCMI-II test, discusses the dependent personality, saying they have a marked need for "social approval and affection."

Many dependent individuals search for a single, all-powerful "magic helper," a partner in whom they can place their trust and depend on to protect them from having to assume responsibilities or face the competitive struggles of life alone. Supplied with a nurturant partner, they may function with ease, be sociable and display warmth, affection, and generosity. Deprived of this support, they withdraw into themselves and become tense, despondent and forlorn.

Arguably, the magic helper, for many years, was Diane Newton King. Dependency, however, should not be equivocated with loss of control. In fact, the opposite is often the case, psychologists say. King's score on the sadistic scale figures into this type of analysis.

While many people associate sadism with overtly cruel sexual acts, sadistic tendencies can take far more subtle forms: Eye to eye intimidation. A crushing handshake. The deprecation of students in a classroom. The frightening of a young sorority girl in a fraternity house bathroom.

Psychiatrist and author Dr. Karen Horney, in her landmark work, *Our Inner Conflicts,* discusses sadistic traits, including the way a sadistic partner acts in a relationship. A sadistic partner, she writes, "enslaves" a partner by being possessive, often isolating them from others, and then exploits. Dr. Horney goes on to say:

> Another sort (of sadistic craving) finds satisfaction in *playing on the emotions* of another person as on an instrument. A man *who expects nothing of his own life* can be entirely absorbed by the game itself. He knows when to show interest and when to be indifferent.

As King said himself, when it came to emotions, with Diane he had "an open book." With the vulnerable partner, the sadist has another tendency, Dr. Horney writes:

> The nature of the exploitation becomes still clearer when we realize that there is simultaneously a tendency to *frustrate* others. It would be a mistake to say that the sadistic person never wants to give anything. Under certain conditions he may even be generous. What is typical of sadism is not niggardliness in the sense of withholding, but a much more active, though unconscious, impulse to thwart others—to kill their joy and to disappoint their expectations. Any satisfaction or buoyancy of the partner's almost irresistibly provokes the sadistic person to spoil it in some way. If the partner looks forward to seeing him, he tends to be sullen. If the partner wants sexual intercourse, he will be frigid or impotent.

Or, if you will, if a TV anchorwoman wants protection by a former cop from an obsessed fan, he may be detached, unconcerned. If a wife has high career expectations, he may go the other way, seeking new levels of underachievement.

Nancy Gwynn was convinced she knew the reason why Diane King had become a "basket case."

"He was trying to drive her out of her mind," she told me. "She kept saying, no matter what I do, what I try, it's not good enough. This all was part of a plan to literally drive her nuts."

Dr. Horney cites a sadist's own self-loathing as the source of his behavior. He must therefore live his life through others, playing a game he must always win, just as Dr. Gary Kaufmann and David Minzy believed.

Dr. Horney writes:

> The emotional gains are achieved by living vicariously. To be sadistic means to live aggressively and for the most part destructively, through other persons. But this is the way a person so utterly defeated can live. The recklessness with which he pursues his goals is the recklessness born of despair. Having nothing to lose, he can only gain. In this sense, sadistic strivings have a positive goal and must be regarded as an attempt at restitution. The reason why the goal is so passionately pursued is that in triumphing over others the sadistic person is able to remove his own abject sense of defeat.

The third personality trait addressed in King's MCMI-II was his abnormally low anxiety levels. King displayed this in his coolness in the courtroom and his indifference to making love in a public park with students. Several studies show low anxiety levels are the hallmark of the psychopath. One reason the psychopath has no conscience, psychologists believe, is that he lacks this internal governor to prevent him from doing wrong. He must take risks and find thrills to feel human. His emotional responses are often flat or forced. Wilson and Herrnstein write in *Crime & Human Nature:*

> The protypical extreme psychopath should be relatively free of anxiety. Fleeting, even if intense, resentments, irritations, or urges should take the place of the more lasting worries or goals of the non psychopath. The pure psychopath's emotional life should compromise pangs rather than aches.

The profile section of Brad King's MCMI-II addressed chilling possibilities of the combination of his personality traits:

> This man exhibits a veneer of arrogant confidence and machismo; however, underlying his narcissistic posture and exploitive style is a basic inadequacy. Able to favorably impress casual acquaintances with his superficial bravado, he routinely displays his characteristic deficiencies, unreliability, impulsiveness, and moodiness to family members and close associates. He persistently seeks recognition. . . . Relationships are maintained only if they are self-serving. With few exceptions they are shallow and fleeting. . . . Almost infantile in his fantasies of himself and in his expectations of others, he often acts on impulse, using minimal deliberation and poor judgement.
>
> Unlikely to admit responsibility for his personal failures or for family difficulties, he usually denies the presence of psychological tension or conflicts. He rationalizes interpersonal problems, and he readily projects blame onto others. Ready to meet his own needs at the expense of those of others, he is self-indulgent and insistent on getting his way. . . . Owing to his basic and extreme dependency, he fears that others will perceive him as being weak and indecisive. Therefore, he presents an arrogant facade, and delights in humiliating those on whom he depends to gain a false illusion of power.
>
> When crossed, subjected to minor pressures, or faced with potential embarrassment, he is provoked to vindictive anger. His undercurrent of defensive vigilance and insecure hostility rarely subsides. Moreover, his surface affability collapses easily, and he is always ready to deprecate anyone who challenges his posture of omnipotence. Although infrequent, his temper outbursts may turn into uncontrollable rage and sudden, unanticipated violence.

Nita Davis saw what she thought was a Brad King crossed. We talked in more detail about their meetings on January 7 when he said his bank account had been "frozen."

"It was the whole intensity I'd never seen before," she recalled. He said he'd told his mother of his marital troubles. "He said that his mother had specifically told him, 'Well, you've blown another one. You screwed up another marriage.' "

At the Knollwood Tavern he seemed to be lumping the significant women in his life all together, his mother Marge, his first wife Gail, and now finally Diane. He had to defeat them by amounting to something, getting his PhD, exceeding their expectations, paying for his daughter's education at Michigan State.

"I'd like to show them," he said.

Then came the stories to Nita Davis about his father denying his Indian heritage, caving in to his mother, stories later shown to be absolutely false, at least in a factual sense.

I wondered if the Indian stories about his father were a form of fantasy, a symbol, especially considering the way King further embraced Native American spirituality and customs after Diane King's death. Did being an Indian constitute independence itself, as with the transformation of the solitary soldier in a movie Brad King had seen six times?

The woman who had denied the Indian seemed omnipresent in his story. Marge Lundeen was the one subject that could elicit the few overt emotional responses I saw, usually displays of anger or frustration. There was much ambivalence as well.

"The truth is I don't give a fuck what my mother thinks," he said of her several times.

In his book *Inside the Criminal Mind,* psychologist Stanton E. Samenow, who studied scores of habitual adult and juvenile criminals, rejects the notion that parents turn children into delinquents. Often, he writes, the parent is the criminal's first psychological and emotional victim. He writes:

> Criminals contend that their parents did not understand them and failed to communicate with them. They are often believed, and as usual, the deficiency is attributed almost entirely to parents. If we could be invisible observers in the homes of delinquent youngsters, we might reach a different conclusion. As a child, the criminal shuts his parents out of his life because he doesn't want them or anyone else to know what he is up to. . . . No matter how hard they try, mothers and fathers cannot penetrate the secrecy, and they discover that they do not know their own child. He is the kid who remains the family mystery.

Brad King, his entire family agreed, was the mystery child, the loner. However, King certainly knew much about his mother and complained often about the same.

He left a trail of resentments as far away as Boulder, Colorado, where I talked to Steve and Donna Boas. Steve Boas had never known Brad King to show any emotional vulnerability, until one day out of the blue he told him a couple of stories about Marge Lundeen. It was just before his arrest.

"It was part of the whole thing he went into about her," Boas recalled. "His mother was very concerned about what people thought. She got pregnant with Brad before she was married. So she came up with a false birthday for Brad after she was married. And Brad never knew that. His birthday is really in January, but she said it was March. He found out in school one day from the principal, and then his father revealed the whole thing. So all this time he was living a lie."

King told me he confronted his mother about it as a teenager. She had nothing to say. They quietly celebrated the real birthday until her parents passed.

There were more secrets to resent. King was in his thirties before he ever knew he had a half sister, that his father was married and divorced before he married Marge. She treated Diane coldly at their wedding, King not finding out until years later that she was furious he'd bought her a large (albeit imitation) diamond ring. There had been many mixed messages.

I heard another secret after I attended a very proper morning service at the local Presbyterian church with the Lundeens one Sunday in Kerrville, Texas. "No, this hasn't been easy for me. No way that I would expect that my son would have done something like this. He's always been so remote from us. And I used to say to Willis, you know I love Brad, but I *really* don't like him very well. That would make his father uneasy."

King blamed her for killing his early aspirations. He'd had a strong interest in Native American culture as a child.

"I wanted to be an anthropologist when I was in high school," he recalled. "And my mother said you can't be that. They don't make enough money. Then I wanted to go in the Air Force and fly jets. She said you can't fly jets. You have allergies. My dreams were met with those things by my mother—*always.*"

One day Brad King came right out with it about her. "Now if I had a reason to be insane, I've got one, don't I?"

Steve Boas had another, more telling, story King told him right before his arrest. "It was about his father, saying that his father wanted to go to California in the early fifties. I guess his brother invited him to Southern California, to go into real estate. But the mother would not leave. It would have been that entrepreneurial adventure that his dad always regretted not doing, and Brad took on that regret for his father and animosity toward the mother. She was in control of everybody's destiny."

King and I talked about that story as well. Under pressure from Marge, he said, Willis took the job with her father at the small-town bank. She was going to stay in her town with her church.

"It's the one thing that disappointed me about my dad, that he didn't stand up to my mother," he said. "I think that was the one thing in his whole life he regretted not doing."

And forty years later, another generation, another woman, this one no longer a magic helper, a celebrity, but now a *mother.* Perhaps the shot to Diane's pelvis was psychological as well as tactical.

"It's the source," maintained state police psychologist Gary Kaufmann. "That's the source of their problems. It's the source of those two kids."

A mother, who wouldn't fall in line, who wanted to be a Christian missionary, saying over and over, no doubt with great force and vilification:

"You're not going to get your PhD. You're going to get off your ass or get out! You're going to go to work so I can stay home with the kids."

A matter of choice.

As February 9, 1991, approached, in the mind of Bradford J. King, the refrain must have been hauntingly familiar.

Almost two years to the date of Diane King's murder, I sat up in the loft of the Victorian barn at 16240 Division Drive, waiting for 6:35 P.M. to come, waiting to run down the steep steps and briskly cover the same track as Travis had.

The weather was unseasonably warm, as it was that deadly night in 1991, and the loft smelled of old straw and barn wood as the sky turned dark gold then gray. A dog tied below, as King's Doberman was, would leave the tack room every few minutes, pulling the links of its chain against the building, causing the entire structure to rumble as though it were haunted.

Mostly it was silent, with only distant country sounds. A car. An airplane. A dog barking somewhere. My own breathing.

Just after 6:35 P.M., I began moving. Past the outbuildings and the silo, down the lane to the footbridge. I crossed Talmadge Creek and crouched through the deer tunnels in the brush, then began moving along the edge of the swamp.

When I neared where the gun was dumped it began, like some kind of primitive celebration. Deer were jumping everywhere, dozens of them, flying out of the marsh, the fields, as though they were exploding out of the brush. For a second they made eye contact before they fled, their white tails shimmering brightly in the dusk.

The deer tails shimmered on the heads of Chippewa at the powwows. They use the white tails as headdresses. They move like the plumes of proud birds in a mating dance with the beating of the big drum.

Native American men. All dancing. In a large circle. In animal skins and other adornments. Warriors and dancers. All eyes on them.

It was at that moment I began to understand. Choices. Risks and the rewards. I believed I knew what Brad King was trying to become.

Back at the barnyard, I noticed some of the wet mud I'd picked up in my run through the field of soy stubble, on my way to Division Drive and the foot of the driveway. It was on my boots and trousers.

There was one thing about all the sand left across Michigan

by the ancient glaciers that had cut out the Great Lakes. Most Michigan boys knew it. All you had to do was give it a few swipes of the hand.

It always fell off with hardly a trace.

5

M ore than twenty years had passed since Bradford King saw Ray Gordon directing traffic on a street corner in Pontiac and followed him into police work. The former Western Teke was in the communications business now in Indiana, but had heard all about King's trial and conviction. The story made some sense to the man King used to call Gordy.

We met to talk in a restaurant in Kalamazoo. Gordon brought his pledge book with Brad King's signature. "Little Napoleon," King called himself, full of "piss and vinegar," Gordon said, until he fell real hard for a blonde named Gail.

Ray Gordon, dressed in a contemporary collarless shirt and fine linen sports jacket, had an engaging, affable personality and quite a story to tell.

They worked together sometimes on the streets in Pontiac PD. "Brad always seemed to do a decent job in the streets. I don't remember anybody ever saying he turned tail and ran on them. I never heard anybody say he didn't back him up. I never heard anybody say he was slow getting to a hot call.

"But I know Brad had a reputation or a tendency to be a little heavy-handed, I guess sometimes, to overstep your boundaries, be it accidentally or intentionally because of the circumstances. You have a bad hair day, something goes wrong on a call, guy takes a swing at you, instead of hitting the guy once, you hit him twice. Brad liked to get a couple extra licks in."

Brad King, he said, also clamped the cuffs one notch tighter than most. Sometimes, without provocation, he used a painful, undetectable maneuver to inflict pain on a captive. "You put the handcuffs behind the guy and you can put your finger between the chains and lift them up high and it hurts in the shoulder blades. I mean, trust me, it hurts."

They saw a lot of each other as friends. They drank together, went to the same parties, played bridge, got together as couples, Brad with Gail, Gordy with his wife, Beth. They also played golf. Lots and lots of golf. King fancied himself a good golfer. He could shoot in the eighties, but he never practiced.

In 1974, Gordon was on a fast track to the detective bureau. Already he was working as a community relations officer, had won citations, and earned a lot of attention from the chief. King was in the surveillance unit. When an opening appeared in community relations, Gordon nominated King. They started the paperwork.

"I thought, hey, this is great," he recalled. "I'll have a friend working with me, and he's got the personality for it."

Then, a rumor had started going around the department. Gordon's wife Beth was having an affair, it went. One thing led to another, and Gordon and his sergeant found the source. The person spreading the slander was Bradford King.

"It didn't make sense to me," Gordon recalled. "To this day, it doesn't make sense. So, I confront him. 'Why the fuck would you do something like that to me?' And there was no answer. Nothing. It's called tacit admission. He wouldn't look me in the eye. He wouldn't talk to me."

Gordon told his sergeant he wanted a transfer if King was coming aboard his unit. The sergeant cancelled King's transfer instead, but not before also considering disciplinary charges on the rumors. The paperwork was still in King's personnel file with the King investigation. Eleven days after his community relations orders came through, King was busted down to uniform patrol.

A week after the cancellation, Ray Gordon received a curious letter from the Oakland *Press*. Somebody had sent the letters-to-the-editor section a typed note complaining about an "uncooperative and obnoxious officer" matching Ray Gordon's description. The open letter asked the Pontiac chief of police for help, adding in the p.s., "Please use my name only if it is necessary."

Ray Gordon's signature was forged at the bottom, underneath it his home address. The editor had sent it back saying the paper wasn't going to run it.

Gordon and his sergeant began taking the letter around to department typewriters, trying to match up the type style. All the department typewriters were new IBM Selectrics, except the one where Brad King typed his reports, which was an old manual. They ran a piece of paper through the spindle.

The type matched.

"I was heartbroken, shocked," Gordon recalled. "I mean, why would somebody just do all this to a friend? My wife said, 'Maybe he's jealous.' I thought, jealous of what? He's got a degree; I got a degree. He's got a dynamite wife; I got a dynamite wife. He's got a nice home; I got a nice home. He's working on his master's; I'd just gotten my master's. I'm in the unit; he's getting transferred. What would he be jealous of? That I could kick his ass in golf?"

"Could you?" I asked.

"Oh, yeah. I loved it. I used to just pound his ass."

Michigan State Police psychologist Gary Kaufmann was intrigued with Brad King's statement at his sentencing, the way he'd railed against the court and jury. I showed Dr. Kaufmann a copy of a newspaper editorial King started writing, but apparently never finished.

"The day I was sentenced I stood a proud man," it began. "The justice system, which I had served so long and had defended, had reached to me its deepest, darkest hour."

Said the psychologist: "He was a student of criminal justice, a former cop. Over and over he'd seen people get away with it. On technicalities. Botched evidence. Poor police work. An inept prosecutor. It's all part of the mix and the mind-set cops get: The real bad guys *always* get off. He'd seen people get away with it. *And he didn't!* So, the criminal justice system didn't work for him. And in that sense, it was unfair."

Dr. Kaufmann believed that the killing of his wife put Brad

King on "a grand stage," offering him all the attention and more that he ever got from his small-town celebrity wife. After her death, the children, who once had been a detraction, became another source of attention, as Marler was when (King) bragged about his brilliance to his students. King made the transformation to the single father of his fantasy trail of lies. Once he was arrested and tried, the children were no longer of psychological use to him, so he let them go to the Newtons without much of a fight. He had Virginia Cairns and a team of lawyers catering to him. Brad King never called or wrote the children once from jail, not on their birthdays, not just to say hello.

Dr. Kaufmann found his name and his taste for clothing in imperial shades telling. "What do you do with a King?" he said. "You cater to him. You take care of his every need."

Randy Wright became troubled the more they learned about the evidence of the murder of Diane Newton King. It bothered Randy Wright that his old friend knew so little about his first gun, or didn't make an all-out effort to locate it . . . if he sold it.

"I don't know," Wright said. "You'd think they could have at least put notices in the Denver paper out there, asking for the guy who bought it to come forward. Something."

At the Gus Harrison Regional Facility, prisoners were not dishing out retribution for King's days as a policeman. Prisoners found the former instructor a valuable addition to the population. King got a job working in the prison law library, doing jail-house lawyer motions and suits.

"Well, I did my first divorce," he said proudly during one of our visits.

King worked with another convicted professional and an imprisoned lawyer. He joked about putting their names together as a firm and hanging out a shingle.

"I've found that many people who sit in this prison—more than one would believe—are here because of the injustice of the justice system," he wrote me one day.

Brad King continued his Native American practices. He

asked prison officials to let him have his ceremonial pipe sent from friends in Colorado, but they refused the request. Soon, however, he was getting regular visits from a Native American medicine man instead of a prison chaplain.

John Van Vleet and his wife Susan stood by their friend and their belief in his innocence. They wrote each other frequently and talked by phone. John visited him when he was in Michigan. But some things didn't sit right.

"You know what I notice?" John Van Vleet said one day. "He's getting along too well in prison. It's not that he doesn't dislike it. He does dislike it. It's like he institutionalizes too easy, and he's only been there a few months. I get queasy feelings about that."

Taking a break from his work at the township treasurer's office, Jim Stadfeld had a theory that killing his wife was a no-lose situation for Bradford J. King.

"He may profess his goddamn innocence to the day he goes to his grave," Stadfeld said. "But I think deep down Brad is exactly where he wants to be. I think unconsciously he knew he was going to get caught. Now he has it all. He can be a prison lawyer, get all the attention, while somebody clothes and feeds him, takes care of all the little bullshit things of everyday life. He's finally going to be somebody. Brad will be one of those guys who will probably never see daylight again, but he'll probably end up with a PhD."

The acrimony between the prosecutor's office, the task force, and the sheriff's department had lessened substantially, but Jim Stadfeld still counted some losses. Stadfeld lost a friendship when a local private investigator he used to work with took work with King's defense.

If they all were part of some kind of small-town conspiracy, they all appeared to be paying a price for it. Gerry Woods nearly paid with his life. He lost something else.

"I don't know," Woods said, sipping on a beer at the Winner's Circle. "It's just not the same after this case. I'm thinking about hangin' it up, you know. But, I'll probably just end up dying on the job."

The Darling family would take months to recover. They considered moving, leaving the hardware business, leaving the town of hospitality for another small village. But now Darling knew there were no perfect towns. He just couldn't understand how his friends and neighbors could let the rumors flourish as long as they did.

"It kind of rips away some things you thought you really believed in," Darling would say. "It's changed me. I'll never be the same."

The blue Ford Escort with the two children in the back rolled south on Mound Road, past the Chrysler auto plants, heading toward Mt. Olivet Cemetery in Detroit, periodically puffing smoke when the gears changed.

The bumper sticker read: "Someone I love was murdered."

The day was April 4, 1993, Diane Newton King's birthday. She would have been thirty-seven.

The summer before, while King was in jail waiting trial, Kateri Tekakwitha King had been baptized with great fanfare at the St. Francis Xavier Mission Church in Kahnawake, Freida's reservation. It was also the home village of the child's namesake, the young maiden they called Lilly of the Mohawks.

The Newton home still had the cut-out pictures, but also a wall full of portraits of Diane Newton King. It featured all her professional accolades and recognition she'd always wanted from her own family. Also in the display was the Dream Catcher framed by Cindy Acosta.

Little Marler King had a request before everyone left for the cemetery. He wanted to take his toy rifle. He was wearing a cowboy hat.

"Grandma, nobody will hear it there," he said.

At the grave site they all gathered: Freida and Royal Newton. Denise Verrier, her husband Don, her children. Allen Marler. The young ones ran among the gravestones, laughing and playing. They were comfortable there. Freida brought the King kids to the cemetery when the days were warm, setting up a lawn chair, having lunch, letting the kids run, working on the flowers.

Her gravestone read: "Beloved daughter, sister, mother." Missing was the word "wife." A sword pierced the stone's Sacred Heart of Mary.

"You know he didn't even get her a stone," Royal Newton said. "We bought it."

Diane King lay next to her father, Herbert Marler. She'd always wished they were close. Over her body and the chilled earth, she was bringing her family together. She always liked to do that, people said.

Freida laid down a basket of flowers she'd made.

It read: "You're so special. I love you. I miss you."

Freida carried her own special pain. She regretted that they didn't talk more, but she was afraid of what she might say about the man her daughter married. She thought Diane wanted to confide in her about her crumbling marriage, but she was afraid what that might start.

"I think she wanted to tell me, but I didn't give her the chance," she said once. "I didn't want her to cry on the phone, because I couldn't reach her. Then again, when we were together, we couldn't discuss it."

They were together the night before her daughter's death, a night that was still very much with the mother at the gravestone. Her daughter lay her head on her tummy. Her granddaughter lay where her mother once carried her, too.

Three generations.

"She didn't stay on that bed just to lay there," Freida said, crying now. "She must have been trying to find a way to bring up the subject."

They watched TV instead.

From the View of

BRADFORD KING

I don't know if you believe in spirit beings. So just read this part and try not to question.

I have been visited by Diane three times since I was arrested. Our conversations were real. She told me she saw nothing when she was shot. She said that when her spirit was released, she stayed close by me and the children. She says that I am innocent and that I will be returned to life as a free man to raise my children. She is becoming a powerful spirit and will be around to help a lot of people.

She says, "I don't know who killed me, but I know you didn't."

The first time I had this happen was after I did a sweat lodge in Colorado. We'd had the feast and I'd come home and put the kids to bed. I couldn't sleep. I felt like I was awake, but obviously was asleep. And she was just there with me, laying on the floor next to me, talking to me and telling me it was okay. It also happened in the jail and here in the prison. She kept telling me that she knows the kids are okay and that it all will turn out for the best.

I picked up a book in our library called *Black Elk and the Sacred Ways of the Lakota*. It was just sitting on top of the book shelf, right where I was sitting doing my legal research. I thought that I was going to have a void in my reading. However, this is the only book of its kind here.

I feel more in touch with the earth again. It is very hard here to maintain that closeness. I pray every day to *Tunkashila*. The lack of the *Chanunpa* makes it a bit more difficult. I'm sure that the spirits understand. Translation time: *Tunkashila*—God, grandfather. *Chanunpa*—sacred pipe. Marker has an Indian name, Tekanatensere. It means Falling Leaves. The most popular translation of Kateri Tekakwitha is Katherine Wild Flower.

I decided that to teach my children their culture I had to live it, and I better assimilate myself. Andre D'Artagnan guided me.

I asked him, "Is that wrong?"

And he said, "It's not wrong. Maybe more people should."

Everywhere I went, in any Indian community, I was accepted as though I were a brother.

Diane and I took the time to learn the traditions, the language. We lived our life as close as we could in these times to those values. Diane practiced both her Catholic religion and the Native American spirituality. I pretty much used the Native American spirituality for myself. I had sweet grass in my office. So did she. We had cedar in our home. I had a medicine bundle. So did she. It was the foundation of the way we lived our lives, especially after having children, it was based in Native American values. Period.

When I was in Colorado after Diane's death, I did sweat lodges once a month. I sat with two of my brothers and we would smoke a pipe and pray. In fact, we would smoke a pipe and pray every time we got together. I found out from those traditions that I am more religious.

Don't tell my mother this. I'll figure out a way to tell her in my own way. But I'm not a Presbyterian anymore. I think you probably figured that out.

I had the Ten Day Feast for Diane based on the Mohawk traditions. I gave away a little round basket that was Diane's to the medicine man. I gave away a lot of jewelry, bracelets, and earrings, stuff like that. She had a couple of things that were very expensive. I kept those for the kids. That's the way it's done. That is the tradition.

The powwows gave me comfort after her death. I liked being with the people who didn't judge me, being there just as another human being. There wasn't a lot of people asking this or that or asking, "How are you doing?" It was also a place Diane loved to be.

I attended five or six powwows before I went to Colorado. The best is the Denver Powwow. The veterans that go in the grand march carry the flags and wear their uniforms with warbonnets. They carry rifles and during the warrior's dance, they shoot the rifles off.

Stella Pamp and Sister Anne Jeffrey said I wasn't supposed to dance for a year. Well, that's a choice. It's ten days of mourning and after that you choose how you're going to honor the dead.

Now Stella Pamp is a Potawatomi. They believe you don't dance for a year, but that's still up to the person. They're pretty much the same as the Ottawa and the Chippewa. You don't dance for a year and then you celebrate seven years on the anniversary of the death with a big feast to help the person pass into the spirit world. It's a seven-year journey.

For the Mohawks, it's an immediate journey. When the ten days are up, the spirit has passed.

I sat and talked with Andre and he said, "You choose. Whichever way you choose is right. It's your choice."

With a little kid who wants to dance, and won't dance unless his dad dances with him, and doesn't understand why he can't dance, I chose to dance. Marler loved to dance.

And Andre said, "Do you want to teach this boy or do you want him to learn from a woman? He needs to learn a man's dance."

I'd danced at powwows before, prior to Diane's death. I didn't have a costume. Diane and I were in the process of making one.

At first I wore a ribbon shirt. In the trial, Sister Anne said I was dancing with a wolf's head costume. It wasn't a wolf. It was a coyote. It's against the law to have a wolf.

It was given to me by a Lakota. He *gave* it to me so I could dance. He was a friend of Andre and Julie's. He knew I was not an Indian, but he said, "Here, I want you to have this. It's been mine, and it's your turn to use it."

After Diane died, I also began wearing paint when I danced. I painted my eye red and circled it with black. The colors symbolize life and death. Red is for life. Black is for death.

Until my year was over, I honored Diane by painting my face that way.

He painted only his right eye. It was the same one that would have beheld her in his gun sight.

HORRIFYING TRUE CRIME
FROM PINNACLE BOOKS

HORRIFYING TRUE CRIME
FROM PINNACLE BOOKS

__**No Safe Place**
by Bill G. Cox   0-7860-0133-X   **$4.99**US/**$5.99**CAN

__**Deacon of Death**
by Fred Rosen   0-7860-1094-0   **$6.50**US/**$7.50**CAN

__**Die for Me**
by Don Lasseter   0-7860-1107-6   **$6.50**US/**$7.50**CAN

__**Murder in the Family**
by Burl Barer   0-7860-1135-1   **$6.50**US/**$7.50**CAN

__**Damaged Goods**
by Jim Henderson   0-7860-1147-5   **$6.50**US/**$7.50**CAN

__**Driven to Kill**
by Gary C. King   0-7860-1347-8   **$6.50**US/**$7.50**CAN

Call toll free **1-888-345-BOOK** to order by phone or use this coupon to order by mail.

Name_____

Address _____

City_____ State _____ Zip _____

Please send me the books I have checked above.

I am enclosing $_____

Plus postage and handling* $_____

Sales tax (in NY and TN) $_____

Total amount enclosed $_____

*Add $2.50 for the first book and $.50 for each additional book.
Send check or money order (no cash or CODs) to: **Kensington Publishing Corp., Dept. C.O., 850 Third Avenue, 16th Floor, New York, NY 10022**
Prices and numbers subject to change without notice. All orders subject to availability.
Check out our website at **www.kensingtonbooks.com**.